The Canterbury Preacher's Companion 2007

Sermons for Sundays, Holy Days,
Festivals and Special Occasions
Year C

Michael Counsell

First published in 2006 by the Canterbury Press Norwich
(a publishing imprint of Hymns Ancient & Modern Limited,
a registered charity)
9–17 St Alban's Place, London N1 0NX

www.scm-canterburypress.co.uk

Scripture quotations are mainly drawn from the New
Revised Standard Version Bible © 1989 by the Division of
Christian Education of the National Council of Churches of
Christ in the USA.
Readings are from *The Christian Year: Calendar, Lectionary
and Collects*, which is copyright © The Archbishops'
Council of the Church of England: extracts and
edited extracts are used by permission.

Readings for days not covered by that book are from
Exciting Holiness, second edition 2003, edited by Brother
Tristram, copyright © European Province of the Society of
Saint Francis, 1997, 1999, 2003, published by Canterbury
Press, Norwich; see www.excitingholiness.org

ISBN 1-85311-709-9/978-1-85311-709-1

Typeset by Regent Typesetting, London
Printed in Great Britain by
St Edmundsbury Press Limited, Bury St Edmunds, Suffolk

Other books by Michael Counsell:

Prayers for Sundays (HarperCollins*Religious*)

More Prayers for Sundays (HarperCollins*Religious*)

Kieu by Nguyen Du, bilingual edition (Thé Gio'i Press, Hanoi)

Every Pilgrim's Guide to Oberammergau and its Passion Play
(Canterbury Press)

Two Thousand Years of Prayer (Canterbury Press and Morehouse
Publishing) (an edited version of this in Swedish is published by
Libris as *Stora Bönboken*)

All through the Night (Canterbury Press and
Westminster John Knox Press)

Every Pilgrim's Guide to the Journeys of the Apostles
(Canterbury Press and Morehouse Publishing)

The Little Book of Heavenly Humour by Syd Little with
Chris Gidney and Michael Counsell (Canterbury Press)

Every Pilgrim's Guide to England's Holy Places
(Canterbury Press)

A Basic Bible Dictionary (Canterbury Press)

INDEX OF ADVERTISERS

All advertisements in this publication have been accepted in good faith, and conform to the Advertising Standards Authority guidelines. Inclusion does not imply any commendation or approval by the Publishers who accept no responsibility or liability for goods or services provided.

To advertise in *Canterbury Preachers Companion 2008*, or any of the other Canterbury Press diaries and yearbooks, please contact Stephen Dutton, Church Times, 33 Upper Street, London N1 0PN   Telephone: 020 7359 4570 or e-mail: stephen@churchtimes.co.uk

Serving the Church of England, the Methodist Church, the United Reformed Church, and USPG

Offering Theological Education, Ordination Training and Mission Partner training that celebrates diversity, stretches the mind, equips for mission and ministry, and nourishes the spirit.

Providing full- and part-time programmes for ordinands, professional development and sabbaticals for serving ministers, and MA, ThD, and PhD degrees in the Research Centre,

For more information see our website www.queens.ac.uk or contact our admissions secretary

Rosemary Maskell
The Queen's Foundation, Somerset Road
Edgbaston, Birmingham B15 2QH
0121 452 2600 – E-mail: r.maskell@queens.ac.uk

Christian Resources Exhibitions

Equipping, empowering and enabling

the Christian community for over 22 years. CRE brings together Christians in all areas of ministry for training, networking and equipping.

More than 700 church suppliers, charities and mission organisations come to inspire, resource and encourage church leaders.

FOR INFO AND BOOKING, VISIT

www.creonline.co.uk

South West CRE

Westpoint EXETER
25-27 January 2007

National CRE

Sandown Park ESHER
15-18 May 2007

Contents

Tax Management for Clergy

PO Box 6621, Grantham, Lincs NG32 3SX

Telephone: 0870 200 3001   Facsimile: 0870 200 3002
e-mail:enquiries@clergytaxuk.com
www.clergytaxuk.com

ARE YOU UNDER PRESSURE?

PUT YOUR TAX RETURN AND TAX CREDITS APPLICATION TO REST

FOR PROFESSIONAL ADVICE ON ALL ASPECTS OF
TAXATION — RING NOW

PERSONAL INTERVIEWS AT 40 NATIONWIDE VENUES

PRESENTATION FOR COLLEGES, COURSES AND CLERGY
GROUPS — RING FOR DETAILS

Independent financial advice is available through our sister
company Independent Financial Management for Clergy

SERMONS FOR SAINTS' DAYS AND
SPECIAL OCCASIONS

Readings are from *Common Worship*, or from *Exciting Holiness* edited by Brother Tristam SSF, second edition, Canterbury Press, 2003.

PETER CHALK & RPP TAXATION SERVICES LTD

Specialists in Taxation for the Clergy

Is your Tax Return still lying on your desk?
Are you claiming all your allowances?
Causing you sleepless nights?
Need help?

LET US HELP YOU!

We offer:
- ✓ Personal service with qualified advisers
- ✓ Affordable, fixed price fee payable by instalments if required
- ✓ Over forty venues nationwide
- ✓ Postal service, if required
- ✓ Free seminars for education/training purposes
- ✓ Financial advice through our sister company Russell Plaice & Partners
- ✓ Authorised Inland Revenue filing by Internet agents
- ✓ Free Tax Credit advice/completion

Contact us now:

Tel: 01476 591333	Post: PO Box 6607
Fax: 01476 577733	Grantham
Email: enquiries@peterchalkco.co.uk	Lincolnshire
Website: www.peterchalkco.co.uk	NG31 7NR

Peter Chalk & RPP Taxation Services Ltd
Registered in England.   Company Number 4551413

xiv

Preface

An encouraging friend asked me whether I had thought of publishing some of my sermons, and I replied with a laugh that nobody publishes sermons these days. Shortly afterwards the Canterbury Press invited me to take on the authorship of the *Church Pulpit Year Book*!

The *Church Pulpit Year Book* has been published for over a hundred years, and the publishers have now decided to change the title to *The Canterbury Preacher's Companion*. I cannot hope to imitate the style of my predecessor, the late Dr Joyce Critchlow, for preaching is a form of communication which flows from the heart of the preacher to the heart of the hearer. These sermons are as I would preach them to a congregation who know me well; for this reason anyone wishing to preach them may need to go through them with a blue pencil first. Some sentiments, illustrations and jokes might go down like a lead balloon, or even cause offence, when spoken by some preachers to some congregations. Be warned!

Who is this book for?

I can imagine this series of books being useful to several sorts of people:

- First is the congregation which cannot obtain the services of a trained preacher on a particular Sunday, or maybe for long periods of time, but has someone who is willing to read a sermon to them so that they may continue to worship together.
- Then there is someone just embarking on the great adventure of preaching, who needs some prepared sermons to get them started until they have the confidence to write their own. For these people I have added some notes on 'How to Preach' which I prepared for a group of Readers in training. I wish I were better at following the good advice given there!

The College of St Barnabas Lingfield

The College of St Barnabas is an independent Charity established in 1896 it fulfils the aims of William Cooper its founder to provide retirement homes for Clergy of the Church of England and their wives.

Residents are accommodated in two roomed flats which all have en-suite facilities. Meals are taken in a central refectory and services such as laundry and room cleaning are all included in the fee. The Eucharist is celebrated and Evensong said daily in the Chapel.

There is a sick wing for Residents who become ill. It is occasionally possible to take applicants directly into this facility for long stay or respite care when there is an unfilled vacancy.

Further details may obtained from the Reverend the Warden, College of St Barnabas, Blackberry Lane, Lingfield RH7 6NJ

Telephone 01342 870650   Fax 01342 871672
E-mail: warden@collegeofstbarnabas.com
Web Site www.st-barnabas.org.uk

As a Charity we are dependent upon the gifts and legacies of our generous supporters. Please help us to care for those who have spent their lives caring for others

Charity Commissioners registered number 205220

- Some busy preachers may have no time some weeks adequately to prepare their own sermon from scratch, but could use one of these sermons, either complete or as an outline.
- Or preachers may look at the readings set for that Sunday and need to find a new angle of approach or some illustrations which will inspire them afresh.
- Some people may be prevented by illness or unavoidable engagements from going to church, but will be able to read one of these sermons at home instead.
- We hope this is a rarity, but some worshippers may have found nothing relevant to their own lives in the sermon they have heard in church, and may go home to seek something inspiring in this book.

What does this book offer?

The sermons for saints' days and special occasions may be used on the nearest Sunday, or on the day of the regular midweek service in the week in which they fall, if required.

After each sermon for the Principal Service on Sundays, there is a suggestion for all-age worship. If young people remain in the church for the main sermon, or if there is a special address suited to their needs during the service, this gives some suggestions for activities that will help them to feel involved. Or these ideas could be used in the Sunday school to link what the young people learn with the readings which the adults hear in church.

I have had a lot of fun choosing 'Suggested hymns' relevant to each sermon. There are some wonderful tunes in our hymn books, and thought-provoking words to go with them, both old and new. Some people learn more theology from what they sing than from what they hear. But most congregations like the majority of the hymns they sing to be familiar, and it may only be possible to introduce one or two of the hymns I have suggested among other better-known ones.

I have aimed to write English as it is spoken. This means short and sometimes incomplete sentences; lots of contractions like 'you'll' for 'you will'; beginning sentences with 'and' or 'but'; and whereas, for instance, 'Jesus' words' is correct in written English, since you cannot hear an apostrophe, I have used 'Jesus's words', as I believe that is the common form in spoken English.

It is a daunting project to produce 150 sermons in a year, but I have enjoyed it. I should be most grateful if readers and preachers

would write to me, c/o The Canterbury Press, with their criticisms
and suggestions for improvement.

Michael Counsell
Birmingham, 2005

How to Preach

Why do we preach?

Life's greatest privilege is to:

- share what God is saying with his people
- proclaim God's love for them
- help them to serve God in the power of the Spirit
- change their lives for the better.

So we must communicate our:

- thoughts about God
- experience of God.

This means exposing who you are, and becoming vulnerable.

Forming the structure

You may have heard the old joke:

> 'Methodist ministers on ordination are issued with a magic hammer: strike any verse from the Bible with this, and it will immediately fall into three points, with introduction and conclusion.'

This is not the only possible structure for a sermon, but it's a good one to begin with. People can't absorb more than three points in one sermon.

- Resist the temptation to put the whole of your training into the first sermon.
      'An author's best friend is her wastepaper basket.'
      'An author must be willing to murder his children.'

- 'Let the skeleton show': for example, 'I've finished discussing the background, now let's look at what it means for us today.' Afterwards they should remember what your three points were, and how one led into the next.

- Sum up the whole of what you want to say in the final sentence. (If you can't, there's too much material and you've wandered.) Then plan everything to lead up to this.

- Write layout notes, with numbered paragraphs, sub-paragraphs and paragraph headings. (When you've been preaching for forty years you can begin to do this in your head without writing it down.)

Notes or full text? Style?

Compiling clear notes first is essential, to make the structure plain. Most beginning preachers need next to write out in full what they're going to say. It mustn't sound like a read essay, or the listeners will fall asleep. So the style must be simple, colloquial, conversational:

- No long subordinate clauses.
- Always use contractions: don't, won't, haven't and so on. (But never use etc. or e.g.)
- No more than one long or new word per sermon, and explain it.
- Commas no more than ten words apart, to show where you breathe.
- Full stops no more than twenty words apart.
- Deliberate use of repetition, but not careless repetition.

There must be plenty of eye-contact: at least once per sentence. Therefore, the preacher needs to read the text through several times beforehand, until it's almost memorized. Then glancing at the first few words will be enough to remind you what you want to say, so that you can say it, while looking the listeners in the eye.

After a couple of years preaching, aim to make the notes longer (always write out quotations in full), till you can tear up the text and preach from the notes. Then you'll really begin to communicate.

A few years after that you may be able to do without writing a full text, making up the sentences in your head based on the notes. But you can never do without making clear notes first.

Length

'I don't know what to preach about.'

'Preach about God, and preach about ten minutes.'

If you're really interesting, you may be able to hold the listeners' attention for 15 minutes; more than that, and they'll fall asleep.

Audibility

It is a waste of time to preach a sermon that nobody can hear. Many people are more deaf than they realize, and such people always sit at the back of the church!

To be able to speak louder, practise singing. Stand up straight but relaxed. Begin to hum with your lips closed: 'Mmmmmmm'. Feel the top of your mouth vibrating. This brings your voice up into your mouth; if you sing or speak from your throat it will turn into a shout and if someone shouts you can't hear the words. Then open your mouth while singing 'Mmmmmmm-eeeeeeee-aaaaaaaah' on any note you like. Feel the top of your mouth still vibrating. Feel your diaphragm pushing up a firm column of air from the bottom of your ribs to the top of your mouth.

Then stop singing and talk using the same part of the mouth to produce the sound. Think of someone at the back of the church and talk directly to them in such a way as to attract their attention.

However, it is often not the volume but the melody which makes people inaudible.

If you speak always on the same note (musical pitch, high or low) it'll be terribly boring. If you always speak with the same melody, which falls at the end of the sentence, nobody will be able to hear the last few words, and the sentence won't make sense. If you vary the melody from sentence to sentence, without being sing-song, you'll be interesting to listen to. 'Elocution is a form of verbal gymnastics between the tip of the tongue and the teeth': always exaggerate the final consonant.

'A preacher needs to be a good actor, but to remember humbly that he or she is acting the part of Christ.'

Communication

'Who has believed what we have heard?' (Isaiah 53:1).

Even if the congregation hear every word, it'll do them no good unless you communicate. You must be quite clear what ideas you want to get across: the words are only aeroplanes for the ideas to ride in. Try to think up striking phrases, graphic images and metaphors; remember the *Readers' Digest* column 'Towards more picturesque language'. Above all you must communicate yourself, your own personality. Eye-contact is essential. Never preach anything you don't personally believe – and you don't really believe anything until you've struggled through doubt to reason it out for yourself. Make it heart-felt, the fruit of your own experience.

If the listeners say, 'I can't remember a word (s)he said, but what a nice/interesting/challenging person (s)he is,' then you've succeeded in communicating. If the listeners say, 'I can't remember a word (s)he said, but my faith is much stronger,' then you've succeeded even better. If you've just preached a brilliant sermon on 'justification by faith', and a listener says, 'Your sermon on "the way to ask for God's guidance" was just what I needed to hear,' then you've allowed the Holy Spirit to succeed!

Personal experience

Preach as well as you can, but don't try to imitate somebody else. Even if it is in stumbling, ungrammatical English, a sermon which tells the listeners what your faith has meant in your own life will have ten times the effect of an abstract theological discourse.

Try to describe at least one event in your life, which has taught you something about God, in each sermon. But avoid embarrassing stories about the charming things your children have said!

Stories

I listened to the people in the supermarket checkout line. Most of them were discussing last night's soap opera on the TV. They were making moral judgements: 'Wasn't it terrible when he did this?' 'What she should have said was that!'

So they were making use of stories to train themselves in moral theology! Next time they're faced with a similar situation, they'll have already made up their minds, subconsciously, how they should behave, and they'll behave a bit better because of the story they've heard. So it is in sermons.

A sermon is dull as ditch-water if it doesn't include at least one story, which can be:

• true or fictional

- from your own experience
- from a book you've read, but put into your own words briefly
- from the Bible
- a joke, so long as it isn't a 'shaggy dog' story!

Exegesis

Jesus is the Word of God. The Bible contains the word of God. The prophets proclaimed, 'Thus saith the LORD.'

'But how shall they hear unless they have a preacher?' (Romans 10:14). Our task is to allow God to speak through Jesus, then through the Bible, then through us. Almost every sermon should be an exposition of the Bible readings set for the day. (Here the liturgical churches have an advantage over the 'free churches', because we're forced to preach on all the important passages in the Bible every three years.) It's good to find a single verse out of the readings that summarizes what you want to say, then repeat this 'text' enough times, at the beginning, in the middle and at the end of the sermon, so that the hearers will learn it by heart, without trying. If they forget the sermon and remember the text, they will have heard God.

Always look for the original context – what the text means when surrounded by the verses which come before and after it, what the text meant to the original Bible writers, what the text meant to the first people to hear it read out – and explain this context to the congregation.

It's very easy to decide on what you want to say, then hunt for a text to hang it on. In this way you're communicating your own prejudices, and not what the Bible says. Exegesis is the art of drawing out what the Bible originally meant *in its own time*, then applying that inner meaning to the changed circumstances of *our* time. This is the task of the preacher, and we dare not miss out either step.

Checklist

When you have prepared your sermon, ask yourself (or have your spouse or honest friend ask you):

1 Where is the gospel?
I have heard Billy Graham and Desmond Tutu preach, and both kept coming back to one simple phrase: 'God loves you.' If you haven't communicated this good news, you ought not to be in the pulpit.

2 What should they do about it?

Unless a sermon results in some practical action or change of behaviour, the listeners will go away frustrated. Don't be 'so heavenly minded that you're no earthly use'.

Practical considerations

- Never use paper any bigger than A5, or you'll lose your place.
- Write or type large, with frequent new lines and much indenting, or you'll lose your place.
- Number the pages clearly, in case you drop them on your way to the pulpit.
- When you find that you've left your sermon notes at home two miles away, and have to preach entirely off the cuff, as I did when I had been ordained only seven years, then you'll discover whether you've learnt anything about preaching!

Leading intercessions

The Anglican minister was asked to preach in the Methodist church, and found he was expected to lead the prayers as well. Fortunately he had brought a spare set of sermon notes, and he found it quite easy to turn these into a prayer . . . until he heard himself saying, 'And now, Lord, I'd like to illustrate this with a funny story, I hope you haven't heard it before.'

Many of the points suggested here about preaching can be applied to leading intercessions, especially:

- careful preparation
- writing it out in your own words
- clear diction
- being always short and concise
- absolute sincerity.

Common Worship (p. 174) suggests five headings:

1 the Church of Christ (worldwide, all denominations, and this congregation);

2 creation (thanksgiving, ecology), human society, the nations of
   the world and their leaders;
3 the local community (families, the caring professions);
4 those who suffer (the sick, at home or in hospital – mention names
   if you have permission – the sad and the hungry);
5 the communion of saints (remember those who have recently died
   – mention names if you have permission – and those who mourn;
   any saints whose saint's day occurs at this time, the patron saints
   to whom this church is dedicated);

and it gives the responses which should be used after each section:

> Lord, in your mercy
All **hear our prayer.**

And after the fifth section:

> Merciful Father,
All **accept these prayers**
     for the sake of your Son
     our Saviour Jesus Christ.
     Amen.

Prayer

St Paul told the Christians in Thessalonica to 'Pray without ceasing'
(1 Thessalonians 5:17). Our preaching and intercessions will fail
unless they are undergirded by constant prayer:

- daily at set times
- as we work
- the evening before we preach
- before the service
- on the way to the pulpit.

Memorized words can help, but if you trust the Lord like a child
trusts his or her father, you can use your own words, or even no
words at all, to draw on the grace he has promised to enable you to
carry out the work to which he has called you.

CHURCH HOUSE BOOKSHOP

serving the Church of England for over 70 years!

A wide range of

Academic Theology,
Bibles, Commentaries,
Preaching Materials,
Church Reports and Music.

Over 30,000 titles available online at

www.chbookshop.co.uk

*or contact our helpful
mail order team on*

020 7898 1300

or visit us at
CHURCH HOUSE BOOKSHOP
31 Great Smith St, London SW1P 3BN

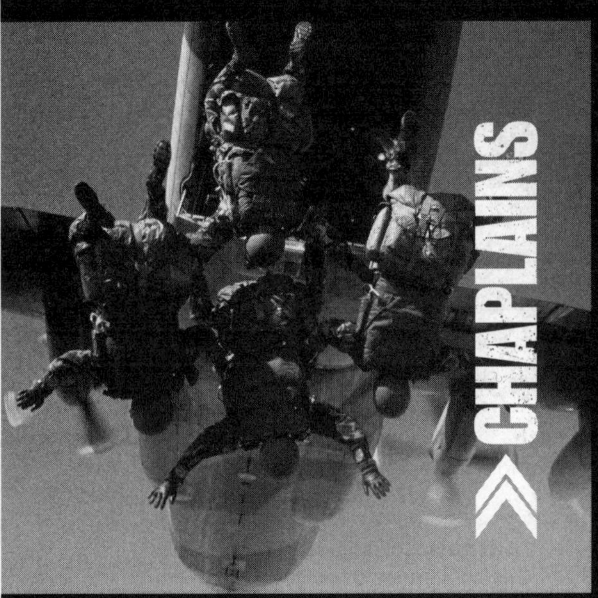

Take a leap of faith

Not all Chaplains jump out of aircraft but if you'd
like to take your ministry to new heights why not
become an Army Chaplain?

Working side by side with the world's youngest
and most dynamic workforce, you'll become a
valued member of our team.

For further information contact,

MOD Chaplains (A) Trenchard Lines,
Upavon, Pewsey, Wiltshire SN9 6BE

www.armychaplains.mod.uk

or call 08457 300 111 and quote ref: CPC

Church Urban Fund

Responding to poverty in our country
Through prayer Through churches Through action

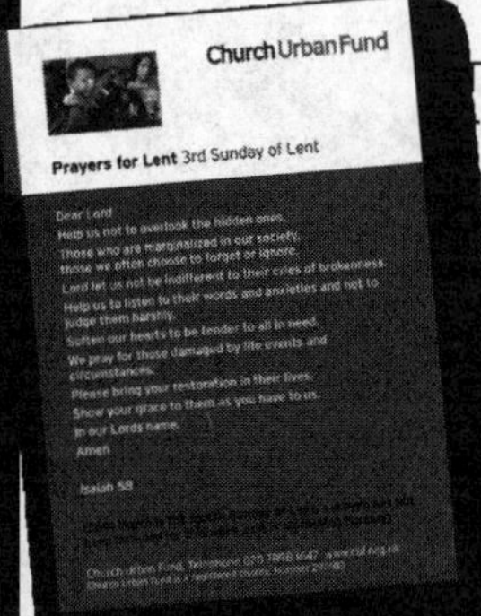

The Church Urban Fund has created four distinct resources to fit in with the Church Calendar:

Prayers for Lent and Easter
A series of six postcards for church or home use, carrying prayers for the Lent and Easter period.

Summer treasure hunt
Material to help congregations celebrate children and childhood, incorporating a hunt in the church or church grounds. Produced for use over July and August.

A harvest of faith
Themes for reflection and action during Harvest.

Make a Different Gift this Christmas
Make a Different Gift challenges us to give to someone we have never met, to be generous to a stranger, helping us to think more closely about our actions over the Christmas period.

To order these materials and find out about other resources please contact us on **020 7898 1649**

Visit: **www.cuf.org.uk** for information on what we do.

Church Urban Fund
Church House, Great Smith Street, London SW1P 3NZ

Fax: 020 7898 1601 Email: enquiries@cuf.org.uk

YEAR C, the Year of Luke

*(Year C begins on Advent Sunday in
2006, 2009, 2012, etc.)*

ADVENT

Advent consists of the four Sundays leading up to Christmas. It is a penitential season, so altar frontals and vestments are purple, and there needs to be an air of solemnity in the services. 'Glory to God in the highest' is often omitted. 'Advent' means 'coming'; there is a sense of eager expectancy looking forward to the coming of Christ into the world at Christmas, but, except in carol services, it is a shame to introduce many Christmas carols during Advent as this robs us of the chance to enjoy some splendid Advent music, and leads to a sense of anticlimax when Christmas comes. We also celebrate the coming of Jesus into our lives daily, at our death, and at the end of the world. Traditional themes for sermons on the four Sundays are Death, Judgement, Heaven and Hell. Candles can be lit, one on the first Sunday, two on the second, and so on, leading up to five on Christmas Eve, mounted on an Advent wreath.

First Sunday of Advent   3 December 2006
Principal Service   **The Coming of the Son of Man**
Jer. 33:14–16 A king is promised; Ps. 25:1–10 Waiting for God;
1 Thess. 3:9–13 Prayer to be blameless at the coming of Christ;
Luke 21:25–36 The coming of the Son of Man

'Then they will see "the Son of Man coming in a cloud" with power and great glory.' Luke 21:27

Politics and religion?

You will often hear politicians say preachers shouldn't meddle with politics. Yet politics is about how we govern our *polis* or state; it affects people's lives, and raises moral or ethical questions. In that sense, everybody ought to be concerned. Certainly nobody should abuse the pulpit by preaching about party politics; but the way our nations are governed is far too important to be left to politicians alone. Bishop Desmond Tutu once said, 'When people tell me there is nothing about politics in the Bible, I wonder which Bible they're reading from.' Of course, in the Old Testament the only politicians were the kings, who had absolute power. The prophets had plenty of criticism for the kings of their day; nonetheless they hoped for a better king one day, a Messiah, which means an anointed one. Isaiah said that the 'house of David' was like a tree cut down to the stump, but there would come 'a shoot from the stump of Jesse'. Jeremiah referred to this shoot as 'a righteous branch . . . called: "The LORD is our Righteousness."' The king in Jeremiah's day was called Zedekiah, which translates as 'the LORD is righteousness'; it was a very political statement.

The Son of Man

When the Book of Daniel was written, the line of Davidic kings had died out, and the Israelites were being attacked by one evil empire after another. Daniel represents these empires by visions of cruel and fantastic beasts. But the symbol for Israel, in the Book of Daniel, is not a beast, but the vision of a human figure; or rather a human-like figure, because he is a heavenly being. The Hebrew language has no word for 'human', so they used the term 'son of man'; and a divine being in human form is 'one like a son of man'. He represents Israel, and he comes to God on the clouds. He is given a kingdom as a reward for his suffering, and judges the earth. But notice the direction of travel: the one like a son of man comes *to* God on the clouds.

Jesus and the Son of Man

The New Testament quotes this passage from the Book of Daniel many times. When Jesus calls himself 'Son of Man', he could mean simply that he is a human being; but the Book of Daniel was in the back of everybody's minds. So to call himself *'the* Son of Man' meant that he was more than human; that he was, in fact, divine. And the only way you can say *that* in Hebrew is by the phrase 'Son of God'. When the New Testament refers to the Son of Man coming on the clouds, it almost always means that Jesus is coming *to* God. He is the representative of suffering humanity, coming to be given the reward for his suffering, and appointed judge of the earth. This will be followed by the resurrection of all those who believe in him. This sounds like a process which began with the resurrection of Jesus, and continues at the death of each one of us. In modern terms, we would say that at our death we are resurrected into the timeless and non-material world of eternity, outside of space and time.

Jesus comes to us daily

We don't have to wait till we die for the coming of the Son of Man. Just as the prophets said that God was concerned for the politics of their own day, so Jesus is telling us that his coming is concerned with today. Jesus comes to us every day of our lives:

- to challenge us to obedience
- to present us with opportunities for love
- to help us to make the right decisions
- to comfort us when we're lonely and sad.

Jesus comes to us each day. We must look out for his invisible presence, welcome him to take charge of our lives, and co-operate with him in building his kingdom of justice and righteousness. A cartoon showed a couple coming out of church. One says to the other, 'I don't know where our preacher gets these bizarre political notions: "The meek shall inherit the earth," indeed!'

All-age worship

When the first candle on the Advent wreath is lit, ask young people to write, draw or mime the changes which happen when people welcome Jesus into their lives.

Suggested hymns

A man there lived in Galilee; Hark the glad sound! the Saviour comes; Son of God, eternal Saviour; The Lord will come and not be slow.

First Sunday of Advent
Second Service   Blessed are the Dead

Ps. 9 The Lord judges the world; Joel 3:9–21 The valley of decision;
Rev. 14:13—15:4 Blessed are the dead; *Gospel at Holy Communion*:
John 3:1–17 Nicodemus

> *'And I heard a voice from heaven saying, "Write this: Blessed are*
> *the dead who from now on die in the Lord." "Yes," says the Spirit,*
> *"they will rest from their labours . . ." And I saw what appeared to*
> *be a sea of glass mixed with fire, and those who had conquered*
> *the beast and its image and the number of its name, standing*
> *beside the sea of glass with harps of God in their hands.' Revela-*
> *tion 14:13; 15:2*

Brahms' German Requiem

When Johannes Brahms wanted to write a Requiem Mass following
the death of his mother and his friend and sponsor Robert
Schumann, he rejected the gloomy words of the Latin *Dies Irae* and
instead chose more optimistic words directly from the Bible. He
called it his 'German Requiem'. One of the solos sings the words,
'And I heard a voice from heaven saying, "Write this: Blessed are
the dead who from now on die in the Lord." "Yes," says the Spirit,
"they will rest from their labours . . .".' These words from the last
book of the Bible, 'The Revelation to Saint John the Divine', draw
out the change which the resurrection of Jesus Christ had brought
in people's attitude to death. It's no longer something to be feared;
to those who believe that heaven is better than earth, death is God's
greatest blessing.

Rest

Death is looked forward to by many people who are weary of the
struggles of life. In Bushey churchyard there used to be an anonymous nineteenth-century 'Epitaph for a Tired Housewife':

> Here lies a poor woman who was always tired:
> she lived in a house where help wasn't hired.
> Her last words on earth were 'Dear friends, I am going
> to where there's no cooking, or washing, or sewing,

for everything there is exact to my wishes,
for where they don't eat there's no washing of dishes.
I'll be where the heavenly anthems are ringing –
but me having no voice I won't join in the singing.
Don't mourn for me now, don't mourn for me never,
I'm going to do *nothing* for ever and ever!'

In the next chapter of Revelation there is a powerful image for the peace of eternity: 'I saw what appeared to be a sea of glass . . . and those who had conquered . . . standing beside the sea of glass.' There was a 'bronze sea' in the Temple of Jerusalem, which probably represented God's triumph over the forces of nature; the sea of glass may represent the crystal firmament of the sky, seen from above. It contrasts the rush and hurry of our life in the world of time, with the changeless peace of timelessness.

Glass mixed with fire

Yet to reach this peace, the believers had to pass through suffering. John 'saw what appeared to be a sea of glass *mixed with fire*'. What a graphic description that is of the life of the Christian! Often, we're able to endure the flame of suffering, because we have a vision that one day it will come to an end. We see the peacefulness of eternity, which awaits us if we bear our suffering bravely for Christ's sake. Glass, mixed with fire. Fire, mixed with crystal. Life is a mixture of suffering and peace. In death, suffering is no more, and all is peace.

Looking forward to heaven

So we ought to look forward to death. Yet so much in the way people of the twenty-first century handle death says the opposite. When death was an ever-present reality, people learned to believe in life after death. Now we have sanitized and hidden death until we almost believe that it is something that happens to other people, not to us. And the belief in an afterlife has grown weaker. Christians don't live in dread of death; we look forward to as long a period of service to God in this world as God will allow us, and then our welcome admission to the greater world of heaven. There we can meet again our loved ones who have died, enjoy the reward for our toil, and be with Jesus, our friend, for ever and ever. Members of the Salvation Army, who are used to moving up from one rank to another in their organization, refer to death as 'Promotion to Glory'! Advent is a season for repenting for our sins, and reflecting on the inevitability of death, but it needn't be all gloom.

'Blessed are the dead who from now on die in the Lord.' 'Yes,' says the Spirit, 'they will rest from their labours.'

Suggested hymns

Give me the wings of faith, to rise; He wants not friends that hath thy love; How bright those glorious spirits shine; Lord, it belongs not to my care; Peace, perfect peace.

Second Sunday of Advent   10 December
Principal Service   **Ready for Christmas**

Bar. 5:1–9 God will lead his people with joy; *or* Mal. 3:1–4 A messenger to prepare the way; *Canticle*: Benedictus, The birth of John the Baptist; Phil. 1:3–11 Completion by the day of Christ; Luke 3:1–6 John the Baptist

'[John the Baptist] went into all the region around the Jordan, proclaiming a baptism of repentance for the forgiveness of sins, as it is written in the book of the words of the prophet Isaiah, "The voice of one crying out in the wilderness: 'Prepare the way of the Lord, make his paths straight.'"' Luke 3:3–4

The king in disguise

It's an old story, some of you will have heard it before. A castle was set in a fertile valley, where a large family lived, with many servants, a long way from the city where the king lived. So nobody in the castle had actually seen the king. But they hoarded up wealth, bullied the servants and were bitchy to each other – why should they bother themselves with thinking about the king? One day a messenger arrived. His clothes were worn out from a long journey. He called everyone together, and announced, 'Your king wants to know what happens in his kingdom, what sort of people live there, and how they treat each other, so he has decided to visit this castle . . .' He never had a chance to finish what he was saying, because an uproar broke out. 'The king's coming,' everybody shouted at once, 'we've got to get ready.' So they got out all the gold and silver, and bullied the servants to polish it, so that they could show off to the king how rich they were. They sent other servants into the fields to gather the crops and kill the beasts and draw wine, so that they could put on a big feast for the king. They started to clean and scour everywhere in the castle, and of course they got in each other's way, so they were even more bitchy to each other, and they shut the children outside, and pushed the messenger out with them.

One little girl soothed the other children who were crying; then she offered the messenger new clothes and food. 'No, thank you,' he replied. 'A cup of water will do, and I'll dress like the other servants.' Eventually all the preparations were finished, and shame-facedly they asked the messenger back in, saying, 'We forgot to ask you exactly when the king's coming.'

'The king's here already,' replied the messenger. 'I am the king. I wanted to know what happens in my kingdom, what sort of people live there, and how they treat each other. I didn't want special treat-ment, because then I would never know, so I decided to visit this castle dressed as a servant. After all, I am your servant, that's what being a king is all about, serving his people. The only preparation I wanted was for you to be kind to each other, so that I could rejoice in how happy my people are. Instead you were absolutely horrid; the only one ready for the coming of the king was this little girl here.'

Getting ready for Christmas

Everyone's very busy getting ready for Christmas, buying presents, cooking food, decorating the house; ready for when we celebrate the coming of King Jesus at Christmas. The spiritual preparations, which are what he really wants, get pushed aside: prayer and love. There's no time for things like that when you're busy.

John the Baptist

John the Baptist said he was a messenger, preparing the way of the Lord. He was not the king, but he warned of a king who would 'bring good news to the oppressed, bind up the brokenhearted, pro-claim liberty to the captives, and release to the prisoners; proclaim the year of the Lord's favour, and . . . comfort all who mourn'. What sort of preparation's needed for the coming of a king like that? As we get ready for Christmas, remember that presents and parties are important as a way of showing our love for people. But far more important is to pray and worship God; repent of the times we've fallen short of the standard of perfect love that Jesus showed us in his life; and accept God's forgiveness, which means forgiving those who trespass against us. Then we must make a fresh start, simply being as loving and kind to each other as we can, so as to be ready for the coming of the king at Christmas. If we live like that, we might actually find that King Jesus has been with us all the time.

All-age worship

Draw, model or act out the story.

Suggested hymns

Hark the glad sound! the Saviour comes; Make way, make way; On Jordan's bank the Baptist's cry; Soon and very soon.

Second Sunday of Advent
Second Service   The Link between the Testaments
Ps. 75 I will judge [76 To save the oppressed]; Isa. 40:1–11 Comfort my people; Luke 1:1–25 John's birth foretold

> *'With the spirit and power of Elijah he will go before him, to turn the hearts of parents to their children, and the disobedient to the wisdom of the righteous, to make ready a people prepared for the Lord.' Luke 1:17*

The beginning of the Gospel

St Luke's writing his Gospel for someone called Theophilus. The name means 'friend of God' and it could be a pseudonym, or a general term for all the godly people who would read his story, such as you and me. But 'most excellent Theophilus' sounds like the title of a high official – like 'Your Excellency'. So it was quite likely that he was a real person. Some have even suggested that he was the lawyer or the judge who was to argue the case for, or hear the case against, St Paul when he arrived in Rome. The Acts of the

Apostles – a continuation of the Gospel of Luke, and which is also addressed to Theophilus – ends when Paul arrives in Rome. This suggests that these two books might be parts of the documentation brought forward in Paul's defence. Most biblical scholars, however, date the Gospels much later than this, but nothing can be proved either way.

Beginning with the Baptist

In any case, it seems a little odd that Luke should begin his Gospel with the prediction of the birth of John the Baptist. The story doesn't occur in any of the other Gospels; where could Luke have got it from? It's possible that while Paul was imprisoned in Caesarea, before he appealed to be tried by the Emperor, Luke had time to travel round gathering facts. He could have met the Virgin Mary, now in her forties, and got all the stories around the birth of Jesus from her. Luke's very careful to emphasize the accuracy of his Gospel in the first few verses, so it's most unlikely that he made it up. The other Gospels agree with him, however, that you can't tell the story of Jesus without beginning with John the Baptist.

John's parents

John's parents, Zechariah and Elizabeth, were both old, and had so far been childless. The birth of their son's a miracle, similar to the births of Isaac, Joseph and Samuel in the Old Testament. Zechariah is a priest and receives his vision in the Temple. The messenger is the angel Gabriel, who appeared to Daniel; Zechariah is struck dumb like Ezekiel; he's told that his son must never drink alcohol, which reminds us of Samson. So by one sign after another we are left in no doubt that John the Baptist was the fulfilment of the Old Testament, the last of the Old Testament prophets, and the hinge who joins the Old Testament to the New Testament.

The connection of the two Testaments

'Testament', of course, means a covenant or contract. God made a contract with his people at Mount Sinai, and promised to protect them provided they behaved themselves. When God's people broke one commandment after another, God sent them prophets, to warn them that without moral behaviour, the old covenant would be made null and void. Jeremiah promised that there would be a new covenant, not based on rules carved in stone, but written in our hearts. John the Baptist's message, when he grew up, was that the time for the new covenant had come. They were to sign this new contract by a public baptism, the ceremony which proselytes, or non-Jewish converts who wanted to join the covenant community of Judaism, went through as their admission ceremony. The Jewish members of the people of God were to make a fresh start, rejoining the family of which they were already members, by a conscious adult decision. But according to John the Baptist, moral behaviour was still required, not as a condition of being admitted to God's family, but as a consequence.

The New rests on the Old

Christians are sometimes tempted to dismiss the Old Testament as unimportant. But you can't understand what the sacrifice of Jesus was all about unless you realize that God can only help people if they're willing to obey him; that he sends prophets to remind us this; and that when we get into a mess because of our disobedience, God steps in to save us. The gospel really does begin with John the Baptist. Think of the Old Testament as a big, bulky book in Hebrew, resting on the edge of a pulpit; and the New Testament as a much smaller book in Greek, lying on top of the big one. Then if you pull the Old Testament away, the New Testament will crash to the ground. That's why Luke began with the Baptist: he links them together.

Suggested hymns

O come, O come, Emmanuel; On Jordan's bank the Baptist's cry; The God of Abraham praise; The people that in darkness sat.

Third Sunday of Advent   17 December
Principal Service   **The Fruit of Repentance**
Zeph. 3:14–20 Sing, daughter Zion, God is in your midst; *Canticle*: Isa. 12:2–6 Great in your midst; *or* Ps. 146:4–10 Justice; Phil. 4:4–7 Rejoice in the Lord; Luke 3:7–18 The witness of John the Baptist

> *'John said to the crowds that came out to be baptized by him, "You brood of vipers! Who warned you to flee from the wrath to*

come? Bear fruits worthy of repentance. Do not begin to say to yourselves, 'We have Abraham as our ancestor'; for I tell you, God is able from these stones to raise up children to Abraham: Even now the axe is lying at the root of the trees; every tree therefore that does not bear good fruit is cut down and thrown into the fire.'' Luke 3:7–9

Unique to Luke

Only Luke's Gospel has any detail about the preaching of John the Baptist. In Luke's account, John uses two striking images.

Fire

The first image John uses is a picture of a forest fire. All the animal inhabitants of the forest come running, flying or crawling out of the trees as fast as they can to escape from the flames. The crowds who flocked to hear John's preaching are compared to a nest of baby snakes wriggling away from danger. The Serpent in the Garden of Eden is a symbol of evil; the people of John's time were still babes in the practice of evil; but they needed to escape from God's judgement. John's call for repentance had turned into a panic over remorse. But repentance in the Bible means a new beginning, a fresh start. So John asked them whether they're willing to do anything about their way of life.

A fruit tree

The second image is of a fruit tree; it occurs in many places in the Bible. What's the use of a fruit tree if it never produces any fruit? God had chosen Israel so that it should produce the fruit of good works, and the harvest of souls, bringing others to worship our loving heavenly Father by their example of love for their neighbours. But they produced none of this. So, says John, the woodsman's axe is lying on the ground by the side of the fruit tree: no fruit, no tree. Christians haven't replaced the Jews; but as St Paul says, we've been grafted onto the same trunk. God has chosen the Christian Church for the same purpose: to bear the fruit of good works. That's why you and I are Christians. If not, 'the axe is lying near the trunk of the tree'. But the answer is not to flee in panic, but to pray for the Holy Spirit who helps us bear fruit, like sap flowing through a tree.

Practical advice

Once again, it's only in Luke's Gospel that we find John the Baptist's practical advice about the sort of fruit that God requires of us.

> And the crowds asked him, 'What then should we do?' In reply he said to them, 'Whoever has two coats must share with anyone who has none; and whoever has food must do likewise.' Even tax collectors came to be baptized, and they asked him, 'Teacher, what should we do?' He said to them, 'Collect no more than the amount prescribed for you.' Soldiers also asked him, 'And we, what should we do?' He said to them, 'Do not extort money from anyone by threats or false accusation, and be satisfied with your wages.'

Try taking that literally. Look in your wardrobe or on the coat-hook and see whether you have two coats. Do you really need them both? How about taking one to the nearest charity shop or refuge for the homeless? They'll be astonished but grateful for your literal response to the Bible's teaching. Then look in your larder. Compared to people in the 'Third World', even the poorest of us is immensely rich; what do you think they would say if they could hear us grumbling about how hard-up we are? Though society may have changed, John the Baptist's advice is still a challenge to us today. If we're really going to enjoy Christmas, we need to look and see whether we are producing 'fruit worthy of repentance': the fruit of good works that proves our repentance to be genuine.

All-age worship

Draw the axe lying near the trunk of the tree. Draw fruit on the tree, and label each one with one of the good works we can do for God.

Suggested hymns

Lo, he comes with clouds descending; On Jordan's bank the Baptist's cry; Rejoice in the Lord always; The Lord will come and not be slow.

Third Sunday of Advent

Second Service **Here is Your God** Ps. 50:1–6 Our God
comes [62 Wait for God in silence]; Isa. 35 Here is your God;
Luke 1:57–66 The birth of the Baptist [67–80 Benedictus]

> *'Strengthen the weak hands, and make firm the feeble knees. Say
> to those who are of a fearful heart, "Be strong, do not fear! Here is
> your God . . . He will come and save you."' Isaiah 35:3–4*

Losing heart

The beautiful poem which is contained in the thirty-fifth chapter
of Isaiah has all the hallmarks of a passage written to encourage
returning exiles. Probably it was written in Babylon almost two
hundred years after the prophet Isaiah died, and literally 'tacked
on' to the scroll of Isaiah to escape the attention of the Babylonian
thought-police. It was written to encourage those Jews who'd been
grabbed from Jerusalem and forced to live in Babylon, and who'd
lost hope. They'd endured a miserable life in Babylon, slaves digging canals for the most part, and their leaders were all dead.

'By the waters of Babylon we sat down and wept.'

Then King Cyrus conquered Babylon and told the exiles they
could go home. You'd think they'd be delighted. But most of the
new generation of Jews had never seen Jerusalem, and they'd been
cut off from their roots. They were thoroughly depressed, and they
thought God had lost interest in them. 'Go back to Jerusalem?' they
said. 'Why bother? And have you seen the road we'd have to travel,
across the desert? No, thank you. We're staying put.'

Returning exiles

Yet God hadn't finished with them. He still had work for his chosen
people to do. But only if they'd return to the promised land. So
the anonymous prophet feels he's called by God to give them new
heart. Even the desert road from the heart of modern Iraq across to
Jerusalem will be made easy for them:

> The wilderness and the dry land shall be glad, the desert shall
> rejoice and blossom; like the crocus it shall blossom abundantly,
> and rejoice with joy and singing. The glory of Lebanon shall be
> given to it, the majesty of Carmel and Sharon. They shall see the
> glory of the LORD, the majesty of our God.

A God who saves

So although they felt personally powerless, they were to recognize that God had a purpose for them. Their return would be God's work, if only they'd recognize it. The result would be a return to paradise, which would make the hardships of the journey well worth it:

> Then the eyes of the blind shall be opened, and the ears of the deaf unstopped; then the lame shall leap like a deer, and the tongue of the speechless sing for joy. For waters shall break forth in the wilderness, and streams in the desert; the burning sand shall become a pool, and the thirsty ground springs of water; the haunt of jackals shall become a swamp, the grass shall become reeds and rushes.

Where there'd been a forbidding wilderness, God would make a new road for his people to travel home:

> A highway shall be there, and it shall be called the Holy Way; the unclean shall not travel on it, but it shall be for God's people; no traveller, not even fools, shall go astray. No lion shall be there, nor shall any ravenous beast come up on it; they shall not be found there, but the redeemed shall walk there. And the ransomed of the LORD shall return, and come to Zion with singing; everlasting joy shall be upon their heads; they shall obtain joy and gladness, and sorrow and sighing shall flee away.

Truly, they had a God who saves. But most of them, most of the time, just didn't recognize that he was at work, and so they failed to co-operate with God as he wanted them to.

Crossing the desert

The frame of mind of the frightened exiles is quite familiar to us, too. We often feel our life's a forbidding wilderness, without joy or consolation, and we lose heart over God's plans for us. Yet if we'll grit our teeth and 'keep right on to the end of the road', God has a place reserved for us in heaven. The proof is that God came down to earth at Christmas; 'God became like us so that we might become like him.' What's the path we must travel to reach paradise? It's a road of self-sacrifice and service to others, and it sounds pretty forbidding. But if we only understood how great the delights of heaven were, no sacrifice would be too great to make in order to get there. This is the 'new and living way' which leads us back to the heart of God. And the guarantee that this is so is the babe in the manger. Do we recognize him? As Isaiah said, 'Here is your God.'

Suggested hymns

From heaven you came, helpless babe (The Servant King); Hark the glad sound! the Saviour comes; Make way, make way; O for a thousand tongues to sing.

Fourth Sunday of Advent (Christmas Eve) 24 December
Principal Service   **Magnificat**
Micah 5:2–5a A leader from Bethlehem; *Canticle*: Magnificat,
Luke 1:46–55; *or* Ps. 80:1–7 Come with salvation;
Heb. 10:5–10 When Christ came into the world;
Luke 1:39–45 [46–55] Mary visits Elizabeth

'He has shown strength with his arm; he has scattered the proud in the thoughts of their hearts. He has brought down the powerful from their thrones, and lifted up the lowly; he has filled the hungry with good things, and sent the rich away empty.' Luke 1:51–53

The need to praise

What a lovely story's told in today's Gospel: Mary visited her cousin Elizabeth. Each was expecting a baby. Mary was too young and Elizabeth too old to expect it in the normal run of events. In both cases, their condition was a miracle. There were Old Testament precedents: Isaiah wrote, 'Behold a virgin shall conceive and bear a son and call his name Immanuel.'

By the word 'virgin' he may have only meant 'a young woman of marriageable age', but this verse shows that every conception and every birth is a miracle, and a sign that God is with us. Elizabeth follows the pattern set by Abraham's wife Sarah. Sarah laughed at the suggestion that she should have a child when she was past the change of life, so that her child was named Isaac, which means 'laugh'. Mary also follows the pattern of Hannah, who gave birth to Samuel, and sang a song beginning 'My heart exults in the Lord'. Mary's song when she visited Elizabeth begins, 'My soul doth magnify the Lord', and it's sung at Evensong under the title of 'Magnificat'. Like a magnifying glass which makes everything bigger, praise shows that God's big in our lives.

John the Baptist

Mary's son was Jesus; Elizabeth's son was John the Baptist. John the Baptist is mentioned by the Jewish historian Josephus – Josephus lived in the same period of time, so he's an eyewitness. Josephus tells us that John was executed by Herod Antipas at Machaerus, above the Jordan, and that he taught a once-in-a-lifetime ceremony of washing. Also that he exhorted to virtue, righteousness between Jews, and reverence towards God. Luke alone tells us that John and Jesus were cousins, and gives us the songs, Benedictus and Magnificat, which were sung at their birth.

A feminist theologian

Magnificat could well have been written by Mary and passed on to Luke; there is nothing specifically Christian in it; but what a revolutionary document it is! God has

> 'Cast down the mighty from their thrones,
> and raised up the humble and meek;
> Filled the hungry with good things,
> and sent the rich people empty away.'

If you sang that in some countries today you would be arrested as a raving Marxist! Mary must have been a remarkable genius, poet, theologian and political philosopher. There was none of your simpering Madonna about the author of the Magnificat. She saw that God cares about political justice, that some people have more money than they actually need – that's you and me – while other people are dying of starvation in their thousands, because we don't care enough about sharing our resources. She's the origin of the strong strain of the social gospel in Christianity.

A revolutionary Christmas

As we approach Christmas, enjoy the celebration of the birth of the baby; but remember that he grew into a man with a challenging message. Jesus isn't for ever 'Gentle Jesus, meek and mild', but one who challenges us to examine our actions. Like his mother and his cousin, Jesus expects us to do something practical about achieving justice in the world. He warns us that 'many who are first will be last'. We can't sing of God who 'has shown strength with his arm, and scattered the proud in their conceit', and be content to let things in the world remain as they are. Mary of the Magnificat won't allow us to retreat from the world into a selfish mysticism. The first disciples were known as 'those who are turning the world upside down'. If that isn't a translation of the word 'revolutionary', I don't know what it is. We have a truly revolutionary gospel; because of Christmas we're going to turn the world the right way up.

All-age worship

Make a collage of pictures of the world's poor, lowly and hungry, and make up a prayer that they will have enough to eat at Christmas.

Suggested hymns

A stable lamp is lighted; Lord Jesus Christ, you have come to us; Tell out, my soul, the greatness of the Lord!; Ye watchers and ye holy ones.

Fourth Sunday of Advent   Christmas Eve
Second Service (not in the evening, see below)
The Jesse Tree Ps. 123 As a maid looks to her mistress [131 My soul is like a weaned child]; Isa. 10:33—11:10 A shoot from the stump of Jesse; Matt. 1:18–25 Magnificat

> *'A shoot shall come out from the stump of Jesse, and a branch shall grow out of his roots.' Isaiah 11:1*

Jesse

The name of the father of King David, in the Old Testament, was Jesse, spelt J E S S E. Not long ago a man died, who'd been given that name by his thoughtless parents. The clergyman who took the funeral had never met him and didn't read his notes carefully enough, and went through the whole service praying for 'her' as though it had been the girls' name Jessie, J E S S I E! Fortunately the family laughed. They said that the deceased had suffered from this mistake all his life and would have been amused when it happened again at his funeral.

The dream of the Messiah

The royal family of Israel were the 'House of David', and traced their family tree back to King David and his father Jesse. But in the time of the prophet Isaiah, the royal family were a sore disappointment. Time after time they'd been defeated in battle, or made disastrous alliances with the wrong side in international disputes. In a graphic metaphor, Isaiah said it was as though the 'family tree' had been cut down, and all that remained was the stump of the tree of Jesse. Yet as Alexander Pope wrote, 'hope springs eternal in the human breast'. New kings at their coronation were anointed with oil, and became the Messiah, which means 'the anointed one'. The Jews always hoped that *this* would be the king they were waiting for, who would lead them back to peace and prosperity. When the royal family died out during the exile in Babylon, a century later, the term 'Messiah' became a dream of an ideal king in the future. In Isaiah's time, everyone hoped it would be now. 'The new king we're crowning today, he's the one,' they hoped. 'New life has come back to the house of David; a new shoot has sprung from the stump of David.'

The birth of the Messiah

Each Christmas we celebrate the birth of the Messiah. We proclaim that Jesus is the fulfilment of prophecies of the Old Testament. So we take each of the titles of the Messiah which is used in the Old Testament and apply them to Jesus. For Christians, Jesus is 'the shoot from the stump of Jesse'. His birthday is an occasion of renewed hope; the world's going to be a better place because of the baby of Bethlehem. And if you believe in him, then for you the world certainly is a better place, spiritually, because of your faith. But Jesus won't necessarily bring peace and prosperity in our day, any more than the new king did in Isaiah's time. That's because too few people believe in him and follow his teachings. Jesus tried to stop people calling him the Messiah, partly because it would bring down the wrath of the Romans, partly because it raised too many false hopes of a military Messiah who would drive the Romans out. That wasn't the sort of Messiah that Jesus was going to be; the birth of the Prince of Peace led him to the cross, the way of suffering and death. Yet when he was directly challenged by the High Priest, 'Are you the Messiah?' Jesus answered, 'I am'.

The Jesse Tree

Jesus is the Messiah, because he's the fulfilment of the hopes of the Old Testament. Matthew and Luke trace his family tree back to King David and his father Jesse, and beyond. Jesus was born in Bethlehem, 'royal David's city', and this emphasizes that he was 'Son of David'. For those who obey him as their king, he brings in the kingdom of God. So in many churches you will find a 'Jesse Tree' window. This takes the form of a tree growing out of the recumbent figure of Jesse. Jesse's lying down with the roots of the family tree in his chest. King David, his son, sits on a branch directly above him, and various other members of the royal family of Israel sit on other branches. Finally at the top of the tree sits Jesus himself. In the days when few could read, the stained-glass windows were the poor person's Bible. Today, as we prepare to celebrate the birth of the Messiah, the Jesse Tree reminds us that Jesus is the fulfilment of all the hopes of the Old Testament – the Son of God and Son of David – the shoot of new life growing out of the stump of Jesse.

Suggested hymns

How brightly shines the morning star; O come, O come, Emmanuel; Of the Father's love begotten; Once in royal David's city.

Christmas Day   25 December

Any of the following sets of readings may be used on the evening of Christmas Eve and on Christmas Day. Set III should be used at some service during the celebration.

Set I   **Room in My Heart** Isa. 9:2–7 A child is born; Ps. 96 Tell of his salvation; Titus 2:11–14 Salvation has come; Luke 2:1–14 [15–20] The birth and the shepherds

> *'And she gave birth to her firstborn son and wrapped him in bands of cloth, and laid him in a manger, because there was no place for them in the inn.' Luke 2:7*

The inn-keeper's wife

A speaker on the radio told how his little niece was in her infant school nativity play. The teacher wanted to give every child a part, so invented some which are not in the Gospels. The speaker asked his niece, 'Is it true that you have a part in a play?' 'Yes, Uncle.' 'And what's the play about?' 'Well, it's all about this inn-keeper's wife'!

No room at the inn

The inn-keeper's wife isn't mentioned in the Bible; nor is the inn-keeper, though it's quite justifiable to invent them for the purposes of a nativity play. In fact Bethlehem may have been too small even to have an inn. The word usually translated as 'inn' means the room in a house where you put up your visitors; the same room is translated 'guestroom' when Jesus asks his disciples, 'Where's the guestroom where I may eat the Passover?' The houses in Bethlehem were so full of visitors coming to register for the census, that none of them had space for Mary and Joseph, and they had to settle down in a stable. Bethlehem is built on a slope, so the stable could easily have been a cave hollowed out underneath the house. There was nowhere to put him in the stable except for the manger, the animals' feeding trough. It was not a beautiful hygienic stable like we see on the Christmas cards, and it probably smelt pretty ripe, but that was the only place where the Son of God could be born, because there was no room anywhere else.

Becoming like us

Jesus was born in a stable. The Son of God didn't come to earth to enjoy a cushioned, protected life. Jesus himself said that those who wear soft robes and fine clothing are only found in kings' palaces. He didn't come to earth to share in luxury. He came to identify himself with the poor and the underprivileged, the sort for whom nothing ever seems to go right. For it was those people he'd come to save. Even though wise people did come to him later, the first to greet him and welcome him to share their life on earth were humble shepherds. Many of us devote a lot of time and energy to the attempt to become wealthy. We want luxury and a sense of our own importance. But Jesus, whose was all the glory and wealth of heaven and earth, was born in a stable. No longer is God a faraway potentate. On Christmas Day, God became one of us, one of the powerless and unimportant people in the world. There's no room for Jesus in the materialistic plans of the wealthy. So he was born in a smelly stable and laid in the hay of the animals' manger. His wasn't a privileged upbringing.

There is room in my heart, Lord Jesus

Jesus will only go where he's welcome. Joseph and Mary welcomed him; the animals welcomed him; the shepherds welcomed him. Are you willing to welcome him? There was no room for Jesus in the inn or the guestrooms of Bethlehem; is there room for him in your heart? Mind you, he'll cause some disruption if you let him in. Out will have to go all your plans for luxury and self-aggrandisement, if you let the humble poor Jesus into your heart. Out will go your selfishness and your self-righteousness if you let the Friend of Sinners into your heart. There's a hymn which we sing all through the year, but the first two verses are particularly appropriate at Christmas time; will you repeat the last two lines after me?

> Thou didst leave thy throne and thy kingly crown,
> when thou camest to earth for me;
> but in Bethlehem's home was there found no room
> for thy holy nativity . . .
> Heaven's arches rang when the angels sang,
> proclaiming thy royal degree;
> but in lowly birth didst thou come to earth,
> and in great humility:
> *O come to my heart, Lord Jesus;*
> *there is room in my heart for thee.*

Say it loud and clear:

> *O come to my heart, Lord Jesus;*
> *there is room in my heart for thee.*

All-age worship

Draw or model Bethlehem's houses on a slope, with the stable-cave hollowed out below them and entered from the down-hill side. Show the manger, the Holy Family and the shepherds.

Suggested hymns

Away in a manger; In the bleak mid-winter; See amid the winter's snow; Thou didst leave thy throne.

Christmas Day   25 December
Set II   **Salvation by Grace** Isa. 62:6–12 Prepare a way;
Ps. 97 God comes to rescue his people; Titus 3:4–7 Salvation by
grace; Luke 2:[1–7] 8–20 Shepherds go to Bethlehem

> *'When the goodness and loving kindness of God our Saviour appeared, he saved us . . . so that, having been justified by his grace, we might become heirs . . . of eternal life.' Titus 3:4–7*

What a beautiful story!

What a beautiful story the Christmas story is! It's a real pastoral idyll, with a loving young mother, a helpless baby, humble shepherds, angels and a star. It's no wonder so many beautiful paintings have been made of the birth of Jesus in Bethlehem, because it has all the elements of a lovely picture in the story already. In an ugly world, here's a moment of real loveliness. When a skilled ballet dancer performs well, we say, 'How graceful! All her movements are full of grace!' And it's as if God had choreographed the entrance of his Son into the world to be as gracious as possible. In the stable at Bethlehem we see the goodness and loving-kindness of God, made visible.

Loving-kindness

For gracious also means kind. People used to say, 'Would you graciously allow me to do this . . . ? Thank you for your gracious gift . . .' In the courtyard of Windsor Castle, and in a few other places, there are small cottages known as 'Grace and Favour Residences'. They are often occupied by retired army officers, or members of the royal household, who have only small resources. When the Queen wishes to reward them for their years of service, she kindly allows them to live in these houses, not as a commercial transaction, but out of her grace and favour. Her loving-kindness. 'Loving-kindness' is a word invented by Miles Coverdale when he was translating the Bible into English, and he couldn't find a word which conveyed the full meaning of God's grace. 'God loved the world so much that he sent his only Son' . . . to be born in Bethlehem to save us. What love! What kindness! What goodness and grace!

Undeserved

Another feature of grace is that it is totally undeserved. What could we possibly do to deserve God's love? How could we possibly earn it? What could we ever pay to God, to make him send his Son to be born that first Christmas Day? No, it's purely out of the kindness of God's heart that he sent Jesus to save us . . . free, gratis and for nothing, as we say. 'Gratis' is another word derived from 'grace'; it means a free gift, which could never be earned. You can remember the meaning of 'grace' from the initials G R A C E. They stand for 'God's Riches At Christ's Expense'!

Saved by grace

The Christmas story's the story of our salvation. When somebody's drowning in the sea, they cry out, 'Help, save me!' We're all drowning in a sea of selfishness and fear, and we can't save ourselves. So we cry out to God, 'Help, save us!' And in his loving-kindness, in his grace, Jesus dives down into this sea of troubles and saves us. What does he save us from? From the habits of sin and the consequences of sin, and from fear of death. Have we done anything to deserve it? No! How can he save us, then, when we can't save ourselves? Because he's a stronger swimmer, he has all the power and the grace of God behind him.

The grace of the Holy Spirit

Which brings us to another meaning of grace. By pouring the Holy Spirit into our hearts, God gives us power to do things we could never do on our own. Grace is power. The lights on the Christmas tree are no use unless they're connected to the power of the electric mains. All the power of God is available to us if we will only switch it on by prayer. Then the Holy Spirit of God will renew our strength, and help us to do anything we want, provided, that is, that God wants us to do it for him. The power of grace will even lift us to the skies, where we could never go on our own. 'This Spirit he poured out on us richly through Jesus Christ our Saviour, so that, having been justified by his grace, we might become heirs according to the hope of eternal life.'

The Christmas story's a very beautiful one, and a very powerful one, because it's the story of God's loving-kindness and grace. It is the story of how heaven came down to earth, to give us on earth the power to get to heaven.

All-age worship

Draw Jesus welcoming people onto his rocket-ship, to take them to heaven, fuelled by the power of the Holy Spirit!

Suggested hymns

Away in a manger; Hark, the herald angels sing; It came upon the midnight clear; Once in royal David's city.

Christmas Day 25 December

Set III   **The Messenger of Peace** Isa. 52:7–10 The messenger of peace; Ps. 98 God's victory; Heb. 1:1–4 [5–12] God speaks through a Son; John 1:1–14 The Word became flesh

> *'How beautiful upon the mountains are the feet of the messenger who announces peace.' Isaiah 52:7*

Suspense

The children's parents were tired of being bounced all over at 6 a.m. every Christmas Day, so they gave strict instructions that they weren't to be woken until seven at the earliest. Of course the children woke up at six as usual, but didn't dare to disobey. There was no clock in their bedroom, so they lay there for an hour holding their breath and wondering just how long the suspense would go on. At last they heard footsteps down the landing, one . . . two . . . three . . . four . . . was it Mummy or Daddy? Was it really 7 o'clock yet? Or were they going to be told to turn over and go back to sleep? It seemed like for ever, but eventually the door handle turned and their dad came in. 'Up you get, kids. It's Christmas. You can open your presents now. It's 7 o'clock.' This was the picture that came to my mind when I read those verses from our Old Testament reading today: 'How beautiful . . . are the feet of the messenger . . . who brings good news'!

Return of the exiles

Of course, they weren't originally written about that particular situation. Most of the Jews had been taken away from Jerusalem into exile in Babylon. A few disheartened stragglers stayed on in the almost deserted city. Then one of the watchmen on the walls shouted out, 'I can see a messenger coming over the Mount of Olives from the direction of Babylon.' What would the messenger bring, good news or bad news? Further humiliation, or the return of the exiles? Defeat, or peace? They all rushed to the walls and peered through the heat haze. First, they could see the cloud of dust that the messenger kicked up with his feet, then they could make out the shape of his body, then they could see his feet as they plodded on towards Jerusalem. He'd come a long way from Babylon and was exhausted. But the watchers on the walls were thrilled to see his progress.

'How beautiful upon the mountains are the feet of the messenger who announces peace,' they said to each other, 'who brings good news, who announces salvation.'

When at last he arrived, weary and travel-worn, he was just able to gasp out, 'The exiles are coming back. The new king in Babylon, Cyrus, is working for our God, though he doesn't know it. God's been away from Jerusalem, but now he's coming back. Our God's in charge, and soon all the world will know it.' Well, I doubt whether an exhausted man said as much as that, but that's what he meant to say! And the stragglers in Jerusalem looked at each other and said:

How beautiful upon the mountains are the feet of the messenger . . . who says to Zion, 'Your God reigns.' Listen! Your sentinels lift up their voices, together they sing for joy; for in plain sight they see the return of the LORD to Zion. Break forth together into singing, you ruins of Jerusalem; for the LORD has comforted his people, he has redeemed Jerusalem. The LORD has bared his holy arm before the eyes of all the nations; and all the ends of the earth shall see the salvation of our God.

The return of the LORD to Zion

So why do we read this passage from the Bible in church on Christmas Day? Listen, and I'll tell you the secret. Today is the day of 'the return of the LORD to Zion'. Of course, God never goes away. He's always here, but he's invisible. Yet sometimes it feels as though he's lost interest in us. Jesus the Son of God has put an end to all that.

He was born on Christmas Day in Bethlehem, which is just down the road from Jerusalem. God came to earth at Christmas. And though we can't see him, he's still here. He's never going away. Now that's really good news. So 'Wake up, it's Christmas Day' is good news, every year. This is the day when Jesus was born. The Lord is with us, and he's never going away. You can't see him, but he'll be with you. He'll enjoy watching you celebrate his birthday.

All-age worship

Draw the people of Jerusalem standing on the city walls, peering at the messenger coming over the Mount of Olives. Put a baby doll or a crib figure in a parcel and unwrap it: Jesus, the best Christmas present of all.

Suggested hymns

Angels from the realms of glory; It came upon the midnight clear; Hark, the herald angels sing; How lovely on the mountains are the feet of him.

Christmas Day
Second Service   Jesus Emptied Himself
Morning Ps. 110 This day of your birth, 117 Steadfast love; Evening Ps. 8 Out of the mouths of babes; Isa. 65:17–25 A new creation; Phil. 2:5–11 Jesus emptied himself; *or* Luke 2:1–20 (*if it has not been used at the Principal Service of the day*)

> *'Let the same mind be in you that was in Christ Jesus, who, though he was in the form of God, did not regard equality with God as something to be exploited, but emptied himself, taking the form of a slave, being born in human likeness.' Philippians 2:5–7*

Truth from poetry

There are some truths which can't be expressed in prose. Arthur O'Shaughnessy wrote:

> We are the music makers,
> we are the dreamers of dreams;

> we are the movers and shakers
> of the world for ever, it seems.

There's a lot of poetry in the Bible, and it's a great mistake to read it as though it were prose. You'll learn far more from one profound Christmas carol about God becoming human in Jesus, than from a dozen weighty tomes about Christology. That's why those who tried to 'demythologize' Christianity never succeeded, for myth is a form of poetry, and if you take the poetry out of the Christian faith, the prose that remains is too cramped to contain the great mystery of God.

St Paul's songs

In several places St Paul's writing seems to take wing as poetry. One such passage was read as our New Testament reading today. Of course, translated into English the lines don't rhyme, but there seems to be a rhythm about them, the phrases fall into groups of three, and most modern translations of the Bible print them in the form of a poem. It's about the humility of Jesus, who was equal to God, but became human and died on the cross. We can't be certain whether Paul had written it himself, or was quoting a song with which his Philippian readers were already familiar. Maybe it was the hymn which Paul and Silas were singing at midnight in the prison on their first visit to Philippi, and which so astonished the jailer that he became a Christian. It certainly proclaims one of the deepest insights into the incarnation of the Son of God.

Jesus emptied himself

It's sometimes called 'The Song of Christ's Glory'. It tells how Jesus, who was equal to God and shared in all the riches and glory of heaven, 'emptied himself' of everything, and dwelt on earth, lived in poverty, and died the shameful death of the cross. 'Therefore God highly exalted him,' raised him to life again, and raised him to the position of supreme glory in heaven, so that everybody on earth should worship him. Paul several times mentions 'the fullness of God', as though the gods which others worshipped were only part of the truth, the whole truth is to be found in Jesus. Jesus, when he was in heaven, enjoyed all the splendour of the universe, he knew everything and he could do anything. But when he was born a helpless baby in Bethlehem, he put aside all his glory and his power and his knowledge, and became as weak and downtrodden and humble and, yes, even as ignorant as you and I are. It was as though he had been full of all these things, sings St Paul, and he deliberately emptied himself. The rediscovery of his knowledge and healing power only came to him gradually as he rediscovered, in prayer and meditation, that he was the Son of God. This daring interpretation is called the 'kenotic theory of the incarnation'. On the Athens Metro, the word for 'Mind the Gap' is *kenos*: the empty space between the platform and the train. So *kenosis* is the theory that Jesus deliberately emptied himself of his divine omnipotence and omniscience when he became human. Quite how far Paul would have gone with it in prose is not certain, but he was quite bold in singing it as a poem.

Imitate his humility

When we realize what Jesus had given up in order to come to earth, it makes the wonder of Christmas absolutely breathtaking. What a paradox, that the babe in the manger is the creator of the universe! What humility! What self-sacrifice! Paul tells us to imitate the humility of Jesus. It sounds almost presumptuous. But when we realize the astonishing generosity of Jesus, who became human for our sakes, we can't cling to our possessions, our greed, our pride and our selfishness. When we *are* willing to pattern our lives on his example of self-emptying, however, the Bethlehem story becomes a marvel again, like it was when we were children. Then every day becomes as happy as Christmas Day.

Suggested hymns

All praise to thee, for thou, O king divine; Hark, the herald angels sing; Long ago, prophets knew; Where is this stupendous stranger?

First Sunday of Christmas   31 December
Principal Service   Understanding God

1 Sam. 2:18–20, 26 Giving children to God; Ps. 148 Young and old together; Col. 3:12–17 The Word of God; Luke 2:41–52 The child Jesus in the Temple

'After three days [his parents] found [Jesus] in the temple, sitting among the teachers, listening to them and asking them questions.

And all who heard him were amazed at his understanding and his answers.' Luke 2:46–47

A normal child

To outward appearances, Jesus was a normal boy of 12 years old. Until he started debating with the teachers of the Law in the Temple in Jerusalem. Then they realized that he already had a quite extraordinary knowledge of 'his Father's business'. Quite how much he knew we may never understand. The Scriptures are quite clear: he was fully human and fully divine. We speak of God's 'omniscience', meaning that God knows everything there is to know. Did Jesus give up his omniscience when he came to earth? Well, all that knowledge couldn't possibly fit into the brain of a baby, even a special baby like baby Jesus. So, for a while at least, Jesus didn't know everything there is to know. But he learned fast. Even by the age of 12 he understood more about God than the experts, because his was heart-knowledge; theirs was head-knowledge. When he was 30, he knew that he was Son of God, that he had to die to save the world, and that his death would be followed by resurrection. Was all that insight already there in the 12-year-old's brain, or was there a learning process all through his life? We don't know. Let's just say Jesus was a normal child who'd developed his knowledge of God to a fantastic degree.

Children's understanding

Other children, too, often astonish us with the depth of their understanding. Many a 12-year-old girl or boy has developed a profound intuition about what's important in life, and knows more about love, and what it is to give it and receive it and to be without it, than their parents. So it's not surprising that many a child would amaze us with their understanding of God. Only we seldom ask them, because we assume they don't know anything worth asking about. The teachers in the Jerusalem Temple, however, followed a question-and-answer method of study. Even today, there's nothing a devout Jew loves so much as discussing the holy books with other Jews. So they weren't surprised when this precocious 12-year-old listened to them and asked them questions. They followed their normal practice and asked him questions in return. All who heard Jesus 'were amazed at his understanding and his answers'.

Jesus wasn't ashamed

Jesus wasn't ashamed to ask questions about how his teachers understood the Scriptures. Neither should we be: if you don't ask, you never learn. The Bible's a wonderful book; useful for the practical business of living, and useful in leading us towards eternal life. We should be ashamed, when we read how diligently Jesus discussed the Scriptures, compared with our own casual ignorance. Take nothing for granted. Study the Bible by yourself, and when you have any questions, be ready to take them to the experts, or look them up in a book. But then don't accept the experts' answers unquestioningly. Question them further, and compare their answers with those of others. Nothing's too much trouble to take, to understand the word of God properly; sadly, many people remain satisfied with a superficial and distorted understanding.

Discussion groups

It's best if you can form a group of friends and meet regularly, say once a week, for several months. Get hold of one of the many series of excellent Bible study notes to start you talking. Then don't be afraid to put forward your questions and your point of view, even if you're afraid they might sound foolish; that's how we learn. And leave plenty of time for even the humblest member of the group to have their say. A little girl was once told to 'Think before you speak!' She answered, 'But how do I know what I think, until I've heard what I say?' She's got a point! Our thoughts, if we have any, are all woolly and muddled until we make the effort to put them into words. We should listen to the experts, and ask them questions. That's what Jesus did. And we shouldn't be too proud to listen to the opinions even of children, and 'babes in the faith'. We can learn from them, as the teachers of the Law learnt from the 12-year-old Jesus.

All-age worship

Make a list of questions about the meaning of the Bible to which you would like answers. Let children do their best to answer them, and compare their answers with those of the experts.

Suggested hymns

Hushed was the evening hymn; I cannot tell why he whom angels worship; Lord, thy word abideth; Once in royal David's city.

First Sunday of Christmas
Second Service   **Adoption** Ps. 132 David's descendants; Isa. 61 The Spirit is upon me; Gal. 3:27—4:7 Children of God; *Gospel at Holy Communion*: Luke 2:15–21 He was called Jesus

> *'When the fullness of time had come, God sent his Son, born of a woman, born under the law, in order to redeem those who were under the law, so that we might receive adoption as children.'*
> *Galatians 4:4*

Inheritance laws

In Bible times, the inheritance laws were absolutely vital to the economy. If a man was farming a piece of land, and had an accident, or became old and frail, who was going to take over? Unless that was completely clear, the land might go to waste, with no food and no income being produced. In that case the frail old man and his wife would probably starve to death. There was no welfare state, no old-age pensions – without an income you'd die. Or suppose the old man died, and nobody succeeded him, who'd support the widow? No wonder life for most people in those days was described by Thomas Hobbes as 'nasty, brutish and short'. Unless there was an heir. That made all the difference. If the oldest son was old enough and strong enough to take over the farm, then he'd grow enough food and make enough money to give the old people a comfortable retirement and look after the women and children until they could look after themselves. So to have someone ready to inherit your property was essential.

Adopting an heir

I've been talking about a farm, but the same considerations applied to every inheritance from a carpenter's shop up to and including a kingdom. So if a couple was childless, or their son was crippled or killed, what could they do? Well, they could adopt. Adoption was much more common than it is today, because it was vital to survival. So you might ask your neighbour who had lots of kids if you could adopt one of his sons to become your heir. Or you could adopt a nephew or a more distant relative. Some people who owned slaves even gave their slaves their freedom, and then adopted them as sons so that they could inherit their property and keep the family line from dying out.

What a privilege!

What a privilege! Imagine if you're somebody's younger son, and you know that when the old man pops his clogs your big brother will take all the land worth having and you'll have to go out to work and scrape a living. Then suddenly your rich but childless uncle says he'd like to adopt you as his son, to inherit all his property. Your life and prospects would be transformed overnight, and you'd leap for joy! Even more if you were a slave, with no prospect of ever being free, and all of a sudden you're told you're going to be cock of the roost. The word 'adoption' had distinctly good vibes in those days.

Becoming a Christian

That's why St Paul uses the word 'adoption' for what happens when you become a Christian. A privilege, a piece of good news which transforms your life. Not a bad metaphor. Don't forget that when you give a slave his freedom, setting him free from the laws which enslaved him, the word used is to 'redeem' him. Then listen again to what St Paul wrote to the Galatians:

> When the fullness of time had come, God sent his Son, born of a woman, born under the law, in order to redeem those who were under the law, so that we might receive adoption as children. And because you are children, God has sent the Spirit of his Son into our hearts, crying, 'Abba! Father!' So you are no longer a slave but a child, and if a child then also an heir, through God.

You are adopted

What a privilege! Now you're free from the code of respectability, which says you must never do anything out of the ordinary if you want to mix with the right people. Free to love your neighbours, and dedicate your life to helping other people in imaginative ways which no code of behaviour could ever suggest. And free to love God. Not to worship him because you're told to, or you're afraid he'll be annoyed if you don't. But because he's given you your freedom. What would you do when the rich uncle set you free from your future as a younger son, or a slave? You'd probably fling your arms round him, and give him a big hug. Why don't you do that to God? If you once take on board what Paul's talking about, your whole attitude to God will be different, and serving him will become an endless joy.

Suggested hymns

Abba, Father, let me be; Fear not, rejoice and be glad; Love came down at Christmas; On Christmas night all Christians sing.

Baptism of Christ (First Sunday of Epiphany)
7 January 2007
Principal Service   **Wind and Fire** Isa. 43:1–7 When you pass through the waters; Ps. 29 The voice of the Lord is over the waters; Acts 8:14–17 Baptism and the Holy Spirit; Luke 3:15–17, 21–22 The baptism of Jesus

> *'[John the Baptist said,] "I baptize you with water; but one who is more powerful than I is coming; I am not worthy to untie the thong of his sandals. He will baptize you with the Holy Spirit and fire."'*
> *Luke 3:16*

Threshing floors

Not long ago in the Holy Land you could still see Arabs threshing and winnowing their wheat on the ancient threshing-floors. Now it's all done by machinery; but in the old days, they cut the wheat with sickles and brought it in sheaves to the threshing-floor. There they separated the grain from the stalk by threshing. This was done either with a flail, or by animals treading all over it, or dragging a 'sledge' with sharp stones over it. After raking away the straw, you're left with grain and chaff. This you gather up with a winnow-ing-fork (which looks more like a shovel) and toss it into the air. The heavy grain falls to the ground, and the wind blows away the chaff.

The valuable grain's shovelled into sacks for the barn; the worthless chaff's destroyed in a bonfire. What's good is separated from the rubbish 'by wind and fire'.

What John the Baptist meant – fire

John the Baptist said of Jesus, 'His winnowing-fork is in his hand, to clear his threshing-floor and to gather the wheat into his granary; but the chaff he will burn with unquenchable fire.' What did he mean? His hearers were all Jews, part of the chosen people, but some took that for granted and did nothing to build the kingdom. God wanted them to live a life of love and service to their neighbours, and spread the good news of the love of God to the rest of the world. But some of them selfishly concentrated on their own concerns. They were real lightweights, no substance to them. As far as being any use to God was concerned, they were rubbish. So John uses a metaphor from the threshing-floor: the grain will be separated from the chaff by wind and fire. We shouldn't take any metaphor too literally. God still loves the selfish people and will do all for them that he can. God doesn't get any satisfaction from seeing them destroyed. So this is not a description of souls burning in the fires of hell. But it's meant to make us sit up with a jolt and ask ourselves: 'Am I really rubbish? Rubbish, as far as making this world a better place is concerned? If so I'd better buck my ideas up; otherwise I'm just chaff, there may be nothing of me worth saving into the next life.'

What John the Baptist meant – wind

But the second metaphor is that of the wind. The same word's used of the Holy Spirit. The Holy Spirit, given to us at our baptism, really sorts out the grain from the chaff. Because the Spirit is given to us to bring us spiritual strength – strength to love our neighbours and witness to unbelievers. Yet most Christians don't realize they have this strength, because they never use it. William Carey, a pioneer missionary in India, said, 'Attempt great things for God, expect great things from God.' We've all been baptized in the Spirit; we have the power if we will use it. So next time you're challenged to love someone rather unlovable, or to speak of the love of God to someone who hasn't yet received it, or to speak in public about your faith, don't just give up and say, 'I can't do that, I'm not the type.' You're not chaff, you're not rubbish. Actually you're God's beloved son or daughter; with you God is well pleased. Instead, try praying for the Holy Spirit. Say, 'God, please give me the power to do this seemingly impossible task for you,' and see what happens. I believe you'll find you can do it. Don't forget that at Pentecost the Holy Spirit came as a mighty wind, and tongues of fire. It sounds like an uncomfortable experience, but to those who were willing to be used by God, the Spirit came as 'power from on high'. The Holy Spirit comes as wind and fire, to separate the grain from the chaff; all it requires is that you should be willing for God to use you in practical deeds of love, through the power of the Holy Spirit.

All-age worship

Make models or draw pictures of the tools used in the old days in harvesting, threshing and winnowing: sickles, a flail, animals treading over the grain, or dragging a 'sledge' with sharp stones sticking out from it, a winnowing-fork.

Suggested hymns

Christ, when for us you were baptized; On Jordan's bank the Baptist's cry; When Jesus came to Jordan; Wind, wind, blow on me.

Baptism of Christ
Second Service   **Birth by Drowning** Ps. 46 There is a river, 47 Clap your hands; Isa. 55:1–11 Come to the waters; Rom. 6:1–11 Baptized into Christ; *Gospel at Holy Communion:* Mark 1:4–11 The baptism of Jesus

> *'Do you not know that all of us who have been baptized into Christ Jesus were baptized into his death? Therefore we have been buried with him by baptism into death, so that, just as Christ was raised from the dead by the glory of the Father, so we too might walk in newness of life.' Romans 6:3–4*

Try to imagine

Picture in your imagination the crucifixion of Jesus. What's going on here? Is it the death of the gentlest man that ever lived? Yes. But it's more. Paradoxically, it's the beginning of new life, the life of the resurrection. Then imagine a baby being baptized. What's going on here? Is it a washing away of the dirt of sin? Hardly, because the baby's had little time or opportunity to commit any sins yet. The water of baptism's like that in which they wash the newborn in the delivery room: it marks the beginning of life. Now, try to imagine a selfish man, grappling with his sinful habits and deciding to give them up so that he can become a Christian. What's going on here? It probably feels like death, having to sacrifice so many things in which he's found his pleasure. But actually, it's new birth; he's setting out on a new way of life which will give him far more abiding joy than the old life ever could. Lastly, picture in your imagination an elderly Christian woman on her death bed. Sometimes death comes to us mercifully in our sleep; we close our eyes and wake up in eternity. But not always. Sometimes dying's quite a struggle. A visitor called on the mother of the German poet Goethe and asked to see her. 'You can't see her now, she's busy,' he was told. 'Busy!' he exclaimed. 'How can an old lady in her eighties be busy?' The reply was quite matter-of-fact: 'Frau Goethe's busy dying.' The struggles of death are like the pains of childbirth; they're the beginning of new life.

Baptism into the death of Christ

When the followers of John the Baptist were baptized, it was a washing away of the past, to make a fresh start in the family of God. They probably went right down under the water as though they were being drowned, and then came up again to begin their new life. It was, in fact, birth by drowning. When Jesus was baptized, he went down into the River Jordan just like all the others. Then he came up again and heard the voice of his Father calling him to begin a new life. When the first Christian converts were baptized in New Testament times, sometimes a whole family was baptized together. Sometimes they went down into a pool or river for their symbolic birth by drowning. Jesus said, 'You must be born again.' St Paul said:

Do you not know that all of us who have been baptized into Christ Jesus were baptized into his death? Therefore we have been buried with him by baptism into death, so that, just as Christ was raised from the dead by the glory of the Father, so we too might walk in newness of life.

Dying to sin, rising to new life

Some of the new converts who were baptized in St Paul's time may have been wicked sinners. Probably most of them were just average-selfish like the rest of us. In either case, Paul says, when you become a Christian all that has to end. The old sinful, selfish human nature has to 'die'. 'How can we who died to sin go on living in it?' he asks. Now, by 'living in sin', he doesn't mean what the newspapers mean by those words today. In fact, the harsh, judgemental people who criticize other people's way of life may be 'living in sin' in a much worse way than those they criticize! It's selfishness and self-centredness which defines sin for St Paul, and Christians have to 'die to self'. This may seem like a sacrifice, but paradoxically it's the way into a new life full of joy. We have to 'die daily'. Every day we die to sin, and are raised to new life; it's a daily birth by drowning. If we've been through this every day of our Christian life, what terrors can the eventual death of the body hold for us? We've experienced the death of the old, and the birth of the new, so many times before.

Suggested hymns

All my heart this night rejoices; Be still, for the Spirit of the Lord; Take my life, and let it be; When Jesus came to Jordan.

Second Sunday of Epiphany   14 January

Principal Service   **Water into Wine** Isa. 62:1–5 Nations shall see your salvation; Ps. 36:5–10 All peoples; 1 Cor. 12:1–11 Many gifts, one Spirit; John 2:1–11 The wedding at Cana

> *'The steward said to the bridegroom, "Everyone serves the good wine first, and then the inferior wine after the guests have become drunk. But you have kept the good wine until now."' John 2:10*

Obsession with purity

It's tragic when somebody suffers from the form of mental illness called an obsessional neurosis. For some, it's a need to go back several times after they have left the house to check that they've locked the door. Others feel the need to wash their hands over and over again, and panic whenever they fear that a single spot of dirt or a germ should have got inside their house. Concern for security and hygiene are good things, but when they become obsessions, it's very hard for the sufferer to live a normal life.

Jewish washings

Yet Jewish society in the time of Jesus had acquired a sort of national obsession with washing. Priests and Levites were commanded in the Scriptures to wash themselves and their clothes before entering the Temple; people who'd been contaminated by disease, or contact with a dead body, had to wash. But it had spread to all areas of life; St Mark's Gospel tells us that

> The Pharisees, and all the Jews, do not eat unless they thoroughly wash their hands, thus observing the tradition of the elders; and they do not eat anything from the market unless they wash it; and there are also many other traditions that they observe, the washing of cups, pots, and bronze kettles.

Most large Jewish houses had special areas set aside for daily ritual washing, and in the remains of some houses in Jerusalem archaeologists have found a distinctive local form of water-pot made not of pottery but of stone.

Moral purity

All these ritual washings weren't to do with hygiene. They may have started that way, but it had become a question of whether dirty human beings could make themselves worthy to enter the presence of God. It became a sign of moral purity, and then a substitute for moral purity. Religious people thought that because they'd washed, they could look down on the immoral people around them.

The marriage at Cana

Jesus and his disciples attended a marriage at Cana in Galilee. It must have been a very religious household, for 'standing there were six stone water jars for the Jewish rites of purification, each holding twenty or thirty gallons' – that's 120 to 180 gallons of water to make a few people feel worthy to talk to God, and more pure than their neighbours. Talk about obsessive! But Jesus changed all that, by turning the water into wine.

Wine for gladness, wine for love

Wine carried a wholly different weight of symbolism. The psalms sing of 'wine to gladden the human heart', the Song of Solomon says, 'Your love is better than wine,' and 'Eat, friends, drink, and be drunk with love.' So wine is a sign of joy and gladness, of parties and love. Above all it symbolizes spontaneity, the very opposite of the nit-picking search for purity of the obsessive washers. Jesus liked to celebrate with the outcasts, who'd given up on the search for purity, telling them that God loves them, and that unselfish love for others is at the heart of morality. Small wonder that he was called 'a glutton and a drunkard, a friend of tax collectors and sinners'!

Gallons of love

Jesus compared his teaching to new wine, which, as it bubbled and fermented, would burst the dried-up wineskins of the old obsessive religion. So at the wedding at Cana, he turned the search for absolute moral purity, which is essentially selfish, into 180 gallons of love! Of course, to be totally loving is much more demanding than to be totally pure, so he wasn't lowering standards but raising them. He was calling us to a life which overflows with love, generosity, tolerance and caring for others. Sadly, there are still Christians who think that religion consists of abiding by a code of rules, and criticize their neighbours for not keeping as high a standard as they do. Well, of course, Jesus wasn't condoning drunkenness. Of course, an alcoholic needs to go for treatment. But the example of Jesus should encourage us to a much more relaxed attitude to life. Life on earth's a preparation for the great wedding feast of heaven, 'the marriage supper of the Lamb'. We should never condemn any other human being because we feel they're less pure than we are. 'Love covers a multitude of sins.' Our water for purification has been turned into the wine of love.

All-age worship

Children can play at wedding parties using soft drinks. Why did Jesus enjoy parties?

Suggested hymns

Bind us together, Lord; Come and join the celebration; Come, my way, my truth, my life; Songs of thankfulness and praise.

Second Sunday of Epiphany

Second Service   **'Speak, Lord, for your servant is listening'** Ps. 96 Tell of his salvation; 1 Sam. 3:1–20 The boy Samuel; Ephesians 4:1–16 Unity in the Body of Christ; *Gospel at Holy Communion*: John 1:29–42 The first disciples

'Eli said to Samuel, "Go, lie down; and if he calls you, you shall say, 'Speak, Lord, for your servant is listening.'"' 1 Samuel 3:9

Hushed was the evening hymn

James Burns was a Scottish minister, who was in charge of the Free Church in Dunblane and then the Presbyterian Church in Hampstead; he died in 1864 and is buried in Highgate Cemetery. The best known of the many hymns he wrote is about the childhood of the prophet Samuel, the story that we heard in our Old Testament reading at this service:

> Hushed was the evening hymn,
> The temple courts were dark;
> The lamp was burning dim
> Before the sacred ark;
> When suddenly a voice divine
> Rang through the silence of the shrine.
>
> The old man, meek and mild,
> The priest of Israel, slept;
> His watch the temple child,
> The little Levite, kept;
> And what from Eli's sense was sealed
> The Lord to Hannah's son revealed.

Respect for children's faith

One of the reasons for the popularity of this very Victorian hymn – the most popular tune was written by Sir Arthur Sullivan, of the 'Gilbert and Sullivan' partnership – is that it treats the faith of a child with respect. Psalm 8 speaks of what God can teach us 'out of the mouths of babes and infants' – 'babes and sucklings' in the old translation – and Jesus stood a child in the middle of the circle and told his disciples to become like children. It is the simple trust that children usually show to their parents that we're to imitate by our faith in God. So the hymn continues, 'O give me Samuel's heart', and 'O give me Samuel's mind, a sweet unmurmuring faith'.

'Speak, LORD, for your servant is listening'

Eli said to the boy Samuel in the story, 'Go, lie down; and if he calls you, you shall say, "Speak, LORD, for your servant is listening."' Samuel did so, and the Lord called him to be a prophet. The hymn in a later verse prays:

> O give me Samuel's ear,
> The open ear, O Lord,
> Alive and quick to hear
> Each whisper of Thy Word,
> Like him to answer at Thy call,
> And to obey Thee first of all.

Samuel's task was not an easy one, for all children want to be liked, and if he did what God told him, Samuel would make himself unpopular. Yet Samuel was called to announce to Eli – who was acting as a father to Samuel – and to Eli's family, that the responsibility of being the Lord's priests at Shiloh was to be taken away from them. The Shiloh sanctuary would be destroyed, because of their failure to live up to their calling. Unpopular as the message was, Samuel gained respect from all because of the sincerity with which he proclaimed it. He went on to become one of Israel's greatest prophets, anointing both Saul and then David as kings.

A listening ear

God seldom speaks audibly to people, as he seems to have done to Samuel. But God still speaks to us today. It may be through reading the Bible that we hear God speaking to us, or hearing the words of a fellow Christian. It may be through the nagging voice of conscience, telling us we ought not to do this, or we should do that. It may be we have to make a choice between two courses of action; we weigh up the pros and cons, and try to consider the will of God as one of the factors, indeed the most important factor in making our decision. Or it may be that, as we go about our daily duties, we come to the deep, quiet conviction that God wants us to do something for him. We should always check this with other people, to make sure we're not projecting our own desires onto God. What God calls us to do may not be easy, and it may not be pleasant. If we decide that's what God wants, we can ignore it, but that way we shall never have peace. Or we can have the strength of our convictions, and step out in faith to put them into practice. Above all, we must expect God to have a purpose for us. Then in our prayers, we are to say, 'Speak, LORD, for your servant is listening.'

Suggested hymns

Hushed was the evening hymn; Lord, speak to me, that I may speak; O Jesus, I have promised; Take my life, and let it be.

Third Sunday of Epiphany   21 January
See also 'Week of Prayer for Christian Unity', p. 293
Principal Service   **Fulfilled Today** Neh. 8:1–3, 5–6, 8–10 Joy in the Commandments; Ps. 19 The heavens declare the glory of God; 1 Cor. 12:12–31a The unity of Christ's Body the Church; Luke 4:14–21 Jesus reads the Scriptures at Nazareth

> *'Then [Jesus] began to say to them, "Today this scripture has been fulfilled in your hearing."' Luke 4:21*

God of surprises

Recently, a Christian asked a Jew, 'What do you think about Jesus?' The quick-witted Jew replied, 'We're always delighted when one of our nice Jewish boys does well for himself!' Probably the people of Nazareth felt similarly proud when the local boy who'd become famous returned to visit the synagogue in their home town. But he wasn't as they had expected him to be. Distinguished visitors were often asked to read from the scroll of the Scriptures, so they handed it to Jesus. He read from Isaiah, chapter 61:

> The spirit of the Lord GOD is upon me, because the LORD has anointed me; he has sent me to bring good news to the oppressed, to bind up the brokenhearted, to proclaim liberty to the captives, and release to the prisoners; to proclaim the year of the Lord's favour . . .

It's the classic statement from the Old Testament of the prophet's call: he's to proclaim good news. He's like a herald who comes to a people ground down by years of war, to tell them that the armistice has been signed. Jesus said that was just what he himself was doing: 'Today this scripture has been fulfilled in your hearing.' What did the people of Nazareth expect Jesus to do? Probably to organize an army to drive out the hated Romans from the 'occupied territories' of Israel. Instead, he showed them that God doesn't just love Jews, God loves everyone, even the hated Gentiles – even the widow in Sidon, even Naaman the Syrian. They didn't like that: it was an offence to their patriotic feelings. Truly God is, as the Jesuit writer Father Gerard Hughes calls him, a 'God of Surprises'. So they tried to throw Jesus down the hill.

A programme of social reform

What Jesus was promising was just what the Nazarenes didn't want to hear: a worldwide programme of social reform. 'He has sent me . . . to proclaim the year of the Lord's favour.' Jesus was describing the Jubilee Year, when debts were written off, slaves set free and allowed to return home, and confiscated lands returned to their original owners. *This* is Jubilee Year, he said – not only now, but every year from now onwards. The slaves are to be set free, not only in Israel but all over the world. The oppressed are to be given justice, allowed to live in peace and grow prosperous, not only in their home country but in every nation. I can assure you, the message of justice and peace is never popular with those who have power. We all live in hierarchies of power, whether we realize it or not. We want justice for ourselves from those who are in authority over us. But we ourselves should also show justice to those whom we have power over, as individuals or as a society or as a nation. That's not such good news, because it means limiting our own power and prosperity. So the message of Jesus was rejected then, and it still is today.

Today

For the message of Jesus still rings out today. The kingdom of God will only come in all its fullness some time in the future, or even in the next world. But if we concentrate only on that, we shall miss the fact that God's kingdom of peace and justice is coming into being today. 'Say not the struggle naught availeth', wrote Arthur Hugh Clough.

> And not by eastern windows only,
> When daylight comes, comes in the light;
> In front the sun climbs slow, how slowly!
> But westward, look, the land is bright!

The justice that Jesus preached about is being brought about all over the world, in obscure corners by unsung heroes. If we want to be a part of the programme he outlined, we'd better get involved with it in our own corner of the globe, wherever we have the power to bring liberty to the captives and release to the oppressed. There's no waiting for the God of Surprises till tomorrow, for 'Today this scripture has been fulfilled in your hearing.'

All-age worship

Make a model synagogue.

Suggested hymns

Hark the glad sound! the Saviour comes; The kingdom of God is justice and joy; Where cross the crowded ways of life; Will you come and follow me?

Third Sunday of Epiphany
Second Service   **God Made Me what I Am** Ps. 33 The greatness and goodness of God; Num. 9:15–23 The cloud of God's presence; 1 Cor. 7:17–24 The life that the Lord has assigned; *Gospel at Holy Communion*: Mark 1:21–28 Authority over an unclean spirit

> 'Let each of you lead the life that the Lord has assigned, to which God called you. This is my rule in all the churches.' 1 Corinthians 7:17

God made we what I am

In the musical *Fiddler on the Roof*, Tevye laments his poverty, singing:

> God, who made the lion and the lamb,
> you it is who made me what I am –
> would it spoil some great eternal plan
> if I were a wealthy man?

God made me what I am. And St Paul, another Jew, exhorts the Christians in Corinth, 'Let each of you lead the life that the Lord has assigned, to which God called you.' He seems to be suggesting that nobody should try to change their life. So those who are married should stay married, not seek a divorce; those who are not married should remain single; those who are slaves shouldn't try to buy their freedom. It's one of the most controversial passages in his writings, and it probably can't be applied directly to our own times without taking into consideration the way our society's changed. It seems that St Paul still believed that there was going to be a Second Coming of Jesus in his own lifetime. So there was no point in anybody changing, as he saw it. He wasn't against marriage in principle, but he saw that marriage might distract Christians from the urgent task of spreading the gospel before the Lord came. However, he conceded that not marrying might also be a distraction for some, so he wrote that 'It is better to marry than to burn with suppressed desire'. Jesus didn't return in Paul's lifetime, and we now face a different situation. We should live today on the assumption that Jesus might come, and plan for the rest of our lives on the assumption that he won't. Paul also knew that to encourage Christians to disobey their husbands, or slaves to demand their freedom, would tar the new Christian movement with the reputation of a revolutionary organization aiming to overthrow the Empire. They weren't yet strong enough to survive the persecution that would result.

Misuse of the Bible

But the best things can be misused, and that includes the Bible itself. Around the time of the American civil war, some of the slave owners of the South quoted this passage from St Paul to justify holding onto their slaves, who were often kept in terrible and demeaning conditions. In the nineteenth century in England, attempts to get decent conditions for working men, women and children were similarly dismissed as dangerous radicalism, and the best that could be said of a servant was that 'he knew his station'. Children and apprentices were told to memorize the phrase in the Catechism that told them to 'order myself lowly and reverently to all my betters' and 'to do my duty in that state of life to which it shall please God to call me'. Anybody from a humble position who tried to 'better himself' was met with a verse from Mrs Alexander's hymn, 'All things bright and beautiful', which mercifully we no longer sing:

> The rich man in his castle,
> the poor man at his gate,
> God made them, high or lowly,
> and ordered their estate.

In Mrs Alexander's defence it should be pointed out that she married a poor Irish clergyman, and knew at first hand about the life of the poor. It was after the hymn was written that her husband became a bishop and they moved into a castle!

Finding God where you are

Yet there's still something important to learn from Paul's words. We sometimes imagine that if our circumstances were different, it would be easier to obey God; that a change of situation will make everything better. If changing circumstances was the solution to difficulties, Adam would have had no problems after he left the Garden of Eden! We forget that God's everywhere, and while we should seek opportunities to serve him on a wider stage, there's still plenty to be done for God in the situation where we now are. There are people to be helped and loved, words of encouragement to be said, and lofty ideals to hold up to people, in the street where you now live, and the place where you now work. And you may be the only person who can do it. Until the time comes when God calls you somewhere else, do your best to lead the life that the Lord has assigned to you for now, to which God has called you for the time being.

Suggested hymns

Awake, my soul, and with the sun; Father, I place into your hands; Forth in thy name, O Lord, I go; Teach me, my God and King.

Fourth Sunday of Epiphany (or Candlemas; see p. 297)

28 January

Principal Service   **What Is Love?** Ezek. 43:27—44:4 The glory of the Lord filled the Temple; Ps. 48 The greatness of God; 1 Cor. 13:1–13 Love; Luke 2:22–40 The presentation of Christ in the Temple

> *'Love is patient; love is kind; love is not envious or boastful or arrogant or rude. It does not insist on its own way; it is not irritable or resentful; it does not rejoice in wrongdoing, but rejoices in the truth. It bears all things, believes all things, hopes all things, endures all things. Love never ends.' 1 Corinthians 13:4–8*

What is love?

During the national census, the enumerator came into the vicarage and read out to the vicar the questions on her clipboard. 'What is your employer's business,' she asked, 'and how long has he been doing it?' After a moment's thought, the vicar answered, 'He's been in the love business since he created the world, and my job is to help him spread it around more.' But what is love? C. S. Lewis wrote a book called *The Four Loves* in which he points out that four words are used for love in the New Testament. There's friendship, brotherly and sisterly love, sexual desire, and self-sacrificing love. All of these are translated into English as love; we have only one word, where the Greeks had four. In the greatest hymn to love in any language, St Paul's First Letter to the Corinthians, chapter 13, he explains what Christians mean by love. It's the fourth word that he uses, *agapē* or self-sacrificing love, and he defines it in four and a half verses in the middle of the chapter: 'Love is patient; love is kind . . .', and so on.

Squabbling at Corinth

The people in the Greek city of Corinth, to whom St Paul wrote this letter, were always squabbling – they were famous for it. It had even infected the church, and there's nothing worse for a church than when its members start squabbling. Sometimes squabbling's the death of a congregation: people stop coming and the church has to close. It was to prevent this happening that Paul wrote not one but two letters to the Christians of Corinth. There were several groups; you can find them all in the Church today. One said the most important thing in Christianity was correct understanding about God, correct teaching and correct doctrine. 'Knowledge', they called it. Some said it was moral behaviour – unless your morals are irreproachable you can't be a Christian, they said. Some said it was practical Christianity: all that matters is how much you're prepared to give and to suffer for other people. Others said that it was mystical experiences that made you a Christian; the form this usually took in Corinth was called 'speaking in tongues'. 'Faith is what matters most', said some; 'No, it's the gift of prophecy that matters most', said others. Yet another group put all their emphasis on the afterlife; our hope for heaven should fill our minds, they said. And the trouble is, they were all right, at least in saying that these things were important. Where they were wrong was in claiming that their favourite aspect of Christianity was more important than all the others. Worse still, they would have nothing to do with the other groups, who didn't share their opinion on what's most important. They'd whisper under their breath, 'The others aren't really Christian.' They'd even try to drive them out of the church, or go off and set up a new congregation of their own where only the pure form of Christianity was taught. And this was dividing the church in Corinth into splinters and destroying it. What was poor Paul to do?

Important, but not as important as love

Well, first he tactfully agreed with each group in turn. Your emphasis is very important, he told them. But not all-important. The most important thing was to maintain the unity of God's people in Corinth in love. What you're teaching is important, but not as important as love. Those who 'spoke in tongues' thought that they were speaking unknown foreign languages, or even the language of angels. But 'if I speak in the tongues of mortals or of angels, but do not have love, I am a noisy gong or a clanging cymbal'. Similarly with prophetic powers, mysticism, faith and giving to charity: they're important, agrees Paul, but not so important that they justify breaking fellowship with other Christians. How much we need to hear that message today!

All-age worship

Write a love-letter to someone you find it difficult to love, telling them that because Jesus loves you both, you intend to love them for Jesus's sake. Then tear it up or burn it, never mention it, but try to show love by your actions.

Suggested hymns

Gracious Spirit, Holy Ghost; Lord of all hopefulness, Lord of all joy; Love divine, all loves excelling; O love that wilt not let me go.

Fourth Sunday of Epiphany
Second Service   **The Test of Experience** Ps. 34 O taste and see; 1 Chron. 29:6–19 Giving to the Lord; Acts 7:44–50 God does not dwell in temples; *Gospel at Holy Communion*: John 4:19–29a True worship

> *'O taste and see that the LORD is gracious; blessed is the one who trusts in him.' Psalm 34:8* (Common Worship)

Suck it and see

There's a rather vulgar expression which was popular at one time in England: 'Suck it and see.' It sounds as though it was an advertising slogan for a lollipop, or a catch-phrase on a comedy radio show. Perhaps it was both. But it enshrines a profound truth. If you are in doubt about the quality of a product, you must try it. The test of the pudding's in the eating. The only way to be sure of anything is the test of experience. The same's true of belief in God. 'O taste and see that the LORD is gracious.' Suck it and see!

Scientific method

And this links up with scientific method. The reason we have so many scientific aids to comfortable living today is because the scientists of the European Renaissance refused to take anything on trust. Too many people had been willing to say, 'Well, my parents believed it, so it must be true,' or, 'The Church says the world is flat so who am I to question it?' But the scientists insisted that nothing should be accepted as true unless it could be tested by experiment. So arose the 'scientific method', which in outline is this:

- Observe as many facts as you can.
- Link them together by a calculation.
- Guess, and I mean guess, at an explanation. Call it a hypothesis, if you like, but a process very like artistic inspiration causes it to come into the scientist's mind.
- Then work out a way of testing it by a controlled experiment in the laboratory. In other words, can you make a prediction: if my hypothesis is true, I would expect such and such to be the measurable result of taking these actions, every time.
- If the results are as you predicted, then you can call your hypothesis a theory. Now you must throw it open to other scientists, who will repeat the experiments and others like them. If, without fail, they get the results your theory predicts, then it gains general acceptance.

The test of experience

Religious language is very like scientific method in this respect. We observe that this is a beautiful world, that it works according to logical laws, that most people have a conscience, that the unexpected often happens, that people fall in love. We guess that all these things may be because there's one powerful God, who loves beauty and morality, is logical and loving. That's the hypothesis. How can we test it by experiment? I'm afraid there's only one way, and that's to trust your life to God. Obey him, and pray to him, and see what happens. If you find that you feel close to him when you pray, and that your life seems to have taken a turn for the better, then you've proved your hypothesis, and you know that God exists. But the experiment takes total commitment. Your faith's the fruit of experience; you've tested it, and found it to be true.

Expertus potest credere

There's a twelfth-century Latin hymn which some people think is by St Bernard of Clairvaux. We know it in English as:

> Jesu, the very thought of thee
> with sweetness fills the breast . . .

The hymn continues:

> to those who ask, how kind thou art,
> how good to those who seek.
>
> But what to those who find? Ah, this
> nor tongue nor pen can show;
> the love of Jesus, what it is
> none but his loved ones know.

The original Latin reads, 'The expert (or rather, the one with experience) can believe.' Isn't this just what we've been saying? It all comes down to the test of experience. If you've experienced the love of Jesus, you know for sure that God exists.

O taste and see

The same thing is said in today's psalm. In the version used in *Common Worship*, Psalm 34 verse 8 reads, 'O taste and see that the LORD is gracious; blessed is the one who trusts in him.' In other words, put it to the test of experience. Make the experiment; put your trust in God, and see whether he behaves graciously towards you. You may continue to suffer misfortunes, but if God gives you the strength to bear them, you've proved, at least to your own satisfaction, that God loves you. That discovery can transform your life, just as much as science changed the lives of our ancestors. But the only way to test it is to commit your life to Jesus. Suck it and see!

Suggested hymns

Come, dearest Lord, descend and dwell; Fairest Lord Jesus; Jesu, the very thought of thee; With wonder, Lord, we see your works.

Third Sunday before Lent (Proper 1)   4 February

Principal Service   **Fish for People** Isa. 6:1–8 [9–13] Holy,
holy, holy; Ps. 138 Faith; 1 Cor. 15:1–11 The resurrection of Christ;
Luke 5:1–11 Fish for people

> *'Then Jesus said to [Peter], "Do not be afraid; from now on you will
> be catching people."' Luke 5:10*

Fishers of men

The Sunday-school teacher at a church in Singapore was a young
Chinese girl. Her English was excellent but her accent wasn't always
perfectly clear. She'd been teaching the children's chorus, 'I will
make you fishers of men if you follow me'. The father of one of the
children came laughing to the vicar and asked, 'What *have* you
been teaching my little girl in your Sunday school?' 'I don't know,'
replied the vicar, 'what's wrong?' 'Well, my daughter came home
last Sunday singing at the top of her voice, "I will make you *vicious
old men*"!'

A metaphor for evangelism

The phrase, 'fishers of men', is, of course, a metaphor for evangelism. When Jesus used it in speaking to Galilean fishermen it was
probably a helpful image: they understood all about the art and skill
needed in the work of fishing; they were fully aware that you must
know and understand your fish, and use different methods with
different fish. So encouraging their fellow Jews to become members
of the new covenant community, which Jesus had instituted, was
very like fishing. Of course the followers of Jesus didn't change religions; they didn't stop being Jews. In the twenty-first century, apart
from the ardent anglers, most people's only experience of fishing is
'fishing for compliments'! So the metaphor resonates too strongly
of entrapment and trickery. Christians have sometimes been guilty
of this, though not all evangelists should be tarred with the same
brush. Sometimes in poor countries, the local people found that
becoming a Christian ensured a good job and economic security.
We can never know the whole truth about another person's motives,
but it's quite possible that although the majority were sincere, some
became Christians for the wrong reasons, what were known locally
as 'rice Christians'.

Emotional manipulation

The other danger is that of emotional manipulation. It's easy to allow the atmosphere of joy and excitement, which arises naturally when the gospel's being preached, to turn into a deliberate attempt to bring unbelievers to such an emotional pitch that they're ready to agree to anything the preacher says. Particularly if there's a collection at the end of the meeting. Sadly, many of those converted in a moment of emotional hysteria don't remain Christians for long. They quickly 'fall by the wayside' when the initial excitement has evaporated. Yet there's a reliable report of two sociologists who went to study 'the techniques of emotional manipulation' at one of the 'Mission England' meetings at Villa Park in Birmingham in 1984. Billy Graham gave a very low-key address, simply outlining the love of God, which had brought Jesus to die on the cross for us. 'Jesus loves you so much,' he said, 'that he gave his life so that you can have peace of mind in this world, and live with him for ever after you die.' So he quietly asked those who wanted to enjoy the love of Jesus to 'get up out of your seats' and go down onto the football pitch where the trained counsellors would help them to give their life to Jesus. The counsellors, on the 'sacred turf' of Aston Villa, thought nothing would happen; then one fold-back seat after another banged back as somebody stood up, until it sounded like thunder as a flood of converts came forward. One sociologist turned to her companion, asking, 'Where's the emotional manipulation in that?' to find that the other was on her knees in tears at the discovery that Jesus loves her!

What is evangelism?

What is evangelism? Evangelism's sharing good news – the good news of God's love. When you know something as exciting as that, it would be indescribably selfish to keep it to yourself. You want others to know and enjoy it too. There shouldn't be any suggestion of persuading people to change their religion, which is 'proselytizing'. If, having discovered God's love, they decide to do this, that must be their own free decision. But the command of Jesus stands: 'make disciples of all nations'. The best way to do this is not by manipulative techniques, but by the example of our joy. Our faces must show people that the gospel of God's love has been good news for us; then they'll want to know the secret of our happiness, so that they can share it.

All-age worship

Draw a fishing-boat. Mark it 'God's love'. Label the net 'Our love for others', and mark the fish with the names of people we know or have read about.

Suggested hymns

Dear Lord and Father of mankind; I danced in the morning when the world was begun; Jesus calls us—o'er the tumult; One shall tell another, and he shall tell his friends.

Third Sunday before Lent

Second Service **Hosea's Family** Ps. [1 Happy are the virtuous]
2 You are my son; Wis. 6:1–21 Kings to honour wisdom; *or*
Hos. 1 Hosea's family; Col. 3:1–22 New life in Christ; *Gospel at Holy Communion*: Matt. 5:13–20 Jesus fulfils the Law

> *'The LORD . . . said to Hosea, "Go and get married; your wife will be unfaithful, and your children will be just like her. In the same way, my people have left me and become unfaithful."' Hosea 1:2* (Good News Bible)

A prophet's family

It must have been terrible for the family of a prophet. He very often gave his children impossible names. Hosea had three kids: his first son he called 'Jezreel', the name of the wide valley where Megiddo and the battlefield of Armageddon is situated. The second, Hosea called 'Lo-ruhamah', poor girl, which means 'Not pitied'. The third child, another boy, was called 'Lo-ammi', which means 'Not my people'. But in those days they believed in 'prophetic symbolism'. It resembled sympathetic magic; they believed that by acting something out, they could bring it about. So by naming his children in this extraordinary way, Hosea believed he was bringing about the punishment of the descendants of King Jehu. Jehu had murdered the 70 sons of King Ahab, in the city of Jezreel on the edge of the valley. The Israelite royal family would be 'not pitied' by God, the people of Israel were no longer God's people.

A prophet's wife

Then what about Hosea's wife, Gomer? It's not easy to be quite sure exactly what happened. Whether or not she was a respectable woman when she married, she was soon unfaithful to her husband, and sank to the depths of degradation. The whole family situation was a mess, and Hosea felt it as a personal tragedy. Yet from this tragedy he learnt something unique about the love of God. The important thing, from Hosea's point of view, was that Gomer symbolized the kingdom of Israel, which had been unfaithful to the LORD, by worshipping other gods. Adultery, harlotry and fornication are common metaphors in the Bible for the worship of idols.

Learning from tragedy

The essence of tragedy, on the stage, is that good people do things with good intentions which have disastrous consequences. The tragedy of real life is that evil people are not punished, but good people suffer horribly. Why this should be we can't tell, though we may suspect that it has something to do with God allowing us free will. It may be hard to explain the evil in the world if God's a god of love; but it would be much harder to explain the good in the world if there were no god at all or an evil god were in control. Jesus didn't say, 'I have explained the world,' but he said, 'I have overcome the world.' Yet the amazing thing about tragedies is that we can learn from them; we can learn things that, without going through the suffering, we should never have learnt in a month of Sundays. Anyone can love a good wife or husband. The amazing thing about love is that so many people manage to love a husband or wife who's far from perfect, and go on loving them for years in spite of everything. Hosea's wife was unfaithful to him, and yet he went on loving her, no matter what. And out of the hell-hole of betrayal he came to the astonishing realization that this is how God loves us. When we're unfaithful to God – when we sin and hurt others, when we worship the idol of our possessions and our prosperity with more ardour than we worship God – God goes on loving us. That's what Hosea learnt from his disastrous marriage, and it's what we learn from the cross, that love never gives up:

> For while we were still weak, at the right time Christ died for the ungodly. Indeed, rarely will anyone die for a righteous person –

though perhaps for a good person someone might actually dare to die. But God proves his love for us in that *while we still were sinners* Christ died for us.

Restoration

In the second part of Hosea chapter 1, the challenge to the nation of Israel to bring its idolatry to an end is followed by a promise of restoration. Once they realized the seriousness of what they'd done, God would forgive them and give them a fresh start in life, as Hosea offered to do for Gomer. His wife would again call him 'My husband'. His son 'Not my people' would be renamed 'My people'; 'Not pitied' would now be called 'Pitied'. And so will God do to the vilest sinner who repents. Our religion's a religion of resurrection. But we only reach that happy point if we face up honestly to the message of the cross.

Suggested hymns

And can it be that I should gain; Morning glory, starlit sky; To God be the glory, great things he hath done; When I survey the wondrous cross.

Second Sunday before Lent   11 February
Principal Service   **Faith in the Creator**
Gen. 2:4b–9, 15–25 Creation; Ps. 65 Creation, harvest;
Rev. 4 The living creatures cry 'Holy!'; Luke 8:22–25 Stilling the storm

> *'[Jesus said to his disciples,] "Where is your faith?" They were afraid and amazed, and said to one another, "Who then is this, that he commands even the winds and the water, and they obey him?"'*
> *Luke 8:25*

Setting the scene

The disciples are on Lake Galilee with Jesus, after a night's fishing. It's smooth as a millpond. Now, storms can come down very suddenly from the mountains to the east of the lake which we now call the Golan Heights. Suddenly, one of these storms strikes the little fishing boat. The waves rise up, they're higher than the mast, and the boat's getting swamped. Soon it'll sink, it seems. The disciples are terrified; they don't want to die. They see that Jesus is asleep. 'They went to him and woke him up, shouting, "Master, Master, we are perishing!" And he woke up and rebuked the wind and the raging waves; they ceased, and there was a calm.'

Jesus stills the storm, and asks the disciples in rebuke, 'Where is your faith?'

Applying it to us

Did they deserve the rebuke? I doubt if I, or any of us, would have been any less frightened than they were when faced with imminent death. A storm at sea is not a very relaxing experience. Most people who've been in one would admit that they weren't very brave. There's another sort of storm, too, which can be pretty frightening. That's the storm when everything seems to go wrong in our lives at the same time. A stormy patch in our lives can be pretty alarming too. But Jesus says to us, too, 'Where is your faith?'

Faith in the Creator

We lack faith, because we don't realize what sort of God we're dealing with. God is the creator of the universe. The writers of Genesis used the stories which other nations told about creation and retold them so as to emphasize that God wanted human beings to love. God created the world to be our home, our workplace, and our artist's studio – as Louis Armstrong sang, 'What a wonderful world'. By studying the world we live in, and enjoying its efficiency and its beauty, we can learn that God loves us, and love him in return. Therefore each one of us has a place in the Creator's eternal plan: to be his pupils in the school of creation.

God will not let us go

So we're all too precious to God, for him to let us go. Even when we disobey, God cares for us and tries to win us back: that's what the story of Adam and Eve is about. When our life's running through a stormy patch, God often advises us how to cope with it, if we'll only listen. God never stops holding on to us, because he loves us. Some time, sooner or later, each one of us will die, but even then God holds on to us; after our death, God takes us to live with him in eternity. Why are you so frightened? Where is your faith?

Faith comes from belief in a Creator

So what have we got to be afraid of, with a Creator and Lover like that? 'Where is your faith?' he asks us. 'Sorry, Lord,' I answer, 'it evaporated, because I was looking at the danger, and not at you. But now I remember, you're that great Creator of the universe, and you made it so that you could love me, and that I could love you. Now I believe that you'll never loose your hold on me, and I'm no longer afraid – well, only a *bit* afraid!' The disciples got back their faith when they realized that Jesus controls the wind and waves, just like the God who made them does. So Jesus must be like God, and God must be as loving as Jesus. Each one of us, if we will keep our eyes fixed on the grandeur and beauty of the creation, and the love of Jesus, will rediscover a God we can have faith in. As Elvis Presley sang:

> Put your hand in the hand of the man who stilled the waters,
> Put your hand in the hand of the man who calmed the seas.
> Take a look at yourself and you can look at others differently
> By putting your hand in the hand of the man from Galilee.

All-age worship

Make plasticine models of Jesus and the disciples and put them in a toy boat; float it in a bowl of water. By fanning it gently, create a storm. Imagine how frightened you would have been in that boat. Write a banner with the words 'Why don't you trust your Creator?'

Suggested hymns

Do not be afraid, for I have redeemed you; Fierce raged the tempest o'er the deep; In the Lord I'll be ever thankful (Taizé); Sweet Sacrament divine.

Second Sunday before Lent
Second Service   **In the Beginning, God**
Ps. 147 Laws of nature, laws of God; Gen. 1:1—2:3 The creation; Matt. 6:25–34 Do not work for the food which perishes

> *'In the beginning when God created the heavens and the earth, the earth was a formless void.' Genesis 1:1*

How did it all start?

The first five books of the Bible are called the Five Books of Moses. The text of the Bible nowhere says that they were written by Moses, and in fact the fifth book contains a description of his death, and what happened afterwards, which would have been hard for Moses to write. Perhaps it would be best to call them Five Books about Moses. Some Christians, known as 'creationists', believe that the first chapter in the Bible, Genesis chapter 1, is a literal description of what happened at the beginning of history, during the course of 7 periods of 24 hours. Others regard this passage as a metaphor for describing the indescribable. These 'liberal' Christians hold that the writer of Genesis, whoever he was, was using the ideas of his own time to teach that God is at the heart of creation. Liberals are quite prepared to admit that theories about a Big Bang, and the Evolution of Species, may be true, without denying the central truth of Genesis. All Christians can agree that the Bible account emphasizes not *how* the world was made but *why* it was made. The important thing to concentrate on is that the world is as it is, because that's how God wants it to be. 'In the beginning, God.' That's all we need to know. Scientists may debate the process by which it occurred; the Bible tells us that God was the cause of creation. When we look at the beauty of the world around us, it's very hard to believe that it all happened by chance.

Why are we here?

A child on a bus pointed to the man sitting opposite and asked his mother in a loud voice, 'Mummy, what's that man for?' The child didn't ask 'Who is he?', but 'What's he for?' When she recovered from her embarrassment, his mother realized that her child had raised one of the most profound questions that face us all: why are we here? What are we for? Most people get through their lives without ever putting this question into words, but their behaviour shows what answer they have subconsciously assumed. If you believe that we're here to get all the pleasure and possessions we can, then you'll ride roughshod over others in the attempt to have your own way. A more sophisticated approach would be to say, 'I can't be happy while others are suffering', and this will restrain your selfish actions to some extent. But if you believe that we are here because God made us, then you'll want to know why God made us, and how God expects us to behave.

Learning to love God

The Old Testament could be described as the sad history of the ways in which human beings have disobeyed their Creator, and the sorry mess he's allowed us to get ourselves into as a result of our misuse of free will. When people had realized this, then God sent Jesus to save us from the consequences of our disobedience. When we realize that it cost Jesus his life to do so, then we shall be filled with gratitude and love for our Saviour. This is a much deeper love than we could ever have felt if we had never sinned and been forgiven. Jesus said that there's joy in heaven when even one sinner repents; of course there is, because this is the purpose of creation, that we should learn to love God with a love that is freely given. *You* are the purpose of creation, when you turn to God and love your Creator with all your heart and mind and soul and strength.

'The chief end of man'

The Scottish *Shorter Catechism* says that 'the chief end of man is to glorify God and to enjoy him for ever'. That's the correct answer to the child's question, 'What's that man for?' We are here so that we can learn to love God. The rest of creation is here to give us an arena in which we can learn to love God and our neighbours; that's why God made it. God began us on the path of learning to love our Creator, and when we've learnt our lessons well, then God will take us to enjoy God's love throughout eternity. The first chapter of Genesis contains a profound truth when it says, 'In the beginning, God'.

Suggested hymns

All creatures of our God and king; Lord of beauty, thine the splendour; O Lord my God, when I in awesome wonder (How great thou art); Thou, whose almighty word.

Sunday next before Lent   18 February
Principal Service   **The Epileptic Boy** Ex. 34:29–35 Moses' face is shining; Ps. 99 God spoke in the cloud; 2 Cor. 3:12—4:2 The Spirit unveils God's truth; Luke 9:28–36 The transfiguration [37–43 The epileptic boy]

'On the next day, when they had come down from the mountain, a great crowd met [Jesus]. Just then a man from the crowd shouted, "Teacher, I beg you to look at my son; he is my only child. Suddenly a spirit seizes him, and all at once he shrieks. It convulses him until he foams at the mouth; it mauls him and will scarcely leave him. I begged your disciples to cast it out, but they could not."' Luke 9:37–40

What happened next?

The first part of the Gospel set for today tells the story of how three of Jesus's disciples saw him transfigured on a mountain-top, and heard the voice of God saying, 'This is my Son.' What happened next? If we read the optional second part of this passage, verses 37 to 43, we find out that after that wonderful experience, the disciples came down to earth with a bump. They met a man whose son suffered from convulsions. In the language of those days he's described as being seized by a demon. A modern doctor would probably ascribe those symptoms to epilepsy, a word which wouldn't have been understood in Jesus's time. The two explanations don't contradict each other: different forms of words are helpful to different types of listener. Epilepsy is a disease of the nervous system; it can be quite mild and relatively harmless, or it can cause occasional distressing loss of consciousness. Many of us suffer from nervous disorders at some time – depression is the commonest – and Christians should be very sympathetic to those who do. Jesus was certain that in the case of this boy, his affliction would respond to prayer. But the disciples couldn't heal him.

Prayer with faith

Why did the disciples fail? Maybe they didn't pray. Maybe they didn't pray hard enough. Or maybe they didn't have enough faith. It's easy to forget about prayer altogether and lose touch with God in the busyness of modern life. So we need a basic minimum; resolving that 'I will never go to bed without having at least said the Lord's Prayer'; or, 'I will try to spend at least five minutes on my knees each day.' These are simply resolutions to help us be self-disciplined; if we fail to keep them on any day we shouldn't feel guilty; simply try again the next day. But occasionally there come moments of crisis when we want to ask God something urgently: a physical need, a spiritual strength, somebody we love is sick, or somebody asks us to pray for them. Then we want to spend half an hour or an hour in prayer: the length of time doesn't matter, but the urgency of the desire does. When we surround somebody with loving prayer, God can use the power of our love to heal them.

Believing prayer works

Perhaps the disciples didn't really believe that prayer works. Jesus described the people of his day as a 'faithless and perverse generation'. For prayer to be effective, you have to trust the God you are praying to, and believe that he really wants the best for all his children. Prayer is always answered, though sometimes God answers 'Yes'; sometimes 'Not yet'; sometimes 'No, because I've something in mind to give you, which is even better than what you're asking for.'

After the mountain-top, the plain

The disciples had a wonderful experience on the mountain-top. Then, 'on the next day, when they had come down from the mountain', they found the village on the plain where the father begged them to heal his sick child, 'but they could not'. They'd thought they could do anything; now they discovered that following Jesus is hard work, and full of disappointments. But if we work hard at prayer, and learn to trust the God we're praying to, then Jesus will step in and give us the things we couldn't obtain on our own. We're given wonderful experiences in our lives so that we can rejoice in the greatness of God, and to empower us to get on with the hard slog of being Jesus's disciple.

All-age worship

Make a prayer board, with a card inviting people to put up details of those they would like prayers for (only mention names if you have permission to do so), and put it in church with a supply of Post-it notes for passers-by to write their prayer requests on, and a pen. If there already is one, make it more attractive.

Come, my soul, thy suit prepare; Lord, the light of your love is shining (Shine, Jesus, shine); 'Tis good, Lord, to be here; What a friend we have in Jesus.

Sunday next before Lent
Second Service   Glorify Your Name
Ps. 89:1–18 The wonders of God; Ex. 3:1–6 The burning bush;
John 12:27–36a Glorify your name

> *'Jesus prayed, "Father, glorify your name." Then a voice came from heaven, "I have glorified it, and I will glorify it again."' John 12:28*

A voice from heaven

St John's Gospel doesn't tell us the story of the transfiguration of Jesus on the mountain-top. Instead, we have another story which contains a voice from heaven. At the transfiguration Jesus appeared in glory, and the voice of God explained who Jesus is: 'This is my Son.' This time, God explains what glory is. We imagine that glory means splendour, a bright shining light which everyone can see, but it's not like that at all.

Glorify your name

We glorify great heroes and heroines. 'How splendidly he plays football.' 'How well he leads his nation to glory.' 'How beautifully she moves and speaks.' But such glory only lasts for a short time, and then the fickle focus of public praise turns onto somebody else. If somebody's worried about their reputation, we say that they're 'concerned about their good name'. So the name of God is God's reputation. To glorify God's name means to make his reputation greater, so that many people will praise him more. Just occasionally our eyes are opened to the glory of God in the world around us, and we have a fresh insight into the beauty of nature. But even then, we quickly forget.

'I have glorified it'

In the passage we've read from St John's Gospel, Jesus asks God his Father to 'glorify your name'. The voice of God answers, 'I have glorified it.' God has glorified his name in the life of Jesus. Yet Jesus didn't lead what's conventionally called a glorious life. An anonymous author wrote:

> How do you explain the greatness of this man? He was born in an obscure village, the child of a peasant woman. He grew up in another village. He worked in a carpenter's shop until he was thirty. Then for three years he was an itinerant preacher. He never wrote a book. He never held office. He never owned a home. He never travelled more than two hundred miles from the place where he was born. He never did any of the things which usually accompany greatness. He had no credentials but himself. Although he walked the land over, curing the sick, giving sight to the blind, healing the lame, raising people from the dead, the top established religious leaders turned against him. His friends ran away. He was turned over to enemies. He went through the mockery of a trial. He was spat upon, flogged and ridiculed. He was nailed to a cross between two thieves. While he was dying the executioners gambled for the only piece of property he owned on earth and that was his robe. When he was dead, he was laid in a borrowed grave, through the pity of a friend. Twenty centuries have come and gone and today he is the central figure of the human race and the leader of the column of progress. All the armies that ever marched and all the navies that were ever built, and all the Parliaments that ever sat and all the kings that ever reigned put together have not affected the life upon this earth as has that one solitary life.

It takes great insight to recognize that true greatness lies in a life of humble service to others. Perhaps that was what God wanted us to understand, after reading the story of the life of love which Jesus lived, when he said, 'I have glorified my name.' Who wouldn't praise a God whose glory shines out from a life like that?

'I will glorify it again'

Now, at the end of Jesus's life on earth, God looks forward to the crucifixion and resurrection. Jesus prayed, 'Father, glorify your name.' Then a voice came from heaven, 'I have glorified it, and I will glorify it again.'

The moment of defeat, the moment when he yields to the suffering imposed on him by men of violence, is his moment of glory. This is the opposite of the way that people usually think. Usually we talk about a glorious victory. Sometimes, after Dunkirk, Kalamata Bay or Souda Bay, we talk about a courageous withdrawal. But a glorious defeat? Yet the death of Jesus shows the glory of love. We have a glorious God: not one who dwells apart in heavenly glory, but one who's prepared to sacrifice his life for others. If you're concerned about your good name, if you want to lead a glorious life, then the only way is the way of self-sacrifice.

Suggested hymns

Glory be to Jesus; Father, we love you, we worship and adore you; Jesus, these eyes have never seen; O Lord my God, when I in awesome wonder (How great thou art).

Lent

Lent is observed in the 40 days leading up to Holy Week. The figure 40 is based on the 40 days that Jesus fasted in the wilderness after his baptism, before he began his ministry. It is calculated either by omitting the Sundays, when the Lenten discipline is relaxed, or by finishing on Palm Sunday. In the early Church, candidates for baptism at Easter prepared for it by 40 days of learning and fasting, and soon the rest of the congregation wanted to join with them. Instead of doing without food, today Christians 'give up something for Lent'. This is a good lesson in self-control, but mustn't lead to self-righteousness. More important is to train oneself to do something good in Lent: to read the Bible, spend more time in prayer, attend extra services or a study group, or do something to help others. Like Advent, Lent is a penitential season, so altar frontals and vestments are purple, or unbleached linen representing sackcloth, and 'Glory to God in the highest' is often omitted. It is good to examine our lives, accept responsibility for our sins, and confess them to God. Sermons in Lent are often linked together on a common theme; a series on the Sermon on the Mount or the Ten Commandments can help with self-examination, or sermons on aspects of Christian living can lead to practical action. There are some fine Lenten hymns, but they can be too gloomy unless mixed with others on lighter but relevant themes.

Ash Wednesday 21 February

Principal Service   **Sinners** Joel 2:1–2, 12–17 Rend your hearts;
or Isa. 58:1–12 Care for the needy; Ps. 51:1–17 Cleanse me from my
sin; 2 Cor. 5:20b—6:10 Suffering of an apostle; Matt. 6:1–6, 16–21
Secret fasting; *or* John 8:1–11 Adultery and forgiveness

> *'Jesus straightened up and said to her, "Woman, where are they?*
> *Has no one condemned you?" She said, "No one, sir." And Jesus*
> *said, "Neither do I condemn you. Go your way, and from now on*
> *do not sin again."' John 8:10–11*

The missing man

Whichever way you look at it, the story of the woman caught
committing adultery is a very beautiful one, and also a very strange
one. One strange thing is that we do now know where in the Bible
it belongs. The footnote to the New Revised Standard Version
says: 'The most ancient authorities lack 7.53–8.11; other authorities add the passage here or after 7.36 or after 21.25 or after Luke
21.38, with variations of text; some mark the passage as doubtful.'
What that all means is that this story's probably not from the pen
of whoever wrote the rest of the Fourth Gospel. Yet nobody seems
to doubt that it's so characteristic of Jesus to have behaved and spoken in this way, that it must be a genuine recollection of an event
that really occurred. Like many others, however, it got left out of
the first draft of the Gospels. But there's something else which is
even more strange, and that is 'The Mystery of the Missing Man'.
To state the blindingly obvious, it takes two to commit adultery.
Deuteronomy, chapter 22, verse 22, lays down the law that 'If a
man is caught lying with the wife of another man, both of them
shall die.' Both of them. But the man who committed adultery with
this woman appears nowhere in the story; he seems to have van-
ished without trace. So the crucial evidence is missing in the charge
against the woman who was brought before Jesus.

A set-up

It all sounds very phoney. Could it be that an innocent woman
was seduced or trapped into a situation where she couldn't defend
herself, in order to bring a test case before Jesus? A real set-up? The
purpose of the arrest was not to trap the woman, it was to trap

Jesus. The Gospel itself says of the Pharisees' question, 'They said this to test him . . .'

Jesus knew that if he declared the woman to be innocent, he was going against the Law of Moses, or, at least, against the Pharisees' interpretation of it. Yet if he declared her guilty, he'd appear so uncaring that he'd lose his popular support from the people. It was to place Jesus in this dilemma that the poor woman had been dragged before him without any proper evidence; her accusers weren't really interested in what happened to her; after all, they thought, she was only a woman.

The escape clause

So Jesus used one of the Pharisees' own traditions to avoid having to condemn the woman. It was his escape clause. They said that only a man who was completely innocent himself was allowed to carry out the death sentence. The woman's accusers probably already knew of Jesus's declaration that somebody who plans to commit adultery, even if he's prevented from carrying out his plans, is as guilty as the one who actually commits the offence. To commit adultery in your head is as sinful as committing it in bed. So Jesus said, 'Let anyone among you who is without sin be the first to throw a stone at her.' Was anyone prepared to stand up in public and claim that they'd never had a sinful thought in their lives? Of course not. So they slunk away, hoist with their own petard.

How to deal with a sinner

Jesus was left alone with the woman, and said to her, '"Woman, where are they? Has no one condemned you?" She said, "No one, sir." And Jesus said, "Neither do I condemn you. Go your way, and from now on do not sin again."' Jesus knew that for many people, to keep to the strict letter of the Law was impossible. The Pharisees wrote these people off scornfully as 'sinners'; Jesus treated them with compassion. He wasn't going to fall into the other trap, of saying that adultery isn't a sin. But like every other sin, it can be forgiven if we're truly penitent, and resolve to avoid temptation in the future. Jesus says the same to each one of us: 'Neither do I condemn you. Go your way, and from now on do not sin again.'

Suggested hymns

Dear Lord and Father of mankind; Father of heaven, whose love profound; Forty days and forty nights; Jesu, lover of my soul.

First Sunday of Lent   25 February
Principal Service   **Worship God Alone** Deut. 26:1–11 First-fruits; Ps. 91:1–2, 9–end God's providence; Rom. 10:8b–13 Faith, salvation and unity; Luke 4:1–13 The temptation of Jesus

> *'The devil said to [Jesus], "To you I will give their glory and all this authority; for it has been given over to me, and I give it to anyone I please. If you, then, will worship me, it will all be yours." Jesus answered him, "It is written, 'Worship the Lord your God, and serve only him.'"' Luke 4:6–8*

Worship

Worship means worth-ship, showing what's worth most in your life. You don't have to say any prayers when you worship. Your actions speak much louder than words in proclaiming what's worth most to you. Someone who polishes their car on a Sunday can rightly be said to be worshipping their car, whether or not they get down on their knees before it – they're showing that their car's worth more to them than God is. In the story of the temptation of Jesus, which we've read in St Luke's version today, the Devil's shown tempting Jesus to worship him. In effect, Jesus is asked to show that the Devil's worth more to him than his Father is, because the Devil can give him earthly power and authority. It was a real temptation, because Jesus really wanted the power to bring peace to this troubled world. But he realized that you can't bring about God's ends by using the Devil's means. Peace can't be brought about by force. So Jesus quoted, or paraphrased, the first two of the Ten Commandments:

> 'I am the LORD your God, who brought you out of the land of Egypt, out of the house of slavery; you shall have no other gods before me. You shall not make for yourself an idol . . . You shall not bow down to them or worship them; for I the LORD your God am a jealous God, showing steadfast love to the thousandth generation of those who love me and keep my commandments.'

The small print

The commandments were given in the form of a covenant or a contract. You should always read the 'small print' before signing any contract: the terms and conditions. If not, you've only yourself to blame if the contract's made null and void because you haven't kept the conditions. In the covenant at Mount Sinai, God made a contract, promising to care for his people Israel; the only condition was, they must keep the Ten Commandments. The commandments were the 'small print' in the contract; if the parties don't keep those conditions, there might as well have never been any contract. They're the basic minimum conditions for life together as a society: God can't easily protect us if we go round killing each other and stealing one another's husband or wife. Our relationship with God's like a marriage – it's an exclusive contract. God simply can't help us if our loyalty's divided. Unless we're wholeheartedly committed to God, there's not much that God can do for us.

Ten headlines

So the first four commandments summarize our duty to God, to love him wholeheartedly; the other six are about our duty to our neighbour. I can't love God while I'm cheating on my neighbour. God loves my neighbour just as much as he loves me. So if I hurt my neighbour, I'm also breaking God's heart. Duty to God and duty to neighbour are inseparably entwined together. The commandments are ten headlines, under which we can write the ways we should show love. What's important to a Christian is not so much keeping the letter of the law, as showing the love, which is the spirit that lies behind it.

Learning the Commandments

It would be a good use of Lent to learn the Commandments by heart, and examine ourselves on how well we have kept them. They used to teach candidates for confirmation a little rhyme:

> Love God, idols away,
> swear not, keep Holy Day.
> Parents honour, do not kill,
> be pure in heart and never steal.
> Tell the truth and never lie,
> shun all evil jealousy.

It's not very profound, but it helps us remember the Commandments. If you know the Commandments, you can quote them to yourself when you need to. When you're tempted, as Jesus was, to divided loyalties, then you can quote to yourself the scripture: '"It is written, 'Worship the Lord your God, and serve only him.'"'

All-age worship

Write the verse above on the shape of two stone tablets, and learn it.

Suggested hymns

Be thou my guardian and my guide; Forty days and forty nights; O for a closer walk with God; O for a heart to praise my God; O Jesus, I have promised.

First Sunday of Lent
Second Service   Repentance of a Wicked City
Ps. 119:73–88 Let those who fear you turn to me; Jonah 3 Nineveh converted; Luke 18:9–14 Pharisee and publican

> *'When God saw what [the people of Nineveh] did, how they turned from their evil ways, God changed his mind about the calamity that he had said he would bring upon them; and he did not do it.'*
> *Jonah 3:10*

Repentance of a wicked city

Nineveh was one of the oldest and largest cities on earth. It had been the capital of Assyria, and from 1300 until it was destroyed in 607 BC, it was the centre of the civilized world. The remains are on the outskirts of Mosul in Iraq, on the east bank of the River Tigris. To the Jews, it was a symbol of pagan unbelief, so Jonah at first refused to preach there; they were so far gone in sin that he didn't think it would do any good. In the story in the Bible, Jonah rejected God's call to preach to Nineveh and took a ship in the opposite direction; but God used a fish to send Jonah back to Nineveh after all. Then Jonah preached to the people there, and to his astonishment, they repented in sackcloth, with fasting, and God forgave them.

To say that God 'changed his mind' is only a figure of speech; this is what God had intended from the beginning. But Jonah was very uptight about this; he was definitely not pleased. Surely God was only interested in his own chosen people? Surely God had promised to destroy Israel's enemies? At the end of the book God explains that he loves everybody, even unbelieving pagans, even the wicked; God said: 'Should I not be concerned about Nineveh, that great city, in which there are more than a hundred and twenty thousand persons who do not know their right hand from their left, and also many animals?'

A rebuke to narrow nationalism

The Book of Jonah was probably written soon after 400 BC, when Nineveh no longer existed. Ezra the priest was exhorting the Jews who'd returned from exile in Babylon to a very narrow nationalism. He even told Jewish men who'd married foreign wives that God wanted them to divorce them. But even in the time of Ezra there were voices raised in protest at his narrowness, and the author of the Book of Jonah seems to have been one of them. The book isn't really about whether or not a fish can swallow a man; a fish-god was the symbol of Babylon; the Jews had been swallowed by Babylon at the Exile; now they were being sent back to proclaim the love of God to the unbelieving Gentiles. If the Gentiles would repent, God would forgive them.

A call to world mission

We mustn't get bogged down in the details of the story of Jonah, and thereby miss its basic message. The whole book's a rousing call to world mission, for Christians no less than Jews. It's important that we should proclaim the good news of God's love to our close neighbours, and in an unbelieving age in Northern Europe we may feel that this takes up all of our energy. But Jesus pointed out that the concept of the neighbour must never be narrowly limited to those of our own race. We must always remember that God loves everybody, and wants all people to be saved. If we can't go to other lands to preach to them ourselves, we can always support the Church in other, poorer nations as they proclaim the good news to their own people.

A call to repentance

The other purpose of the Book of Jonah is to serve as a call to repentance. 'Since all have sinned and fall short of the glory of God,' writes St Paul, 'they are now justified by his grace as a gift, through the redemption that is in Christ Jesus.' The glory of God is God's universal love, and all of us fall short of that standard. Lent's a good time to examine ourselves, and see just how far short of the standard of Jesus's love we've fallen in the past year. Then, if we're willing to repent, as the Ninevites did, God will surely forgive us because he loves us, as he forgave and loved the people of Nineveh.

Suggested hymns

God is working his purpose out; Rock of ages, cleft for me; The day thou gavest, Lord, is ended; There's a wideness in God's mercy.

Second Sunday of Lent   4 March
Principal Service   **The Wrong End of the Stick**
Gen. 15:1–12, 17–18 God's promise to Abraham; Ps. 27 Faith in
God's providence; Phil. 3:17—4:1 Citizens of heaven;
Luke 13:31–35 Jesus's lament over the city

> *'Jesus said, "Jerusalem, Jerusalem, the city that kills the prophets and stones those who are sent to it! How often have I desired to gather your children together as a hen gathers her brood under her wings, and you were not willing!"' Luke 13:34*

The wrong end of the stick

How frequently we get hold of some new idea, which could be a blessing to us, and yet we turn it into a curse by grasping the wrong end of the stick! The man who buys an expensive piece of technology and only uses it for trivial purposes is the most obviously ridiculous example. The Old Testament reading today tells how God promised land to the descendants of Abraham the nomad, from the Sinai desert as far as the middle of Iraq; what miseries ensue when politicians take that literally! The psalm tells how God's people hunger to worship him in his Temple. But Jeremiah gave a telling-off to those who thought Jerusalem was impregnable, simply because it contained the Temple. The inhabitants of Philippi were proud that their city, being a Roman colony, gave them citizenship of the Roman Empire, but St Paul said it was far more important to remember that they were 'citizens of heaven'. Jesus rebukes Herod Antipas as a 'crafty fox', because he was using politics, not as a way of serving other people, but as a means for gaining power and holding on to power. All these people had grasped a good idea, intended by God as a blessing: property, places of worship, national pride, political power; but by getting hold of the wrong end of the stick they turned each of these blessings into a curse. The stick they were meant to pull on, to bring them closer to God, became a stick they used to beat other people and drive them away.

The Ten Commandments

The Ten Commandments are like that, too. The command to keep the Sabbath day holy was intended to set people free to worship God regularly. Our week never feels right if we haven't started it in fellowship with God and God's family. Yet 'Sabbatarians' make it a weapon to persecute people for enjoying themselves. Jesus had fierce words for those who used the law of the Sabbath to prevent sick people being healed on the Lord's day. The command not to take the Lord's name in vain was intended to prevent unscrupulous people from manipulating God to their own advantage, and claiming the Lord's support for their own plans and prejudices. But many people do just that when they make the Commandment refer to strong language, which is an entirely different issue. They get hold of the wrong end of the stick.

Jesus and Jerusalem

Jesus loved Jerusalem and its inhabitants. He said he felt towards them like a mother-hen trying to protect her chicks under her wing feathers. Yet they refused to come to him. Jesus was following Jeremiah: he loved the Temple, but he knew it wouldn't protect Jerusalem from destruction if they ignored the law of love.

The ideal church

Visitors to Jerusalem in recent years have been shocked by the political violence and the materialism of the so-called Holy City, forgetting that those were the features that Jesus would have seen there in his day. We have to keep the tension in our minds between the ideal, heavenly Jerusalem, Jerusalem as she ought to be, and the real, earthly Jerusalem, which, with all its faults, Jesus loved. Many people love their church as much as Jesus loved the Temple. It's always those inside an institution who can see the failings of that institution, however, and their love for it gives them more right to criticize it than those on the outside. Some people use the Church and its faults as a stick to beat others with, but that's the wrong end of the stick. We need to remember that, although it's not ideal, the Christian Church is the means Jesus chose to draw us closer to God, and there's no alternative. An old story tells of Jesus being questioned by the angels when he returned to heaven, as to how he was going to continue his work on earth. 'I have chosen twelve fishermen,' he replied. 'Twelve fishermen!' exclaimed one of the angels. 'It'll never work.' 'I have no other plan,' replied the Saviour. God has no other way for spreading his love in the world than through the Church. With all its faults, it deserves our love.

All-age worship

Draw a hen gathering her chicks under her wings; find a picture of the Temple in the time of Jesus and copy it.

Suggested hymns

Jerusalem the golden; Light's abode, celestial Salem; The Church's one foundation; Thy hand, O God, has guided.

Second Sunday of Lent
Second Service   **Counting the Cost** Ps. 135 Praise for God's goodness; Jer. 22:1–9, 13–17 Sin in Jerusalem; Luke 14:27–33 Counting the cost

> *'Jesus asked his disciples: "Which of you, intending to build a tower, does not first sit down and estimate the cost, to see whether he has enough to complete it? Otherwise, when he has laid a foundation and is not able to finish, all who see it will begin to ridicule him, saying, 'This fellow began to build and was not able to finish.'"' Luke 14:28–30*

An unequal society

'Annual income twenty pounds, annual expenditure nineteen nineteen six, result happiness. Annual income twenty pounds, annual expenditure twenty pounds ought and six, result misery.' This is the wisdom of Mr Micawber in *David Copperfield*; it's thought that Charles Dickens based the character on his own father. Some people today live comfortably in the black on this balance sheet, and know nothing of the struggle of those who live constantly in fear of going into the red. It was the same in the unequal society of Jesus's time; some people had to stand all day in the marketplace, waiting for someone to hire them; some could afford to build themselves expensive towers to protect their property. But woe to the man who lived in the Micawber poverty trap; the man who thought he could build a tower, but, when it was half-done, ran out of money because he hadn't done his sums. Forever after he'd be laughed at as the Dreamer of the Half-finished Tower.

Materialism

In Jesus's time, just like today, a person's value was measured by how much they owned. Jeremiah, too, warns against the one 'who builds his house by unrighteousness, and his upper rooms by injustice; who makes his neighbours work for nothing, and does not give them their wages.'

There's nothing new in materialism. But we mustn't make our possessions into our idol. People matter more than things, and relationships matter most of all: 'Money can't buy me love.'

The cost of discipleship

In fact, in some situations, possessions can be an obstacle. It's good to work hard to provide for your family, but not if that means you have no time for your family. If you never invite anyone into your home for fear they'll make it dirty, you'll soon have no friends. How can you serve God, if you're too mean to help other people? Jesus told the story of the half-finished tower to make us laugh at our own materialism, and then ask ourselves 'What's the cost of discipleship?' How much does it cost us, not just in money but in time and effort, to be a follower of Jesus? Jesus gave up everything to come to us, and it cost him his life. He calls each one of us to follow him, and warns that this will mean taking up our cross. Maybe that won't mean dying for Jesus, but it'll certainly mean living for him.

Giving up and keeping

What does this mean in practice? For the rich young ruler, Jesus said it meant giving away all he possessed to the poor, because Jesus knew his possessions were his idol, and he wouldn't be a free man until they were gone. Jesus didn't demand this extreme of all his disciples, and, thank God, he doesn't demand it of all of us. Wealth can be used to provide employment for other people. The Old Testament provided a very simple guideline on how much money most people need to give up: if you give away one tenth of your income, you're free to enjoy the other nine-tenths with a clear conscience. There are rich and poor Christians today who are happy people because they tithe their after-tax incomes. There is also the story of a woman who, hearing the words of Jesus read out, 'none of you can become my disciple if you do not give up all your possessions,' stood in the middle of her house and looked at each of her possessions in turn, saying aloud, 'Jesus, that table, that vase, that book belongs to you now. What do you want me to do with it?' In some cases she felt Jesus wanted her to enjoy it, in some cases to share it, and in a few cases to sell it or give it away. Then she did the same with how she spent her time, because all of that, too, belongs to Jesus, though he wants us to relax and enjoy ourselves in some of it. That's what counting the cost means: the cost of discipleship is giving up everything, and then being astonished at how much God gives us back.

Suggested hymns

O Jesus, I have promised; Take my life, and let it be; Take up your cross, the Saviour said; Will you come and follow me?

Third Sunday of Lent   11 March
Principal Service   **The Fig Tree** Isa. 55:1–9 A call to conversion; Ps. 63:1–8 I will bless you as long as I live; 1 Cor. 10:1–13 Temptation; Luke 13:1–9 The parable of the fig tree

'Jesus told this parable: "A man had a fig tree planted in his vineyard; and he came looking for fruit on it and found none."' Luke 13:6

What does a fig make you think of?

What does a fig make you think of? If you were one of those unlucky children who were made to take a dose of syrup of figs, the associations in your mind will be unpleasant. If you've bought dried figs at Christmas, you'll think that the flavour's quite pleasant, in spite of the pips which get stuck between your teeth. Only if you have eaten a fresh fig, however, will you know just how delicious they can be. The Old Testament includes figs among the delights of the promised land; and the Jews looked forward to the day of *shalom,* of prosperity and peace, when everyone should sit under their own vine and their own fig tree. So the mention of a fig tree would give to any Jew pleasant thoughts of peace and prosperity for God's chosen people.

Failure to produce

Yet the prophet Micah writes of a fig tree which is a *big* disappointment:

> Woe is me! For I have become like one who,
>   after the summer fruit has been gathered,
>   after the vintage has been gleaned,
> finds no cluster to eat;
>   there is no first-ripe fig for which I hunger.
> The faithful have disappeared from the land,
>   and there is no one left who is upright;
> they all lie in wait for blood,
>   and they hunt each other with nets.
> Their hands are skilled to do evil;
>   the official and the judge ask for a bribe,
>   and the powerful dictate what they desire;
>   thus they pervert justice.

God wanted to gather the fruit of good works from his people, and instead they're corrupt, selfish, materialistic and vicious. This is the idea that Jesus took up in his parable: 'A man had a fig tree planted in his vineyard; and he came looking for fruit on it and found none.' It's a parable of judgement; God looks for us to care for each other, and we're like a fruit tree that fails to produce.

Jesus reinterprets the Ten Commandments

For instance, the Ten Commandments tell us not to murder or to steal. God can't lead his people through the wilderness if they're killing each other and taking each other's property. But Jesus, in the Sermon on the Mount, went beyond that. If you hate another person, it's as bad as murdering them, he said. Storing up wealth on earth involves depriving others of it. So if God finds us full of hatred and greed, where's the fruit of love that he made us for?

Time's running out

Jesus doesn't say that God's given up on the Jews. Jesus doesn't say that God's given up on us. But he does say that time's running out. God, represented by the landowner, would be quite justified in saying that he 'doesn't give a fig' for those who fail to produce. But the gardener replied, 'Sir, let the fig-tree alone for one more year, until I dig around it and put manure on it. If it bears fruit next year, well and good; but if not, you can cut it down.'

God doesn't want to destroy us, but we mustn't presume on God's patience. It's urgent that we should decide to be on God's side, producing the fruit of good works that he made us for. Stop putting off till tomorrow what you could possibly do today!

Judgement on all

Jesus wasn't only speaking of the Jews, he was talking about all of us. Jesus was a Jew and he loved his own people. Anti-Semitism arises when people think that Jesus was only condemning the Jews, and forget that he was expressing God's judgement on the whole human race. In particular, on the Christian Church, those who've been allowed to join the Jews among the Chosen People of God. We're chosen not for privilege, but to serve. If we stop serving our neighbours, stop winning new believers, stop loving each other, then God would be quite justified in giving up on his Church. Thank God, then, for his patience; he never will give up on us finally, any more than he's finally given up on the Jews. But we need to spend some time, each Lent, thinking about what God made us for, what God chose us for, and what God calls us to do, and repenting of our failure to produce fruit.

All-age worship

Draw a farmer tenderly caring for his fruit tree, even though it bears no fruit.

Suggested hymns

Ah, holy Jesus, how hast thou offended?; Drop, drop slow tears; My God, I love thee – not because; Where cross the crowded ways of life.

Third Sunday of Lent
Second Service   **A Ladder to Heaven** Ps. 12 No longer any godly, 13 How long?; Gen. 28:10–19a Jacob's ladder; John 1:35–51 The call of Nathanael

> *'Jesus said to Nathanael, "Very truly, I tell you, you will see heaven opened and the angels of God ascending and descending upon the Son of Man."' John 1:51*

Jacob's ladder

'As Jacob with travel was weary one day,' begins an anonymous eighteenth-century hymn, 'at night on a stone for a pillow he lay.' We can vividly imagine the scene as it's described in Genesis 28. Jacob had cheated his brother Esau out of his birthright, and run away to escape from his fury. His father had instructed him to travel all the way from southern Israel back across the desert to northern Mesopotamia to find himself a wife. When he made himself a hard bed on a stone in the hills, north of where Jerusalem would later stand, he must have felt that God was far away, and had lost interest in him. If only there was a way he could speak to God! If only God would speak to him! Then he had a remarkable dream. Heaven was not far away. He saw in his dream a ladder or staircase, with its foot at the stone where he lay, and its top in heaven, and the angelic messengers were carrying prayers straight up to God from that place, and bringing God's blessings straight down to him where he was. So Jacob named that place 'Bethel', which means 'the House of God'; it later became an important place for worship, for communication with God. And Jacob said, 'This is none other than the house of God, and this is the gate of heaven.' Those words are often painted over the door of a church, though a story is told of one church where they fixed a notice on the door below, so that it read: 'This is the gate of heaven. This door is kept locked during the winter months'!

A Greek joke

Here's another joke, which they tell in Greece. The Archbishop of Athens visited the Pope in the Vatican to resolve the differences between their churches, and they decided to telephone heaven to seek advice. The Pope suggested that as the bill for the telephone call would be rather expensive they should share the cost. The same thing happened when the Pope went to Athens, but the Archbishop said there was no need to worry about the cost: 'To call heaven from Athens,' he said, 'is only a local call!'

'Heaven lies about us'

People worry about how they're going to communicate with God. 'What can we do to make sure that God hears our prayers?' they sometimes ask. Well, God always hears our prayers, though he may not always give us what we want at the time we want it, if he has something better in mind for us. Or they may go on pilgrimage. This is fine if it's a way of helping us to feel closer to God; but God's no closer to us in one place than another. William Wordsworth wrote that 'heaven lies about us in our infancy'. He meant that heaven's all around us all the time, but as we grow older, and more distracted with material things, we stop noticing it. But God never goes away; he's always 'closer to me than breathing, nearer than hands and feet'.

Francis Thompson

Another poet, Francis Thompson, was living in poverty in London selling matches or newspapers, and addicted to opium. He must have felt that God was miles away. But later he wrote a poem teaching that even in the gutters of London the kingdom of God was close to him:

O world invisible, we view thee . . .

The angels keep their ancient places; –
Turn but a stone, and start a wing!
'Tis ye, 'tis your estranged faces,
That miss the many-splendoured thing.

But (when so sad thou canst not sadder)
Cry; – and upon thy so sore loss
Shall shine the traffic of Jacob's ladder
Pitched betwixt Heaven and Charing Cross.

Nathanael

Jesus described Nathanael as 'a true Israelite': a worthy descendant of Jacob. Jesus saw him sitting under a fig tree; probably that was where Nathanael sat to pray. Jesus wanted him to know that he, Jesus, was the way in which we can communicate with God and God can communicate with us, so Jesus said, '"Very truly, I tell you, you will see heaven opened and the angels of God ascending and descending upon the Son of Man."'

We can always talk to God through Jesus, and God can talk to us through his very human Son. And Jesus is close to us at every place and at every time. Jesus is Jacob's ladder. The lines of communication never close.

Suggested hymns

As Jacob with travel was weary one day; Nearer, my God, to thee; O for a closer walk with God; Prayer is the soul's sincere desire.

Mothering Sunday is celebrated in the UK on the Fourth Sunday in Lent; Americans celebrate Mother's Day on the second Sunday in May. 'Mid-Lent Sunday' has for long been a time for a relaxation of the Lenten fast. Domestic servants and apprentices were allowed the day off, and gathered flowers from the hedgerows on their way home to give to their mothers. The readings for the Principal Service are concerned with the family, but instead of a sermon for the Second Service this book provides a special sermon for Mothering Sunday. If there is a special service, young people can make flowers into posies, or draw pictures of flowers on greetings cards. These can be blessed with words such as the following, then given out at the Peace, or at the end of the service, for those present to give to their mothers, or put in a suitable place in memory of her, saying 'Thank you, mother, for all you have done for me.'

O God, bless these flowers, bless us, and bless our mothers. May the flowers remind us how much our mothers have done for us; may they remind our mothers that we love them; and may they remind us all that God cares for us better than any mother ever could. **Amen.**

Fourth Sunday of Lent   18 March

(For Mothering Sunday, see the Second Service; for the Eve of St Joseph's Day, see page 305. If the Principal Service readings have been displaced by Mothering Sunday provisions, they may be used for the Second Service.)

Principal Service   **The Prodigal Son** Josh. 5:9–12 Eating the Passover in Canaan; Ps. 32 Repentance; 2 Cor. 5:16–21 Forgiveness and reconciliation; Luke 15:1–3, 11b–32 The prodigal son

'I will get up and go to my father, and I will say to him, "Father, I have sinned against heaven and before you; I am no longer worthy to be called your son; treat me like one of your hired hands."' Luke 15:18–19

The Prodigal Son

One of the Ten Commandments forbids adultery; it's intended to establish the family as the basis of society. But there's more than one way to destroy the family. The parable in today's Gospel's often called 'The Prodigal Son'; using 'prodigal' to mean 'wasteful'. The sons were entitled to share out their father's property when he died, but the younger son in the story wanted his share now; it was tantamount to saying to his father, 'I wish you were dead!'

Honouring our parents

That's not honouring our parents, as the Commandments tell us to. Then instead of buying land, trading with it or investing it, he squandered the lot on having a wild time in the big city. But at last, he 'came to himself'; that is, he realized that this juvenile delinquent wasn't really him, and he had the potential to be a very different and much better person. The first good thing he ever did in his life was to make up his mind to go home and say sorry. He knew he could never claim back his position as a son, but he hoped he might get a much lower position as one of the workmen whom his father employed. Christians have always seen this as a parable about how we can return to God, claiming nothing, but accepting the unearned gift of salvation which God offers to us.

The forgiving father

For the truly remarkable person in the story, the real hero, isn't the prodigal son but his father. The father would have had every right to refuse to speak to the son who had insulted and impoverished him. Yet he went out to meet him half-way, and threw a party for him, slaughtering the calf which had been fed on the best food to provide a meal for some special occasion. Those who listened to Jesus must have known full well that none of them had it in them to treat a runaway like that. In fact, no human father could be expected to behave in such a loving way. Jesus told the story, to make us realize that, yes, God is like a human father, but much, much better.

'There's a wideness in God's mercy like the wideness of the sea.' How different the picture of God that Jesus gives us is from the usual idea of God as a stern, unforgiving judge. It should really be called the Parable of the Forgiving Father.

The older brother

A child was asked the question, 'Who do you think was not glad to see the prodigal son come home?' Not knowing what the correct answer was, the child guessed: 'Probably it was the fatted calf'! Well, probably the child was right. But the answer expected was that the older brother wasn't pleased at the return of the prodigal. He wouldn't join in the celebrations; he wouldn't call the prodigal his brother, but called him 'this son of yours'; he's the first to say anything about prostitutes. He wasn't going to lose anything by the prodigal's return, but he resented the love which the father offered to one who hadn't earned it, when he thought that he himself had.

Little Jack Horner

The Parable of the Prodigal Son was probably told to remind the Jews, who'd obeyed all the Commandments and thought that they'd earned the right to be called the Chosen People, that God isn't only interested in Jews. God, in his love, wants to forgive all races, if they will only turn to him in repentance. But are we Christians any better? Don't we sometimes come to church feeling like Jack Horner, 'O what a good boy – or girl – am I'? Don't we sometimes resent it if we see someone in church who's not as good as we imagine we are, and resent them for being there? Don't we sometimes despise other nations and other races? Surely we all need to say, 'I will get up and go to [God my heavenly] father, and I will say to him, "Father, I have sinned against heaven and before you; I am no longer worthy to be called your son [or daughter]."' Surely we all need humbly to accept the undeserved forgiveness which God offers to everyone without distinction.

Suggested hymns

Amazing grace; Father, I place into your hands; Just as I am, without one plea; There's a wideness in God's mercy.

Mothering Sunday   18 March
Look After Mother

(*The Christian Year: Calendar, Lectionary and Collects* gives two Old and New Testament readings, Psalms and Gospels for Mothering Sunday, either of which may be used in any year. *The Canterbury Preacher's Companion* will set the first of each for Year B and the second for Year C, and offer a new set of readings for Year A.)

1 Sam. 1:20–28 His mother offers Samuel to the Lord;
Ps. 127:1–4 Children a gift from the Lord; Col. 3:12–17 Love and care; John 19:25–27 Mary is your mother

A falling-out in the family

Every family's unique. The family that Jesus belonged to certainly was. After Jesus had been a guest at the wedding in Cana, we read in St John's Gospel that 'he went down to Capernaum with his mother, his brothers, and his disciples; and they remained there a few days'. There's no mention of Joseph, so some people guess that he was already an old man and had died, leaving Mary a widow, with Jesus and his brothers to look after her. At this point in the story the whole family seem to be friends, and supportive of each other. Later on, however, it says that 'not even his brothers believed in him'. When they discovered that Jesus was determined to become a travelling preacher and healer, they tried to stop him, 'for people were saying, "He has gone out of his mind."'

Mary, his mother, stayed with Jesus till the last, but there's no mention of his brothers when he went up to Jerusalem, so they must have fallen out with him completely, and left him to look after his mother all by himself. The good news is, they seem to have given up their opposition to Jesus after he was crucified, because the Acts of the Apostles says that the disciples 'were constantly devoting themselves to prayer, together with . . . Mary the mother of Jesus, as well as his brothers'.

A falling-out in the family can usually be healed eventually, with a bit of patience; perhaps it was Mary herself who talked them into a reconciliation.

Meanwhile, a crisis

Meanwhile, there was a crisis. When Jesus was crucified, Mary and the other women who looked after Jesus were there, looking on, even though most of the men had run away. Jesus knew that when he died, there'd be nobody to look after Mary if his brothers kept up their hostility. So he called her to him, together with his best friend, the one whom the Bible calls 'the disciple whom he loved'. Jesus asked them to look after each other:

When Jesus saw his mother and the disciple whom he loved stand-ing beside her, he said to his mother, 'Woman, here is your son.'

Then he said to the disciple, 'Here is your mother.' And from that hour the disciple took her into his own home.

Looking after Mother

Jesus knew that everyone needs a mother to look after them, totally when they're small, tactfully and discreetly as they learn to stand on their own two feet. We know very little about the Beloved Disciple, but perhaps his own mother had died and he was missing her. So, even in the midst of his intense pain, Jesus thoughtfully gave his own mother to his best friend, to be a mother to him. Mothers, too, need someone to look after them. Again, it needs to be done tactfully, letting her know that we are proud of her and grateful to her, but without being a nuisance to her. Then, as she gets older, her children have to work together to care for her.

'Mary's your mother'

Mothering Sunday's a good chance for families to do a stocktaking of their relationships. Have we fallen out with any of our family members, and is there anything we can do to bring about a reconciliation? Are you doing all you can to look after Mother? Are you giving her a chance to look after you? Do you have any friends with no mother of their own, who need someone to care for them, and someone for whom they can care? Every family's unique, with its own problems and opportunities. But we can all follow the example of Jesus, his best friend and his mother Mary. We can always think about what our family and friends need, and help them to live a full and happy life.

All-age worship

Flowers can be blessed, then given out at the end of the service, see the note above.

Suggested hymns

For the beauty of the earth; Lord of all hopefulness, Lord of all joy; Shall we not love thee, Mother dear?; Ye watchers and ye holy ones.

Principal Service   **The Fragrance of the Perfume**
Isa. 43:16–21 Salvation; Ps. 126 Salvation and joy;
Phil. 3:4b–14 Perseverance; John 12:1–8 Mary and Martha

> *'Mary took a pound of costly perfume made of pure nard, anointed Jesus' feet, and wiped them with her hair. The house was filled with the fragrance of the perfume . . . Jesus said, "Leave her alone. She bought it so that she might keep it for the day of my burial."'*
> *John 12:3–8*

Mary and Martha

The sisters Mary and Martha are only mentioned in two passages in the Gospels. In Luke 10 we read that when Jesus visited their house, Mary sat and listened to him, but Martha was too busy preparing the meal. In John 11 we read how Jesus raised their brother Lazarus, and the story continues into John 12, today's Gospel, where Mary anointed Jesus's feet with perfume and wiped them with her hair. It was unusual to find adult women who were not married, unless they were widowed or divorced. Perhaps some man gave the expensive perfume to Mary as a pledge that he'd marry her, but never came back. This is only speculation, but if true, it would make her act of self-sacrifice in 'wasting it' on Jesus, as Judas called it, doubly moving. It was an action which spoke louder than words how much she loved Jesus, and 'the house was filled with the fragrance of the perfume'.

The fragrance of the perfume

Of all the five senses, the sense of smell is the most evocative. Nobody who was present when Mary poured out her jar of 'pistic nard' to show her love will have ever forgotten it. The house was filled with the fragrance, just as Mary's life was filled with love; her love permeated her whole personality. There is a similar incident when Jesus was anointed by a sinner woman in Luke 7. On that occasion Jesus said, '"Therefore, I tell you, her sins, which were many, have been forgiven; hence she has shown great love. But the one to whom little is forgiven, loves little."'

It seems that the self-righteous couldn't accept the forgiveness that Jesus offered, because they didn't realize that they needed

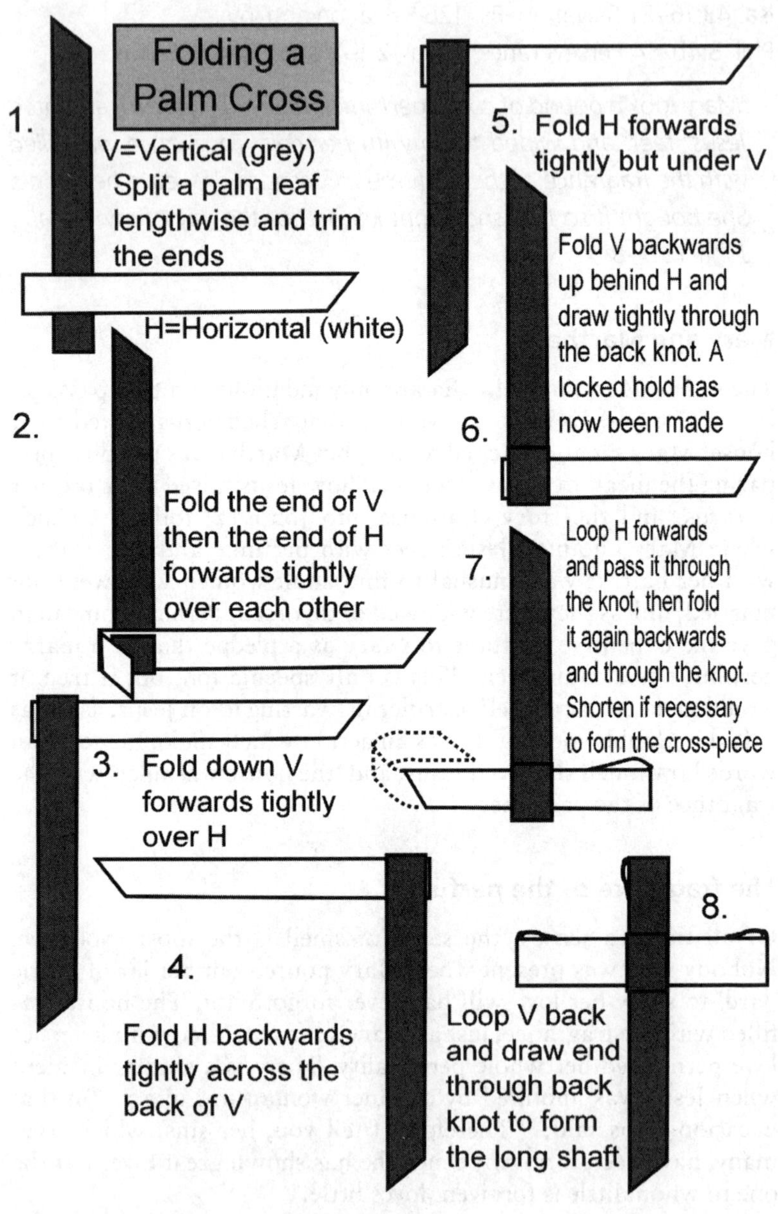

Folding a Palm Cross
1.
V=Vertical (grey)
Split a palm leaf lengthwise and trim the ends
H=Horizontal (white)
2.
Fold the end of V then the end of H forwards tightly over each other
3. Fold down V forwards tightly over H
4.
Fold H backwards tightly across the back of V
5. Fold H forwards tightly but under V
Fold V backwards up behind H and draw tightly through the back knot. A locked hold has now been made
6.
7.
Loop H forwards and pass it through the knot, then fold it again backwards and through the knot. Shorten if necessary to form the cross-piece
8.
Loop V back and draw end through back knot to form the long shaft

forgiving. The smug hypocrisy of those who think they're good is very unappealing, contrasted with the genuine love of those who've repented. The ninth and tenth Commandments are about the sinful inner attitudes of lying and coveting, which it is perfectly possible to combine with an outward appearance of righteousness.

Anointed for burial

Jesus said that Mary had anointed him ready for burial. It was as if she'd unwittingly seen into the future. This was just before Jesus entered Jerusalem to be crucified; nobody else thought he was going to die, but Jesus knew. In a warm climate dead bodies are covered in perfumed oil before they're buried. In Jesus's case, it was Mary Magdalene, Mary the mother of James and Salome, who came to do it for him on the Sunday morning following his death. The tomb was in a garden, and with the spices and the flowers the air must have been heavy with perfume on that occasion also.

The love of Jesus

Jesus had said, 'Greater love can nobody show than this, to lay down your life for your friends,' and, 'the Son of Man has come . . . to give his life as a ransom for many.' So the women knew that it was in love for his friends that Jesus had sacrificed himself on the cross. Love had filled his whole life, and now it filled their hearts in gratitude to their crucified Lord. What they didn't yet know, however, was that burial is followed by resurrection. They had yet to understand that Jesus is now alive. He leads the way to heaven, for all of us forgiven sinners to follow him.

The perfume of love

As we approach Holy Week, Good Friday and Easter, let's be on the lookout for signs of love. The love of Jesus, who voluntarily accepted suffering and death on behalf of you and me. And let's allow ourselves to love Jesus wholeheartedly in return, as a response of gratitude for his love. Once you allow the love of God to occupy even a small corner of your heart, it doesn't just stay there, but spreads until it permeates your whole life. Will you let the odour of love fill your life, until the house of your soul is filled with the fragrance of the perfume?

All-age worship

Prepare small sachets of spices, and hang them in your home to represent the pervasive love of Jesus. Make palm crosses.

Suggested hymns

My song is love unknown; O the deep, deep love of Jesus; Were you there when they crucified my Lord?; When I survey the wondrous cross.

Annunciation of our Lord to the Blessed Virgin Mary

(The Annunciation is transferred to Monday 26th, so the sermon at the Second Service is for the Eve of the Annunciation.)

Willingness Isa. 7:10–14 The sign of Immanuel; Ps. 40:5–10 I love to do your will; Heb. 10:4–10 I have come to do your will; Luke 1:26–38 The angel's message

> *'Then Mary said, "Here am I, the servant of the Lord; let it be with me according to your word."' Luke 1:38*

Nine months' pregnancy

It was decided that the birth of Jesus should be celebrated on 25 December, for no better reason than that it elbowed out a pagan festival of the winter solstice. Next it was decided to celebrate his conception on the 25 March, because that's exactly nine calendar months before his alleged date of birth. An elderly deaconess once expostulated, 'Exactly nine calendar months between conception and birth? Only a man could have imagined that would be so!' The story of the Annunciation of our Lord to the Blessed Virgin Mary is worth celebrating, whatever day we celebrate it, because the whole mystery of the incarnation of the Son of God begins there. Our salvation from sin and our hope of eternal life, coming from the death and resurrection of Jesus, wouldn't have been possible if God hadn't become human at Bethlehem. And *that* wouldn't have been possible, if one young girl hadn't been willing to say 'Yes'. 'Here am

I, the servant of the Lord,' said Mary to the angel; 'let it be with me according to your word.'

A remarkable woman

Mary was a truly remarkable woman. The birth of Jesus was remarkable because she was a virgin, and it had never previously happened that a woman had conceived without losing her virginity. Yet we oughtn't to be surprised at that: God can do anything, and God had never become human before, so we have no precedent for saying how it ought or ought not to have happened. Even more remarkable, however, was that Mary allowed it to happen. How much did she understand of what the consequences would be? Of course there would be all the usual discomfort of pregnancy and the pain of childbirth. Then there was the shame of being known to have been unmarried at the time the child was conceived. Mary knew she would be pilloried for that, but she was willing to accept it. Gabriel said that Mary's son would be King of Israel, and being the mother of a king is a difficult role to play. Her son was also Son of God, and she had no idea what that would mean for her. Later, when she went to the Temple in Jerusalem after the baby was born, the old priest Simeon warned her that her son's suffering would drive a sword through her own heart also. Did she have any inkling as to what she was taking on? Yet she said that she was the Lord's handmaid, the closest domestic servant whose task is to do everything her master or mistress demands, immediately and without question. Whatever God required of her, that she was willing to do, no matter what it might cost.

Willingness

So Mary's obedience undid Eve's disobedience. Whether or not you regard the story of the Garden of Eden as historical, the point it focuses on is that all our human troubles originate in disobedience. 'Adam' is a Hebrew word which means 'the human race'. The story of how he lost his opportunities for happiness, by doing what God had forbidden, is the story of Everyman. Jesus is called 'the Second Adam' because he obeyed his Father's call to travel the way of the cross, and so his obedience undid the harm that human disobedience had caused. Mary, then, is often compared to Eve. In the story of the Fall, Eve was unwilling to do what God told her; in the story of the Annunciation, Mary was willing, and so evil was destroyed.

Thus was fulfilled the prediction that the son of a woman should crush the serpent's head.

Barkis is willin'

In Charles Dickens's novel, *David Copperfield*, the character Barkis is famous for the phrase, 'Barkis is willin''. The Blessed Virgin Mary should be honoured for many things, but first of all, because she was willing to take on the task to which God had called her. Sometimes, each one of us may come to the conviction that God's calling us to do something for him. Our conscience tells us that this is the right thing to do, even though it may not be very pleasant. In fact, if we had been left to choose for ourselves, we'd probably have chosen to do the opposite. Are we ready, when that happens, like the Virgin Mary, to say that we're willing to do what God wants us to, no matter what the consequences?

Suggested hymns

For Mary, Mother of our Lord; Her Virgin eyes saw God incarnate born; Sing we of the blessed Mother; The angel Gabriel from heaven came.

Holy Week

The final week of Jesus's life on earth is celebrated from Palm Sunday to Easter Eve. Long readings of the Passion narrative are set at all the services. Palm Sunday is often marked with a procession of palms, Maundy Thursday by the washing of feet, Good Friday by the veneration of the cross, and Easter Eve by a vigil with the lighting of the new fire. An informal Passover supper to commemorate the Last Supper can be held on any day but is especially suitable for Maundy Thursday. A series of sermons on the Passion, or on the seven words of Christ from the cross, can be preached throughout Holy Week, or to mark the Three Hours on Good Friday. Most of the sermons provided in this book for specific days in Holy Week could be used on other days instead.

Palm Sunday   1 April
Principal Service   No Cross, No Crown

Isa. 50:4–9a I gave my back to the smiters; Ps. 31:9–16 Assurance
in suffering; Phil. 2:5–11 Jesus's obedience unto death;
Luke 22:14—23:56 The Last Supper to the burial; *or*
Luke 23:1–49 The trial before Pilate to the death on the cross

> *'[Jesus] said to [the disciples], "Who is greater, the one who is at the
> table or the one who serves? Is it not the one at the table? But I am
> among you as one who serves."' Luke 22:27*

A Quaker, a Baptist and an Anglican

William Penn was sent down from Christ Church College in
Oxford in 1661 because he refused to conform with the newly re-
established Anglican Church. After some years of travel he became
a Quaker, and wrote pamphlets attacking the doctrines of the
Trinity, the atonement and the Calvinistic understanding of
justification. For this he was imprisoned in the Tower of London,
where he wrote the spiritual classic *No Cross, No Crown*. This
includes the words: 'No pain, no palm; no thorns, no throne; no
gall, no glory; no cross, no crown.' After his release he sailed to
America and set up the colony of Pennsylvania, with a constitution
that allowed freedom of religion to all monotheists.

In the nineteenth century, a paper was found on the desk of the
famous Baptist preacher Charles Spurgeon when he died, which
read:

> No cross, no crown; no loss, no gain;
> They, too, must suffer who would reign.
> He best can part with life without a sigh,
> Whose daily living is to daily die.
> Youth pleads for age, age pleads for rest,
> Who pleads for heaven will plead the best.

In the twentieth century, an Anglican, George Briggs, Canon of
Worcester, expressed the same idea in a prayer:

> Holy Father, who hast shown us that the brave bearing of the
> cross is the beginning of wearing thy crown: help us by thy grace
> to bear patiently our pains and disappointments, as thy beloved

Son bore his; and to present them to thee as the pure gift of our faithfulness to our crucified Lord . . .

Whether or not they'd read each other's writings, which seems unlikely, these three Christians from very different backgrounds focused on one phrase to sum up the choice facing Jesus on Palm Sunday: no cross, no crown. There would be no glory unless he was willing to go the way of the cross.

Riding on a donkey

On the first Palm Sunday, the people waved palm branches and shouted Hosanna, the traditional greeting for a triumphant king. But a battling king would have been riding on a war-horse, and Jesus wasn't that sort of king. So he rode a donkey instead, to show that he was the Prince of Peace. The people wanted to make him a military Messiah to drive out the Roman army, but he knew that the only way he could become a king was the way of the cross: no cross, no crown.

The way of the cross

In harrowing detail the four Gospels describe the hostile forces opposed to Jesus, and the suffering he endured. To follow this way with him in your imagination is a gruelling journey. Yet we must travel with him, because otherwise we can't understand why Easter is such a triumph. Try to picture the scene in your mind's eye, hear the sounds, feel the heat, smell the crowds and the horses and the blood. It may be a difficult experience, but it will make Easter that much more wonderful.

How to be a VIP

The same choice faces us in our daily life as faced Jesus. We all want to be a VIP; we would all like our moment of glory; we enjoy the admiration of other people; we may even have our delusions of grandeur! But Jesus warns us that there's only one way to be placed on a pedestal, and that's the way of self-sacrifice:

The kings of the Gentiles lord it over them; and those in author-ity over them are called benefactors. But not so with you; rather the greatest among you must become like the youngest, and the leader like one who serves. For who is greater, the one who is at the table or the one who serves? Is it not the one at the table? But I am among you as one who serves.

For us, as for Jesus, the choice is stark: no cross, no crown.

All-age worship

Make a model of Jesus riding on a donkey, and carry it at the front of a procession in which you wave palm crosses or branches from potted palms or bushes, shouting 'Hosanna – save us now!'

Suggested hymns

All glory, laud and honour; Give me joy in my heart, keep me praising; Hosanna, hosanna, hosanna in the highest (Tuttle); Ride on, ride on in majesty.

Palm Sunday

Second Service　**The Song of the Vineyard** Ps. 69:1–20 Zeal for your house consumes me; Isa. 5:1–7 The Song of the Vineyard; Luke 20:9–19 The parable of the wicked tenants

> *'The vineyard of the Lord of hosts is the house of Israel, and the people of Judah are his pleasant planting; he expected justice, but saw bloodshed; righteousness, but heard a cry!' Isaiah 5:7*

Caring for a vineyard

What a lot of work some people put into their gardens! Whether it's vegetables or flowers, the garden-lovers seem to be out there at all hours, digging and weeding and watering. If their garden doesn't produce the champion marrows or prize-winning roses they'd hoped for, they're very disappointed, and wonder whether all their hard labour has been in vain. A few British people recently, not satisfied with gardening in their home town, have travelled to France and bought a vineyard there. If they try to look after it themselves, they soon find that the toil of caring for a vineyard is back-breaking hard work.

God's vineyard

In the Book of Isaiah we find the quite beautiful but tragic Song of the Vineyard. Israel and Judah are God's vineyard, sings the prophet, and he has laboured hard in caring for them. But there's been no vintage; a few withered grapes perhaps, but not the harvest he'd hoped for. God's heartbroken. Now what harvest was that, which God was expecting? God made the Jews his Chosen People, not because they were better than anybody else. He chose them because they were slaves in Egypt and had nothing. They had no homeland, no God of their own, and no purpose in life.

A God who saves

So God saved them out of Egypt, hoping they'd learn that God is a god who saves. Unlike the other gods, our God doesn't ignore the cries of those who call on him for help, but intervenes in history to get us out of the mess that we've got ourselves into. But even though we've no claim to deserve God's pity, he intervenes and saves us.

A God who cares

God also showed the Jews that he's a God who cares. Yes, he'd save them from their enemies, but all the gods claimed to do that. More importantly, he'd save them from themselves. If they travelled through the wilderness stealing, lying, stealing other men's wives and coveting their property, society would fall apart. So God gave them the Ten Commandments, to show that he cares about how we treat each other.

A God who looks outward

Then the Lord gave the Jews a homeland and the city of Jerusalem. This was to be their base. The message was to spread out from here until the whole world had heard what the Jews had learnt. They were to be a light to lighten the Gentiles, because all the isles and coastlands were waiting for God's Law. So the Jews were called to teach the rest of the world about a God who saves, and a God who cares: 'ethical monotheism' to give it its technical name. And what did they do? They sat at home and squabbled among themselves.

A heartbroken God

So God was heartbroken. After all that work he'd put into caring for his vineyard, it produced no fruit. God's Chosen People were a great disappointment to him, so he threatened to take the vineyard of Israel away from them unless they started doing what he'd chosen them for.

The wicked tenants

Jesus is obviously referring to Isaiah's prophecy when he tells the story of the wicked tenants, whose vineyard has been taken away from them and given to others. On the first Palm Sunday, Jesus rode into Jerusalem hoping that the people would welcome him and follow him; instead they crucified him. But we mustn't make this a text for anti-Semitism. All the first Christians were Jews, and they did spread the gospel to us Gentiles, as God told them to. We Christians haven't replaced the Jews, we've been privileged to be grafted into the vine to become part of the Chosen People with them. But then the same requirements apply to us. We've been chosen for service, not for privilege. We've been chosen to bear the fruit of good works, the fruit of the Spirit, and the harvest of souls. God wants more and more people to put their trust in him, because they've heard from us that he's a God who saves and who cares. As we follow Jesus through Holy Week we need to remember that it's our failure to bear fruit, as much as the sins of the Jews and the Romans, that broke the most loving of all hearts on the cross. We're all to blame. Yet still he cries, 'Father, forgive them, for they know not what they do.'

Suggested hymns

I am the vine, you are the branches; Make way, make way; My song is love unknown; The great Creator of the worlds.

First Three Days in Holy Week   2–4 April
Why Did Judas Do It?

(Following are the Wednesday readings but this sermon may be used on any day this week.)

Isa. 50:4–9a I gave my back to the smiters; Ps. 70 Those who say Aha! Aha!; Heb. 12:1–3 Suffering and perseverance on the cross; John 13:21–32 Judas betrays Jesus

> *'After receiving the piece of bread, [Judas] immediately went out. And it was night.' John 13:30*

Why did Judas do it?

Why did Judas do it? Why did he betray Jesus? Judas went to the High Priests and offered to tell them where and when Jesus could be arrested in a quiet place, without attracting a riotous crowd. So Judas led the soldiers to the Garden of Gethsemane, and identified Jesus for them in the dark by kissing him. Why? What were his motives?

A trick?

Jesus knew that Judas was going to betray him. Jesus knew that his own death on the cross would lead to the salvation of the world. So it's sometimes suggested that God wanted Judas to become a traitor, and Jesus tricked him into it. Poor Judas! He certainly played an unwitting part in God's eternal plan, but to suggest that God caused him to do it is to make the fundamental error that all theories of predestination make. God, outside of time, can look at all times simultaneously, and know what's going to happen. But he doesn't take away our free will. The choice to do something bad is always ours alone, and there's always the possibility of turning back at any time, until the inevitable chain of cause and effect has been set in motion.

Love of money?

Was it from love of money? The priests paid Judas thirty silver shekels, which was about three months' wages for a labourer; not very much. When an ox gored a slave to death, according to the Book of Exodus, the ox's owner had to pay the slave's owner thirty pieces of silver in compensation; that's all a slave's life was worth. The cynics say that every man has his price, but surely Judas valued his own integrity higher than that! When he realized the consequences of what he'd done, he threw the money back at the priests. He'd not been bought.

Covering his crimes?

Did Judas betray Jesus in order to cover up crimes he'd already committed? John's Gospel says that Judas 'was a thief; he kept the common purse and used to steal what was put into it'. Perhaps it was from fear of being found out that he created a distraction. But this sounds a bit like the sort of unfounded allegation that others might make in their bitterness after Judas was dead, and we can't know whether or not it was true.

Provoking a revolution?

Judas may have been a zealot; the word 'Iscariot' may possibly come from the Latin word *sicarii*, meaning dagger-men. Possibly Judas wanted to start a revolution to drive out the Roman army, and hoped that the attempt to arrest Jesus would provoke him into taking up arms and beginning the fight.

Disappointment?

More likely Judas already realized that Jesus wasn't going to be a violent revolutionary and a military Messiah. Perhaps he was so disappointed in Jesus that he wanted to get him out of the way so that somebody else could have a go.

Mental breakdown?

John and Luke suggest that Satan entered Judas and made him do it. Everyone, including Jesus himself, can be tempted by evil impulses; but everyone has the power to 'just say no'. Unless, that is, their mind's gone. If the word 'Iscariot' doesn't mean a dagger-man, Judas could have been named after his home-town, Kerioth. If so he was from Judah, and the only one of the Twelve who wasn't a Galilean; he was an outsider. This, together with all the conflicting emotions we have just discussed, could have led to a mental breakdown. The Bible, lacking modern psychological language, usually calls this demon possession.

Might we?

So the answer to our initial question is that we really don't know why Judas did it. But we mustn't demonize Judas; he wasn't a monster. Jesus loved him, and chose him to be one of the Twelve; he must have seen the potential that Judas had for much that was good. He was a human being like us. We too, subjected to the same tensions, could have toppled over the edge. Judas deserves our sympathy, and a humble look at our own frailty.

How much forgiveness?

Did Jesus forgive Judas? I hope so. Judas committed suicide, the sin of despair. But maybe as Judas fell, it was like in those lines written by William Camden about a man who broke his neck falling from his horse:

> My friend, judge not me,
> Thou seest I judge not thee.
> Betwixt the stirrup and the ground
> Mercy I asked, mercy I found.

Suggested hymns

All ye who seek for sure relief; Father, whose everlasting love; Just as I am, without one plea; There's a wideness in God's mercy.

Maundy Thursday   5 April
Foot-washers to the World

Ex. 12:1–4 [5–10] 11–14 The Passover; Ps. 116:1, 10–end (*or* 9–end) The cup of salvation; 1 Cor. 11:23–26 The last supper; John 13:1–17, 31b–35 Foot-washing

"'[Jesus said,] If I, your Lord and Teacher, have washed your feet, you also ought to wash one another's feet." John 13:14

By royal appointment

Certain suppliers in Britain are granted a royal warrant by the Queen, and are allowed to put the royal coat of arms over their door and on their stationery, with the words, 'By royal appointment', butchers or bakers or candlestick-makers or whatever 'to her Majesty Queen Elizabeth'. This is counted as a very great honour. You and I, as Christians, are the servants of the King of kings. What honour could we put over our own doorways? The highest title we could lay claim to, as Christians, is 'By royal appointment, foot-washers to the world'.

The job of a slave

Washing the feet of those who'd come into the house from the dusty roads of Palestine was the task of the lowliest slave in the household. When Jesus ate the Last Supper with his disciples, there were probably far more disciples present in the room than just the Twelve – never mind what Leonardo da Vinci showed in his beautiful painting. Some women travelled round Galilee with Jesus ministering to his needs, and it's unlikely that they were absent at Passover, the great family festival. At least they'll have been in and out of the kitchen. So who was going to do the lowliest slave's job, the foot-washing?

Jesus did it

The answer, as we all know, is that Jesus did it. He did it, to teach humility. Over and over he'd taught his disciples that anyone who wants to be important must be the servant of all. Now he was putting his teaching into practice himself. It symbolized his whole life and also his death. All his life he'd been serving others: making their tables and chairs for them when he was a carpenter, healing the sick, cheering the sad, forgiving the guilty, and reminding the outcasts that God loves them. When he rebuked the hypocrites, he was serving them, for he was doing what was in their best interests, in the hope that they would listen and change their proud ways. There were so many people making demands on him that his time was not his own, and he had to go away into the hills at night if he wanted to pray. So he showed by his example what a life of self-sacrifice meant.

Foot-washers to the world

If that was how Jesus lived, that's how we must live. 'If I, your Lord and Teacher, have washed your feet, you also ought to wash one another's feet,' he said. There's no room at Jesus's side for arrogance or pride. You can't be a Christian and be totally self-centred. The way of a Christian is one of denying self: saying no to your selfish desires, denying your right to control your own belongings, your own time, your own actions, and putting them all under the control of Jesus. What he wants you to do is to use them all in the service of others. It may seem hard, but when we look at Jesus's example of self-denial in his own life, we can at least make it our goal, even if we often fall short. We start with humble service to those closest to us. Then we go on to serve those around us in ever-increasing circles. Our target is to be foot-washers to the world.

A sacrificial death

Jesus acted out this visual parable at the Last Supper, which was his opportunity to explain to his disciples the meaning of his death. In the broken bread and the poured-out wine, he was illustrating that his body was to be broken and his blood outpoured, for them. Pages of theology have been written on what this meant, and how the death of Jesus resembled the sacrifices of the Old Testament. But a good starting-point for us is to look at what he'd already taught, in the foot-washing, about humble self-sacrifice. 'Having loved his own who were in the world, he loved them to the end,' to the uttermost limits, even to the extent of dying for them. He died as he had lived, in total self-sacrifice, forgetting his own needs and wishes and, in the end, sacrificing even his own life for others. There was no limit to his self-sacrifice. Neither can there be to ours, if we are his disciples.

Suggested hymns

An Upper Room did our Lord prepare; Broken for me, broken for you; Great God, your love has called us here; O thou, who at thy Eucharist didst pray.

Good Friday 6 April
Principal Service **The Suffering of Christ**

Isa. 52:13—53:12 The suffering servant; Ps. 22 Why have you forsaken me?; Heb. 10:16–25; *or* Heb. 4:14–16; 5:7–9 Jesus the priest; John 18:1—19:42 The blood of the covenant

'There they crucified him.' John 19:18

The gift of tears

Many people who find it difficult to express their emotions, nevertheless find there's moisture in their eyes on Good Friday. Peter Ustinov in his autobiography *Dear Me* writes of a relative who had 'the readiest gift of tears. The story of the crucifixion was enough to set her off, as though it were not so much a monumental tragedy as a personal misfortune.' The fifteenth-century Norfolk mystic Margery Kempe used to thank God for the 'gift of tears', and prayed, 'Lord, make my eyes walls of tears, that when I receive your body, tears of devotion may pour down my cheeks.'

Those who are brought up to be stiff upper-lipped probably miss some of life's deeper experiences. You can't force yourself to be either emotional or unemotional, you must just accept yourself as you are. Yet when we think of the suffering of Jesus, there are few people who can withhold a tear or two. Jesus must have seen many people crucified when he was a boy. He knew what suffering crucifixion involved, so why did he go ahead and submit to it? This is something we should ask ourselves whenever we look at a crucifix.

The reason why

There have been many answers to the question, 'Why did Jesus die?' Doctrines of the atonement are grouped under different headings: a sacrifice for sin, a victory over death, to reconcile us to the Father, and so on. They're all true in their way, but none of them contains the whole truth. They're like photographs of a mountain taken from different angles; none of them is untrue, but you need to consider all of them if you are to get a rounded picture of the whole. In the modern age we want to ask a different, psychological question: what were the personal motives of Jesus which made him go through with the crucifixion, when he could easily have escaped?

How to avoid crucifixion

You think he couldn't have avoided the cross? Oh yes he could. He could have stayed at home in peaceful obscurity as the carpenter of Nazareth. The temptations which he said the Devil had presented to him in the wilderness, to use the wrong means to achieve the right ends, must have stayed with him all his life. He could have deserted his friends in Gethsemane and left them to face the music. He could have told Pilate that he was not a king. He could have told the High Priest that he was not the Son of God. Yet he had spent his whole life trying to convince people that God is a loving Father, because he himself was like God: 'like father, like son'. So if he'd denied that he was God incarnate, when challenged, or if he'd run away, his actions would have contradicted his words. Then the world would have gone on thinking that God's a cruel tyrant who ignores his people in their hour of need. So Jesus continued boldly to proclaim the truth, fully aware of the suffering it would involve.

The pain of crucifixion

The skeleton of a man who'd been crucified was found in the twentieth century in Jerusalem. He was only one of hundreds who were executed in this way around the time of Jesus. A nail was still jammed through his ankle bones, and fragments of the wood were still on it. Other features of the skeleton told us details of how crucifixion was carried out. The nails were driven not through the hands, where the flesh would have torn free, but through the ganglia of nerves which pass through the wrist bones. The arms were almost vertical, so that the ribs were compressed and it was impossible to breathe. All that a man could do was to heave himself up on the nail through his feet, gasp a lungful of air, and fall back to hang from the nail through the wrists. Over and over for three hours, until the soldiers broke the legs in a coup de grâce, and you died of suffocation. And the reason Jesus willingly submitted to the most painful form of execution that's ever been invented was because he loves you. He's willing to sacrifice himself to save you from the consequences of your sins and from the fear of death. He wants you to know that God loves you. There was only one way Jesus could convince us of this, and he accepted what it cost him. 'If you have tears, prepare to shed them now.'

Ah, holy Jesus, how hast thou offended?; Drop, drop slow tears; Were you there when they crucified my Lord?; When I survey the wondrous cross.

Easter

The forty days of Easter, up to Ascension Day, are a season of joyful celebration. We celebrate the resurrection of Jesus from the dead, and are filled with hope as inheritors of eternal life. The altar frontals and vestments are white, or gold on Easter Day, and the wonderful Easter hymns resound with alleluias. If the 'Gloria in excelsis' has been omitted in Lent, it is sung again for the first time at the Easter vigil. At the vigil, the Easter candle may be lit; it then burns at all services during the season, and at baptisms in the rest of the year. At the vigil, or some other service, there may be a renewal of baptism promises. There may be an Easter garden with a model of the empty tomb. Eastertide sermons expound our reasons for believing that Jesus is alive, and for hoping for an eternal future for ourselves.

Easter Vigil   7–8 April
At Early Dawn

(A minimum of three Old Testament readings should be chosen. The reading from Ex. 14 should always be used.)

Gen. 1:1—2:4a Creation, Ps. 136:1–9, 23–26 Thank the Lord who delivered us; Gen. 7:1–5, 11–18; 8:6–18; 9:8–13 Noah, Ps. 46 Our refuge and strength; Gen. 22:1–18 Sacrifice of Isaac, Ps. 16 The path of life; Ex. 14:10–31; 15:20–21 The exodus, *Canticle*: Ex. 15:1b–13, 17–18 The song of Moses; Isa. 55:1–11 Come to the waters, *Canticle*: Isa. 12:2–6 Great in your midst; Bar. 3:9–15, 32—4:4 God gives the light of wisdom *or* Prov. 8:1–8, 19–21; 9:4b–6 Wisdom, Ps. 19 The heavens declare God's glory; Ezek. 36:24–28 I will sprinkle clean water on you, Ps. 42 and 43 Faith and hope; Ezek. 37:1–14 The valley of dry bones, Ps. 143 A prayer for deliverance; Zeph. 3:14–20 I will bring you home, Ps. 98 Salvation and Justice; Rom. 6:3–11 Baptism, death and resurrection, Ps. 114 The exodus; Luke 24:1–12 The empty tomb

> *'On the first day of the week, at early dawn, [the women] came to the tomb, taking the spices that they had prepared. They found the stone rolled away from the tomb, but when they went in, they did not find the body.' Luke 24:1–3*

At early dawn

> I got me flowers to strew Thy way;
> I got me boughs off many a tree:
> But Thou wast up by break of day,
> And brought'st Thy sweets along with Thee.

So wrote George Herbert, the seventeenth-century courtier-turned-country-parson. The first people to see that the tomb of Christ was empty arrived at early dawn, so the resurrection took place before then, sometime in the night, when nobody was about. The mysteries of God often take place in the dark, as though they were too holy to be observed. The creation took place before there was light; the angel of death passed over the Israelites during the night; the shepherds were told to find the newborn baby Jesus at night.

The Easter vigil

In the early Church, Easter was the most important day of the year. Baptisms took place on Easter Day, and the whole congregation joined the candidates who were to be baptized in an all-night preparation or vigil, and renewed their own baptismal promises when the candidates took theirs. All fires were put out and a new fire was kindled from flint, to symbolize that resurrection is the beginning of a totally new life. Still today, in many churches, the Easter candle's lit from the new fire. It burns until Ascension Day, to symbolize the 40 days in which the risen Christ was visibly present on earth. Servers light their candles from the Easter candle and pass the flame to others in the congregation, symbolizing the spreading of the light of Christ from person to person throughout the world.

The Church, which until then has been pitch dark, gradually fills with light as the flame is passed on. Alleluias, which haven't been sung since before Lent, fill the air. Passages from the Bible, relating to baptism, resurrection and light, are read, and suitable psalms are sung. So is the beautiful hymn known as the *Exultet*:

This is the night when of old you saved our fathers, delivering the people of Israel from their slavery, and leading them dry-shod through the sea. This is the night when Jesus Christ vanquished hell and rose triumphant from the grave. This is the night when all who believe in him are freed from sin and restored to grace and holiness. Most blessed of all nights, when wickedness is put to flight and sin is washed away, lost innocence regained, and mourning turned to joy. Night truly blessed, when heaven is wedded to earth and all creation reconciled to God!

New light

Few churches can provide an all-night service these days, but many will celebrate the Easter Vigil in the dark on Saturday evening, or at dawn on Sunday morning. Increasingly, Protestants are finding a hilltop or high ground to celebrate what they call a 'Sonrise Service', spelt S O N R I S E ! If it's arranged ecumenically, Anglicans sometimes introduce some elements of the Easter vigil, and find that the Easter candle's a welcome symbol of new light. For until Jesus came to earth, the world dwelt in the darkness of sin, fear of death and fear of God. There were individuals who thought it was 'better to light a candle than to curse the darkness'. Their light flickered and died 'like a candle in the wind'. But with Jesus, 'The light shines in the darkness, and the darkness did not overcome it . . . The true light, which enlightens everyone, was coming into the world.'

Suggested hymns

A brighter dawn is breaking; Come, ye faithful, raise the strain; Light's glittering morn bedecks the sky; Lord, the light of your love is shining (Shine, Jesus, shine); Thou, whose almighty word.

Easter Day   8 April
Principal Service   **Witnesses**

Acts 10:34–43 Peter and other witnesses to the resurrection; *or*
Isa. 65:17–25 New heavens and a new earth; Ps. 118:[1–2], 14–24 I
shall not die but live; 1 Cor. 15:19–26 The last enemy destroyed is
death; *or* Acts 10:34–43; John 20:1–18 Magdalene at the tomb; *or*
Luke 24:1–12 The women see Jesus

> *'Jesus said to [Mary Magdalene], "Do not hold on to me, because I
> have not yet ascended to the Father. But go to my brothers and say
> to them, 'I am ascending to my Father and your Father, to my God
> and your God.'"' John 20:17*

Testimony of an actress

In 1994 a young British actress went to Israel to make a video,
in which she performed the part of Mary Magdalene telling her
life story. The camera crew were all secular Jews, and on the first
couple of days' filming they remarked what a good actress she
was. But on the final day's shooting, she told the story of meeting
the risen Christ in the garden. At that point she stopped looking
towards the camera and speaking to the viewers, and started speaking to Jesus and telling him how she'd tried to do what he'd told
her to. The camera crew said afterwards, 'At that point she wasn't
acting. We couldn't see Jesus, but we knew he was there listening
to her, because she really believed it herself.' Many people watch us
Christians, to see whether our actions really show that we believe
what we say in church, or whether we betray our insincerity. In that
sense, we are all witnesses, whether we like it or not.

Go and tell

Jesus told Mary Magdalene to 'Go and tell'. She had proved to
herself that Jesus was alive. But this good news was too precious
to keep to herself. She had to tell others. By the conviction with
which she spoke, they'd know that what she said was true. Women
were not allowed to give evidence in the law courts of Jesus's day,
because their testimony wasn't regarded as reliable. But Jesus chose
women to be the first witnesses of his resurrection, so that they
could 'go and tell' what they knew from their own experience.

What is your experience?

Could you be a witness to the resurrection? Maybe you think not, because you've never seen Jesus. But you've often spoken to him. Maybe it was only the unthinking recitation of a prayer like a formula. Maybe sometimes you were not very clear in your own mind whether there was anybody listening, or whether you were just speaking into a void. But just occasionally you've felt that there really was somebody there on the other end of the line, listening to your prayers. And just occasionally they were answered. You got what you were asking for. Or you didn't get it, but you received a spiritual strength which enabled you to cope with your disappointment and feel that all was for the best. You couldn't have had any of those experiences, if the Jesus you prayed to had died 2000 years ago and never come to life again. Your experience proves to your sceptical mind that Jesus rose again and is alive today, listening to your prayers. So, amazingly, you too are a witness to the resurrection, out of your own experience.

Baptism and ordination

Many churches have a renewal of baptism promises on Easter Day. At our baptism we promised, or our godparents promised for us and we took the promises for ourselves at confirmation, to reject evil, repent of our sins and turn to Christ. Then we were baptized into the death of Jesus 'so that, just as Christ was raised from the dead by the glory of the Father, so we too, might walk in newness of life'.

Sometimes baptism and confirmation are spoken of as 'the ordination of the laity', when we're each given our ministry to perform in the Church. As well as achieving our own salvation, we all promise to serve others in the Church. Some are called to preach, others to give a word of warm welcome before the service and to lend a sympathetic ear afterwards. And we're all being watched, to see whether we're sincere witnesses to the resurrection of Jesus, by our words or by our deeds. All Christians, without exception, are ordained to this ministry. Pray to God for the power that raised Jesus from the dead to be revealed in your life, in the love shown by your actions and the way you recount your own experience of answered prayer. Like Mary Magdalene, once we've received the gift of God's love, we have to 'go and tell'.

Make model figures of Peter, John, Mary Magdalene, Mary the mother of James, Joanna, Salome, Jesus and the angels to go in the Easter garden.

Suggested hymns

Alleluia, alleluia, give thanks to the risen Lord; Good Joseph had a garden; Thine be the glory; Walking in a garden.

Easter Day
Second Service **Resurrection Appearances**
Morning Ps. 114 The exodus, 117 Praise the Lord; Evening Ps. 105 The exodus, *or* 66:1–11 God holds our souls in life; Isa. 43:1–21 You are my witnesses; 1 Cor. 15:1–11 Witnesses of the Resurrection; *or* John 20:19–23 Sunday evening appearance

> 'Then [the Risen Christ] appeared to more than five hundred brothers and sisters at one time, most of whom are still alive, though some have died.' 1 Corinthians 15:6

What do Christians believe?

It sounds as though the Christians in Corinth were confused about the resurrection. Well they might be! Those who were Greeks had hoped, after the soul flew free from its imprisonment in the body, like a bird from a cage, for nothing better than that their ghost should journey in Charon's ferry boat across the River Styx to the gloomy land of Hades, were they'd sleep for ever. Then came Jews and built a synagogue in Corinth, and they appeared to believe that at some future date, some of the dead would come back to earth and resume their fleshly bodies. Not so much a resurrection as a resuscitation. What, the Corinthians asked St Paul, do Christians believe about resurrection? Paul wrote them a long answer. He draws illustrations and analogies from all over the place to help them towards a new concept. This Christian teaching is neither the Greek idea nor the Jewish idea, but draws on both. But he begins with the resurrection of Jesus.

Hysteria?

Now, if only a few people had seen Jesus after he died, we might have thought they were deluding themselves with wishful thinking. Many people have had hallucinations, and thought they saw something or someone that wasn't there. Sometimes you get a string of hallucinations as a sort of hysteria spreads. Occasionally, but very rarely, two people may have the same hallucination at the same time. But the resurrection of Jesus wasn't like that at all.

Resurrection appearances

The four Gospels agree that it was a group of women who first saw that the tomb was empty, and went to tell the other disciples. St John says that Mary Magdalene was the first to see the risen Christ. St Paul says that St Peter – whom he calls 'Cephas' – saw Jesus. So did James. Then Jesus appeared to the Twelve; this is the Sunday evening appearance behind closed doors, mentioned by St Luke and St John, who also mentions another appearance the following Sunday when Thomas also was present. Then there was the appearance to seven disciples on the lakeside in Galilee, also reported by St John, who may have been one of them. Luke mentions the two disciples who saw Jesus on the road to Emmaus, one called Cleopas, the other possibly his wife. But St Paul goes on to say that Jesus appeared to more than five hundred people at one and the same time, a quite remarkable number. Many of them were still alive, and could be questioned about their experience; they were reliable witnesses to an actual historical event. Lastly Paul mentions that Jesus appeared to him on the road to Damascus. This wasn't a dream, he said, but an actual appearance of the risen Christ. There are very few historical events which have as many reliable witnesses as the resurrection of Jesus Christ.

What did they see?

What, then, did these witnesses see? It wasn't an ordinary physical body like ours, because it seems that Jesus could appear and disappear at will, even when the disciples were behind closed doors. So much for the Jewish idea of resuscitation. Yet it wasn't a ghost, for Jesus apparently ate with them and invited Thomas to touch his side. So much for the Greek concept. St Paul had to invent a whole new terminology for what he called 'the spiritual body'. But it wasn't a hallucination – not with all those witnesses to say that it was a historical event – it was an appearance.

A vision

An appearance is when somebody outside your mind causes you to see them. The initiative is with the one who appears, not, like a hallucination, the febrile invention of a sick mind. There's an over-whelming weight of evidence that appearances have happened, and continue to happen today all over the world. It doesn't really matter to us in what way Jesus was 'really there' when he appeared, even if we could understand what the words mean. What matters is that we should believe the evidence, and hold on to the fact that he's 'real-ly here' today, though we can't see him; that he loves us, and can hear and answer our prayers. Now that's really important; but if we ever have any nagging doubts whether it's true, we can turn back to the reliable accounts of the resurrection appearances to convince us.

Suggested hymns

Alleluia, alleluia, hearts to heaven and voices raise; Alleluia (3) O sons and daughters, let us sing!; The day of resurrection!; Thine be the glory.

Second Sunday of Easter   15 April
Principal Service   **That You May Believe**
Ex. 14:10–31; 15:20–21 The exodus (*if used, the reading from Acts must be used as the second reading*); or Acts 5:27–32 Peter and other witnesses to the resurrection; Ps. 118:14–29 I shall not die but live; *or* Ps. 150 Praise in Heaven; Rev. 1:4–8 The firstborn from the dead; *or* Acts 5:27–32; John 20:19–31 Thomas's doubt and faith

> *'These [things] are written so that you may come to believe that Jesus is the Messiah, the Son of God, and that through believing you may have life in his name.' John 20:31*

Why bother?

The Andrew Lloyd-Webber/Tim Rice musical *Jesus Christ Superstar* is more a study of what people thought about Jesus, than a life of Jesus. At the Last Supper, the tipsy disciples sing:

> Always knew I could be an apostle;
> knew that I could make it if I tried.
> Then when we retire, we can write the Gospels
> so folk will talk about us when we've died.

The disciples certainly had delusions of greatness, and Jesus often had to teach them humility. But if they imagined that leadership in the Church would bring them cosy luxury, they had a nasty shock coming. It soon turned into a career of scorn and mockery, of suffering and martyrdom. If they wanted a life of ease, they should have retired into obscurity. Why bother being an apostle when it only brings you trouble? Fortunately for us, they didn't give up, but faced the painful consequences of their vocation with unwavering faith. And then they wrote the Gospels. Why? Not in search of fame as the musical suggests. St John tells us why he wrote his Gospel: 'These [things] are written so that you may come to believe that Jesus is the Messiah, the Son of God, and that through believing you may have life in his name.'

An axe to grind

All four Gospels were written with a purpose. They weren't an abstract analysis of history written in the cold detachment of an academic study. Such dispassionate books have never been written until comparatively recently. The ancient historians all had an axe to grind. They wrote history as a way of persuading the readers to their point of view, and their writings were all the better for it. You can read the lifeless dissections of modern historians and say to yourself, 'So what?' But when you read someone who really cares about the events they're describing, you may agree or disagree, but you'll do so passionately, and it may change your insight into the people of the past, and your attitude to your own life today. Because the Gospel-writers were describing the incarnation of the Son of God at a particular moment in history, they took pains to get their history as right as they could, without being able to visit a reference library and check the back numbers of the newspaper! This was no spiritual other-worldly religion where facts are unimportant; this was God coming into the world of matter, to redeem the material world and send history off in a new direction. But it wasn't only to describe historical events that the Gospels were written; they were written to persuade. They were written 'that you might believe'.

Through believing, have life

But I repeat, this was no abstract theory that the Gospel-writers wanted us to believe. The Gospel-writers don't want us to believe *that,* but to believe *in.* Not to believe that certain miracles happened, but to believe in the Saviour who could make them happen if he wanted to. They wanted us to trust Jesus, and follow where he leads. If you trust your guide, you'll follow him through thick and thin, like the first disciples did. They believed in the resurrection; they believed in a Saviour who's alive, and can lead us to fullness of life. 'Eternal life', in St John's Gospel, is something we can begin to experience here and now, a more joyful and exciting life because it's a life of love and service to others; 'life in all its fullness'. The Gospels were written, not for the sake of the writers, but for the sake of the readers, you and me. They were written so that we might come to know Jesus, who died and is now alive again. Then, knowing him as our living friend, we might come to believe in him. Thus we shall share in the vigorous and vital life that Jesus is living, which begins here and now, and goes on getting better until it turns into eternity.

All-age worship

Draw the symbols of the four Gospels: the man for human Matthew, the lion of bold Mark, the ox for domesticated Luke, and the eagle with its wide vision for John.

Suggested hymns

Dear Lord, we long to see your face; Hail, thou once despised Jesus; Thine be the glory; Alleluia (3) O sons and daughters, let us sing!

Second Sunday of Easter

Second Service **The Suffering Servant** Ps. 16 The path of
life; Isa. 52:13—53:12 *or* 53:1–6, 9–12 The Suffering Servant;
Luke 24:13–35 The road to Emmaus

*'When you make his life an offering for sin, he shall see his off-
spring, and shall prolong his days; through him the will of the Lord
shall prosper.' Isaiah 53:10*

The prophet's dilemma

Imagine you're a Jew in exile in Babylon, around 538 BC. The Persian
Emperor Cyrus has just signed a decree allowing all the foreign
exiles in Babylon to return home to their own lands, but the Jews
are too demoralized to do so. They think that their God can no
longer do anything for them, now that they have left his territory
and entered the land where the Babylonian gods are all-powerful.
What can you, the prophet, do to encourage them? Well, you can
write a long poem beginning 'Comfort, O comfort my people',
describing how God will lead them home because he still has a
purpose for them. But how are you to distribute this poem so that
groups of Jews all over what's now Iraq can read it? Suppose Cyrus
or his secret police get their hands on a document which says that
the Jewish God is more powerful than the idols of Babylon, what'll
they do? If it says that Cyrus is merely a tool in God's hands to bring
about the future greatness of Israel, they'll regard it as a seditious
pamphlet. If they can catch you they'll throw you into jail. And
they'll certainly cancel the edict allowing the Jews to go home.

Second Isaiah

So you hit on the brilliant idea of disguising your poem, by literally
'tacking it onto the end' of a document which is nearly two hundred
years old. You sew your seditious poem by invisible mending onto
the end of the scroll of the prophet Isaiah. The join is so seamless
that at first sight it looks as though they're all the same book. But
most people today accept that chapters 40 onwards are by someone
else, whose name we don't know, so we call him 'Second Isaiah'.
There's nothing dishonest or irreverent about this. We believe it
was God's brainwave, to make sure that the writings of two of his
greatest prophets survived until today.

The Servant Songs of Second Isaiah

This anonymous prophet wanted his fellow Jews to understand that even their suffering during the Exile had a purpose. The suffering of the Jews, he taught, was a necessary preparation for the task that God had in mind for them. They were to sacrifice their own needs and their own glory, so that they could be God's servants and tell the world about their God – a God who sacrifices *his* needs and his glory, to rescue the people he loves from the mess they've got into. Interspersed through the scroll of Second Isaiah are what we call the four Servant Songs, describing the career and character of someone called the 'Servant of the Lord'.

- One: 'Here is my servant . . . my chosen . . . I have given you as . . . a light to the nations.'
- Two: 'You are my servant, Israel, in whom I will be glorified . . . I will give you as a light to the nations, that my salvation may reach to the end of the earth.'
- Three: 'I gave my back to those who struck me, and my cheeks to those who pulled out the beard; I did not hide my face from insult and spitting.'

The fourth Servant Song, which we read today, is the classic description of the Suffering Servant of the Lord, so famous from quotations in the New Testament and in Handel's *Messiah*.

Who is the Servant?

Who is the 'Servant of the Lord' described in these four songs? They probably describe the vocation of God's servant Israel to rebuild their nation and bring justice to the others, to be a 'light to the Gentiles'. The Songs are a challenge to Israel to learn from its suffering during the Exile, and carry the message of a saviour God to the rest of the world. Later they helped Jesus and his followers explain *his* suffering on the cross, understanding that anyone called to serve God may suffer, but self-sacrifice is redemptive. So we're quite justified in applying them to the death of Jesus:

- 'a man of sorrows and acquainted with grief';
- 'and the LORD has laid on him the iniquity of us all';
- 'by whose [injuries] we are healed'.

But they also describe his vindication when people listen to his message and put their faith in him: 'When you make his life an offering for sin, he shall see his offspring, and shall prolong his days; through him the will of the LORD shall prosper.'

Suggested hymns

Broken for me, broken for you; Hail, thou once despised Jesus; My God, I love thee – not because; The strife is o'er, the battle won.

Third Sunday of Easter   22 April
Principal Service   Do You Love Me?
Zeph. 3:14–20 The Lord is in your midst (*if used, the reading from Acts must be used as the second reading*); or Acts 9:1–6 [7–20] Paul's conversion; Ps. 30 God brought me up from Death; Rev. 5:11–14 Worshipping the Lamb; *or* Acts 9:1–6 [7–20]; John 21:1–19 The Lakeshore

> *'[Jesus] said to [Peter] the third time, "Simon son of John, do you love me?" Peter felt hurt because he said to him the third time, "Do you love me?" And he said to him, "Lord, you know everything; you know that I love you." Jesus said to him, "Feed my sheep."'* John 21:17

'I'm going fishing'

The Big Fisherman was out of his depth. He was a practical man, who worked with his hands, and he could talk about business, but all this God-talk was too much for him. Now he'd seen Jesus alive after he'd died on the cross, and this was forcing him to think out afresh what he believed about resurrection. So to get away from all this theology, he made a practical suggestion: 'I'm going fishing.' This was his trade, he knew all about fishing, more than anybody else, in fact. No need to think new thoughts here; in a fishing boat he was never out of his depth. And then he and his mates fished all night and never caught a thing; not a nibble.

A miraculous catch

In the morning, Jesus appeared to them again. Standing on the lake-shore, he called to Peter and told him he was doing it all wrong; a carpenter giving instructions to a master-fisherman about fishing – how humiliating! But Jesus isn't satisfied with a little corner of our lives, the 'religious' part, what we do on Sundays. Jesus wants to take charge of the whole of life, seven days a week, what we do at work and what we do in the home, as well as what we do in church. Wisely, Peter took the carpenter's advice and cast his net on the other side of the boat, and they caught 153 fish. There may have been a natural explanation, but the disciples were wise enough to recognize that it was yet another sign, pointing to who Jesus was. Peter jumped into the shallow waters and floundered his way to shore; now he didn't care whether he was out of his depth or not.

'Do you love me?'

After breakfast, Jesus asked Peter, 'Do you love me?' Many young lovers have asked each other that question, 'Do you love me?', in astonishment, or disbelief, or simply to test the other's genuineness. But love has so many levels and means so many things. Elizabeth Barrett Browning asked: 'How do I love thee? Let me count the ways,' and spent the rest of the poem answering her own question. At first Peter didn't understand what the question meant: 'Yes Lord, you know I love you,' he replied. But in what way did Peter love Jesus? 'More than these?' asked Jesus – these friends, this fishing, this beautiful lake – are you willing to turn your back on all of these for my sake? Jesus never demands anything less than our total loyalty, in every corner of our life. He asked Peter three times, to match the three times that Peter had denied even knowing Jesus. Jesus uses two different words, both translated as 'love'. At first, Jesus asks whether Peter loves him sacrificially, as Jesus loves Peter. The only answer Peter can give is the other word, the word for friendship, 'You know I'm your friend!' So the third time Jesus lowers his sights, and asks, 'Are you *really* my friend?' Have you even worked out what friendship means?

'Feed my sheep'

If Peter truly was his friend, Jesus told him, he must 'Feed my sheep'. From fisherman to shepherd was quite a career change, and Peter probably didn't welcome it: he was stepping out of his depth once again. Jesus had already told him that the sign of a good shepherd is one who is willing to lay down his life for his sheep. No more thinking about what he'd rather be doing, he had to be a pastor of the

Church, whether he liked it or not. Jesus asks you and me, too, 'Do you love me?' If we want to be friends of Jesus, our whole lives, at home, at work and in the Church, must be devoted to serving Jesus, by serving other people. Even if we feel inadequate; even when we feel out of our depth.

All-age worship

Make origami fish and write on each the name of one of the countries of the world. Make a big net, and try to catch them for Jesus.

Suggested hymns

Forsaken once, and thrice denied; I will make you fishers of men; Jesu, my Lord, my God, my all; Thou art the Christ, O Lord; Will you come and follow me?

Third Sunday of Easter
Second Service   Jesus Wept
Ps. 86 You have delivered me from death; Isa. 38:9–20 The living thank you; John 11:[17–26] 27–44 The raising of Lazarus

'When Mary came where Jesus was and saw him, she knelt at his feet and said to him, "Lord, if you had been here, my brother would not have died." When Jesus saw her weeping, and the Jews who came with her also weeping, he was greatly disturbed in spirit and deeply moved. He said, "Where have you laid him?" They said to him, "Lord, come and see." Jesus began to weep. So the Jews said, "See how he loved him!"' John 11:32–36

Grief

There's nothing wrong with grief. It's a natural response to the loss of someone you love. Maybe, the measure of your grief is the measure of your love, though different people express their grief in different ways, and just because someone doesn't show it openly, doesn't mean they're not grieving. When his friend Lazarus died, we read that 'Jesus began to weep.' In the old translation it's the shortest verse in the Bible, just two words; 'Jesus wept.'

HOW TO MAKE AN ORIGAMI FISH

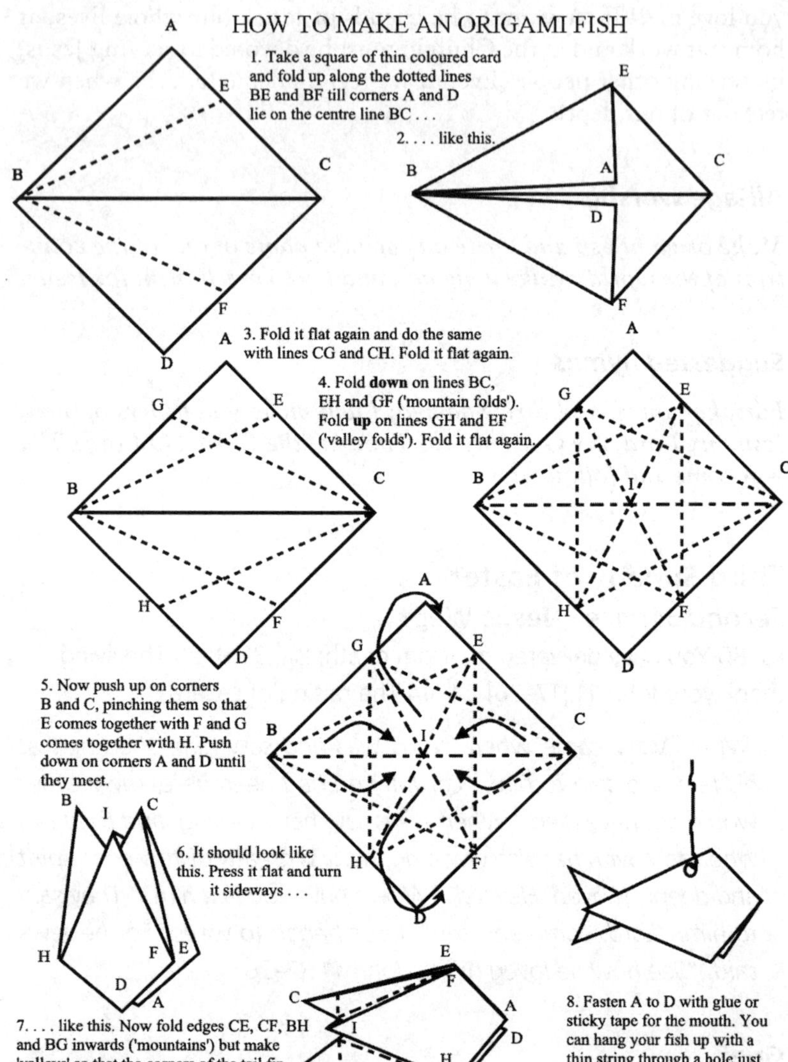

So the bystanders exclaimed, 'See how he loved him!' Jesus was completely human, as well as being completely divine. So he was capable of strong human love for his friend Lazarus, and he wept to express his sense of loss when Lazarus died. He was also capable of strong human sympathy, and he was deeply moved by his love for Martha and Mary, the sisters of Lazarus, when he saw how they were grieving. Their grief was to be expected. So was Mary's anger with Jesus, when she said peevishly, 'Sir, if you'd been here, my brother wouldn't have died!' At times of loss, many people look for someone to blame. It may be some other relative, or the doctor, or the hospital, or the government. It needn't even be a rational anger; looking back we may reflect that it was quite unjustified; but it's a way of releasing the pent-up emotion. Jesus didn't blame Mary for blaming him; he just wept with her. At times of grief, that's the best thing to do; it may be the only thing we can do. Jesus wept.

If you'd been here . . .

Was Mary right when she cried out in frustration to Jesus, 'If you'd only been here when you were needed, my brother wouldn't have died'? It showed great faith; she believed that Jesus was capable of preventing people from dying. Why didn't he? Well, if death's the gateway to life eternal, then it's not a disaster but a blessing. When God, in his love, calls someone to himself, it may be a disaster for those who're left behind, and have to cope on their own. Logically, we should weep for the mourners, not for the departed. We some-times temper our grief by saying, 'It was a happy release for him or her.' But we're very far from logical at a time of loss. In one of their serious moments, Gilbert and Sullivan wrote a song which goes,

> Is life a boon?
> If so, it must befall
> that Death, whene'er he call,
> must call too soon.

Jesus knew that death's not an end but a new beginning, a heavenly birthday: 'I am the resurrection and the life,' he said to Martha. But Mary and Martha didn't know that, yet. It wasn't until Jesus rose from the dead that people could be sure that there is life after death.

Jesus wept

Yet even so, Jesus wept. In spite of his divine foreknowledge, he feared death, in the Garden of Gethsemane, and he grieved at the loss of those he loved. No, there's nothing wrong with grief; it doesn't mean that we have no faith. It's quite justified to cry out, 'Lord, I believe; forgive my unbelief!' At times of loss, we're *all* like the disciples, whom Jesus called 'you of little faith'. But our faith must be like a grain of mustard seed: small, but growing. We need to pray for growing faith, then eventually we shall grow through our grief. You must never ask anyone in grief, 'Have you got over it yet?' because that would mean that they've forgotten the person who has died, and no longer miss them. We never 'get over' our grief. But with a growing belief in the resurrection, we may progress towards acceptance of our loss. Yet even for the best of us – those whom others imagine to have a strong faith – there may be bad times. Then we shut the bedroom door, and remember that – with all his divine foreknowledge of the resurrection, when we shall all be reunited with those we love who have gone before us into the bliss of eternity – still, 'Jesus wept.'

Suggested hymns

Alleluia, alleluia, give thanks to the risen Lord; Alleluia, alleluia, hearts to heaven and voices raise; Thine be the glory; Who is he, in yonder stall?

Fourth Sunday of Easter   29 April
Principal Service   **My Sheep Hear My Voice**

Gen. 7:1–5, 11–18; 8:6–18; 9:8–13 Noah's flood (*if used, the reading from Acts must be used as the second reading*); or Acts 9:36–43 Peter raises Tabitha; Ps. 23 The Lord is my shepherd; Rev. 7:9–17 The Lamb their shepherd; John 10:22–30 My sheep hear my voice

'Jesus said, "My sheep hear my voice. I know them, and they follow me. I give them eternal life, and they will never perish. No one will snatch them out of my hand."' John 10:27–28

The Good Shepherd

Last week we heard in the Gospel how Jesus called Peter to 'feed my sheep'. Peter was called to be a shepherd of Christ's flock, a shepherd of Christ's followers, gathered together into the Christian Church. 'Feed' is a strange word to use in an English translation of the Bible, because most English-speakers associate it with feeding a toddler. It would be an odd sort of shepherd who picked the grass and put it into the sheep's mouths for them! It means, of course, leading them to good pastures where they can feed themselves. In the twenty-third Psalm, David said that the Lord God is our shepherd. Jesus takes up this idea at the beginning of the tenth chapter of St John's Gospel, where he says, 'I am the good shepherd.' He takes on himself God the Father's role of being a shepherd to his people, by defending them from spiritual dangers, and leading them to where they can find spiritual nourishment.

Spiritual dangers

What are the spiritual dangers that Jesus, the Good Shepherd, is going to defend us from? The perils that Jesus means, when he says that 'No one will snatch them out of my hand', are the things which can take us out of the fellowship of the Church, where we're surrounded by his loving embrace. That includes the danger of false teaching, the sort of alternative religion which denies the reality of sin and the dangers of self-centredness, and the power of the risen Christ to save us from them. Today an even greater danger is the siren voice of the secular world, which despises belief in God as old-fashioned and irrelevant, and tempts many who used to be churchgoers with the delusion that there are much better ways of spending Sunday. But if you've really listened to the voice of Jesus, then, even if these temptations do draw you away from his Church for a while, you'll always hear the voice of the Good Shepherd calling you back, and sooner or later you'll return. 'No one will snatch them out of my hand,' he says.

Spiritual nourishment

The twenty-third Psalm sings of the green pastures and still waters to which the shepherd leads his sheep. Jesus says, 'I give them eternal life, and they will never perish.' When we're in the sheepfold of the Church, we come to know the voice of Jesus the Good Shepherd, to know him as a friend, and to be close to him in prayer. We embark on a new way of life, the Christian life, which is full of joy. The Christian life feeds us with the guidance and promises of God, and joins us to Jesus in love. Once you're joined to Jesus in love, nothing can separate you from him, not even death itself. So he gives us eternal life; we can live with him for ever in the green pastures and by the still waters of heaven.

'My sheep hear my voice'

But although the Christian life's a very joyful one, it's also a very demanding way of living. We hear the voice of Jesus calling us to serve our neighbours, beginning with our family, then spreading out into our neighbourhood, our whole society, and even nations far away, whom we can help by working for peace and justice. And the only way to live this new life is through the strength we receive by listening to the voice of Jesus. We listen to him by daily Bible-reading, prayer and regular attendance at church. Jesus said, 'My sheep hear my voice. I know them, and they follow me. I give them eternal life, and they will never perish.' Therein lies our hope; so let's remain faithful to Jesus, and faithful to his Church.

All-age worship

Model sheep can be made from wool or curled paper. The shepherd's crook is shaped so that it can be hooked round the leg of a sheep who strays. Make a model crook and practise this with model sheep. Listen to each other's voices when blindfolded, and try to recognize who's speaking.

Suggested hymns

God be with you till we meet again; Loving shepherd of thy sheep; The Lord's my Shepherd, I'll not want; Thine for ever, God of love.

Fourth Sunday of Easter
Second Service   **God Led Them Through the Depths**
Ps. 113 God raises the poor from the dust, 114 The Exodus;
Isa. 63:7–14 God led them through the depths;
Luke 24:36–49 Words of the Risen Christ

Tonus Peregrinus

The music of the Church in the Middle Ages is called 'plainsong'
because there's a single line of melody without any accompaniment.
One of the chants, however, is more elaborate. It's called *Tonus
Peregrinus*, perhaps because the melody wanders around, like a
peregrine falcon. It's also been formed into one of the melodies of
the Anglican chant used in cathedrals and larger churches. Sometimes it's used to sing the Nunc Dimittis, but it's especially associat-
ed with Psalm 114, 'When Israel came out of Egypt'. Perhaps that's
because this psalm describes the wanderings, or peregrinations, of
the Israelites at the Exodus.

The Christian Passover

The descendants of those first Israelite pilgrims used to remember
the Exodus every year in the Passover festival. They ate unleavened
bread to remind them that their ancestors had to leave Egypt in a
hurry, without allowing the dough time to rise. They remembered
that the angel of death had 'passed over' the houses where the blood
of the paschal lamb was splashed on the doorposts. Those inside
were saved from death by the blood of the lamb. So, naturally, when
Christians began to celebrate the resurrection of Jesus, who was
killed on the eve of the Passover festival, they compared him to the
paschal lamb who had saved them from death by his blood. The
whole story of the Exodus became fixed in the Christian minds
as a metaphor, prediction and 'type' of the resurrection of Christ.
The New Testament, and our Easter Worship, are full of Passover
language.

A God who saves

It's not just the coincidences of language that make the Exodus
important for understanding the resurrection of Jesus. At a deeper
level, both Exodus and the resurrection proclaim the same profound

truth: that God is a God who saves. When we're in a mess, and can't get out of it on our own, God steps in and rescues us. The Israelites were slaves in Egypt and couldn't save themselves, so God led them through the Red Sea and saved them. The human race were slaves to sin, and couldn't save themselves from slavishly repeating the same selfish actions over and over again. So God sent his Son to die on the cross, so that we might see what harm sin does, and be saved from the guilt and power of sin by the blood of Jesus. We were driven to despair by our fear of dying, when all our efforts in life would come to naught. So God's Son rose again from the tomb to save us from death and lead us to the promised land of heaven. What a joyful Easter message! A God who saves us from sin and death.

All life a pilgrimage

The Letter to the Hebrews says that the people of the Old Testament 'all died in faith, not having received the promises, but having seen them afar off, and were persuaded of them, and embraced them, and confessed that they were strangers and pilgrims on the earth'. There's a sense in which all life's a pilgrimage. Some people are tourists in their journey through life, some are travellers, some are pilgrims. G. K. Chesterton once said, 'The traveller sees what he sees, the tourist sees what he came to see.' There's a joke about travellers being those who don't know where they're going, and tourists being those who don't know where they've been! In that case, pilgrims are those who set out for a place where they can meet God, and find that God's been with them throughout the journey. In our wanderings we often get stuck, and God has to step in and save us. We're helped, as the Israelites were, as we wander through life's wilderness, to remember that we're not alone, by remembering God's mighty acts of salvation in the past. Then we can cry to God to rescue us, as he saved the Israelites through the waters of the Red Sea. And when our turn comes to die, we can trust God to lead us through the deep waters of death, and raise us to new life as he raised Jesus his Son at the resurrection.

Suggested hymns

At the Lamb's high feast we sing; Come, ye faithful, raise the strain; God sent his Son, they call him Jesus (Because he lives); Thank you, Jesus.

Fifth Sunday of Easter   6 May
Principal Service   **Known by Your Love**

Bar. 3:9–15, 32—4:4 Wisdom; *or* Gen. 22:1–18 Abraham willing to sacrifice Isaac (*if used, the reading from Acts must be used as the second reading*); *or* Acts 11:1–18 Baptism of the Gentiles; Ps. 148 Nature praising God; Rev. 21:1–6 Death will be no more; John 13:31–35 The commandment to love

> *'[Jesus said,] "I give you a new commandment, that you love one another. Just as I have loved you, you also should love one another. By this everyone will know that you are my disciples, if you have love for one another."' John 13:34–35*

Would there be enough evidence?

'If you were put on trial for being a Christian tomorrow, would there be enough evidence to convict you?' Those are the words of a poster which was popular in the days when many Christians in communist countries were being put in prison. The challenge in the wording is that it asks us to examine ourselves for the proof that we're Christians. It's not enough to say 'I live in a Christian country; my parents brought me up as a Christian; I was baptized as a baby; I often watch religious programmes on the television.' It's not enough to say 'I go regularly to church.' There's a saying in America, 'Just because the mouse is in the cookie-jar, it doesn't mean it's a cookie!' Just because you're in a church building doesn't make you a Christian. Nor, dare I say it, does the fact that you had a wonderful conversion experience some years ago and your prayer-time leaves you with beautiful warm feelings. It's very dangerous to categorize people according to their religious experience. Many people dismiss others saying, 'He (or she) hasn't had the same religious feelings as I have, so that means he (or she) isn't a real Christian.' Jesus told us never to judge others; and Queen Elizabeth I is reputed to have said, 'We will not make windows into people's souls.' It's none of our business to decide whether other people are or are not Christians. No, the only question for us is, 'Am *I* a Christian?' The test for that's given us by Jesus: 'By this everyone will know that you are my disciples, if you have love for one another.'

The proof of the pudding

The proof of the pudding's in the eating. The evidence for faith is loving behaviour; it's the fruit which proves that the roots are sound. When Jesus speaks of love, he's not talking about mushy emotions. His new commandment's to do with the way we treat each other. 'Just as I have loved you, you also should love one another,' he said. Well then, how does Jesus love us? If you read the Gospels carefully, you find that his was a very special kind of love. He loved the whole human race. He was not hidebound by nationalist prejudices; he loved Roman soldiers, a Canaanite woman, and the Greeks who came to learn from him. He loved his own nation, but his eyes were wide open to its faults. He loved his hometown, but there he was a prophet without honour. His was a tolerant love; he loved those whom society had outcast, the prostitutes, cheating tax-collectors, and other sinners. He loved his closest friends, he even loved Judas, and he told them to love each other. But what comes over most clearly is that Jesus loved people as individuals. He wanted to find out all about people, he accepted them as they were, and loved them for what made each of them unique. Then he found out what their needs were – sometimes he knew what people needed better than they knew themselves – and set about meeting their needs. His was an active love; a love which issued in practical service, healing and restoring people so as to bring out their hidden potential. That's how Jesus loves us. And that's how he commanded us to love each other: inclusively, tolerantly and as individuals to be respected, encouraged and served.

The greatest love story in the world

The Bible is the greatest love story in the world, because it is about a love that sacrifices itself to meet the needs of others. 'If you were put on trial for being a Christian tomorrow, would there be enough evidence to convict you?' Probably not a lot; but if you're really trying to love other people in the self-sacrificing way that Jesus loves you, then the prosecution might just be able to make out a case against you!

All-age worship

Work out at least one way in which you can help somebody else in the coming week. Ask Jesus to help you to do it, and thank him for loving us more than we shall ever understand.

Suggested hymns

A new commandment I give unto you; I want to walk with Jesus Christ; Love divine, all loves excelling; Where cross the crowded ways of life.

Fifth Sunday of Easter
Second Service   Israel, the World and the Universe
Ps. 98 God has done marvellous things; Dan. 6:[1–5] 6–23 The lions' den; Mark 15:46—16:8 The resurrection

> 'Sing to the Lord a new song, for he has done marvellous things.'
> Psalm 98:1

Superman

In one of the Superman stories, a disaster is set to happen at a fixed time by the clock. To give himself time to prevent it, the hero grabs hold of the rotating earth and turns it the other way by half an hour! It's too fantastic to be anything other than science fiction, but it arouses a wistful feeling in us. Wouldn't it be wonderful if just one human being had the power to alter the operations of the universe. Suppose we could change the way the forces of nature work. What if we could halt the inevitable tramp of death, of change and decay, of return to zero entropy and primitive chaos, which seems to fill the universe with frustrated hope? Well, I have news for you. One man has done just that.

A victory for Israel

The glimmerings of hope are seen right back in the early history of the Israelite people. Though they were small and apparently insignificant, they believed that what happened to them mattered to God. God had chosen them to do something for him, which they couldn't do if they were destroyed. So a victory in battle for the army of Judah was a victory for the Lord God. Now, you can see the dangers in this: if they identified their military successes too closely with the will of God, they'd have an excuse for slaughtering their enemies, and if they were vanquished they'd believe that God had let them down. But they were saved from this by enlarging their idea of God: the Lord is not just the tribal god of the Jewish people, he's the God of all the earth. A victory for the people who are committed to obeying God is a victory for the whole human race. It means that justice and godliness are triumphant over the godless forces of evil, and that's good news for everyone. So in the ninety-eighth Psalm, the psalmist calls on us to

> Sing to the Lord a new song, for he has done marvellous things.
> His own right hand and his holy arm have won for him the victory . . .
> He has remembered his mercy and faithfulness towards the house of Israel,
> and all the ends of the earth have seen the salvation of our God.

Even the inanimate creation seems to benefit:

> Let the sea thunder and all that fills it; the world and all that dwell upon it.
> Let the rivers clap their hands, and let the hills ring out together before the Lord.

How can this be? Is it just poetry, or does even a small victory for the Creator affect the universe that he created?

The hope of Israel and the world

On the first Easter Day, Jesus rose again from the dead to live for ever. Thus he defeated the 'last enemy', death itself. What Israel had been struggling for, justice and obedience, was seen to have an eternal significance. And not only for Israel. The resurrection of Jesus fulfils the hope of the world. The universal reign of death is at an end. Oh yes, our bodies will die, but our souls, our inner personalities, our self-awareness will go on into another dimension, and live for ever with Jesus. What's the point of God creating human beings to love him, if they only live for three score years and ten? But if through faith they can live for ever, then love's triumphant and our hopes are vindicated.

The resurrection fulfils the hope of the universe

The resurrection also fulfils the hope of the universe. The universe is the context in which human life and love have been created. Even should the myriads of galaxies spin off into extinction, our memory of them, our admiration for nature's power and our wonder at nature's beauty, will go with us into eternity. Then God's purpose in creating it will have been fulfilled. Jesus was the superman who changed the universe; the resurrection of Jesus means that nothing in the whole cosmos will ever be the same again.

Seizing the opportunity

The resurrection of Jesus fulfils the hope of Israel, of the world and of the universe. These are ideas too big for us to grasp. But they present us with an opportunity that must be seized. Eternal life's not an automatic immortality: resurrection is the gift of God, but it's only possible when we have faith. You may not be Superman or Superwoman, but by seizing the opportunity of faith, you *can* start the world of injustice and oppression turning in the opposite direction, the direction of love and hope, in your part of the universe at least.

Suggested hymns

I praised the earth, in beauty seen; Lord of beauty, thine the splendour; Morning glory, starlit sky; The spacious firmament on high.

Sixth Sunday of Easter (Rogation Sunday)   13 May
Principal Service   A Place of Prayer
Ezek. 37:1–14 The valley of dry bones (*if used, the reading from Acts must be used as the second reading*); or Acts 16:9–15 The baptism of Lydia; Ps. 67 Let the peoples praise you; Rev. 21:10, 22—22:5 The heavenly Jerusalem; John 14:23–29 Going to the Father; *or* John 5:1–9 The paralysed man at the pool

> *'On the sabbath day we went outside the gate by the river, where we supposed there was a place of prayer; and we sat down and spoke to the women who had gathered there.' Acts 16:13*

Philippi

St Paul saw a vision of a man from Macedonia calling him, 'Come over and help us.' He obeyed, and the first major town in Macedonia he and his companions came to was the colony of Philippi. There was 'gold in them thar hills', so Alexander's father, King Philip of Macedon had fortified the city to protect the gold mines, and named it Philippi after himself. In Shakespeare's play *Julius Caesar*, he describes how, after Caesar's murder, Octavian and Mark Antony defeated Brutus and Cassius at the Battle of Philippi. The victorious soldiers were allowed to retire there and turn it into a 'colony'. In Paul's time most of the population were retired veterans or descendants of soldiers. They were very proud of their Roman citizenship, which is why Paul in his letter to the church in Philippi writes '*our* citizenship is in heaven'. But when he first arrived he was surprised to find that there was no synagogue. The only place the handful of Jews could find to worship was on the river bank, 'where . . . there was a place of prayer'. What faith! Many people will say, 'We don't have a synagogue building (or a church building in our case) so we can't hold services.' But the Jews of Philippi knew that you can pray anywhere, even on the river bank.

Lydia

Among them was a woman who was not a Jew. Lydia was a merchant, dealing in purple cloth. This was a luxury commodity; the purple dye was made from scarce murex shells; and the cloth was only worn by very rich people, or members of the Emperor's household like the retired soldiers of Philippi. She was probably a widow, and had taken over, from her late lamented, a thriving international trading company. She came from Thyatira, where there was a guild of purple-dyers. But though she was a Greek, she had no time for the debased superstition of the pagan temples. She wanted to find a real god, who would answer her prayers and insist on fair dealing between his people, as she did in her business. So she joined the Jews at the place of prayer on the river bank, and became, not a convert but a 'God-fearer'. She listened to Paul, and found that the Christian religion was the answer to her prayers. Soon after, Paul baptized her there in the river, together with all the people who worked for her, and she invited Paul, Luke and their companions to sleep among the bales of cloth in her spacious home-cum-business premises. So Paul's prayers, too, had been answered: he'd made his first European converts, and from this tiny acorn, a mighty oak would grow.

A place of prayer

Everywhere's a place of prayer. We thank God for beautiful churches, with their special feeling of holiness, where we can pray with the encouragement of other Christians beside us. But we can also pray beneath the open sky – Jesus said, 'For where two or three are gathered in my name, I am there among them' – or in the privacy of our bedroom – he said, 'Whenever you pray, go into your room and shut the door and pray to your Father who is in secret; and your Father who sees in secret will reward you.' This Sunday is observed in country districts as Rogation Sunday – the name comes from the Latin word for asking – when we pray for God's blessing on the growing crops, a reminder that God wants us to pray about every detail of our lives. And Thursday's Ascension Day, when we think of Jesus going to the Father, where he can present our prayers to the Father as the perfect Mediator, both God and human. As William Cowper wrote:

> Jesus, where'er thy people meet,
> There they behold thy mercy-seat;
> Where'er they seek thee thou art found,
> And every place is hallowed ground.
>
> For thou, within no walls confined,
> Inhabitest the humble mind;
> Such ever bring thee when they come,
> And, going, take thee to their home.

All-age worship

On a map of the world, stick flags with the name of somebody you know who lives there. Pray for that person, for that country, for the food which is grown there, and thank God for those who pray for us.

Suggested hymns

Come, my soul, thy suit prepare; Great Shepherd of thy people, hear; Jesus, where'er thy people meet; What a friend we have in Jesus.

Sixth Sunday of Easter

Second Service   **Go, Teach** Ps. 126 The Lord has done great
things for us, 127 Unless the Lord builds the house; Zeph. 3:14–20
God is in your midst; Matt. 28:1–10, 16–20 The ascension command

> *'"Go therefore and make disciples of all nations, baptizing them in
> the name of the Father and of the Son and of the Holy Spirit, and
> teaching them to obey everything that I have commanded you.
> And remember, I am with you always, to the end of the age."'*
> *Matthew 28:19–20*

Famous last words

There seems to be a fascination with famous last words. Somehow,
the final words that anyone moderately famous utters seem to take
on a special significance, as if they somehow summed up all that
the celebrity has learnt in their lifetime. Shakespeare wrote, 'The
tongues of dying men enforce attention like deep harmony.' Here's
a selection:

Ethan Allen, when a friend said 'The angels are waiting for you':
  'Well, let 'em wait.'
Beethoven: 'Friends applaud, the comedy is over.'
Charles II: 'Let not poor Nelly starve.'
Douglas Fairbanks, Snr: 'I never felt better.'
Heinrich Heine: 'God will pardon me. It's his trade.'
St Lawrence on his gridiron: 'Turn me, I'm roasted on one side.'
Ramon Narmez: 'I don't *have* to forgive my enemies. I've had
  them all shot.'
Lord Palmerston: 'Die, my dear doctor? That's the last thing I'll
  do.'
General Sedgwick: 'Might shoot me? They couldn't hit an
  elephant at this dist . . .'
Emperor Vespasian: 'I think I am becoming a god.'
And King George V, when told by his doctor he would soon be
  well enough to convalesce in Bognor, told him in very nautical
  language what he could do with Bognor.

The last words of Jesus

Well, those were just for laughs. More seriously, wouldn't you pay attention to the last words on earth of Jesus Christ? No, they weren't the seven words from the cross, though those are important too. St Matthew's Gospel tells us that after the resurrection, coming to the end of his 40 days when he was visible to his disciples here on earth, before he ascended into heaven and was no longer visible, Jesus spoke some last words. They were:

> Go therefore and make disciples of all nations, baptizing them in the name of the Father and of the Son and of the Holy Spirit, and teaching them to obey everything that I have commanded you. And remember, I am with you always, to the end of the age.

Go

He begins by telling them to 'Go'. Jesus says the same to us. We're not to sit down comfortably indoors and wait for things to happen. If we've heard the good news that God loves us, we must share it with others far and near; in our own street, or, if circumstances allow, to the ends of the earth.

Baptize

Jesus tells us to baptize all nations. To baptize someone is to proclaim that their sins are forgiven, and they've been welcomed into God's chosen people. This is for all nations, there can be no racial prejudice here. The Church is not a select club for 'people like us'. The gospel can be translated into any culture, and finds new riches when it is expressed through the cultures of different peoples.

Teach

But baptism's only the beginning of the process. We have to teach. The word 'disciple' simply means someone who is being taught. Becoming a Christian is a never-ending process. You never stop learning, and you're never too old to learn. When Jesus told us to love God with all our minds, he suggested that we should have to do some pretty serious thinking about our faith. The early Christians are said to have won over the Roman Empire because they were better than the pagans at everything: they out-lived them, out-died them and out-thought them. If Jesus calls us to teach, then first we must learn, and go on learning. Christians have learnt about God from the lips of the Son of God. This is not to deny that there are indeed great truths in other faiths, from whom we can learn. But if Christians hadn't been willing to share what they had learnt, you and I should still be worshipping gods like Thor and Woden.

With you always

But Jesus doesn't send us out to baptize and teach on our own. He comes with us. 'And remember, I am with you always, to the end of the age.' Wherever we go, his invisible presence is always with us, guiding, teaching, consoling and inspiring. We know he is, because he promised it in his last words before he ascended.

Suggested hymns

Alleluia, sing to Jesus; Jesus shall reign where'er the sun; Lord, thy church on earth is seeking; One more step along the road I go.

Ascension Day   17 May
Principal Service   A Cloud Took Him

Acts 1:1–11 The Ascension (*must be used as either the first or second reading*); *or* Dan. 7:9–14 The Son of Man; Ps. 47 God has gone up; *or* Ps. 93 The Lord is king; Eph. 1:15–23 Christ is seated beside God; Luke 24:44–53 The Ascension message for all nations

> *'Jesus said to his disciples: "You will receive power when the Holy Spirit has come upon you; and you will be my witnesses in Jerusalem, in all Judea and Samaria, and to the ends of the earth." When he had said this, as they were watching, he was lifted up, and a cloud took him out of their sight.' Acts 1:8–9*

A stained-glass window at Fairford

Fairford Parish Church in Gloucestershire contains some of the finest medieval stained-glass windows in the country. Those in the chancel show the life of Jesus, and the one of the ascension shows the disciples gazing up into heaven, with just the feet of Jesus appearing in the top of the window as he rises into the clouds. But is that what the disciples actually saw? Is this what St Luke meant by 'he was lifted up'? What did he mean by 'heaven'?

The three-storey universe

The astronomers of Babylon thought that the stars were fixed to a vast sphere which moved over a flat earth. These ideas were accepted by the authors of the biblical story of creation: they described a three-storey universe, with the heavens at the top, the earth at the centre and 'the waters under the earth', together with the abode of the dead, somewhere under the earth. Since God created the heavens, he must be beyond them. But although the Bible speaks of heaven as God's dwelling-place, it also says that heaven cannot contain him, and that he is also on earth – in fact that God is everywhere.

The Greek and medieval universes

But, at the same time, the ancient Greeks were thinking about the shape of the universe. In about 600 BC Pythagoras said that the earth's a sphere. This was generally accepted as true because you can see its shadow on the moon during an eclipse. His followers also suggested that the earth rotates, and revolves around the sun; unfortunately these ideas were quickly forgotten. Plato, on the other hand, said that heaven's a world of pure ideas, which has no location in space. St Luke, a sophisticated Greek doctor, was surely not unaware of these ideas. But Aristotle went back to a fixed earth with heavenly spheres moving round it, and this became a dogma of the medieval Roman Catholic Church. For them, heaven was a fixed place above the stars. This is why Galileo was persecuted for suggesting that the sun is at the centre of the universe.

Poetic language

But many writers use poetic language without meaning it literally. Job talks about God measuring out the heavens with the span of his hand, but Jesus said 'God is spirit'. When Luke spoke about Jesus ascending into heaven, did he mean it literally or metaphorically?

A cloud received him

The clue's probably to be found when Luke writes that 'a cloud took him out of their sight'. A cloud was the symbol of the presence of God in the Old Testament – think of the pillar of cloud that led the Israelites out of Egypt, and the cloud and smoke on top of Mount Sinai. So what Luke means is that Jesus entered the intimate presence of his Father, which he had left when he came to earth. Jesus had been visible to his disciples for 40 days after the resurrection. Now he needed to teach them that they were never going to see him again, but that, nevertheless, he'd still be invisibly with them. So he caused them to see the vision of him entering a cloud, to show them that he was now with God. But God's everywhere, so Jesus is with us everywhere, 'even to the ends of the earth'.

'Out of the everywhere into the here'

A sentimental poem speaks of a newborn baby coming 'out of the everywhere into the here'. We could describe the ascension of Jesus as being when he passed 'out of the here, into the everywhere'. You no longer have to go to Jerusalem and fight through the crowds to talk to Jesus; he's right here and ready to listen to you now. Heaven's the state of being with God; it is, if you like, a 'higher plane of existence'. Jesus was promoted to a higher position of authority at his ascension; the disciples had a vision, and the symbolism of 'going up' was used. Heaven's the joyful state of being close to God our Father; Jesus entered that state on Ascension Day, and we can enjoy it here and now.

Suggested hymns

Christ triumphant, ever reigning; Hail, thou once despised Jesus; Jesus is Lord! Creation's voice proclaims it; The head that once was crowned with thorns.

Seventh Sunday of Easter

(Sunday after Ascension Day)   20 May

Principal Service   **Jesus Prays for Us** Ezek. 36:24–28 I will put my Spirit in you (*if used, the reading from Acts must be used as the second reading*); Acts 16:16–34 Baptism of a jailer; Ps. 97 The Lord is king; Rev. 22:12–14, 16–17, 20–21 Come!; John 17:20–26 That we may be with Christ and see his glory

> *'Jesus prayed, "Father, I desire that those also, whom you have given me, may be with me where I am, to see my glory, which you have given me because you loved me before the foundation of the world."' John 17:24*

'I'll pray for you'

Sometimes when you have a problem or some sadness in your life, you may share it with a friend, who'll say, 'I'll pray for you.' You may have said it yourself when a friend of yours is in distress. Then we kneel and lift this child of God to our loving heavenly Father in our imagination, and ask him to do for them whatever best meets their needs. It's good to try to put ourselves mentally in our friend's shoes as we pray for them. Then we may understand what they most need; we may even see that there are things we ourselves could do to help. Or we may not ask for anything specific, because we don't know what will be most helpful for our friend in the long term. But if you surround the person you're praying for with love, God may be able to help them because you've prayed. Love's a very powerful force; and as Tennyson wrote, 'More things are wrought by prayer than this world dreams of.'

To know you're being prayed for

What a comfort it is, then, to know that you're being prayed for. At times of loneliness, to know that others are thinking of you. In times of danger, to know that they're asking God to protect you. When you've no time to pray for yourself, or don't know what to ask for, it's marvellous to know that others love you enough to hold you up in their minds before God. Then God's love can combine with your friends' love to bring you healing and strength. But if your friends' prayers are powerful, how much more wonderful it is to know that Jesus himself is praying for you. And he is; he promised.

The High Priestly prayer

The seventeenth chapter of St John's Gospel has often been called the High priestly Prayer. The Jewish High Priest would cleanse and sanctify himself before going into the Holy of Holies in the Jerusalem Temple to pray for the people on the Day of Atonement. Similarly Jesus prays for his disciples: '"Sanctify them in the truth; your word is truth. As you have sent me into the world, so I have sent them into the world. And for their sakes I sanctify myself, so that they also may be sanctified in truth."'

Then he goes on to pray, '"I ask not only on behalf of these, but also on behalf of those who will believe in me through their word, that they may all be one. As you, Father, are in me and I am in you, may they also be in us, so that the world may believe that you have sent me."' That's you and me he's talking about. We're the ones who've come to believe in Jesus because of the words of those first disciples. Jesus was praying for us. How marvellous! In Stainer's oratorio *The Crucifixion* come the words:

> Wonder of wonders, oh! how can it be?
> Jesus, the Crucified, pleads for me!

Jesus is still praying for us

Jesus is still praying for us. This is also called the Sunday after Ascension, to remind us that at the end of his life on earth, Jesus went to be at God's right hand, where he continues to ask his Father to bless us. We're one in love with Jesus, because we love him. Well, Jesus wants that unity to go on into the next life. He wants *us* to be as close to his Father, in love, as *he* is, now that he's in heaven. So he prays, '"Father, I desire that those also, whom you have given me, may be with me where I am, to see my glory."'

Jesus wants you to be with him in heaven and see his glory. If ever you're feeling low or lonely, and wondering whether you'll make it to heaven; if you feel unable to pray for yourself, don't worry! Jesus is praying for you. With Jesus in your fan club rooting for you, you're bound to win!

All-age worship

Design a stained-glass window showing Christ in glory (the tapestry in Coventry Cathedral will give you some ideas). Use coloured pencils, or make a collage of coloured paper or transparent film.

Suggested hymns

Hail the day that sees him rise; Hail, thou once despised Jesus; Jesu, our hope, our heart's desire; Our eyes have seen the glory of our Saviour, Christ the Lord.

Seventh Sunday of Easter (Sunday after Ascension Day)

Second Service   **Gifts** Ps. 68 Let God arise; Isa. 44:1–8 I will pour my spirit; Eph. 4:7–16 Gifts of the ascended Christ; *Gospel at Holy Communion*: Luke 24:44–53 I am sending upon you

> *'Therefore it is said, "When he ascended on high he made captivity itself a captive; he gave gifts to his people."' Ephesians 4:8*

Presents

'It's time to distribute the presents.' What excitement those words arouse in the hearts of children at Christmas-time. Each child wondering whether they'll get the gift they've set their heart on, and whether there'll be any pleasant surprises. Even when we grow up and go shopping, it seems as if nobody can resist buying something that is advertised as having a 'free gift attached'. In the olden days, when a king was crowned or when he won an important victory, he would ride in triumph into the city, and would distribute gifts to his people. It might be a shower of golden coins tossed into the crowd, or the gift of important positions to his followers. Such a procession is described in Psalm 68; in the Greek version which St Paul quotes from, God gives gifts to his people.

The ascension

In his Letter to the Ephesians, Paul takes these words and applies them to Jesus. When Jesus ascended into heaven, after his ministry on earth was finished, says Paul, he gave gifts to his people. We can imagine Jesus entering heaven in triumph. Then comes the time to distribute the presents. Jesus pours gifts on the members of the Church on earth. They're not necessarily the presents we'd have asked for, but Jesus knows that they're the gifts we need. The Church that Jesus had left behind, to continue his work after he had gone, was very small and weak. It still is, compared with the mighty task that confronts us: that of telling the whole world how much

Jesus loves them. So Jesus gives us what's needed to achieve church growth; and the list of gifts shows what the strategy is.

Gifts

There are some specialists in the Church, but everyone's got a job to do. The five specialist gifts that are mentioned are:

- Apostles. That simply means missionaries. There'll always be a need for pioneers who move into an area where Jesus has never been heard of, or where he's been forgotten.
- Prophets. They sometimes foretell the future, but more especially they proclaim what God's view is of the present. Often they point out how corruption or politics are ruining the lives of the people. We need bold preachers like that in every church.
- Evangelists. Once the missionaries have settled, some are needed to proclaim the good news of what God has done for us in Jesus; that's what the word evangelist means.
- Pastors. These are the shepherds who care for the needs of Christ's flock, by visiting individuals in their homes, listening to them and meeting their emotional and material needs.
- Teachers. When people have become Christian, they need to learn how God expects them to live. This is the task of the teachers in the Church.

Ordinary church members

Most members of the clergy possess one or two of these specialist gifts; very few have them all. Yet we expect our vicars to be a jack of all trades. That's not what the Bible says. The task of the specialists is to train the rest for every-member ministry. St Paul uses the word 'saints' to describe all the ordinary members of the Church. So, says Paul, the specialists are 'to equip the saints for the work of ministry, for building up the body of Christ'. The work of ministry's done by the ordinary church members, caring for each other and their neighbours. The growth of the Church depends on them.

Maturity

The Church has to grow, not just in numbers, but in maturity. If you think back to what you were like when you first attended church, you'll realize that through God's gifts, you're now considerably more mature as a Christian than when you were a 'babe in Christ'. But when you look ahead to the goal, which is nothing less than to grow 'to the measure of the full stature of Christ', you realize there's a long way to go yet! But don't be downhearted. Thank God for the gifts he's given you already, and use them. Make sure you're always willing to learn. Aim for perfection, but be content even when you can't reach it. On the wall of a teenager's bedroom there's a poster which reads: 'I'm not perfect yet. But parts of me are excellent'!

Suggested hymns

All praise to our redeeming Lord; Forth in the peace of Christ we go; Help us to help each other, Lord; O Holy Ghost, thy people bless.

Day of Pentecost (Whit Sunday)   27 May
Principal Service   **The Spirit of Truth**

(The reading from Acts must be used as either the first or second reading.)

Acts 2:1–21 The day of Pentecost; *or* Gen. 11:1–9 The tower of Babylon; Ps. 104:24–34, 35b The Spirit in creation; Rom. 8:14–17 Spirit, adoption, guidance, suffering; John 14:8–17 [25–27] The Spirit of truth

> *'Jesus said, "I will ask the Father, and he will give you another Advocate, to be with you forever. This is the Spirit of truth, whom the world cannot receive, because it neither sees him nor knows him."' John 14:16–17*

The Holy Ghost

We do use some misleading words in church. Or we used to. Take that great hymn called the 'Te Deum'. In the traditional English translation it requires us to say that we believe in 'the Holy Ghost, the Comforter'. Most people these days think ghosts are spooks, and the thought of sharing your life with one's the very opposite of comfortable! But of course 'ghost' is the old English word for a 'spirit', and the Holy Spirit's not at all spooky. The Holy Spirit is best defined as God working through people; it's the powerful force of love available to us all.

The Comforter

Then how about this word 'Comforter'? If you ever played with toy soldiers, you know that they live in a castle or 'fort', a strong place that can be 'fortified'. So in old English a Com-*fort*-er was one who gave you strength. We'd be wrong to think that the Holy Spirit is cosy. In the Bayeux tapestry, the pictures are explained by Latin words along the top. At one point the caption reads, 'Bishop Odo comforts the lads.' You would expect from those words to see him letting the soldiers cry on his shoulder; but in fact he is coming up behind them and prodding them with a spear! He's comforting them by putting strength into them, encouraging them and sending them forward to fight. That's what the Spirit does for us.

The Paraclete

'Comforter' is the old English translation of a Greek word sometimes rendered as 'Paraclete'. It crops up in a few of our hymns. It's said that a new convert was having the doctrine of the Trinity explained to him, and got confused when the Spirit was symbolized by a dove and called the Paraclete. He protested, or so it's alleged, 'Holy Father I understand. Holy Son I understand. But Holy Parakeet I can't understand!' Actually the word means somebody called to your side. Specifically it means an advocate, called to your side in a law court to plead for you, and draw out of you the evidence that you couldn't, on your own, put into words. This is what the Holy Spirit does; the Spirit helps you to speak for Christ. Jesus warned that some of his disciples would have to defend themselves before kings and governors. Today, we're more likely to have to defend ourselves against the scorn of those who think that Christianity's stupid and irrelevant. Don't worry that you don't know what to say, or aren't a natural speaker; the Holy Spirit will come to your side as your advocate and give you the words to say. Provided they're said with courtesy and respect, they'll be more persuasive than you expect. The Holy Spirit put them there.

The Spirit of truth

Jesus promises us 'the Spirit of truth'. The truth that Jesus is talking about, however, is not one that can be put into words or argued about. When the Spirit's in us, we're in direct contact with God, who's the designer of the universe. You can't get any closer to absolute truth than that. The 'Thirty-nine Articles of Religion', at the back of the Book of Common Prayer, says that 'Holy Scripture containeth all things necessary to salvation'. That doesn't mean that there's no truth outside the Bible; it doesn't even mean that you have to believe every word of the Bible, in order to be saved. But it does mean that you don't need any of the truths that are not mentioned in the Bible in order to come to God. And all that you need to know, in order to live with God for ever, is in the Bible, and the Holy Spirit, the Spirit of truth, will help you to find it. This is 'saving truth', and this is what's brought to us by the Holy Spirit, our Advocate, called to our side to help and fortify us.

All-age worship

Find out all you can about the work of an advocate or barrister in the law courts, and try to bring some pictures. What does this teach us about how Jesus pleads for us to God the judge, and how the Holy Spirit helps us defend our faith before those who don't know God?

Suggested hymns

Come down, O Love divine; Holy Spirit, come, confirm us; Spirit of holiness, wisdom and faithfulness; Spirit of the living God, fall afresh on me.

Day of Pentecost
Second Service   **Letter and Spirit** Morning Ps. 36:5–10 In your light we see light, 150 Everything that breathes; Evening Ps. 33:1–12 The breath of his mouth; Exodus 33:7–20 My presence will go with you; 2 Cor. 3:4–18 Letter and Spirit; *Gospel at Holy Communion*: John 16:4b–15 The Spirit of truth

> 'God . . . has made us . . . ministers of a new covenant, not of letter but of spirit; for the letter kills, but the Spirit gives life.' 2 Corinthians 3:6

The letter of the law

Sometimes, if you're in a dubiously legal situation, it's safer to stick to the letter of the law, just so that nobody can accuse you of wrongdoing. But at other times, sticking to the letter of the law can lead you into harming other people, whereas a more flexible approach might have enabled you to bend the law slightly and achieve a much fairer result. We all know the petty official, 'dressed up in a little brief authority', who refuses an application because 'Oh no, that's against the regulations, that is. It's more than my job's worth to allow that.' The letter of the law can be a prison whose bars won't bend an inch to allow the prisoners to escape.

Paul the Pharisee

Saul the Pharisee, who later became St Paul the apostle, had found the Law of Moses like that. Its rules, which had been given for a pastoral and agricultural society, were hard to apply in the city of Tarsus. It covered every department of life, and if the Law didn't tell you exactly what to do in any given circumstances, the Pharisees had drawn up complicated traditions to interpret it. What's more, it was mostly negative. It told you 'Thou shalt not do this, thou shalt not do that.' It took all the fun out of life, and put nothing in its place. In some cases it quite literally brought death, for the list of capital offences was a long one, including adultery, cursing your parents, incest, eating non-kosher food and visiting a spiritualist medium, to name but a few. Apart from that, all these impossible regulations resulted in a vain struggle to please God. Because you could never be completely successful, God became a bugbear, a remote and implacable judge, ready to trip you up when you least expected it. Not all Jews found the Law as oppressive as this, but Saul the Pharisee certainly did. It killed his spontaneity, and left him spiritually dead. It was because the followers of Jesus were teaching people to sit lightly to the Law that he rode to Damascus to root them out and have them executed for blasphemy.

Filled with the Spirit

We all know what happened to Saul on the road to Damascus. He then spent several years working out what it means to be a Christian. The amazing thing was, he found that the law was now irrelevant. Yes, God still expected him to behave in a moral way. But morality was not a matter of obeying pernickety rules, but of listening to the voice of God within him, telling him what to do – the inner voice that Christians, quoting the Hebrew Scriptures, called the promised Holy Spirit of God. What the Holy Spirit told them to do was to love. You had to cudgel your brains sometimes to work out what was the most loving thing to do. But it was much more spontaneous than following a set of laws, and life was fun again. The one thing the early Christians were absolutely certain of was that they were filled with the Spirit. And that the Spirit gave them liberty, a new quality of life together here, and the certainty of eternal life with God hereafter. 'The letter kills,' said Paul, referring to the law, 'but the Spirit gives life.'

Morality

That doesn't mean that Christians can behave how they like. They must set an example to the world around them, by being more moral than their neighbours. But this must be a spontaneous morality growing out of love, not adherence to petty regulations. Alas, some Christians today seem willing to give away all the freedom that St Paul fought for; the freedom that Jesus won for us at the cost of his life. You can find far too many Christians today with a 'thou shalt not' religion. They try to reimpose the laws of the Old Testament on the totally changed society of today, and keep thinking up new things to forbid. In the process they forget what Jesus, in his quarrel with the Pharisees, called 'the weightier matters of the law: justice and mercy and faith'. There's nothing wrong with making rules to govern your own life, provided you're willing to bend them when love requires it. But you must never ever condemn somebody else, because they aren't following your rules. If they're spontaneous and loving, that's OK. The letter kills, but the Spirit gives life.

Suggested hymns

Come, Holy Spirit, come; Gracious Spirit, Holy Ghost; O thou, who camest from above; Spirit of God, unseen as the wind.

Prov. 8:1–4, 22–31 Wisdom's call, wisdom in creation;
Ps. 8 Stewardship of nature; Rom. 5:1–5 God's love and Spirit;
John 16:12–15 Spirit, Father and Jesus

> *'Jesus said, "When the Spirit of truth comes, he will guide you into all the truth . . . All that the Father has is mine."' John 16:13–15*

A Jewish joke

This is a joke told by a Jew. A certain Jewish gentleman, he said, was knocked down by a bus. A Christian priest rushed up to him, thinking to give him the last rites, but before he began he questioned the victim to see whether he was a Christian. 'Do you believe in three persons and one God,' he asked, 'three in one and one in three, neither confusing the persons nor dividing the substance?' 'My God,' exclaimed the Jew, sitting up suddenly, 'I'm dying and he sets me a mathematics exam!'

The Trinity in the Bible

You won't find, in the pages of the Bible, the fully developed doctrine of the Trinity, which the priest in the story was insisting on. What you do find is many passages which imply, or require, a belief in the unity of Father, Son and Holy Spirit, and at the same time that Jesus and God the Father and the Holy Spirit are independent personalities. One such passage is in today's reading from St John's Gospel: 'Jesus said, "When the Spirit of truth comes, he will guide you into all the truth . . . All that the Father has is mine."'
   We should also remember other words of Jesus:

- 'Go therefore and make disciples of all nations, baptizing them in the name of the Father and of the Son and of the Holy Spirit'. (Matt. 28:19)
- 'The Father and I are one.' (John 10:30)
- 'And I will ask the Father, and he will give you another Advocate, to be with you forever. This is the Spirit of truth.' (John 14:16–17)

It's very hard to talk about these quotations without using language about three persons and one God. St Patrick illustrated this by pointing to the shamrock, which has three leaves within one leaf.

Trinitarian wars

Yet one of the most depressing things about the history of the Church is to read how some worthy Christians in the first few centuries were willing to argue with, to excommunicate and even to kill other very worthy Christians, simply because they couldn't agree over the form of words in which the triune nature of God was to be expressed. The Emperor Constantine locked all the bishops he could find into a church at Nicaea, and told them not to come out until they'd produced a statement of what Christians believed. How was he to unite the Roman Empire around the Christian faith, unless Christians could agree with each other? The result was what we call the Nicene Creed, but the arguments went on for centuries.

Lead you into all truth

Jesus promised that the Holy Spirit would lead his followers 'into all truth'. This suggests a lengthy process, as under the guidance of the Holy Spirit, Christians will discover new facets of God's nature, and new developments in how he expects us to behave. In the first few centuries the Spirit was leading the Church into a doctrine of the Trinity. Yet it's been wisely said that the most convincing proof of the existence of the Holy Spirit is that the Church arrived at the truth in spite of, rather than because of, the Councils of the Church. If so, the Spirit must be leading us into new truths today also: for instance the abolition of slavery and apartheid, the concern for human rights, equality and tolerance. These are new developments in human thought, but they come because God's been working through the Church to lead us into new truth. The Church, then, should welcome these developments, and never resist them.

Too big for words

We must never be trapped into arguments about mere words. St Paul said in Athens, 'The God who made the world and everything in it, he who is Lord of heaven and earth, does not live in shrines made by human hands.' God's also too big to be contained in any formula constructed by human minds: God's too big for words. So Trinity Sunday should remind us to welcome the promises of

Jesus that, through him, we can pray to the Father, who'll give us his Spirit to dwell in us. We're not required to understand the doctrine of the Trinity to be Christians, though it's dangerous to deny it. Trinity Sunday reminds us to fall down in reverence before the greatness of God, who 'surpasses all understanding'. Otherwise we deserve the accusation of the Jew in the story, that we've turned Christianity into an examination in mathematics!

All-age worship

Draw some of the symbols of the Trinity: a shamrock, a triangle and circle, three interlocking circles, three fish, etc.

Suggested hymns

Affirm anew the threefold name; Holy, holy, holy, Lord God almighty; I bind unto myself today; Immortal, invisible, God only wise.

Trinity Sunday

(For Corpus Christi, the Thursday after Trinity Sunday, see page 319.)

Second Service   **I am** Morning Ps. 29 The Lord enthroned; Evening Ps. 73:1–3, 16–28 Hard to understand; Ex. 3:1–15 I am; John 3:1–17 God so loved

> *'God said to Moses, "I am who i am . . . Thus you shall say to the Israelites, 'The Lord, the God of your ancestors, . . . has sent me to you'. This is my name forever, and this my title for all generations."'*
> *Exodus 3:14–15*

I think, therefore I am

The French Philosopher René Descartes was puzzled about the question of existence. How can I know that anything at all exists, he asked. Maybe the whole universe is just a figment of my imagination? Or do things exist when I'm looking at them, but cease to exist when they're no longer being observed by anybody? Eventually he decided that everything's open to doubt, except his own conscious experience, and the fact that he himself must therefore exist, even if nothing else did: 'I think, therefore I am.' The Roman Catholic scholar Fr Ronnie Knox wrote a limerick parodying this position:

> There once was a man who said, God
> must think it exceedingly odd
> if he finds that this tree
> continues to be
> when there's no one about in the Quad.

The reply's probably anonymous:

> Dear Sir, Your astonishment's odd:
> I am always about in the Quad.
> And that's why the tree
> will continue to be,
> since observed by
> Yours faithfully, God.

The existence of God

This puts the boot on the other foot. God exists, therefore we are. If God hadn't thought of the universe, there would be no universe. We are a good deal more than 'ideas in the mind of God', but our existence is entirely dependent on his. So those who try to prove the existence of God or the contrary are going about it the wrong way. Yip Harburg, who wrote the lyrics for *The Wizard of Oz*, also wrote this little verse:

> No matter how I probe and prod
> I cannot quite believe in God,
> But oh! I hope to God that he
> Unswervingly believes in me!

God exists, whether we believe in him or not. Perhaps that's why the name of God, in the Bible, is 'I AM'.

The name of God

The words 'I am' in Hebrew sound a bit like the name by which some at least of the Jewish patriarchs had known God. That name was pronounced something like 'Yahweh', only they never pronounced it for fear of breaking the Commandment against taking the Lord's name in vain. When they wrote it, they only put the consonants with no vowels, to prevent anyone from accidentally pronouncing the sacred name. Underneath they wrote the vowels of the word 'Adonai', meaning 'my Lord', which was what they actually said. William Tyndale's sixteenth-century translation of the Bible into English was one of the first to put the consonants of Yahweh together with the vowels of Adonai. This formed the word Jehovah, which doesn't exist in Hebrew and would never be spoken by a Hebrew-speaker. 'Yahweh' is usually translated in English Bibles by the words, 'the LORD', in small capitals. But, asked the Israelites, what does this name mean? The answer to this question was given when God appeared to Moses in the burning bush: 'Yahweh' means 'I am'.

> God said to Moses, 'I AM WHO I AM . . . Thus you shall say to the Israelites, "The LORD, the God of your ancestors, the God of Abraham, the God of Isaac, and the God of Jacob, has sent me to you".'

It could be translated slightly differently, as 'I will be who I will be', or even 'I am becoming what I am becoming'. But essentially this is a rebuke to excessive curiosity: all that reason can say about God is that he exists; what he's like has to be revealed to us.

Our dependence on God

But if we exist because God exists, that means we're totally dependent on God. He's not just a superman sugar-daddy we call for in cases of emergency. As the hymn says, 'I need thee every hour.' He's the God who cared for Abraham and Isaac, and saved Moses from Egypt. That means that he's a loving God. If the universe exists because God made it, and God is a God of love, then the universe is on our side in the great struggle to exist. A woman named Margaret Fuller is supposed to have made a particularly stupid remark when she said, 'I accept the universe.' The writer Thomas Carlyle commented, 'Gad! She'd better!' Thank God, then, that whoever he is, God exists! Believe in him. Keep the faith. God's there for us when we need him; in fact he's there for us all the time. We exist because God exists. 'I AM' loves us.

Suggested hymns

Bright the vision that delighted; Firmly I believe and truly; I need thee every hour; The God of Abraham praise.

Ordinary Time

Sundays after Trinity are referred to as 'Ordinary Time'. Other seasons are preparing for or responding to Christmas and Easter; this is just a season of steady growth, which is why the church hangings and vestments are green, the colour of growing things. Under the present lectionary, the Collect and Post-communion Prayer depend on the number of Sundays since Trinity Sunday, but the readings depend on the calendar date ('Proper 5' means the readings 'proper', or 'appropriate', for 'the Sunday between 5 and 11 June inclusive (if after Trinity Sunday)'). At the Principal Service, there are two alternative series of Old Testament readings and Psalms, which the minister may choose between. The 'Continuous' series follow the chapters of an Old Testament book in sequence Sunday after Sunday. The 'Related' series are chosen to illuminate the set New Testament reading and Gospel. If a Saint's Day falls on the Sunday, the minister may choose to use the readings for the saint instead of those for the Sunday. In these cases, this book provides a sermon on the Saint's Day readings in place of the Second Service.

First Sunday after Trinity (Proper 5)   10 June
Principal Service   **A Dead Son**
(*Continuous*): 1 Kings 17:8–16 [17–24] The widow's jar; Ps. 146 God upholds the widows, trust not princes; *or* (*Related*): 1 Kings 17:17–24 Elijah heals the widow's child; Ps. 30 You restored me to health; Gal. 1:11–24 Paul's conversion and authority; Luke 7:11–17 Raising the widow's son at Nain

'The dead man sat up and began to speak, and Jesus gave him to his mother.' Luke 7:15

A dead son

The times seem out of joint when a son dies before his parents. It's hard enough for children to be bereaved of their parents, but how are parents to bear the loss of their child? In the case of the widow of Nain it was even worse, because since her husband died, her son had been the breadwinner. Now she'd starve, probably. Jesus's compassionate heart went out to her. He stopped the funeral procession, and raised her son to life again. If only he would do that every time! Yet it would be no sort of world to live in if God was always preventing the natural process of death. Sometimes there has to come release, and rest. It's just that when somebody dies young it seems such a waste.

A true story

An English vicar was leading his parishioners on pilgrimage in the Holy Land. Among them was a newly qualified anaesthetist, and the girl he loved; he was even carrying an engagement ring in his back pocket in case he plucked up courage to propose to her. Mount Tabor, the traditional site of the Transfiguration, is so steep the coaches can't climb it, and numbers of taxis race up and down the hairpin bends instead. The English pilgrims hired three taxis, and the vicar was in the front one. A little Arab boy ran out in front of the second taxi and was knocked down. The anaesthetist leapt out of the third taxi and tested for vital signs. No breathing, no pulse; in layman's terms the child was dead. But the doctor promptly gave mouth-to-mouth resuscitation and heart massage, and, as we would put it, 'brought the child back to life'. Then the group looked at their maps, and realized that they were eight miles from Shunem, where Elisha brought a dead boy to life, and five miles from Nain, where Jesus did the same. It seemed to them that miracles were almost commonplace occurrences in the Holy Land; as though somehow they were fulfilling prophecy!

The sequels

There are two sequels to this true story. The doctor did propose to his lady-love, on the shore of Galilee; they both thought they'd lived through a moment of truth. They were happily married and had lovely children. The vicar had a young son, who, a year later, was knocked down by a car and killed. There was a doctor passing by, but the lad's neck was broken. The vicar had to learn that you can't have miracles on demand. God can't take away our free will, or rather, he won't, because that would take away our freedom to love. So God won't prevent us killing each other, even if the victim is young and doesn't, as we say, 'deserve to die'. But then who does deserve to die, if death is an unmitigated tragedy?

Is death a blessing?

But there are always two sides to every question. Perhaps death isn't always a tragedy; perhaps death is God's greatest blessing? The vicar struggled with this thought through many dark nights. Why had the Arab boy been saved from death, but his own son was not? Where's the little lad now? The vicar hoped his son was with Jesus. Well, that mustn't be too bad. It was only the parents who were suffering, not the child; he was out of the world of pain and sin, and 'the streets of [the heavenly] Jerusalem are full of the sound of children playing'.

Sacrificing a son

Painful as it was, the vicar had to learn to give up his son into the loving arms of God. But then he visited the Oberammergau Passion play, which depicts the death of Jesus, the Son of God, on a cross. 'God understands what I'm going through,' he thought. 'God, too, has looked on the body of his dead Son!' Then it didn't seem so bad. God doesn't ignore our pain. God's right down here in the midst of the blood and dust, suffering with us. Through the sacrifice of Jesus, God gives to us all the hope of resurrection, of new life in happiness, where we shall meet again with those we love. Somehow, that makes it bearable.

All-age worship

Make shadow-play puppets of the funeral procession, Jesus coming up to them, the dead man getting up from the stretcher (there were no coffins) and returning to his mother's arms.

Suggested hymns

Lead, kindly light, amid th'encircling gloom; O love that wilt not let me go; There is a green hill far away; There's a song for all the children.

First Sunday after Trinity

(For the Eve of St Barnabas see page 321.)

Second Service   **The Rainbow** Ps. 44 Come to our help;
Gen. 8:15—9:17 God's covenant with Noah; Mark 4:1–20 Parable of
the Sower

> *'God said, ". . . I have set my bow in the clouds, and it shall be a
> sign of the covenant between me and the earth."' Genesis 9:13*

A shaggy-snake story

This is a shaggy-dog story, or perhaps a shaggy-snake story. Noah
told all the animals as they left the ark, 'Go forth and multiply!'
A year later he made a tour of inspection and was delighted to
find a pair of each species surrounded by offspring. Then he heard
some sobbing in the forest, and found two snakes crying. 'What's
the matter?' he asked. 'Well you told us to go forth and multiply,
and we can't,' wailed the snakes. 'Why not?' asked Noah, and the
snakes answered: 'Because we're adders!' (But the story doesn't end
there. The second part of the story will be quite incomprehensible
to those who can't remember the time before we had pocket cal-
culators.) 'Go and ask the wise old owl for advice,' recommended
Noah. Another year later he came by and found lots of pieces of
wood chopped up and formed into a palisade. Inside this were Mr
and Mrs Snake and dozens of baby snakes. 'Splendid,' exclaimed
Noah. 'What did you do?' 'Well, you see all these pieces of wood?'
replied the snakes. 'Any adder can multiply with the aid of logs!'

The promise to protect the earth

According to the story in Genesis, the whole human race was so
wicked that they deserved to die. But God, in his mercy, decided
to spare one human family, and a pair of every animal and bird, so
that they could build a new future. So the amazing fertility of the
natural creation is pleasing to God. How it must distress him, then,
when we cut down millions of acres of rainforest, and destroy the
diversity of species. God tells the humans, in the story, that they're
in charge of the world of nature. That means, in modern terms, caring for the environment and a responsible use of natural resources.

God promises to do his bit, too. He doesn't promise that there'll be no more natural disasters, though many people believe that with responsible planning the harmful effects of disasters could be reduced. But God does promise that never again will he destroy the whole animal kingdom. Human beings could do it, but God won't. 'As long as the earth endures, seedtime and harvest, cold and heat, summer and winter, day and night, shall not cease.'

God's covenant with Noah

Then God signs a contract, or covenant. He promises on his side to protect the natural creation. Noah and his descendants, on their side, have to promise to do three things: not to eat raw meat; not to murder; and to multiply. The Jews considered that the whole human race was descended from Noah, so the covenant with Noah contained the only commandments that were binding on non-Jews as well as Jews. These laws are referred to, though somewhat muddled, at the Council of Jerusalem in Acts 15. Probably the secretary got it down wrong in the minutes, and what the apostles declared was that the only Old Testament laws which are binding on us, the Gentile Christians, are those in the covenant with Noah.

The sign of the covenant

God promises that he'll keep his side of the bargain with Noah. So that human beings will never forget this, God signs the contract, not with pen and ink, but with a most dramatic symbol. He takes his battle bow, the bow and arrow with which he was about to destroy all life on earth, and hangs it up in the clouds, never to be taken down and used again. There it hangs today, for everyone to see, says the story; and that's why we call it the 'rain-bow'. The children's musical *Captain Noah and his Floating Zoo*, by Michael Flanders and Jacob Horowitz, sings it like this:

> Oh what a beautiful scene,
> the rainbow overhead:
> violet, indigo, blue and green,
> yellow, orange and red.

A sign of hope

Many people marvel at the rainbow and regard it as a symbol of hope. 'Somewhere over the rainbow'; 'Follow every rainbow'; 'At the rainbow's end'. Wordsworth wrote:

> My heart leaps up when I behold
> a rainbow in the sky.

In the Book of Revelation, the glory of God is represented as a rainbow round his throne. It's the sign that, however unfaithful we humans may be, God will never break his promises.

Suggested hymns

God whose love is everywhere; Great is thy faithfulness, O God my Father; O love that wilt not let me go; We plough the fields, and scatter.

Second Sunday after Trinity (Proper 6)   17 June

Principal Service   **Forgiveness and Love**

(*Continuous*): 1 Kings 21:1–10 [11–14] 15–21a Naboth's vineyard; Ps. 5:1–8 God's justice; *or* (*Related*): 2 Sam. 11:26—12:10, 13–15 David's repentance; Ps. 32 Forgiveness; Gal. 2:15–21 Law, faith and grace; Luke 7:36—8:3 A woman's repentance

> *'Jesus said, "Therefore, I tell you, her sins, which were many, have been forgiven; hence she has shown great love. But the one to whom little is forgiven, loves little."' Luke 7:47*

A woman of the town

There are probably some people you just wouldn't want to be seen talking to. Let alone welcome them into your home. For Simon the Pharisee, his worst moment came when a certain 'woman of the town' came into his house at Bethany while he was giving a dinner to a visiting rabbi. The Gospel doesn't say what is meant by 'a woman of the town', beyond the fact that she was regarded with scorn by the Pharisees as 'a sinner', but I think we can guess. As far as Simon was concerned, she was the dregs. The guests weren't sitting, but reclining on couches, which was the custom in smart society at that time. The woman came and stood behind the couch where Jesus was lying, near his feet. Then she produced a perfume bottle. 'This is too much,' thought Simon. 'Where did a woman *like that* get a valuable bottle of perfume like that from?' There was only one possible answer; which was disgusting, he thought. The last straw was when *that woman* started sobbing: her tears fell on Jesus's feet, so she used her long hair to wipe them dry, and then poured the perfume from the bottle all over them, until the bottle was empty. Simon didn't have a high opinion of Jesus, either; he was heard to say in a stage whisper, 'If *this man* had been a holy man, he'd have known what sort of woman *that woman* was.' If Jesus had been respectable, he meant, he wouldn't have allowed her to touch him. So obviously he wasn't.

The two debtors

The only answer to a remark like that was to tell a story. So Jesus made up a tale of two debtors who were let off their debt. They both owed money to the same lender; one owed a lot, the other owed comparatively little, but neither had to pay a penny. They'd obviously both be grateful to the generous lender, but the question Jesus asked was, which would be most grateful? Simon gave the obvious answer: 'The one who was let off the bigger debt.' Well, said Jesus, the woman who was a sinner has been forgiven her many sins, so she loves God greatly. Simon's love for Jesus was little, because he hadn't been forgiven for much. Indeed, he may not have been forgiven for anything, because he hadn't asked for forgiveness. He thought he didn't need forgiveness. So he had nothing to be grateful for, and no reason to love Jesus. He didn't even bother with the simple courtesies which were expected from a host to a guest in his house.

Big sins and little sins

If Jesus had told Simon that he, too, was a sinner, he would have huffed and puffed and ignored it. Yet he *was* a sinner. The word the Bible uses for sin means 'missing the target'. The target is perfect love, like that of Jesus; nothing less will do. You can't talk about big sinners and little sinners, 'since all have sinned and fall short of the glory of God'. Simon's biggest sin was the sin of snobbery. By despising the woman of the town, he cut himself off from God, because he thought *he* had no need of God's love. But that wasn't how God saw it. The woman had sinned greatly, and asked for forgiveness; she had been forgiven, and so she loved God greatly. That's what God wants, our love. He doesn't want a perfect obedience to a code of morality, if that means ignoring the simple duty to love your neighbour.

Forgiveness and love

Aim for perfection, even though none of us ever reaches it. We should none of us be satisfied 'until all of us come to the unity of the faith and of the knowledge of the Son of God, to maturity, to the measure of the full stature of Christ'. But when you fall short and miss the target, confess your sins to Jesus, and he'll forgive you. Then you'll be grateful to him, and you'll love him. Then you'll love other people, because we're all sinners, and we can all be forgiven. That's what God really wants; that's what it's all about. Forgiveness leads to love, and love leads to forgiveness. Without love there can be no forgiveness; if we don't think we need forgiving, we shall never experience love.

All-age worship

Practise the long jump (or draw it if that's impractical). The target is to love others as much as Jesus loves us. What will Jesus say if you fall short?

Suggested hymns

Drop, drop slow tears; Just as I am, without one plea; Rock of ages, cleft for me; We pray thee, heavenly Father.

Second Sunday after Trinity
Second Service   **You Get What You Give**
Ps. 52 A tree in God's house [53 Fools say]; Gen. 13 Abram and Lot; Mark 4:21–41 Parables and a storm

> *'Jesus said to [his disciples], "Pay attention to what you hear; the measure you give will be the measure you get, and still more will be given you."' Mark 4:24*

A hidden parable

I think there may be a hidden parable behind this saying. It comes in a chapter full of parables, and Jesus must have told far more stories than there was space for in the Gospels. The clue's in the word 'measure'. Maybe it went something like this.

The crooked corn merchant

Once there was a crooked corn merchant. When farmers brought him grain, he measured it out in bushel-baskets, and paid them accordingly. When his customers came to buy corn for baking, he measured it out in baskets and charged them so much a bushel. Only they weren't the same baskets! For the farmers he used large baskets, so they had to sell him more than they bargained for. For the customers he used smaller baskets, so they didn't get as much as they expected. One day an astute farmer realized what was happening. He waited till he saw a housewife going into the shop to buy corn. Then he brought in his grain to sell, before the crooked merchant had time to swap the measures over. The humiliated merchant had to use the same, smaller baskets that he'd just used to sell with, for measuring out the corn he was buying. So he finished up paying the farmer for his grain far more than it was worth. All the farmers and customers laughed at the crooked corn merchant, telling him, 'The measure you give will be the measure you get!'

A parable about judging others

The parables of Jesus are often very funny. They usually end with a question. Something like 'What do you think about this character?' 'Which of these acted in a neighbourly way to the man who was attacked by robbers?' The lost parable of the crooked corn merchant, I suggest, is a parable about judging other people. You can either be generous in what you say or think about somebody else, or you can be mean. If you're generous you'll think of reasons why somebody acts as they do. Maybe it's in the way they were brought up. Or maybe we don't know all the circumstances, and it was perfectly reasonable to act in that way if you knew what the other person knew. For instance, somebody jumps the queue at the doctor's surgery. Maybe he's naturally impatient and never thought about the others. Maybe he was never brought up to be considerate. Or perhaps his wife's desperately ill and a wait of a few minutes might make the difference between life and death. We don't know.

If you're generous in judgement you'll make allowances. If you're mean-spirited, you'll condemn him without waiting for an explanation. The mean-spirited are like the crooked corn merchant, cheating with his two sets of baskets. When we laugh at the corn merchant, we may find we're laughing at ourselves.

Judgemental

Yet most of us are far more judgemental than we realize. We jump to conclusions, and don't wait for explanations. We're quick to condemn, and slow to praise. We like to pass on bad opinions about other people, without admitting that they're mere gossip. We write people off too soon, without giving them a chance to find their feet and put right their mistakes. We never give them any encouragement to say what they feel; we may not even give them a chance to say sorry. We don't take time to explore ways of being encouraging, or helping people to change, like saying, 'You're such a clever person; perhaps if you'd thought about it longer you might have chosen a better way of doing that.' Instead we just say, 'You were wrong!'

'Judge not, that you be not judged'

If we give mean measure in judging other people, we shall get mean measure when we are judged by other people. If you're generous and make allowances, people will usually make allowances for you. But if you're judgemental and mean-spirited, nobody will make any allowances for your mistakes. When our life is over, God won't ask how many of the Commandments we've broken. God's so generous that all of these can be forgiven. God *will* ask, were you judgemental? Were you generous and understanding about other people's faults, or were you always rubbing their noses in it? Jesus says to you, 'Do not judge, so that you may not be judged. For with the judgment you make you will be judged, and the measure you give will be the measure you get.' Remember the crooked corn merchant: you get what you give. The way to avoid condemnation from God, is to be generous in your judgement of other people.

Suggested hymns

'Forgive our sins as we forgive'; God forgave my sin in Jesus' name (Freely, freely); Make me a channel of your peace; There's a wideness in God's mercy.

Third Sunday after Trinity (Proper 7)
(The Birth of St John the Baptist)   24 June
Principal Service   **Demons**

(*Continuous*): 1 Kings 19:1–4 [5–7] 8–15a The still small voice; Ps. 42, 43 Faith and hope; *or* (*Related*): Isa. 65:1–9 God's judgement; Ps. 22:19–28 Salvation; Gal. 3:23–29 The Law our tutor till faith comes; Luke 8:26–39 Demons sent into pigs

> *'Jesus . . . asked him, "What is your name?" He said, "Legion"; for many demons had entered him.' (Luke 8:30)*

A story of its own time

The story of the man whose name was Legion is very much a story of its own time. By which I mean that the words and ideas it is told in belong to the first century, and wouldn't be the words and ideas we'd choose to use today in the twenty-first century. That's not to say whether it's true or untrue, though if you say it's true you'll have to go on to ask, *in what way* is the story true? In the first century, everybody believed in demon possession, and the Jews considered that pigs were not fit for food, and not worthy of consideration. In the twenty-first century, we'd be more likely to talk about mental breakdown, and we'd be concerned with the animal rights issues raised by the drowning of the poor pigs! Now, I'm not going to take sides in a dispute between the centuries. Some philosophers would have us believe in the relativity of truth. What's true for you may not be true for me, they say, and each person has their own truth. Well, that makes the search for truth irrelevant and any form of reasoned discussion impossible. But it may be true that each of us has aspects of the truth, like facets of a jewel. The whole truth, if it's ever to be known here below, must take each of these facets into account. So there may be something we can learn from studying the first-century way of speaking, and also something to learn from today's psychotherapists. Both of them may be true in their own way. So I shall talk about demons, then I shall talk about mental illness.

Demons

Up until modern times, most people believed the world was infested with evil spirits. The man in the story believed that a whole regiment or legion of them had taken possession of him. Jesus told his disciples to cast out demons, and many spectacular cures have followed a ceremony of exorcism. But the fact that Jesus spoke about demons doesn't help us to decide whether they exist. He couldn't very well give the sick man a course in Freudian psychoanalysis! So he spoke in language that would be meaningful and helpful, though in what sense it was 'true', you must decide for yourself. Today, great harm can be done by Christians who persuade somebody that they're possessed when they aren't. This may bring about an unnecessary violent interlude, and prevent them from seeking more helpful cures. But if anybody already believes that they're possessed, we have to take them at their word and speak in a way that'll be helpful to them. We can all reassure such unfortunate people that the power of Jesus is greater than any other power, and that Jesus can heal and wants to heal. We can all pray with anyone who's sick. But before attempting anything approaching an exorcism, remember that it's very dangerous not to call in the official diocesan expert in this field, or the equivalent in other churches.

Mental illness

Amateur dabbling in things we don't fully understand is equally dangerous in the field of mental illness. Anybody can and should be ready to listen sympathetically to somebody who's troubled. Everyone can pray. But if a sick person talks about hearing voices which tell them what to do, then a qualified psychotherapist is needed. Yet Christians shouldn't be afraid of mental illness or shun the sufferers. Sympathy, compassion and prayer are a vital Christian ministry to the sick, which should go hand in hand with medical treatment.

What is truth?

So, was the man called Legion possessed by demons, or was he sick? We can't tell. And it doesn't really matter. Jesus loves everyone, and wants them to be whole. In a battle of that importance, we shouldn't be fighting each other over different interpretations of the truth; we should use every weapon we have – prayer, medicine and psychotherapy – in the attempt to bring healing and peace.

All-age worship

Ask a missionary society for the names of Christian doctors or nurses who have gone to other countries to heal people. Mark the places they have gone to on a map of the world, and pray for them.

Suggested hymns

Be still, for the Spirit of the Lord; Make way, make way, for Christ the king; O God, by whose almighty plan; Thine arm, O Lord, in days of old.

The Birth of St John the Baptist   24 June
(or may be transferred to 25 June)
Birth of the Baptist Isa. 40:1–11 A voice in the wilderness; Ps. 85:7–13 Salvation is at hand; Acts 13:14b–26 A baptism of repentance; *or* Gal. 3:23–29 The Law our schoolmaster; Luke 1:57–66, 80 Birth of the Baptist

> '[Zechariah] asked for a writing tablet and wrote, "His name is John."' Luke 1:63

An unusual birth

The story of the birth of John the Baptist's an unusual one. First, Zechariah and Elizabeth are of an age when it's usually impossible to have children. Then an angel appears to Zechariah, telling him that he's to have a son and name him John. John's to be a great man, after the pattern of Elijah, and is to prepare the people for the Lord. Zechariah's disbelieving, so he's punished by being struck dumb till after the baby's born. When the baby's circumcised, Elizabeth says he's to be named John. This surprises everyone; usually a child was named after one of his or her relations, but none of the family bore this name. So Zechariah sends for a writing tablet, a piece of wood with a coating of wax. In the wax he scratches with a stylus, 'His name is John.' Then he can speak again, and sings a remarkable song which we call the Benedictus. A most unusual story, and the prelude to a remarkable life. John the Baptist lived in the desert, and called the members of God's covenant community to apply for readmission, by being baptized. He proclaimed a baptism of repentance for the remission of sins. Then, after an uneasy relationship with his cousin Jesus, he was beheaded by King Herod Antipas.

Sources

John the Baptist was a historical figure. He was mentioned by the Jewish general and historian Josephus, writing towards the end of the century, and Josephus had no interest in writing Christian propaganda. John seems to have had disciples or followers, who reported John's doubt to Jesus, and who continued to proclaim his message after his death. Where does the story of the birth of the Baptist come from? Well, it shows many traces of the way the Hebrew and Aramaic languages were spoken, and it's quite unlike the Greek in the rest of Luke's Gospel. Probably the story was first told in Aramaic, and then translated into Greek before Luke got hold of it. Perhaps it was a story told among John's disciples, showing how important their master was in their eyes, as he was to Josephus.

What's in a name?

Why then was there all this fuss about what the baby was to be named? As everyone knows, Juliet asks Romeo, 'What's in a name? That which we call a rose by any other name would smell as sweet.' But to her, their names do matter, because they indicate that 'the star-crossed lovers' come from different families who are at war with each other. So the name of John is important, because it tells us something about his character and his place in history. John, or originally Yohanan, was one of the commonest names given to Jewish baby boys. It means 'The Lord is gracious'. That's a common enough statement in the Hebrew Scriptures, but even today people find it hard to believe. Despite all assurances to the contrary, an awful lot of people believe that God is a remote and stern despot, looking for every little slip we make so that he can punish us for it. John was committed, by the name he was given, to proclaim the opposite. Perhaps that's what the angel meant when he said, 'With the spirit and power of Elijah he will go before him, to turn the hearts of parents to their children, and the disobedient to the wisdom of the righteous, to make ready a people prepared for the Lord.'

Before Jesus could begin his ministry, some people at least had to be prepared to believe that God is gracious. How would people believe that Jesus had come to save them from their sins, unless they already believed in a God who saves? If we're to prepare the way for the Lord in our own generation, we must begin by disabusing people of the popular prejudice that Christians are a gloomy puritanical people who worship a harsh and judgemental God. No, 'God is gracious'. John called the people to repent, so that God could forgive them their sins. Jesus told people who felt guilty, 'Your sins are forgiven.' Jesus also said:

> 'John the Baptist has come eating no bread and drinking no wine, and you say, "He has a demon"; the Son of Man has come eating and drinking, and you say, "Look, a glutton and a drunkard, a friend of tax collectors and sinners!"'

The cousins were almost opposites. Yet each in his own way was proclaiming that God is gracious.

Suggested hymns

Lo, from the desert homes; On Jordan's bank the Baptist's cry; The great forerunner of the morn; Ye that know the Lord is gracious.

Fourth Sunday after Trinity (Proper 8)   1 July
Principal Service   **No Looking Back**
(*Continuous*): 2 Kings 2:1–2, 6–14 Elijah's spirit given to Elisha; Ps. 77:1–2, 11–20 Remembering God's saving acts; *or* (*Related*): 1 Kings 19:5–16, 19–21 Elijah calls Elisha; Ps. 16 The path of life; Gal. 5:1, 13–25 The fruit of the Spirit; Luke 9:51–62 Endurance in following Christ

> *'Jesus said . . . "No one who puts a hand to the plough and looks back is fit for the kingdom of God."' Luke 9:62*

You can't force love

Jews and Samaritans hated each other. A Samaritan village refused to admit Jesus, because he was heading for Jerusalem, which was a rival to their holy place on Mount Gerizim. His disciples wanted God to destroy the Samaritan village, because the Samaritans were different from Jews, but only slightly different – always the hardest sort of foreigner to love! But Jesus didn't want forced obedience, he only wanted love, and you can't force love. So he refused to punish the Samaritans. This is the paradox of free will: God created us so that we can love him, so he gave us freedom. There'd be a lot less suffering in the world if God forced wicked people to obey him. But people without free will would be mere machines or robots, and a robot can't love.

Excuses

The Samaritans' excuse for rejecting Jesus was their xenophobia – hatred of foreigners. It's not unknown today. Other people had other excuses for not following him: some used the insecurity of life as a disciple as their excuse, they didn't want to become homeless. Jesus replied that foxes have holes, birds have nests, but he has no home at all, except where he's welcomed. Or their legal duty to their family was used as an excuse: my father's just died, or might die any minute, or I don't know how many years he has to live. 'Let the dead bury their dead,' answered Jesus – the duty to proclaim the gospel overrides all other obligations. Excuses, excuses; if you don't want to make the effort to be a follower of Jesus, if you're frightened that it might involve making sacrifices, you can always find an excuse. Many people who claim to have intellectual doubts about Christianity are simply finding an excuse to avoid the effort involved in being a Christian. Many of the attacks that the newspapers launch against the Church are simply to provide their guilty-feeling readers with an excuse, because they've stopped going to church services.

Ploughing

In this context, Jesus spoke about ploughing. Few people today have any experience of ploughing a field by hand. When ploughs were drawn by horses, or oxen, a man was needed to press down on the handle so that the ploughshare should dig below the surface, and guide it in a straight line parallel with the furrows that had already been made. You had to concentrate, and keep looking at the line of furrows stretching out in front of you. If you kept looking over your shoulder, the ploughing would be a mess. Jesus used this as a metaphor: we need to concentrate on our discipleship, he said: 'No one who puts a hand to the plough and looks back is fit for the kingdom of God.'

You can always think of an excuse for being half-hearted in your Christianity, but half-hearted Christians are no use. God wants Christians who are totally committed, who work hard for the Church and allow the gospel to influence their actions and decisions every moment of every day.

No looking back

Nostalgia's a very dangerous thing: 'Things were so much better when I was younger,' and all that nonsense. You can easily spend so much time thinking about the past, that you don't concentrate enough on the present; then you can't build a satisfying future. Endurance and perseverance, that's what's needed. Having put our hand to the plough there must be no looking back. 'Keep right on to the end of the road', as in the old song. Then, remember the musical *Salad Days*. The enthusiasm and joy in the song, 'We said we wouldn't look back', shows that there's no true satisfaction in being half-hearted; even if our plans have to be constantly adjusted, true happiness is found by the optimist looking to the future.

All-age worship

Draw or model a plough drawn by two horses in line, or two oxen yoked together. Show the ploughman keeping the furrows parallel. Can he afford to look over his shoulder? What excuses do people make for not coming to church today?

Suggested hymns

Father, I place into your hands; Thou didst leave thy throne and thy kingly crown; Who would true valour see; Will you come and follow me?

Fourth Sunday after Trinity

Second Service   **Sibling Rivalry** Ps. [59:1–5, 16–17 You are my fortress] 60 Human help is worthless; Gen. 27:1–40 Jacob cheats Esau; Mark 6:1–6 Jesus rejected at Nazareth

> *'[Isaac said to Esau,] "Your brother came deceitfully, and he has taken away your blessing."' Genesis 27:35*

Sibling rivalry

The American comedian Danny Kaye had a song about how
agonizing it is to be one of triplets. The three apparently sweet little
girls sang:

> We do everything alike,
> we look alike, we dress alike,
> we talk alike, we walk alike,
> and what is more we hate each other very much . . .
> how I wish I had a gun, a little gun,
> it would be fun
> to shoot the other two and only be one!

I suppose we should call it black humour! It gets a laugh by painting
the extreme case of what is quite a common phenomenon, known
as 'sibling rivalry'. Brothers and sisters in childhood compete for
toys, for time and space and for their parents' affections. Fortunately most children grow out of it when they become adults; but
if you have a brother or sister with whom your relationship has
always been one of sweetness and light, you should count yourself
very blessed.

Jacob and Esau

Jacob and Esau never grew out of it. They were twins who fought
each other in the womb. Esau was the elder of the two by a few
minutes, so he should legally have inherited twice as much of their
father Isaac's property as Jacob did. This was his 'birthright'. But
one day Esau came in starving from a hunting trip, and Jacob persuaded his brother to sell the birthright to him in exchange for a
dish of red lentil stew, what the Geneva Bible of 1560 called 'a mess
of pottage'. Later, when their father was nearly blind and dying,
Jacob disguised himself as Esau and claimed the special blessing due
to an elder son, including ruling over his brothers. The story was
probably told to explain the later rivalry between the Israelites, the
descendants of Jacob, and the Edomites, descended from Esau. But
very few of the people portrayed in the Old Testament are 'admirable' people. It's no use recommending children to read the Old
Testament in search of moral examples. There are some, but there
are far more ghastly examples of character traits to be avoided.
The lesson it teaches is that God doesn't only work through perfect

people. God can take people who are absolute beasts, and use them to carry out his will. Which is just as well, as there are a lot of them around! We often don't recognize that God's trying to teach us a useful lesson, even though it's through an unpleasant experience inflicted on us by somebody we hate.

Jesus and his relatives

Jesus knew something about sibling rivalry, too. The people of Nazareth said of Jesus, '"Is not this the carpenter, the son of Mary and brother of James and Joses and Judas and Simon, and are not his sisters here with us?" And they took offence at him.' Apparently Jesus had at least four brothers and some sisters in Nazareth. You would have thought that some of them would stand up for Jesus. Not a bit of it. His siblings seem to have been part of the opposition. They tried on several occasions to persuade Jesus to withdraw from the apparently crazy course he had started on, and to give up his ministry altogether. After the resurrection, however, they joined his disciples, and 'James the brother of the Lord' became the leader of the church in Jerusalem. An example of sibling rivalry being overcome by generous love, perhaps?

Life in the real world

There's no doubt that the whole Bible's about life in the real world. In a perfect world there'd be no sibling rivalry; but there is no perfect world. Sometimes people appeal to the Bible for support for 'Christian family values'. The family's very important in God's plan for human life, not because it's a paradise of idyllic love, but precisely because it's extremely difficult. You can choose your friends, but you can't choose your relatives. So you've just got to learn to get along with the set you've been issued with. And that's what love's all about. Love isn't about living happily with people you like. Love is the struggle to accept, tolerate and do good to people who are extremely difficult to like. Thank God that God loves us, though he must often find it impossible to like us. So God set us on earth in families, in order that, in the family, we can begin to learn to love the unlovely, and then extend it beyond the family into the whole world. Learning to love each other in spite of, or even because of, our differences, as God loves us. Even to the extent of transcending sibling rivalry.

Suggested hymns

Bind us together, Lord; For the beauty of the earth; Lord of all hopefulness, Lord of all joy; My song is love unknown.

Fifth Sunday after Trinity (Proper 9)   8 July
Principal Service   **Dealing with Atheists**
(*Continuous*): 2 Kings 5:1–14 Naaman healed from leprosy;
Ps. 30 Healing; *or* (*Related*): Isa. 66:10–14 The motherhood of God;
Ps. 66:1–9 God's grace; Gal. 6:[1–6] 7–16 Righteousness;
Luke 10:1–11, 16–20 Sending out the seventy disciples

> *'[Jesus said,] "Whenever you enter a town and they do not welcome you, go out into its streets and say, 'Even the dust of your town that clings to our feet, we wipe off in protest against you. Yet know this: the kingdom of God has come near.' "' Luke 10:10–11*

Dust from our feet

How should we deal with atheists? Jesus tells us to be quite firm with the opposition; he said: 'Whenever you enter a town and they do not welcome you, go out into its streets and say, "Even the dust of your town that clings to our feet, we wipe off in protest against you."' There's no point in wasting time on sterile argument. Yet St Peter tells us that we must be able to explain our reasons for believing if anyone asks us: 'Always be ready to make your defence to anyone who demands from you an accounting for the hope that is in you; yet do it with gentleness and reverence.' So what are the reasons we believe in God?

Probability

Nobody can prove there is a God. Equally, nobody can prove there isn't. But like many of the things we believe in science, belief in God is based on probability. Nobody can prove that there's such a thing as an electron; we can't see them; but we can see what they do, and it would be foolish to deny their existence. Nobody can prove the truth of Darwin's theory of evolution, but it's the most probable explanation for how a lot of things we observe in nature came to pass. But when we look at the complexity and efficiency of the world around us, although it's possible that these things *all* happened purely by chance, that's a very unlikely explanation. It's far more likely that God was behind the whole process, directing the apparently random events to produce the world he'd planned. The same applies to the other 'arguments for the existence of God' – they're not proofs, nobody ever said they were. It's extremely improbable that our awareness of purpose and progress in creation, our awareness of beauty, our sense of right and wrong, and the lives of good people down the ages could *all* be based on a fallacy. You'd be a fool to take the least likely explanation in every case. The modern theory of probability was invented by the French philosopher Blaise Pascal. He said that, as there are no proofs of the existence or the non-existence of God, we're bound to gamble on the most likely choice. If you assume that there's no God, then, when you die, you find there is, you'll be very sorry. But if you live assuming there is a god, and there isn't, you'll be none the worse!

What sort of God?

Yet when you've argued that the idea of God gives a probable explanation for the world we live in, you've said nothing about what sort of God he is. If you ask an atheist to describe the god he or she doesn't believe in, I think in most cases we'd have to say that we Christians couldn't believe in that sort of God either! They've rejected the picture of God as a fierce judge, whereas today's reading from Isaiah shows that God has many of the characteristics of a patient mother. We believe in a God of love, who in his courtesy allows us free will, including the choice of whether to believe in him or not.

The problem of evil

But then the atheist will raise the problem of evil. If God is a loving God, why does he allow all the suffering in the world? The answer to that's tied up with the issue of free will: the only way God could stop us hurting each other would be if he took away from us the power of choice.

Capitalize on your successes

Jesus wants us to love and pray for the atheists we know. But we shouldn't worry about them. Leave God to handle them. What

Jesus told the 72 disciples would be good advice for anyone in business: ignore your failures and capitalize on your successes. Rejoice because so many people do respond to God's love, and leave the rest to him, because he still cares for them.

All-age worship

Take a bag of Scrabble™ letters and throw them at random on the floor. While the rest close their eyes, one person arranges some of the tiles into as long a word as possible. Then open your eyes. Can you recognize the pattern (the word)? Do you think it got there by chance? Can you prove that somebody arranged them? Can you prove that it happened by chance? Which is the most likely explanation? What's the most likely explanation for the beautiful world around us?

Suggested hymns

For the fruits of his creation; Immortal, invisible, God only wise; Jesus is Lord; O Lord my God.

Fifth Sunday after Trinity

Second Service   **Jacob Loved Rachel** Ps. 65 God in nature [70 Don't delay!]; Gen. 29:1–20 Jacob loved Rachel; Mark 6:7–29 The death of John the Baptist

> *'Jacob loved Rachel; so he said, "I will serve you seven years for your younger daughter Rachel."' Genesis 29:18*

Matchmaking at the well

To nomadic people, wandering in a dry land, an abundant water source was essential, to provide drink for people and animals. Be it an oasis, or a small well with a stone over it to prevent contamination or theft, they'd lead their flocks for miles to reach it, and the tribes from afar would gather at the well. Important social business, including matchmaking, took place at the well. A generation before, Rebekah had been selected to marry Isaac because she was kind to Abraham's messenger, and watered his camels at the well for him. The messenger recognized that the character of the girl made her a suitable match for Isaac. Now their son Jacob came to a well in a remote region, and rolled the stone from the well's mouth and watered the flocks. There, for the first time, he saw a graceful and beautiful young girl called Rachel, and fell in love with her. That day he determined that she should be his wife.

Keeping it in the family

That was what Jacob had come for. Isaac, his father, like *his* father Abraham before him, was determined that his son shouldn't marry one of the local Canaanite women. The Old Testament was concerned for the purity of the Jewish religion; whenever the Israelites married local women, their simple faith in Jehovah became diluted with fertility cults and superstitions. So Isaac was sent to find a wife from the branch of his own family which had stayed in Mesopotamia. Rachel was Laban's daughter, and Laban was Jacob's uncle, his mother's brother. Laban was also Abraham's brother's grandson. So Rachel was – wait for it – Jacob's first cousin through his mother; and also his second cousin once removed through his father. That really was keeping it in the family! But this was a great strength for an ethnic minority living as expatriates among a strange people. Blood's thicker than water, and the family can be a great support network.

The dangers of tradition

The family was a great tradition. Yet almost immediately Jacob ran into the dangers of over-reliance on tradition. He loved Rachel so much that he was willing to work for seven years to pay the bride-price for her. Then Laban tricked him by bringing him Rachel's elder sister Leah, disguised under a veil, so that Jacob unwittingly married Leah instead. 'But it's our tradition,' protested Laban, trying to justify his chicanery. 'In our family, the elder sister always gets married before the younger. You can't change that!' Such was Jacob's love for Rachel that he now worked a further seven years, so that he could take her as his second wife. There's nothing in the tradition at that time against polygamy, you notice, or against marrying two sisters. Tradition is constantly changing under the force of circumstances. Tennyson wrote:

> The old order changeth, giving place to new,
> And God fulfils himself in many ways.

A chosen romance

What was new, and a radical break with tradition, was that Jacob chose his own wife, on the basis of love. Even his father Isaac had married Rebekah in an arranged marriage, and it was only after they were married that he discovered that he loved her. For Jacob, it was love at first sight, and then he waited 14 years for the marriage. 'The heart has its reasons which reason knows nothing of,' wrote Blaise Pascal, and to allow the choice of the heart to override family tradition was the early dawn of romanticism. God gave us passionate human love so that we should learn something of the strength and depth of God's love for us. Romantic love is a stepping-stone to divine love, a manifestation of divine love and a sharing in the love of the Trinity. Parents always prefer their children to marry someone from a similar background; it avoids the frequent misunderstandings that come with different cultures. Yet, amazingly, people of different social, cultural or ethnic groups sometimes fall in love despite the opposition of both families; in many cases they overcome the problems, and their love becomes a thing of stability and reconciliation. Tradition's a great strength, guiding our lives in tried and tested ways. But tradition's always changing, and it's no use fighting the changes, because they'll come about whether we oppose them or welcome them. Then perhaps, in a generation or two, we shall forget that it ever changed, and start defending the new customs as though they stretched back for centuries!

Suggested hymns

Let there be love shown among us; Love divine, all loves excelling; O love that wilt not let me go; O perfect love, all human thought transcending.

Sixth Sunday after Trinity (Proper 10)   15 July
Principal Service   The Good Samaritan
(*Continuous*): Amos 7:7–17 The plumb line: judgement on the city; Ps. 82 Justice; *or* (*Related*): Deut. 30:9–14 The word is near you; Ps. 25:1–10 Truth and guidance; Col. 1:1–14 Bear the fruit of good works; Luke 10:25–37 The Good Samaritan

> *'Jesus asked, "Which of these three, do you think, was a neighbour to the man who fell into the hands of the robbers?" [The lawyer]*

said, "The one who showed him mercy." Jesus said to him, "Go and do likewise."' Luke 10:36–37

Singapore story

The priest of a multiracial parish in Singapore decided to take a series of photographs to illustrate the parable of the Good Samaritan. He chose members of his congregation to be photographed acting scenes from the parable in modern dress. As it happened, the cast included a Chinese, an Indian, a Eurasian and a Malay. The priest asked the Malay to take the part of the Samaritan. Then the cast went on strike. 'What's the problem?' asked the priest. 'Don't you see?' they answered. 'This is a parable about race. The Samaritan belongs to an outcast and despised race. But he's actually a better person than any of the others. If we make the Malay be the Samaritan, that means, first, that we Chinese and Indians despise the Malays. Secondly, that the Malays are better than we are. We don't want to say either of those things!' When the problem was talked through, everybody agreed there was no problem. But all of them had learnt a lot about race relations.

The despised race

So who were the Samaritans? After the death of King Solomon, the Israelites split into two kingdoms. When the capital city of the northern kingdom moved to the city of Samaria, the region changed its name from Ephraim to Samaria. When the northern kingdom was conquered by Assyria in 722, some of the population was deported. Propagandists for the southern kingdom alleged that it was the majority, and that they were replaced by foreigners; the Samaritans claim that it was a few only who returned later. They built a sanctuary on Mount Gerizim, and kept part of the religion of Israel: the worship of the LORD, the Five Books of Moses, circumcision, the Sabbath and festivals; but they rejected later developments of Judaism. This mixture of similarity and difference led to mutual loathing and enmity between Jews and Samaritans. Jews avoided the area and 'had no dealings with the Samaritans'. Until we realize the depth of this mutual hatred, we don't appreciate how revolutionary it was for Jesus to use a Samaritan as the hero of his parable. The Singapore youngsters didn't want to admit that they despised the Malays. So I wouldn't dare to suggest that there's any race that you, dear friends, despise and fear today. You must search your own consciences on that. But if there is, try putting the name of that race in the title, 'The parable of the Good . . .'.

Who is my neighbour?

The parable's about neighbourliness. The basic meaning of the word 'neighbour' is quite clear, it's somebody who lives next door, whose property abuts onto yours, or who at least lives in the same street or the same village. But think of problems with neighbours about boundaries, hedges, drains, noise and so on, and you'll realize that neighbours are some of the most difficult people to get on with. The Book of Leviticus challenged the Jews: 'You shall love your neighbour as yourself.' Now that's pretty difficult. 'You mean that man whose overhanging tree is stopping my flowers from growing? I'm to love him? Well, I'll think about it!' So the lawyer's question was: how far does neighbourliness extend? My own street? My own town? Or the whole nation? Not only them, answered Jesus; you must love the whole world as much as you love yourself. Especially those whom you hate and despise. We live in a global village, and everyone's my neighbour.

The needy

Then Jesus moved the goalposts. He didn't answer the question about who the Jew was to love; instead he talked about who we're to accept love from. He said that anybody who needs our help is our neighbour and deserves our love. Because sometime we may need their help. We're mutually interdependent. So go and do likewise. Love everybody you meet, the chance encounters, the despised races, the people you see on the television. Love them, for Christ's sake! Finally, we must never be too proud to allow other people to help us. The young people in Singapore were right: neighbourliness knows no boundaries of race or religion.

All-age worship

Take a series of photographs of congregation members acting the parable of the Good Samaritan, to make a wall display, a slide show or a PowerPoint™ presentation. Remember the Samaritan was a foreigner; what's the message of your display for today?

Brother, sister, let me serve you; When I needed a neighbour, were you there?; Where cross the crowded ways of life; Will you come and follow me?

Sixth Sunday after Trinity
Second Service   **Wrestling Jacob** Ps. 77 Remembering the past; Gen. 32:9–30 Wrestling Jacob; Mark 7:1–23 Tradition

> *'Jacob was left alone; and a man wrestled with him until daybreak.'*
> Genesis 32:24

Ancient questions, ancient answers

The story of Jacob wrestling with the 'man' – who turns out not to be a man at all, but is actually God in disguise – is a very primitive one. When it was told round the nomads' camp fire, it must have answered a number of questions which were bothering them. They're not the questions which concern us today, but here they are:

1 Why do Jews not eat meat from the thighs of their animals; and in fact have special butchers able to remove that meat before the rest is cooked? Do you lie awake wondering about that? No, nor me.
2 Why does Jacob have two names in their stories; sometimes he's called Jacob, sometimes Israel; and Israel sounds like the Hebrew words for 'Struggles with God'?
3 Why is there a place near the River Jabbok called Peniel or Penuel, which means 'the face of God'?
4 What is God's name? Is he El, as he's called in the north of the country, or Yahweh as he's known to the tribes who live round Jerusalem? Why doesn't God tell us his name?

So those are the questions which lie behind the story of Wrestling Jacob. And as I've hinted, I think they're of absolutely no interest to us today.

Wrestling in prayer

But I think there's another question which is illustrated by the story, which is absolutely crucial for today's Christians. That is, why do we ourselves spend so much time wrestling with our faith? Why isn't life simple and straightforward? From that question there follow a whole lot of other thorny questions. Why's it so difficult being a Christian? Why do we find it so hard to pray? Why's there so much suffering in the world? Why doesn't God explain? Why do bad things happen to good people? We have flung our questions at heaven's gate: Why . . . why . . . why? 'But answer came there none.' Yet it's important that we should ask the questions. No, more than that, it's absolutely *vital* that we should ask the difficult questions of faith, and go on asking them over and again. Because the answer doesn't come in words, it comes in the relationship we build up with God while we wrestle with him. God doesn't want us to pretend that everything's easy, he wants us to come to him as we are, with all our weakness, all our puzzlement, our impossible questions, our feeble faith and our muddled minds, to lay them at his feet. And leave them there, trusting him, whether he gives an answer now, or later, or never.

Charles Wesley's hymn

Charles Wesley, the younger brother of John Wesley, the founder of Methodism, wrote two hymns referring to wrestling in prayer. The first is 'Shepherd divine, our wants relieve':

> The Spirit's interceding grace
> give us in faith to claim;
> to wrestle till we see thy face,
> and know thy hidden name.
> Till thou thy perfect love impart
> till thou thyself bestow,
> be this the cry of every heart,
> 'I will not let thee go.'

The other is one of the greatest hymns that great hymn-writer ever wrote. There are two wonderful eighteenth-century tunes which it's sung to, one by the author's grandson Samuel Sebastian Wesley called, appropriately, 'Wrestling Jacob', and one by Robert King called 'David's Harp'. The words go like this:

Come, O thou traveller unknown,
Whom still I hold, but cannot see,
my company before is gone,
and I alone am left with thee;
with thee all night I mean to stay
and wrestle till the break of day . . .

Verse 4:

Yield to me now, for I am weak,
but confident in self-despair;
speak to my heart, in blessings speak,
be conquered by my instant prayer!
Speak, or thou never hence shalt move, –
and tell me, if thy name is Love?

'Tis Love! 'Tis Love! Thou diedst for me!
I hear thy whisper in my heart!
The morning breaks, the shadows flee;
pure universal Love thou art!
To me, to all, thy mercies move;
thy nature and thy name is Love!

And another verse which is left out in most hymn books:

My prayer hath power with God; the grace
unspeakable I now receive;
through faith I see thee face to face,
I see thee face to face, and live:
in vain I have not wept and strove;
thy nature and thy name is Love.

You can never get to this point, the point of recognizing that God is Absolute Love, without wrestling in prayer. Go to it!

Suggested hymns

Come, my soul, thy suit prepare; Come, O thou traveller unknown; Prayer is the soul's sincere desire; Shepherd divine, our wants relieve.

Seventh Sunday after Trinity (Proper 11)
(St Mary Magdalene)   22 July
Principal Service   **Too Busy to Pray**

(*Continuous*): Amos 8:1–12 Justice for the needy; Ps. 52 Justice for the needy; *or* (*Related*): Gen. 18:1–10a Abraham welcomes three guests; Ps. 15 Justice; Col. 1:15–28 Christ the head of the Church; Luke 10:38–42 Martha and Mary, works and prayer

> *'Jesus said, "Martha, Martha, you are worried and distracted by many things; there is need of only one thing. Mary has chosen the better part, which will not be taken away from her."' Luke 10:41–42*

Poor Martha

Poor Martha! I think everyone, when they first hear the story, feels a wave of sympathy for Martha. It was all so unfair. She had all the housework to do. She was doing all the cooking, 'slaving all day over a hot stove, working her fingers to the bone', as they say. Whereas Mary, that lazy, idle, good-for-nothing sister of hers just sat near Jesus, soaking up what he had to say. Where's the justice in that? Then Jesus, instead of telling Mary to take her fair share of the household chores, said that Mary had chosen the better way. For poor Martha, that must have been the last straw. Few people who haven't had to do it themselves can realize just how much hard work is involved in the care of a house and the preparation of a meal. It's exhausting.

Why was Jesus so unfair?

So why was Jesus so unfair? Instead of sticking up for Martha he gave her a gentle rebuke. Didn't he care that she was overworked? I think what he was trying to do was to make her look at her own life in a new light. She was very busy, and it's good to have high standards in what you do. But was it actually all necessary? Might not everyone have been a lot happier if Martha hadn't worked so hard? Who'd have cared if the house was less than spotless, and the meal was a simpler one than the one she'd planned, so long as there was a bit more time to listen. Some busy people, men and women, are so absorbed in what they're doing, they never pay attention to anyone else. Maybe Mary was quietly suffering, ignored and neglected, because Martha had no time for her sister's feelings. Maybe Martha had no time for feelings at all, her own or anybody else's. And in this way she caused a lot of hurt to others, without realizing what she was doing. She was also hurting herself. Who knows how much more profound and helpful, thoughtful and considerate – even happy – a person she could have grown into, if she'd only allowed herself a little more time? She was so busy doing, she had no time to be. To be herself; to be the person she could have become. Do you allow yourself time simply to be? There has to be time in every life when you stop being busy doing, and make a pause for reflection and calm.

Listening to God

Mary, however, was listening to Jesus, and Jesus was talking about God. God's got all the time in the world, because God is the maker of time. So if we want to come to know God, we too have to make time. We have to make time to pray. And that doesn't mean constantly rushing to God with a shopping list of requests. A large part of prayer is simply being quiet and listening. Not for audible sounds, but listening with the ears of the heart to discover what God's thinking. Are we too busy with our own plans to discover what God's plans for us are? The only way to do that is as God says in the Psalms, 'Be still, and know that I am God.' That's what Mary, listening to Jesus, was doing. That's what Martha wasn't allowing herself to do, because she was so busy. Most of the things we make ourselves busy with are important, but they're not as important as listening to God. If we're too busy to pray, we're simply too busy. Will you find time today to stop doing, and simply make space to be, with God, what he wants you to be?

All-age worship

Learn to relax. Think of each group of muscles in your body in turn, tense them and then consciously relax them. Steady, slow breathing, neither too deep nor too shallow. Then, before you fall asleep, remember that God is right here! 'Closer is he than breathing, nearer than hands and feet.' Listen to God in the silence. Imagine that God is telling you what he wants you to become.

Suggested hymns

Be still, for the Spirit of the Lord; Let me have my way among you, do not strive; O love divine, how sweet thou art; Teach me, my God and King.

St Mary Magdalene   22 July

(or may be transferred to 23 July)

Put the Past Behind You S. of Sol. 3:1–4 Seeking and finding; Ps. 42:1–7 As deer long for water; 2 Cor. 5:14–17 A new creation; John 20:1–2, 11–18 Go and tell

> *'So if anyone is in Christ, there is a new creation: everything old has passed away; see, everything has become new!' 2 Corinthians 5:17*

Who was she?

Mary Magdalene was one of the most important people in the story of Jesus. All four Gospels agree that she was one of the principal witnesses of the crucifixion and resurrection of Jesus, and that she was sent to tell others the good news. St Luke tells us that she was one of the women who supported Jesus financially during his ministry, and that Jesus had cast out seven devils from her. Apart from that, everything's guesswork about Mary Magdalene; but there's no doubt she was what's called, usually in capital letters, 'A Woman With A Past'.

You may believe that she was literally possessed by seven devils. In which case, what wicked deed had she done to get into such a state?

You may believe that this was what would be called in modern terms a bout of mental illness. Even today, with all our knowledge of psychology, the stigma of such an attack is very hard to live down.

You may identify her with one of the other women in the Gospels with a shady background, who anointed Jesus's feet and burst into hysterical tears.

You may accept the widespread tradition that Mary Magdalene was a prostitute.

You may even believe the fantastic legend, peddled by several bestselling books, that she was married to Jesus, for which there's absolutely no evidence at all.

Whatever your theory about Mary Magdalene, it's quite clear that she carried with her a bad reputation, which must have been almost impossible to overcome.

How Jesus handled her

Many men would run a mile from a woman with a past like that. But not Jesus. He handled her with courtesy, respect and affection. He didn't push her away, as other people did, and that showed her that she was not all bad. He healed her, and that showed her that God still loved her. He allowed her to wait on him, and that gave her a role in life, which gave her back her self-respect. He chose her to be his principal witness, and that showed her that a shady past is no hindrance to a glorious future.

People can change

People can change. You're not condemned to go on repeating your mistakes and your sins, if you genuinely want to reform. Repentance can be followed by forgiveness, and forgiveness can be followed by a fresh start in life. When you're loved, you make the discovery that you're not totally unlovable. The love of Jesus turned Mary Magdalene from a sinner into a saint. The love of another human being can turn the most downtrodden mouse of a person into a radiantly confident, creative and compassionate colleague. I doubt if there's anyone in this world who doesn't have something in their past to be ashamed of: some spiteful word, some thoughtless action, some yielding to temptation. But the message of Mary Magdalene, and the message of the Christian gospel, is that you can put your past behind you.

'So if anyone is in Christ, there is a new creation: everything old has passed away; see, everything has become new!'

The religion of the second chance

Christianity really ought to be known as the religion of the second chance. Our churches are not a hothouse for saints but a seedbed for repentant sinners. The Christian Church ought to be famous as the place where those with a shady past are helped to make a new beginning. If the Church doesn't do that, for Christ's sake, who will? The Church must welcome, and love, people with a shady past

– like you and me, if the truth were known. Fred Astaire sang a song by Jerome Kern:

> Nothing's impossible I have found,
> for when my chin is on the ground,
> I pick myself up,
> dust myself off,
> and start all over again.

Wouldn't it be wonderful if the Church really was widely recognized as the place where everybody can put the past behind them, and have a second chance in life? At its best, the Church is just that. And that's the good news that Mary Magdalene was sent to proclaim. You and I could be spreading the same gospel, by our words and by our actions, by our compassionate, tolerant attitude and our affirming, encouraging love. Let's get on with it!

Suggested hymns

And can it be that I should gain; Just as I am, without one plea; To God be the glory, great things he hath done; Walking in a garden.

Eighth Sunday after Trinity (Proper 12)   29 July
Principal Service   **Ask, Seek, Knock**
(*Continuous*): Hos. 1:2–10 Hosea's family; Ps. 85 Forgiveness; *or*
(*Related*): Gen. 18:20–32 Abraham's prayer for Sodom; Ps. 138 Faith in God's mercy; Col. 2:6–15 [16–19] Resurrection with Christ; Luke 11:1–13 Ask, seek, knock

'[Jesus said,] "Ask, and it will be given you; search, and you will find; knock, and the door will be opened for you. For everyone who asks receives, and everyone who searches finds, and for everyone who knocks, the door will be opened."' Luke 11:9–10

A poem and a promise

In these verses we have a perfectly crafted poem. It has six lines, the last three echoing the first three. It doesn't rhyme, but Hebrew poetry never did; it was the parallelism – words echoing the words

that had gone before them – that shaped it into verse. Listen to it
again:

> [Jesus said]
> 'Ask, and it will be given you;
> search, and you will find;
> knock, and the door will be opened for you.
> For everyone who asks receives,
> and everyone who searches finds,
> and for everyone who knocks, the door will be opened.'

Why did Jesus put what he said into poetry? I'm sure he savoured
the rhythm of the words, but there was a much more important
reason than that. Jesus would preach a long sermon, certain that
nobody could remember all of what he said. So he would sum up
the nub of his message at the end in a short, memorable phrase. And
everybody finds verse easier to memorize than prose.

Imagine a family

Imagine a family where one of the family members had been unable
to go to hear Jesus preach, due to sickness or work. When the others
get home, the questions begin. 'What did Jesus preach about today?
Tell me, tell me!' 'He preached about prayer.' 'What did he say about
prayer? What did Jesus say?' 'Well, he said something like, we'll get
anything we ask for, if we, sort of, ask hard enough.' 'Tell me the
exact words. What did Jesus say, precisely?' 'Well, I can't remember
all of it. But he ended up with a little poem. I can remember the
poem word for word.' And so the message about prayer in faith
spread to many more than were able to hear Jesus preach. The
promise that we shall get what we pray for is remembered, because
the promise is a poem.

Unanswered prayer

But just a minute. The poem with a promise about prayer brings a
problem. Do we always get what we pray for? We can all think of
examples of unanswered prayer, and times when God seems to be
deaf to our requests. Jesus said that God will answer prayers when
they are made 'in my name': 'The Father will give you whatever
you ask him in my name.' Now, asking in the name of Jesus doesn't
just mean tacking the mumbled words 'through Jesus Christ our

Lord. Amen' on the end of every prayer. It means praying in the spirit of Jesus, as his representative, praying for the sort of things Jesus would pray for. Now Jesus wouldn't be praying for extravagant worldly possessions, would he? He'd more likely pray that we should have the grace to be content with what we've got, and the grace to make us more caring and loving people. It's often been said that there is no such thing as an unanswered prayer. God always answers prayer, but his answer may be

> Yes; or
> Yes, but wait; or
> No, because I've got something better in mind to give you.

Very often the answer to prayer may be a change in the person who prays; we may become more patient; or more contented; or we may realize that if we're to get what we ask for, we need to do something about it ourselves.

Persistence and faith

The poem about 'ask, seek, knock' teaches us persistence in prayer. Don't give up if your prayer seems unanswered at first, or you can't see what the answer is. If at first you don't succeed, pray and pray and pray again. 'Pray without ceasing.' It's the very act of praying passionately that brings you close to God and builds up your faith in him. You begin to realize how God, as a good parent, loves his children to talk to him, to share their innermost, deepest feelings and desires with him. God may very much want to give you what you're asking for, but he is just waiting until you realize how completely dependent on him you are. Waiting till you're desperate. Waiting till you pray with urgency and faith. The relationship you build up with God through prayer's more important even than the thing you're praying for.

All-age worship

Can you turn one of your own prayers into a verse that you could memorize and repeat?

Suggested hymns

Come, my soul, thy suit prepare; Father, hear the prayer we offer; Jesu, the very thought of thee; What a friend we have in Jesus.

Eighth Sunday after Trinity
Second Service   Endurance Tests

Ps. 88 Let my prayer come before you; Gen. 42:1–25 Joseph tests his brothers; 1 Cor. 10:1–24 Examples for us; *Gospel at Holy Communion*: Matt. 13:24–30 [31–43] Weeds

> *'No testing has overtaken you that is not common to everyone. God is faithful, and he will not let you be tested beyond your strength, but with the testing he will also provide the way out so that you may be able to endure it.' 1 Corinthians 10:13*

Endurance tests

In the army they set the raw recruits endurance tests. They have to yomp in full kit across rough terrain for hour after hour, until every muscle is screaming for mercy. 'It's doing you good, soldier,' yells the sar'major. 'Strengthening your feeble little muscles. Giving you the guts to keep going. Very necessary in battle. Come on, you horrible little people, left, right, left, right!' Of course, nobody believes him at the time. But the next time they do it, incredibly, it's not as bad as the first time. Getting to the end of an endurance test does make you stronger.

Tests to destruction

In the metallurgy workshop they have another sort of test. The test to destruction. A new metal object is subjected to greater and greater pressure until it collapses. Or greater and greater tension until it snaps. Measuring the pressure, or the tension, at which it gives way, shows how strong that type of object or that batch of raw material is. But the sample will never be any use afterwards. It's been tested to destruction.

Testing times

There are testing times in every life. Times of pain, times of loneliness, times of temptation. The question is, are they endurance tests or tests to destruction? We only wish we knew. Am I going to give way under this experience, or am I going to come out of it stronger? St Paul thinks he knows the answer. It's doing us good. You may not believe it at the time, but it's making you morally stronger. Of course! What good would it do God if he let us be destroyed? He's gone to all the trouble of making us, and revealing that he loves us; what use would a moral wreck be to God? This isn't a test to destruction. God doesn't want his children to suffer, but in a world where people have free will to choose whether or not to hurt each other, suffering's bound to happen. You never think you can stand up to it. 'But God, I have a very low pain threshold!' Yet incredibly, every time we pass through testing times, putting our trust in God, he gives us the grace, the inner strength – the guts, if you like – to bring us through it. Suffering doesn't *necessarily* make you a better person, it depends how you use it. If you put your trust in God, and ask for his help, it can give you a strength of character which you can acquire in no other way. Suffering is an endurance test, not a test to destruction.

It's doing you good

St Paul wrote:

> No testing has overtaken you that is not common to everyone. God is faithful, and he will not let you be tested beyond your strength, but with the testing he will also provide the way out so that you may be able to endure it.

You may think you're unique in the awful things that happen to you, but there's always someone worse off. As the Chinese proverb puts it, 'I had no shoes, and I grumbled, until I met a man who had no feet!' We shouldn't jump to the conclusion that because we've come to a sticky patch in our lives, we're completely finished. God knows us better than that, and with the testing he always provides a way out – or a way through. We realize our need of God when we're stretched to the limit. The suffering which lies ahead of you is just enough to be an endurance test, and leave you a better person. It's not going to be enough to break you, if you'll only cry out for God's mercy and grace – it's not a test to destruction. We should try to avoid suffering if we can. But if we can't evade it, a hymn at midnight's in order.

> No testing has overtaken you that is not common to everyone. God is faithful, and he will not let you be tested beyond your strength, but with the testing he will also provide the way out so that you may be able to endure it.

That'd be a good verse to commit to memory, so as to be ready for anything the world can throw at us: 1 Corinthians 10:13. Look it up when you get home.

Suggested hymns

Be thou my guardian and my guide; God moves in a mysterious way; O love that wilt not let me go; Sometimes a light surprises.

Ninth Sunday after Trinity (Proper 13)   5 August
(Eve of the Transfiguration, see page 330.)
Principal Service   Stewardship
(*Continuous*): Hos. 11:1–11 Fatherhood of God; Ps. 107:1–9, 43 Guidance; *or* (*Related*): Eccles. 1:2, 12–14; 2:18–23 Vanity and wisdom; Ps. 49:1–12 Wisdom and death; Col. 3:1–11 Righteousness and unity; Luke 12:13–21 The rich fool

> *'[Jesus] said to them, "Take care! Be on your guard against all kinds of greed; for one's life does not consist in the abundance of possessions."' Luke 12:15*

Parson Woodforde

James Woodforde became Rector of Weston Longville in Norfolk in 1776. Clergy in those days were known as the Parson, or person, of the parish. Parson Woodforde wrote *The Diary of a Country Parson*. It gives a rare insight into the life of the Church in the eighteenth century, but what astonishes many readers is his description of the enormous meals which he and his companions ate. If to enjoy the good gifts of God's creation is a form of worship, then James Woodforde was a devout believer! Some might call it gluttony or greed, yet it seems to have done no harm to his health, for he lived to 62, which was a good age in those days. Conspicuous consumption, of food or wealth, is wrong because it harms your health, or deprives other people of what they need. But we all consume far more than people in the Third World, so never mind about judging other people, we should all examine ourselves to see whether we're guilty of the sin of greed.

The Rich Fool

First let me say that I sympathize with anyone in the congregation who's genuinely very poor; this sermon's not addressed to you. Jesus told us to look at the lilies of the field and the birds of the air, which depend entirely on God. And he told what we know as the parable of the Rich Fool, who gathered more and more grain in his barns until there was no more room. So he pulled down the barns, intending to build bigger ones, but before he could, he died and his wealth became the property of someone else. His riches were no use to him then, after he'd died. Perhaps we should think about our death a little more often; it puts a lot of things in perspective.

Materialism

Good food, beautiful clothes, great music, are all good things to spend your money on. We should enjoy them and thank God for them, as Parson Woodforde did. But to have more gives us an added responsibility to care for those who have less. Is our conspicuous consumption causing others to go hungry? It's hardly surprising that there's so much hatred in the poor nations of the South against the prosperous North. We're only storing up trouble for ourselves if we ignore these imbalances. Rich fools indeed!

What can I do about it?

But what can I do about it? The child who was told to eat up his rice pudding, because there were people starving in China, was quite right to protest, 'Well send it to them, then!' If I cut back on my consumption, it's not going to help the poor. But there's a perfectly good way described in the Bible to be rich and still have a clear conscience. It's called tithing. The Jews gave one-tenth of all their crops and income to the Temple. Ultimately this money was for social projects, building works and the relief of poverty. Nowadays many of those things are paid for out of the income tax, so a modern adaptation of what the Jews did would be to give away one-tenth of your *after-tax* income. Our churches are very gentle with us, and only ask us to give to the church a 'half-tithe', or one-twentieth part of our after-tax income: 5 per cent. Actually, most of our lovely churches would fall down if the members gave less than that. But it's kind of assumed that this isn't all you'll give away. Another 5 per cent is to be given to other charities, for the homeless and the poor in the Third World. That's not easy to do immediately, you may need a year or two to work up to the standard of tithing. Curiously, the poor find it easier to achieve than the rich. But if you do manage to give away one-tenth of your after-tax income, you've done all that God demands of you. You can enjoy the other nine-tenths with a beautifully clear conscience, and revel in what God has lent you in the certainty that you have used it responsibly. Nobody could compare you with the rich fool in the parable. Of course, you still have to think about stewardship of your time and talents, but that's another sermon!

All-age worship

Learn about poor people in other countries, and think of things to do to help them.

Suggested hymns

God of grace and God of glory; In a world where people walk in darkness; O God of earth and altar; Where cross the crowded ways of life.

Ninth Sunday after Trinity

Second Service **Communion** Ps. 107:1–32 Thanksgiving for deliverance; Gen. 50:4–26 Deaths of Jacob and Joseph; 1 Cor. 14:1–19 Tongues and prophecy; *Gospel at Holy Communion*: Mark 6:45–52 Walking on water

> *'If the bugle gives an indistinct sound, who will get ready for battle?' 1 Corinthians 14:8*

Speaking in tongues

Probably only those who've had contact with the Charismatic Movement, or have visited a Pentecostal church, will have had first-hand experience of speaking in tongues. It's a form of spiritual experience in which words come from your mouth, but it is not you, it's the Holy Spirit speaking. This can give great encouragement to new Christians – 'Just think of it, God can speak even through me!' St Paul himself spoke in tongues often. But in Corinth, he found that there was a danger that those who did speak in tongues despised those who didn't, suggesting that they weren't real Christians. So he spends several chapters dealing with what they called 'spiritual gifts'. Paul didn't deny that 'speaking in tongues' comes from the Holy Spirit, though he thought it better that it should be done at home than when they met for worship. The trouble with speaking in tongues, he says, is that it's wonderful for the person to whom it happens, but it doesn't communicate anything to anyone else.

Prophecy

So he prefers prophecy, says Paul. Now prophecy's an ambiguous word. It can mean foretelling the future, and there were certainly people in the early Church who did that. But Paul is talking about something which happens every Sunday during worship, and surely fortune-telling was not a regular feature of their church life? So he must have been taking the second meaning of the word prophecy. The prophets in the Old Testament, it's often said, were not only in the business of 'foretelling' the future. They were also 'forth-telling' God's view of the present; telling forth what the life of the people looked like to God. So Paul, when he recommends prophecy to the Christians in Corinth, must mean preaching – preaching which helps the congregation to see things from God's point of view. This is better than the other spiritual gifts, he said, because it communicates.

Communication

God wants to communicate with us. Jesus died to save us from sin and death, and to make us better people. But we shouldn't understand what God's doing – we shouldn't be able to benefit from it – unless God communicated with us, to explain it. John's Gospel says that Jesus is the Word of God, because the words of Jesus tell us what God's thinking: God speaks to us through Jesus. But the words of Jesus will never reach us unless someone repeats them and explains them. St Paul asks, 'How shall they believe in him of whom they have not heard? And how shall they hear without a preacher?' The art of communication is a question of taking ideas which are in one person's mind, and putting them into the mind of another. Effective preaching requires understanding what God's thinking, choosing the right words, putting them in the right order, and pronouncing them clearly. Unless the preacher does this, St

Paul asks, 'If the bugle gives an indistinct sound, who will get ready for battle?' That's why he prefers preaching to speaking in tongues: because it communicates.

What is God trying to communicate?

What an amazing idea it is, that God has ideas in his mind which he is desperate to communicate to our minds! It's very humbling to think that he should condescend so. It actually matters to God what we're thinking. God's trying to tell us that he made the universe, that he loves us, that he wants us to live with him for ever. God the Father's telling us that he loves the world so much that he gave Jesus his Son. The death of Jesus is how God forgives us all our sins; his resurrection's how God assures us of eternal life. God's telling us that he wants us to love our neighbours for his sake; this may not be easy, in fact Paul describes it as a battle against the evil in the world and in our own hearts. But God will give us his Holy Spirit to make it possible. If God's trying to communicate all that to us, we should listen with wrapt attention. Preachers must do their best, but no communication will happen unless congregations are prepared to work at their listening. Ask each other questions about the sermon on your way home from church. After all, you're supposed to be preparing yourself for a battle; nobody wants to go into the fight ill prepared because they haven't listened to the orders of the day and the pep-talk.

Suggested hymns

Dear Lord and Father of mankind; Fight the good fight with all thy might; God has spoken to his people, alleluia; Onward Christian soldiers, marching as to war.

Tenth Sunday after Trinity (Proper 14)   12 August
Principal Service   **Treasure in Heaven**
(*Continuous*): Isa. 1:1, 10–20 Sins like scarlet shall be like snow; Ps. 50:1–8, 22–23 God's covenant; *or (Related)*: Gen. 15:1–6 Promise to Abram and his faith; Ps. 33:12–22 Faith in God; Heb. 11:1–3, 8–16 Abraham's faith; Luke 12:32–40 Treasure in heaven

> *'[Jesus said,] "Make purses for yourselves that do not wear out, an unfailing treasure in heaven, where no thief comes near and no*

moth destroys. For where your treasure is, there your heart will be also.'' Luke 12:33–34

A *Punch* cartoon

In the days when people employed servants, there was a cartoon in *Punch* magazine showing a wealthy woman praising her house-maid to the vicar. 'She's an absolute treasure,' she said. 'I do hope when I die she will go to heaven too so that we can be together.' The vicar realized the woman was still expecting to be waited on after she died, so he replied, 'I don't think that's quite what Jesus meant when he spoke of having your treasure in heaven!'

What Jesus meant

What *did* Jesus mean by those words? He said, 'Make purses for yourselves that do not wear out, an unfailing treasure in heaven, where no thief comes near and no moth destroys. For where your treasure is, there your heart will be also.' He was poking gentle fun at the wealthy of his time. The rich people had so many belongings they didn't know where to put them. If they put them in a locked storeroom, the iron things turned rusty and the expensive clothes got moth-eaten. But if they kept their belongings lying round the house, burglars could break in and steal them.

The heavenly balance sheet

Those dangers still exist today. But most people's wealth, if they have any, is invested in stocks and shares today, if only in the indi-rect form of a pension fund. So instead of worrying about moth and rust these days, most wealthy people worry about the stock market, and spend their time studying balance sheets. Maybe Jesus would have said, 'You'd be better off worrying about the heavenly balance sheet.' The Jews believed that this was kept in what they called 'the book of life'. Saint Paul wrote to the Philippians, 'Yes, and I ask you also, my loyal companion, help these women, for they have struggled beside me in the work of the gospel . . . whose names are in the book of life.' And in the Revelation, John writes: 'And I saw the dead, great and small, standing before the throne, and books were opened. Also another book was opened, the book of life. And the dead were judged according to their works, as recorded in the books.' Perhaps it's only a metaphor, but if there is something corresponding to a heavenly balance sheet, we'd do far better to worry about that than the stock market. Fortunately, for Christians, the whole negative balance of sins over good deeds can be written off at a stroke, when we claim the forgiveness of sins brought to us by the death of Jesus on the cross. But we shouldn't presume on God's kindness, or add to Christ's suffering by our continued sinning. Far better to build up a healthy credit balance of little acts of kindness and consideration, to be on the safe side!

Death benefits

There's a joke which in one form runs like this: 'The job of a Christian is unlike any other job: the pay is awful and the hours are appalling, but the retirement benefits are out of this world!' Perhaps that means you never do retire from active Christian service until you die, so that it would be better to call them 'death benefits'. But then people might not get the joke, for few people think of death as a benefit. Yet for the Christian, death *is* a benefit, if we've built up a store of treasure in heaven – a healthy credit balance of good deeds in the book of life. Lay up treasures in heaven. They're safer than equities.

All-age worship

Write down the bad things you have done, or as many as you can remember, and silently tell God you're sorry. Then fold up the paper without showing anybody, put it in a metal bowl and burn it. God has forgiven and forgotten everything that was on the list; now you must forgive yourself and only remember with gratitude how much God has forgiven you.

Suggested hymns

God forgave my sin in Jesus' name (Freely, freely); O Lord of heaven and earth and sea; There is a land of pure delight; When I survey the wondrous cross.

Tenth Sunday after Trinity

Second Service **God's 'Yes'** Ps. 108 Love as high as heaven [116 The cup of salvation]; Isa. 11:10—12:6 Return from exile; 2 Cor. 1:1–22 God's 'Yes'; *Gospel at Holy Communion*: Mark 7.24–30 The foreign mother

> *'The Son of God, Jesus Christ . . . was not "Yes and No"; but in him it is always "Yes." For in him every one of God's promises is a "Yes." For this reason it is through him that we say the "Amen," to the glory of God.' 2 Corinthians 1:19–20*

Childish voices

'Dad, can we go for a walk in the rain?' 'No!'

'Mum, will you buy me an ice-cream?' 'No!'

'Dad, can't I stay up a little longer?' 'No!'

'Mum, is it time to switch on the telly yet?' 'No!'

Some people's recollections of childhood seem to consist of the constant repetition of the word 'No!' How we wished that some-body would say 'Yes' to us sometimes! Now, our relationship with God is usually based on our relationship with our parents. Thank God we usually grow out of those childish misconceptions eventually, but there are many people who still feel that every time they address a question to God they get the answer 'No!'

'God, would you make me rich?' 'No!'

'God, would you take away my sickness?' 'No!'

'God, please can I always be happy?' 'No!'

Perhaps the reason is that we keep on asking the wrong questions. Instead of always demanding instant gratification, we should try asking God what he wants us to do, so that he can help us. You know the story of the man who prayed, 'Give me a break, Lord, let me win the lottery.' God replied, 'Give me a break, son, first go out and buy a ticket!' But it isn't as simple as that. Sometimes God requires a long period of obedience to his wishes before he's able to give us what we asked for. And by that time, we often realize that what we originally asked for wasn't what we really needed, and now we don't want it after all! God sometimes has to answer 'No!', because what we ask for wouldn't be good for us at that particular moment.

Jesus is God's 'Yes!'

What we really need is a change of heart – our own heart, not God's. We need to become ashamed of the times we have disobeyed God's wishes, and to understand what pain it causes him when we do. We need to appreciate that love's more important than possessions. We need to realize how much God loves us. We need to understand that a lifetime of frustration and suffering is far outweighed by the eternal joys of heaven which come as our reward. In a word, what we need is Jesus. Jesus is God's 'Yes' to what we really need. Jesus on the cross shows us, yes, exactly how much our sin hurts God. The simple lifestyle of Jesus, the servant of all, shows us, yes, just how little possessions matter compared with love. Jesus not only tells us that yes, God loves us – he shows it, by laying down his life for us. We stop grumbling about our own life, when we compare it with the life of Jesus. The resurrection of Jesus proves to us that, yes, there is life after death, and it's far more wonderful than we're capable of imagining. Jesus is God's 'Yes' to the questions we haven't even thought of asking yet.

Amen

We usually end our prayers with words something like '. . . through Jesus Christ our Lord. Amen.' 'Amen' is a Hebrew word; the Jewish people use it to end their prayers with, and it means 'truth', or 'may it be so'. Or, in effect, 'Yes, I agree with this prayer.' But when we say 'through Jesus Christ' it means, 'Yes, I think Jesus would agree with this prayer'. Jesus told us to pray in his name, and that probably means always trying to pray prayers that Jesus could say 'Yes' to.

God's promises

The Bible's full of promises. Some Christians keep a 'promise box', full of little slips of paper or card on which they write the verses from the Bible which contain the promises of God. Then they can pull out one card every day, and remind themselves of just what wonderful things God has promised to those who love him. To each of those promises, God in Jesus says 'Yes', he will surely give them to us eventually, when he knows that the time is right. Or, as St Paul put it:

> The Son of God, Jesus Christ . . . was not 'Yes and No'; but in
> him it is always 'Yes.' For in him every one of God's promises is

a 'Yes.' For this reason it is through him that we say the 'Amen,' to the glory of God.

Suggested hymns

Come, my soul, thy suit prepare; God has spoken to his people, alleluia; Lord, thy word abideth; Seek ye first the kingdom of God.

Eleventh Sunday after Trinity (Proper 15)   19 August
Principal Service   Signs of the Times

(*Continuous*): Isa. 5:1–7 The song of the vineyard; Ps. 80:1–2, 9–20 The vine; *or* (*Related*): Jeremiah 23:23–29 The word of God; Ps. 82 Justice; Heb. 11:29—12:2 Faith and perseverance; Luke 12:49–56 Interpreting the time

> *'[Jesus said,] "You hypocrites! You know how to interpret the appearance of earth and sky, but why do you not know how to interpret the present time?"' Luke 12:56*

Weather forecasting

The weather's a national obsession with British people, who never stop talking about it. We religiously check the weather forecast, and from it we decide what to wear when we go out. Some people, however, hang up a piece of seaweed, or rely on folklore: 'Red sky at night, shepherd's delight; red sky in the morning, shepherd's warning.' In Israel the rain clouds always come up from the Mediterranean, and the dry winds from the desert, so Jesus complimented his fellow countrymen on their proficiency at weather-forecasting: 'When you see a cloud rising in the west, you immediately say, "It is going to rain"; and so it happens. And when you see the south wind blowing, you say, "There will be scorching heat"; and it happens.'

But then he challenged them: if they were so knowledgeable about the weather, how come they were completely lacking in common sense about spiritual matters?

Recognizing Jesus

In Studdert-Kennedy's poem, 'When Jesus came to Birmingham', he describes how Jesus wept because the people totally ignored him.

Does God sometimes come to us, in the form of somebody who needs our help, and we give God the brush-off? When there's a chance to do something for Jesus, do we give him the cold shoulder? How many of us could sing, 'I let my golden chances pass me by'? Lots of knowledge, yet spiritually almost blind. How sad! From now on, let's be on the look out, so that we recognize Jesus when he comes to us.

Interpreting politics

But Jesus may have had something else in mind when he said, 'You know how to interpret the appearance of earth and sky, but why do you not know how to interpret the present time?' He lived in a time of political turmoil. His land was occupied by the Romans, who had brought to it a world civilization, good roads and public services, and stability. Yet many Jews thought that only God ought to rule over Israel, and waited for the Lord's Messiah to come and drive the Romans out. There was muttering and sedition. Some Jews encouraged it; others said that politics was nothing to do with them, and if you ignored it, it was sure to go away. Forty years later it would erupt into secret stabbings, what we would today call acts of terrorism, and then open revolt. In AD 70 the Romans would march into Jerusalem and destroy the Temple. It took very little political nous to recognize that this was the way things were going. The revolutionaries should have recognized they were leading their nation to disaster, the people who pretended not to care should have done something to stop the terrorists. How many people today, who think that violence will solve political problems, or who have nothing to do with politics, are equally blind? In the words attributed to Edmund Burke, 'All that is needed for evil to triumph is for good people to do nothing.'

What will future generations think we were blind to?

We often look back on past generations and ask, 'How could they have been so blind?' How could the eighteenth century have ignored the evil of slavery, and the next century the hardships of the children working in the factories? How could the twentieth century have condoned racial discrimination and apartheid? I wonder how future generations will weigh us up, when they look back at us. Will they shake their heads at the widespread dismissal of moral values, and the assumption that anyone can do 'what's good for them', no matter what effect it has on others? Will they be astonished at our assumption that the Church will somehow keep going although the majority of people do nothing to support it? At the way we push God into a marginal position in our lives, an optional extra for those who like that sort of thing? Will people in future ask of us, 'How could they have been so blind?' So good at weather-forecasting, but no spiritual common sense! Perhaps it's time we took a good hard look at ourselves, and decided to do better.

All-age worship

Copy out and enlarge the weather-forecast map from the newspaper. What signs does the weather-forecaster look for to recognize that rain is coming? Are there any signs elsewhere in the newspaper that show what God thinks of the way we live today? Draw some of them.

Suggested hymns

Be still, for the Spirit of the Lord; Jesus, stand among us; O God of earth and altar; O thou who camest from above.

Eleventh Sunday after Trinity
Second Service   **The Foundation Stone**
Ps. 119:17–32 Your decrees are my delight; Isa. 28:9–22 A foundation stone; 2 Cor. 8:1–9 Generosity; *Gospel at Holy Communion*: Matt. 20:1–16 Labourers in the vineyard

> 'Thus says the Lord GOD, See, I am laying in Zion a foundation stone, a tested stone, a precious cornerstone, a sure foundation: "One who trusts will not panic." And I will make justice the line, and righteousness the plummet; hail will sweep away the refuge of lies, and waters will overwhelm the shelter.' Isaiah 28:16–17

Collapse of an orphanage

In Saigon in 1969 a Christian orphanage collapsed, killing all the children inside it. It only merited a small paragraph in the papers, which were full of the news of the war in Vietnam. But it turned out that the contractor who built the orphanage thought he'd save money on the foundations, and in a heavy storm the foundations were washed away and the building collapsed, with the loss of dozens of innocent lives. Foundations are the last thing we should skimp on.

Isaiah's foundation stone

In a modern building, the foundation stone is often purely decorative, with a carved inscription to indicate that some VIP has been present to lend kudos to the building project. But in ancient times the foundation stone was the first one to be laid, providing a firm base that will guarantee the stability of the whole structure. The prophet Isaiah uses this picture to criticize the basis on which the life of the nation was being erected:

> Thus says the Lord GOD, See, I am laying in Zion a foundation stone, a tested stone, a precious cornerstone, a sure foundation: 'One who trusts will not panic.' And I will make justice the line, and righteousness the plummet; hail will sweep away the refuge of lies, and waters will overwhelm the shelter.

They thought they could do everything themselves, and had no need of faith. But without faith in God, says Isaiah, troubled times lead to panic. Even those who've never watched *Dad's Army* know about Corporal Jones and the unexploded bomb, when he rushed around shouting, 'Don't panic, don't panic!' In this way he wound himself up into such a state of panic that he was of no practical use to anyone. But if you build your nation on the foundation stone of trust in God, then even when things are going badly, you'll have no need to panic.

The house on the rock

Maybe Jesus was thinking of this passage from Isaiah when he told the parable about the house built on the rock. You remember how the house built on sandy soil collapsed when the rains came and the floods rose, but the house built on the firm foundation of the bedrock lying below the surface of the ground withstood everything. Jesus, like Isaiah, was challenging us to look at the foundations of our lives. If we construct our lives on the basis of faith in God and obedience to his word we shall stand firm, no matter what troubles come our way. As Mother Julian of Norwich put it, 'God did not say, Thou shalt not be tempested, thou shalt not be travailed, thou shalt not be afflicted; but he said: Thou shalt not be overcome.'

The cornerstone

The first stone in the foundation was often laid at the corner of the building, to define its layout. So in Psalm 118 there's an oft-quoted verse: 'The stone that the builders rejected has become the chief cornerstone.' Jesus cites it at the end of the parable of the Wicked Tenants. St Peter applied it to Jesus himself: 'This Jesus is "the stone that was rejected by you, the builders; it has become the cornerstone."'

Living stones

Peter says that the Christian Church is a temple, with Jesus as the foundation stone:

> Come to him, a living stone, though rejected by mortals yet chosen and precious in God's sight, and like living stones, let yourselves be built into a spiritual house, to be a holy priesthood, to offer spiritual sacrifices acceptable to God through Jesus Christ. For it stands in scripture: 'See, I am laying in Zion a stone, a cornerstone chosen and precious; and whoever believes in him will not be put to shame.'

St Paul writes:

> So then you are no longer strangers and aliens, but you are citizens with the saints and also members of the household of God, built upon the foundation of the apostles and prophets, with Christ Jesus himself as the cornerstone. In him the whole structure is joined together and grows into a holy temple in the Lord; in whom you also are built together spiritually into a dwelling place for God.

Each one of us has a role to play in God's plan for the world, provided we're prepared to accept the place he gives us, to co-operate with others, and make our faith in Jesus the foundation of our lives.

Suggested hymns

Christ is made the sure foundation/Blessed city, heavenly Salem; City of God, how broad and far; How sweet the name of Jesus sounds; Ye that know the Lord is gracious.

Twelfth Sunday after Trinity (Proper 16)   26 August
Principal Service   Healing on the Sabbath

(*Continuous*): Jer. 1:4–10 Jeremiah's call; Ps. 71:1–6 Be a stronghold; or (*Related*): Isa. 58:9b–14 Care for the needy; Ps. 103:1–8 The Lord forgives and heals; Heb. 12:18–29 The mediator of a new covenant; Luke 13:10–17 Healing on the Sabbath

> *'[Jesus asked them,] "Ought not this woman, a daughter of Abraham whom Satan bound for eighteen long years, be set free from this bondage on the Sabbath day?"' Luke 13:16*

An admirable rabbi

A church magazine misspelled the word 'rabies', saying that the Christian minister 'was taking his dog to be inoculated against rabbis'. But when the same group met their local rabbi, they found he was a lovable and admirable person. He sang his Sabbath prayers with sincere devotion, and he spent long hours studying the Scriptures. He told the story of Rabbi Akiba, who lived between AD 40 and 135, and was asked if he could recite the whole Law of Moses while standing on one leg. 'Certainly,' replied Akiba. 'Love God, and love your neighbour as yourself' – the same answer that Jesus had given when asked to summarize the Law. But when it came to the Sabbath laws, the Christians didn't know what to think of their local rabbi. 'I mustn't travel on the Sabbath; I mustn't light a fire; I mustn't switch on the light or drive a car because both of those involve making fire; I mustn't carry a burden. Even if it's only a piece of paper, I mustn't carry it from one room to another,' he said. Such conscientious care in carrying out the perceived will of God is surely admirable. But is this really what God wants, asked the Christians? Probably it was loyalty to the Law which formed the Jews into a people and enabled them to survive for thousands of years as a people. But doesn't such meticulous attention to detail, they wondered, distract us from the love which Akiba and Jesus spoke about?

The ruler of the synagogue

Jesus obviously came up against some very narrow and scrupulous Jews. Jesus healed a sick woman on the Sabbath day. We read:

> The leader of the synagogue, indignant because Jesus had cured on the Sabbath, kept saying to the crowd, 'There are six days on which work ought to be done; come on those days and be cured, and not on the Sabbath day.'

The implied criticism of Jesus was obvious.

Fulfilling the Law

Jesus said, 'Don't think that I've come to abolish the law or the prophets; I've come not to abolish but to fulfil.' The devotion which many Jews show to the Law of the Hebrew Scriptures is surely admirable; we have a lot to learn from them in carefully seeking and following God's will. But we must be careful never to lose sight of love, which is at the heart of morality. Jesus told us, 'Unless your righteousness exceeds that of the scribes and Pharisees, you'll never enter the kingdom of heaven.' We must be more meticulous in applying love to every situation and choice that face us than any Jew is in applying the Law. There can be no room for criticism or anti-Semitism. Christianity's not an easy option; it's more demanding than Judaism.

The gospel of release

When Jesus healed a crippled woman on the Sabbath day, he was declaring that love doesn't fall short of law, love goes beyond law. Jesus obviously saw sickness as bondage and healing as release. So when Jesus commanded us to heal, this included medical work, but it went beyond it. Many people are already crippled by a burden of guilt, struggling to live up to some code of behaviour, often self-imposed. The Christian isn't to make them feel more guilty, by binding yet more rules and regulations on their backs. We're to proclaim the gospel of release from the guilt of sin. Many people are crippled by sinful habits which they think they can't break. We are to proclaim that the power of the Holy Spirit can overcome sinful habits, changing and reinvigorating our crippled lives. The gospel of release is good news to all of us. We don't need inoculation against rabbis, we need to imitate them in their devotion to God, and to strive towards ever greater care for those who are oppressed.

All-age worship

Make a list of sick people you know or know of. Write some prayers to say for them. Use these prayers in the all-age worship, without mentioning any names unless you have permission to do so.

Suggested hymns

Dear Lord and Father of mankind; This is the day, this is the day; This is the day the Lord has made; Immortal love, for ever full.

Twelfth Sunday after Trinity
Second Service **Conscience** Ps. 119:49–72 I was humbled that I might learn; Isa. 30:8–21 This is the way; 2 Cor. 9 A collection; *Gospel at Holy Communion*: Matt. 21:28–32 The two sons

> *'When you turn to the right or when you turn to the left, your ears shall hear a word behind you, saying, "This is the way; walk in it."'*
> *Isaiah 30:21*

Condemned by his conscience

> My conscience hath a thousand several tongues,
> And every tongue brings in a several tale,
> And every tale condemns me for a villain.

So says the king in Shakespeare's play *Richard III*. He's not the only person to have known the nagging of a guilty conscience. Most people only realize they have a conscience when it begins to torment them. Then they try to persuade themselves that they're innocent, but they know perfectly well that they aren't, and at every turn they are met by a voice coming from somewhere inside them telling them that they've committed a sin.

A voice behind you

The prophet Isaiah talks about a voice, which many readers have taken to refer to the conscience: 'When you turn to the right or when you turn to the left, your ears shall hear a word behind you, saying, "This is the way; walk in it."' But unfortunately our consciences never tell us what to do, much as we wish they would. The job of the conscience is to condemn us when we've done wrong. The 'voice' which Isaiah refers to is not conscience but 'Your Teacher', and Christians will understand this to be a reference to Jesus. Jesus told us the way to live, and demonstrated it in his own life. But he only pointed out the way to go, he didn't give us a detailed road map with every turning plotted and described, 'Turn left at the Dog and Duck' and so on. Still, if we read the words of Jesus in the Gospels and commit them to memory, they'll act as a constant reminder of the voice of Jesus. It's a good idea to try to memorize a verse a day, with its reference, like this: 'Matthew seven, verse one: Do not judge, so that you may not be judged.' Say it a few times at the beginning of the day, and repeat it at odd moments, and you'll build up quite a treasure-store of quotations. Then they'll serve you as 'a word behind you, saying, "This is the way; walk in it"'; and the voice will be the voice of Jesus.

Prisoners of conscience

The voice of our conscience can be a very positive thing, too. 'Liberty of conscience' is the freedom to do what you believe to be right, without any compulsion to do what you think is wrong. If this liberty's taken away, then you get 'prisoners of conscience', the modern martyrs who spend years in prisons or prison camps because they've had the temerity to speak out for what they believe to be the truth. Amnesty International has a long list of prisoners of conscience who are languishing in stinking jails today, and you'd be surprised at the outwardly respectable countries where this sort of thing happens on a daily basis. We should always remember the prisoners of conscience in our prayers.

Conscience must be followed

In the old days there was a carefully worked-out science of how you apply moral principles to particular cases; it's rather fallen into disrepute these days. But one law that the moral theologians taught can still be applied today: 'Conscience must always be followed.' If your inner voice tells you it's wrong to do something, you shouldn't do it.

Conscience must be educated

But there's a consequence of this rule that people sometimes forget. 'Conscience must always be followed; and conscience must always be educated.' Your own inner feelings don't automatically tell you what's right and what's wrong. Very often the inner voice is that of your own prejudices. The person who refuses to think logically about their behaviour is a menace: 'My mind's made up,' they say, 'don't confuse me with facts.' But we need facts if we're to behave ethically, and then we need to think carefully about the consequences of our actions.

What tells you?

So the job of the conscience is not to help you make up your mind what to do. The words of Jesus, the advice of others, the experience of the past and the calculation of future consequences of your action provide that sort of guidance. When we've already worked out what's right and what's wrong, then conscience is what torments us when we do what we already know to be wrong. Hamlet decides he's not brave enough to face death if it leads to an eternity of regret, and he laments, 'Thus conscience doth make cowards of us all.' And a good thing too, if it stops us doing wrong, from fear that our conscience will condemn us.

Suggested hymns

Breathe on me, breath of God; I want to walk with Jesus Christ; O Jesus, I have promised; Our blest Redeemer, ere he breathed.

Thirteenth Sunday after Trinity (Proper 17)
2 September

Principal Service **Status** (*Continuous*): Jer. 2:4–13 Living water; Ps. 81:1, 10–16 God's justice; *or* (*Related*): Ecclus. 10:12–18 Pride and judgement; *or* Prov. 25:6–7 Pride and humility; Ps. 112 Righteousness; Heb. 13:1–8, 15–16 Righteousness; Luke 14:1, 7–14 Pride and humility

> *'[Jesus said,] "When you are invited, go and sit down at the lowest place, so that when your host comes, he may say to you, 'Friend, move up higher'; then you will be honoured in the presence of all who sit at the table with you."' Luke 14:10*

Status symbols

A satirical song by Michael Flanders and Donald Swann began

> Playing on the status symbols, laying out the ready cash
> bigger, better, newer, smarter, hear the status cymbals clash

and continued with many examples of not only 'keeping up with the Joneses' but making it clear that you are better than they are:

> 'My car horn goes ah-ee, ah-ee,
> your car horn goes hoot, hoot, hoot.'
> 'I've just bought a Mini Cooper.'
> 'Oh yes, I've got one in my boot!'

That sort of social one-up-manship didn't end in the 1960s when that song was recorded; it's with us still. If it isn't having a bigger car or a smarter house than your neighbours, it's measured by the number of square feet of carpet in your office.

Being admired

Let's face it, for many people, being admired by those around them is the most important thing in life. Hence our obsession with status. But Jesus would have none of this. He asked, 'How can you believe, when you accept glory from one another and don't seek the glory that comes from the one who alone is God?' And in another place, Jesus said to his disciples:

> 'You know that among the Gentiles those whom they recognize as their rulers lord it over them, and their great ones are tyrants over

them. But it's not so among you; but whoever wishes to become great among you must be your servant, and whoever wishes to be first among you must be slave of all.'

Life in the kingdom is the very opposite of the scramble for status that characterizes the rat race. St Paul writes to the Christians at Philippi:

> Let the same mind be in you that was in Christ Jesus, who, though he was in the form of God, did not regard equality with God as something to be exploited, but emptied himself, taking the form of a slave, being born in human likeness. And being found in human form, he humbled himself and became obedient to the point of death – even death on a cross.

Pride before a fall

So Jesus tells a story. Like many parables, it's told to make us laugh. But then suddenly we realize we're laughing at ourselves. The guests at a banquet were probably arranged in a U-shape, with the most important guests reclining to the left and right of the host. So the story tells of a self-important man who was invited to a banquet, and immediately he arrives, without asking anybody, he goes straight to the most important place. But no sooner is he settled, than another guest arrives who's more important than he is, and he has to give up his place to the newcomer. There's no more room at the top table, so blushing scarlet with embarrassment, he has to move down and sit with the less important guests, while everybody laughs at him. How humiliating! How shameful! But then, how well deserved. Pride comes before a fall.

Humility

So we need to cultivate the grace of humility. It's not the hand-wringing humility of Dickens's Uriah Heep: 'I'm a very 'umble man, Mr Copperfield.' It's a realistic facing of our place in God's plan for the world. We may have a very important role to play, but none of us is indispensable. 'By the grace given to me,' says St Paul, 'I say to everyone among you not to think of yourself more highly than you ought to think, but to think with sober judgment, each according to the measure of faith that God has assigned.' 'Be kindly affectioned one to another with brotherly love; in honour preferring one another.' It's like the recommendation to a shy person at a party: 'Try to find out as much as you can about the other people who're there. Then by concentrating on others and forgetting about yourself, you'll soon lose your shyness.' In life in general, if you concentrate your attention on other people, you'll soon stop worrying about your own status. After all, you have, each one of you, the status of a forgiven sinner, destined for heaven. There's no higher status than that.

All-age worship

Make a seating plan for a banquet in heaven. Mark the places nearest Jesus, 'For the really humble people', and the ones furthest from him, 'Reserved for the proud'.

Suggested hymns

From heaven you came, helpless babe (The Servant King); Gentle Jesus, meek and mild; Just as I am, without one plea; Tell out, my soul, the greatness of the Lord.

Thirteenth Sunday after Trinity
Second Service   **I Must Decrease** Ps. 119:81–96 Like a wineskin in the smoke; Isa. 33:13–22 To see the king in his beauty; John 3:22–36 I must decrease

'"He must increase, but I must decrease."' John 3:30

The readings at this service contain three remarkable images: the wineskin in the smoke; seeing the king in his beauty; and John the Baptist voluntarily decreasing his influence to make way for Jesus.

Wineskins

Wineskins are leather bottles. In ancient times glass was a rare luxury, so glass bottles were only used for perfume. Wine was transported in pottery amphora. But for household use, it was kept in a leather bottle made from the skin of a goat. When it was new, the leather was flexible and would swell with the pressure built up by continued fermentation of the wine. But when the wineskin was old, the leather was dry and brittle, and would split if new wine was put in it. That's why Jesus said that his bubbly new teaching was like new wine; it would burst the rigid containers of the old orthodoxies, and needed a new type of mind and a new type of society: you can't put new wine into old bottles, he said.

The wineskin in the smoke

Psalm 119 is a hymn of praise to God's law. Each of its 176 verses contains one of the words meaning law: commandments, instruction, word, and so on. It's arranged in groups of eight verses, and each verse in the group begins with the same letter of the Hebrew alphabet. The author longed for the time when God would impose the rule of law over all the earth, to bring injustices to an end: 'My soul is pining for your salvation,' he wrote. But that day seemed an awful long time a-coming. In the meantime he felt dried up and withered with disillusionment and despair about human society. So he uses the first of our three vivid images; he writes, 'I have become like a wineskin in the smoke.' A leather bottle, hung up over the fireplace, or in a smoky room, dries out and becomes brittle. So he felt that all hope had evaporated out of him.

Seeing the king in his beauty

Isaiah also longed for the kingdom of God. His land was being attacked by enemies, but one day, he believed, God would bestir himself and rescue them. Then the righteous, those who had refused to accept bribes, will dwell at peace in the land. Then, says Isaiah, 'Your eyes will see the king in his beauty.' The kings of Israel were regarded as God's representatives, so this is a dream of the day when the Messiah would sit on the throne of Israel and rule the land with justice. What a beautiful sight that would be! But Christians know that the Messiah came in an unexpected way, not like a king at all. Now, however, Jesus reigns in heaven, and one day, Christians believe, we shall go to heaven and see him there. If we come close to the invisible God in our prayers, then one day, if not in this life then in the life to come, our 'eyes shall see the king in his beauty'.

'He must increase, but I must decrease'

Finally, we come to the remarkable words of John the Baptist. John had built up a loyal following. People were flocking into the wilderness to hear him and be baptized. He was well on the way to forming a new People of God, membership in which was by choice, not by heredity. He could have gone on to be a popular Messiah, if he'd wanted to. But instead he humbly stepped back and let his cousin, Jesus of Nazareth, take his place. 'He must increase, but I must decrease', said John. There's only room for one Messiah, and if Jesus is to grow in influence, John must shrink in importance to make way for him.

Sacrifices for the kingdom

In their different ways, the Psalmist, Isaiah and John the Baptist hoped for the kingdom of God to come. But each knew that it would not come without some sacrifices on their part. The author of Psalm 119 must go through a dark night of the soul before he sees his hope fulfilled; he feels like a wineskin in the smoke. Isaiah knows that his nation will be attacked many times by their enemies before he can see the king in his beauty. John the Baptist has to step out of the limelight so that Jesus can take his place. For each of us, too, there are sacrifices to make; maybe we shan't know what they are until the time comes to make them. But if we reject the easy path of selfishness and corruption, the day will come when we shall enjoy the vision of God in his heavenly kingdom.

Suggested hymns

Immortal, invisible, God only wise; My God, how wonderful thou art; O thou who camest from above; Soon and very soon, we are going to see the king.

Fourteenth Sunday after Trinity (Proper 18)
9 September
Principal Service   **The Runaway Slave** (*Continuous*): Jer. 18:1–11 The potter; Ps. 139:1–6, 13–18 God knows us; *or* (*Related*): Deut. 30:15–20 Choose life; Ps. 1 Righteousness; Philemon 1–21 The runaway slave; Luke 14:25–33 The call to take up the cross

> *'Perhaps this is the reason [your slave] was separated from you for a while, so that you might have him back forever, no longer as a slave but more than a slave, a beloved brother.' Philemon 15–16*

The slave called 'Useful'

He was a friend of St Paul, and his name, though it looks like 'WUN-see-muss', was pronounced 'o-NEE-simm-muss'. Onesimus was a slave. His name means 'useful'. And that's a dead giveaway. He was called 'useful' because he was a good slave. But that can't have been the name his mother called him by when he was a tot. So he no longer had any individual personality left. He wasn't a person whom his mother loved. He was merely a slave who was useful to his master. Some slaves were treated abominably; others were raised to quite high positions. But because they were slaves, they were somebody else's property, and they had no say in their own future at all. Onesimus was the property of a slave-owner called FILL-ee-monn or fie-LEE-monn, whichever you prefer. He lived in what we now know as Turkey, in a town called Laodicea. We know from the Book of Revelation that it was famous for its lukewarm water, which people drank and bathed in for their health. Maybe Philemon owned a bathing establishment, and Onesimus had one of the unpleasant jobs cleaning up at the end of the day. So Onesimus ran away, which was stealing his owner's property – himself! His owner could pursue him to the ends of the earth, and flog him to death if he chose to. The slave wasn't a person, just a piece of property, and had no rights under the law.

Going to St Paul

The only thing the runaway could do was find one of his owner's friends, and ask him to mediate. Onesimus had heard his master talking of a man called Paul. So Onesimus ran all the way from Turkey to Rome to find him. When he met St Paul, he found that he was at present a prisoner – he had even less freedom than Onesimus had. But Paul didn't regard the slave as a piece of property. Paul told him that he was actually a person, beloved by God! Amazing! So he joined the apostle Paul's religion and became a Christian.

The Letter to Philemon

What was Paul to do now? He couldn't keep the runaway slave; that would have been stealing another man's property. He couldn't hand him over to receive a flogging. So he wrote a very diplomatic letter. It's the shortest book in our New Testament, only one chapter, called Paul's Letter to Philemon. He starts off by praising Philemon;

it was essential for Paul to get Philemon on his side to begin with. Then he suggested that Philemon owed his life to Paul – his spiritual life, because Paul had told Philemon about Jesus, and so he'd received eternal life. Now, Paul was going to call in the debt. He wanted Philemon to welcome Onesimus back, not as a useful slave, but as a Christian brother. 'Now just a moment,' thought Philemon. 'Welcome him? Welcome my property as a brother? That's not the way we slave-owners behave with what's ours! If you treat everybody as equal in the sight of God, where's it going to end? It'll mean the abolition of slavery, you mark my words. Who ever heard of such a thing!'

A biblical time bomb

So Paul had set a time bomb. A biblical time bomb. It didn't go off for 1900 years. But it meant exactly what Philemon was afraid it meant: the abolition of slavery, and the equality of every child of God. Why didn't Paul just say so? Probably because the people of his time weren't ready to hear it, and he had no interest in starting a revolution. But the time bomb exploded eventually, and slavery was abolished as a result of Paul's Letter to Philemon.

Counting the cost

Have we counted the cost of discipleship? Do we understand how much we have to give up, if we want to be followers of Jesus? Philemon had to give up his slave, but he also had to give up one of the foundation principles of his life: the idea that one person can own property in another human being. What priorities or prejudices does Jesus call you to give up?

All-age worship

Try making a jar, either with clay on a wheel or using plasticine. If it's not right, what would you do? Jeremiah says the potter has the right to squash the clay flat and make a new jar. God made us, so we can't complain if it's painful while he remakes us when we go wrong.

Suggested hymns

O God of earth and altar; Once to every man and nation; Take my life, and let it be; The kingdom of God is justice and joy.

Fourteenth Sunday after Trinity

Second Service   **I Lift My Eyes** Ps. [120 Deliver me] 121 I lift
my eyes; Isaiah 43:14—44:5 A new thing; John 5:30–47 You search
the Scriptures

*'I lift up my eyes to the hills – from where will my help come? My
help comes from the LORD, who made heaven and earth.' Psalm
121:1–2*

Tao Fong Shan

Among the mountains north of Hong Kong there's a valley, and
as you walk up the valley and lift up your eyes, you see a building
in Chinese style near the summit of one of the mountains. It's in
fact a Protestant mission, founded by a Norwegian Lutheran, Dr
Karl Reichelt, in 1930, but it was built in the style of a Buddhist
monastery. This way, he hoped it would attract Buddhist monks
from all over China who wanted to find out about Jesus. In
familiar surroundings they could 'search the Scriptures', meaning the Christian Bible, meditate and ask questions. There was no
aggressive evangelism, but many of the monks responded to this
gentle approach and became Christians. They couldn't return to
their monasteries, so they supported themselves by painting Bible
stories in Chinese style, on scrolls or plates, and selling them to
visitors. The name of the mission is Tao Fong Shan, which means
The Mountain of the Spiritual Way. Their favourite subject for
painting was Psalm 121:

> I will lift up mine eyes unto the hills
> from whence cometh my help.

That's the Coverdale translation found in the Book of Common
Prayer, which has become one of the most familiar phrases in
the English language. I'll talk about the modern translations in a
moment.

Steady as a rock

The reason those words are so popular, I suppose, is because so
many people feel threatened by what a famous prayer calls 'the
changes and chances of this mortal life'. They long for something

unchanging and settled, something they can depend upon and rest on in life. Among all the shifting sands of this world, the mountains rise up, unchanged for generations, and, as we say, 'steady as a rock'. So people turn to Jesus Christ, 'the same yesterday, today and for ever', to find security. The unchanging God is compared to the solid mass of the mountains: a few psalms further on we find the words:

> As the mountains surround Jerusalem,
> so the LORD surrounds his people,
> from this time on and for evermore.

The message of the Bible, which the Buddhist monks found in their meditation, is that God's utterly dependable; you can rely on the Lord Jesus to take care of you in all circumstances. When life gets a bit scary, that's nice to know.

The hills of the robbers

The modern translations of the Bible, however, translate our text as a question:

> I lift up my eyes to the hills –
> from where will my help come?

This doesn't change the meaning of the passage, just reinterprets it. Scholars have learnt a lot more about the Hebrew language since Coverdale's time. They now believe that, although it's still God's protection and dependability that is being emphasized, the metaphor of the hills is part of the threat. They were known as 'the hills of the robbers', and you needed courage to travel through the mountains. The psalm asks where we're to find help in times of danger. The answer is the same as in the old translations: 'My help comes from the LORD, who made heaven and earth.'

Words of inspiration

The rest of the psalm continues the theme of God's protection:

> He who keeps Israel will neither slumber nor sleep.
> The LORD is your keeper; the LORD is your shade at your right
>   hand.

The sun shall not strike you by day, nor the moon by night.
The LORD will keep you from all evil; he will keep your life.
The LORD will keep your going out and your coming in
from this time on and for evermore.

These have inspired several great musical settings. The Scottish metrical version sings,

I to the hills will lift mine eyes; from whence doth come mine aid?

The wonderful music of Mendelssohn's *Elijah* soars to the words,

He, watching over Israel, slumbers not nor sleeps.

And one of the loveliest of the modern hymns has a delightful melody, by Bishop Michael Baughen, to the words by Bishop Timothy Dudley-Smith:

I lift my eyes to the quiet hills
in the press of a busy day;
as green hills stand
in a dusty land
so God is my strength and stay.

Those Buddhist monks who referred to the Christian God as 'The Mountain of the Spiritual Way' knew a thing or two. God's dependable protection is good news indeed.

Suggested hymns

God is our strength and refuge; I lift mine eyes to the quiet hills; I to the hills will lift mine eyes; O strength and stay, upholding all creation.

(If you want to find out more about Tao Fong Shan, see www.tfssu. org)

Fifteenth Sunday after Trinity (Proper 19)

16 September

Principal Service   **Lost Sheep** (*Continuous*): Jer. 4:11–12, 22–28 Judgement; Ps. 14 The fool has said; *or* (*Related*): Ex. 32:7–14 The golden calf and a prayer for forgiveness; Ps. 51:1–10 Prayer for forgiveness; 1 Tim. 1:12–17 Christ brings salvation; Luke 15:1–10 A lost sheep, a woman's lost coin, forgiveness

> '[Jesus said,] "Just so, I tell you, there will be more joy in heaven over one sinner who repents than over ninety-nine righteous persons who need no repentance."' Luke 15:7

A lost sheep

In the parable of the Lost Sheep, Jesus tells the story of a shepherd who has a hundred sheep, and is pasturing them on the scant grass in the area known as 'the wilderness'. Most sheep move together as a crowd. But one of the flock goes off on its own, and gets lost in one of the perilous gorges. It was stuck. It couldn't do anything except bleat. The shepherd counted his flock and found one missing; then he heard its cries. 'In that situation,' asked Jesus, 'what would you do?' 'Cut your losses and let it die,' most would answer. You have to accept some losses in any business. If you abandoned the 99 other sheep in the wilderness, they might stray, and a wolf might eat the lot. Common sense tells you to leave the lost sheep to its fate. But shepherds who spend all their time with the sheep, get to know the sheep as individual characters. The sheep become almost like family to the good shepherd. So the good shepherd would risk all to rescue the one lost sheep, because he cares for it. Then he carries it home over his shoulders, and calls his friends and neighbours to rejoice with him. He's won back the lost sheep.

The Whiffenpoof Song

Perhaps it's because judgemental preachers have over-used the image of the lost sheep that people like to ridicule it. Or perhaps it's to avoid the challenge of the parable. In the 1952 film *The Road to Bali*, Bing Crosby and Bob Hope find they've no money to pay for the meal they've just eaten. They overhear others in the restaurant talking about Yale University, so they sing a song called 'The Whiffenpoof Song', which is a Yale University anthem. The others are deceived into thinking that Bing and Bob are fellow alumni, and pay for their meal. The Whiffenpoofs were a male chorus founded at Yale in 1909, and their anthem, based on a poem by Rudyard Kipling, runs like this:

> We're poor little lambs who have lost our way,
> Baa, baa, baa.
> We're little black sheep who have gone astray,
> Baa, baa, baa.
> Gentlemen songsters off on a spree,
> Doomed from here to eternity,
> Lord have mercy on such as we,
> Baa, baa, baa!

The parable of the Lost Sheep says something quite extraordinary about God's attitude to sinners: God doesn't condemn them; God loves them.

Forgiven sinners

There were two sorts of people in Jesus's time: the Pharisees, who kept the laws of the Old Testament; and the rest, who'd given up trying. The Pharisees called them, in a voice filled with disgust and contempt, 'the sinners'. But they were decent people on the whole. Jesus enjoyed going to parties with them. He told them about a God who doesn't reject people when they slip up, but comes in search of them, trying to win them back to become his friends, because he loves them. So pleased is God when even one so-called 'sinner' decides to reform, that heaven joins in a great triumphal shout.

You bring pleasure to God

The parable describes a God who loves sinners more than he loves respectable people, 'who need no repentance'. Because, in fact, everybody needs to repent, because 'all have sinned and fall short of' God's all-embracing love. The respectable Pharisees didn't realize how narrow and unloving they were, so they never saw the need for them to repent. Every one of us needs to repent, on a daily basis, because we daily fall short of the love and tolerance shown by Jesus. And each time you repent, you bring pleasure to God. Have you ever thought of that? Whenever you turn to God and say, 'I'm sorry, I'll try to do better next time', then a broad grin of happiness spreads across God's face, and all the angels and the souls of the faithful departed join in a great whoop of joy. And it's all because of you!

All-age worship

Make a 'flannelgraph' of the parable of the Lost Sheep. You'll need a fluffy background, e.g. flannelette, with the same (or Velcro) on the back of the paper cut-out figures to make them stick to the background. Cotton-wool sheep will stick to the flannel anyway, but the lost sheep must be thin enough to fit over the shepherd's shoulders.

Suggested hymns

I cannot tell why he, whom angels worship; Loving Shepherd of thy sheep; The king of love my shepherd is; There were ninety and nine.

Fifteenth Sunday after Trinity
Second Service   **The Open Church** Ps. 124 If the Lord were not on our side, 125 Those who trust in the Lord; Isa. 60 Arise, shine; John 6:51–69 I am the living bread

> *'Your gates shall always be open; day and night they shall not be shut, so that nations shall bring you their wealth, with their kings led in procession.' Isaiah 60:11*

The new Jerusalem

Isaiah dreams of a new Jerusalem. The Old City of his day was full of soldiers and corrupted by trade. It's not much different today. Isaiah dreamt of a day when Jerusalem would 'Arise and shine, for your light has come.' When God returns to Jerusalem and rebuilds it, then

> Nations shall come to your light,
> and kings to the brightness of your dawn . . .
> so that nations shall bring you their wealth.

Foreigners are to share in the blessings of what the Jews have learnt about God, and are to bring the wealth of their cultures into the worship of the Jewish God. There's no room for nationalism here. This picture is taken up in the Book of Revelation, where the New Jerusalem comes down from God.

> The nations will walk by its light,
> and the kings of the earth will bring their glory into it.
> Its gates will never be shut by day –
> and there will be no night there.
> People will bring into it the glory and the honour of the nations.

In the New Testament the New Jerusalem represents the Christian Church, with open gates, *as it should be*.

Cultures

Few today would dare to suggest that God prefers one race over another. But there is an unspoken assumption that the way *we* do Christianity is the right way. Yet God has allowed many different cultures to arise in the world, and in the Church. If some Americans choose to accompany their singing with electric guitars and some Indians with sitars, and some African Christians choose to dance their way for joy from village to village, that's no more wrong or right than pointed arches and *Hymns Ancient and Modern*. It's just different. If only we could recognize that our customs, like the others, are just different cultures which have grown up over time, we might become more tolerant. The gates of the New Jerusalem are never to be shut; and the Church must always be open to admit new cultures.

Class

The vision of the New Jerusalem, with its open gates, is a vision of an open Church: open to different cultures, different classes, open to change, open to castaways. Society may be less class-divided than it was, but there are still some who don't want to meet and get to know those who are 'not one of us'. Yet if the Church is being what it ought to be, all the classes of society ought to meet on equal terms as Christian brothers and sisters on Sundays. During the Vietnam war, outside a church one soldier was heard calling to another, 'You're going my way, Fred – like a ride in my Jeep?' The chaplain turned round to see that a General was speaking to a GI – in the Lord's house they were all equal.

Change

The Church should be open to change. The gospel doesn't change; nor does the faith once delivered to the saints. But the way Christians express the gospel is bound to change from century to century, that we may 'by all means win some people'. God called us to love him with all our minds, and promised that the Holy Spirit would lead us into new truths, or new understandings of the old truths. The Church can't do this if it keeps its gates closed to all possibility of change. A bishop said to a churchwarden, 'You must have seen a lot of changes in your church during your years as warden.' 'Yes, bishop,' growled the churchwarden, 'and I've resisted every one of them.'

Castaways

'New occasions teach new duties,' and the Church is constantly discovering new opportunities of service to others, and new groups it needs to serve. There are always people who are castaways: those who are outcasts from society, those whom respectable people won't be seen talking to. It's on them we should be focusing our message of God's all-embracing love, just as Jesus did to the outcasts of his day. In his time it was the prostitutes and tax-collectors who needed his love. In our time should we be adding those who are gay, divorced or suffering from AIDS to that list, and opening the doors of our church to any of them who feel excluded? Who else can you think of?

The wealth of the nations

If the Church is even to begin to approximate to the New Jerusalem it must have gates which are open at all times. It must be an open Church; open to all cultures, classes, changes and castaways. Isaiah pictures the nations bringing their wealth into the New Jerusalem. When you find a congregation which is truly open – open to what different sorts of people can bring into its common life – don't you feel it's incredibly rich?

Suggested hymns

Glorious things of thee are spoken; Once to every man and nation; O worship the Lord in the beauty of holiness; Thy kingdom come, O God.

Sixteenth Sunday after Trinity (Proper 20)
23 September

Principal Service   **The Shrewd Manager**

(*Continuous*): Jer. 8:18—9:1 Balm in Gilead, healing the nation;
Ps. 79:1–9 Suffering, prayer for forgiveness; *or* (*Related*):
Amos 8:4–7 The needy; Psalm 113 The needy; 1 Tim. 2:1–7 Those in
authority; Luke 16:1–13 The shrewd manager

> *'[Jesus said,] "His master commended the dishonest manager because he had acted shrewdly; for the children of this age are more shrewd in dealing with their own generation than are the children of light. And I tell you, make friends for yourselves by means of dishonest wealth so that when it is gone, they may welcome you into the eternal homes."' Luke 16:8–9*

Absentee landlords

Absentee landlords are the curse of the economy in many nations today. We're talking about people who buy up agricultural land, often at knock-down prices, make no investment in drainage, irrigation or fertilizers, but charge an extortionate rent to their tenants who do the actual work in the fields. The tenants often become deeply in debt to the landlords, and are trapped in a no-win, no-escape situation of near starvation. The Americans are often criticized for what they did in Vietnam, but one of their projects was an astonishingly socialist programme of land reform. This involved surveying the whole country by aerial photographs, and registering on a computer the title deeds for each field in the name of the peasants who were actually digging that field. It was called the 'Land to the Tiller' programme. There was a similar problem in Jesus's day, and nobody proposed introducing land reform then. Much of the agricultural land was in the hands of absentee landlords, who employed a manager, steward or land agent to supervise the tenants who worked in the fields. Jesus told a parable about one of these managers, who was a very shrewd man.

I cannot dig, to beg I am ashamed

The absentee landlord suspected his manager of cheating over the payments he sent him. The landlords were so hated in Jesus's time that most people wouldn't blame a manager who fiddled the books as far as he dared, for the sake of the tenants. But this one had been caught out, and was told to submit his accounts before he got the sack. How was he to earn his living from now on? In the memorable words of the Authorized Version, he said to himself, 'I cannot dig, to beg I am ashamed!' So the shrewd manager encouraged each of the tenants who owed money to the landlord to make new receipts with much lower figures of indebtedness. The manager promised to endorse these and submit them in place of the originals. Then, when he was sacked and homeless, the grateful tenants would take him into their homes! An ingenious scheme, and according to the story the landlord found out, but instead of sacking the manager, praised him for having a sound head for business.

A puzzling parable

It's a good story, but it's puzzling to hear it coming from the lips of Jesus. Was Jesus actually commending dishonesty? The written word, however, can't convey the expression on Jesus's face when he told it. Maybe there was a broad grin; maybe even a forefinger rubbed knowingly up the side of the nose. Certainly the story was told as a joke, and any oppressed tenants in the audience will have roared with appreciative laughter. Probably we should categorize it as broad satire. Anybody who reads a joke and comments on it seriously is sadly bound to miss the point. But what was the point?

Wise as serpents, harmless as doves

The point is that we all put a great deal of effort and concern into money affairs. By contrast, we hardly ever think about our eternal future, which is far more important. Whereas we could be using what little money we have wisely, to help other people on behalf of God. Christians have to be wise as serpents, harmless as doves, in what we do with our money, if we're to make any friends at all. Scrooge-like selfishness and greed in handling our money is no way to win God's approval. Nor is selfishness and greed in any other department of life. So maybe we've all got a lesson to learn, even from a dishonest but shrewd manager: be generous, selfless and open, and make friends with the people round you. For heaven's sake!

All-age worship

Jesus said, 'Nobody can be a slave to two slave-owners.' Make up a story about a slave who tried, and the disaster that followed when he was caught out. Jesus went on to say, 'You can't be a slave to God and to money at the same time.' What does it mean to be a slave to money?

Suggested hymns

And didst thou travel light, dear Lord?; From heaven you came, helpless babe (The Servant King); Son of God, eternal Saviour; Where cross the crowded ways of life.

Sixteenth Sunday after Trinity

Second Service   **Sent on a Mission** Ps. [128 Domestic bliss] 129 Cursing the persecutors; Ezra 1 Permission to rebuild; John 7:14–36 The one who sent me

> *'Then Jesus cried out as he was teaching in the temple, "You know me, and you know where I am from. I have not come on my own. But the one who sent me is true, and you do not know him. I know him, because I am from him, and he sent me."' John 7:28–29*

The one who sent me

St John's Gospel was written by a Jew who'd become a Christian. He makes the connection between Jesus and the Creator of the universe quite clear: Jesus comes from the Father. Jesus calls the Creator 'The one who sent me'. God had a job which needed doing, and he sent Jesus to do it. Simple as that. Some of the Jews recognized Jesus and followed him; some didn't. John reports the words of 'Jesus the Jew' to those Jews who hadn't accepted him yet. In not recognizing Jesus, he says, they're rejecting the one who sent him. There's no anti-Semitism here, nor any excuse for us to be anti-Jewish. This is one group of Jews arguing with another group of Jews, and Jews love arguing, especially about religion. But it's an internal dispute within Judaism; and we Gentiles are privileged to have been grafted into the Jewish nation.

The mission of Jesus

Jesus says he has a very special role in the history of the world, however you define it. Jesus has been sent out from his Father to do a job for him. He's 'the one who was sent'. Next question: what was Jesus sent to do? What was his mission? Answer this question in stages. First step: Jesus was sent to remind his fellow Jews that they're still God's Chosen People, and God loves them. But some of them were going the wrong way about responding to God's love. God gave you the Law, says Jesus, to show that he cares about how you treat each other. But you don't have to earn God's love by slavish adherence to the letter of the Law. All you have to do is respond to God's love by loving him back, and loving other people for his sake. Then God will give the Holy Spirit to all his children, who'll show them what to do, and give them the power to do it. So far we've come several steps along the way of answering the question, 'What was Jesus sent to do?' The nationalistic Jews he was speaking to had a nasty feeling they knew what the next stage was going to be, and they didn't like it.

> The Jews said to one another, 'Where does this man intend to go that we will not find him? Does he intend to go to the Dispersion among the Greeks and teach the Greeks? What does he mean by saying, "You will search for me and you will not find me" and "Where I am, you cannot come"?'

There were many Jews dispersed outside the Holy Land, speaking Greek in preference to Hebrew, and living among a population of Greek people who were not Jews. The Jews of Judaea (and that's usually what St John's Gospel means when it speaks of 'the Jews') weren't interested in the Jews of the Dispersion. And they were horrified at the thought that non-Jews might be included among the Chosen People. But Jesus wasn't proposing to do that in his lifetime, he was going to heaven, the spiritual dimension, where those who argued with him couldn't follow because they couldn't see any further than the ends of their noses.

Your mission and mine

But the mission to the rest of the world *was* part of the programme, though not until after the resurrection of Jesus. It started with the apostles: St John wrote his Gospel in Greek. But it didn't end with them. It continues with you and me: we're sent by God to continue the mission that Jesus began. Your mission and mine's to carry the love of God to those around us. You don't have to go abroad to be a missionary: you just have to know that you're sent by God. To do what? To tell those who haven't yet recognized the love of Jesus, about the all-loving Father that Jesus spoke about – a God who doesn't demand that we earn his love by obeying a set of rules, but who gives us his Holy Spirit to show us the way to love, and provide us with the power to love everybody for God's sake.

Suggested hymns

God forgave my sin in Jesus' name (Freely, freely); I danced in the morning when the world was begun; Spirit of holiness, wisdom and faithfulness; Will you come and follow me?

Seventeenth Sunday after Trinity (Proper 21)
30 September
Principal Service   **The Rich Man and Lazarus**
(*Continuous*): Jer. 32:1–3a, 6–15 Buying a field; Ps. 91:1–6, 14–16 Providence; *or* (*Related*): Amos 6:1a, 4–7 Possessions; Ps. 146 The needy; 1 Tim. 6:6–19 Possessions, the needy; Luke 16:19–31 A rich man and Lazarus

> *'"[Abraham] said to him, 'If they do not listen to Moses and the prophets, neither will they be convinced even if someone rises from the dead.'"' Luke 16:31*

Purple and fine linen

A certain bishop once admitted with a smile that he was very embarrassed to preach on the story of the unnamed rich man and the poor man named Lazarus. Lazarus is the hero, and although he suffers in this life he's rewarded in the afterlife. The rich man, villain that he is, refuses to feed the hungry man at his gate, and is punished in the next world for his selfishness. But what embarrassed the bishop is that the rich man is described as being dressed in purple and fine linen, 'and I', commented the bishop, 'am the only person in this church who is wearing exactly the same – purple and fine linen!'

The furniture of heaven and the temperature of hell

The parable that Jesus told is in the style of a folk tale. In fact it may have been based on a popular tale told in Egypt at that time in which a passer-by, seeing two funerals, is granted a vision of rewards and punishments in the afterlife. If Jesus used a popular folk tale, we mustn't look too closely at the details. The purpose of the parable's not to describe the furniture of heaven or the temperature of hell. What Jesus *is* insisting on, however, is that there really is going to be another life for us after death. We need to bear that in mind in deciding whether we shall be generous or selfish in this life.

Rewards and punishments

Lazarus, who'd been poor, changed places with the rich man after he died. Lazarus was the one enjoying the fine food at the party in heaven. The host at this party was none other than Abraham, the ancestor of all of the Jews, of the poor as well as the rich. The guests were reclining on couches Roman-style. Lazarus was in the position of honour on Abraham's right, and since each was leaning on his left arm, that meant Lazarus was close to Abraham's bosom. The rich man was concerned about the fate of his brothers. They didn't believe in an afterlife, so they were eating and drinking as though there was no tomorrow. He realized that they'd be punished with the same suffering that he was enduring, so he asked Abraham to send Lazarus back to earth to warn them. But, Abraham says, the brothers wouldn't listen to Lazarus, even if he did come back from the grave. God cares about right and wrong, and rewards those who treat others with kindness with the gift of eternal happiness. God may very well not be able to do anything at all for the selfish, because their hearts are closed and their ears are deaf to God's messages of love.

Not one of us

This parable's the subject of a very old English folk song, which was arranged by the composer Ralph Vaughan Williams. We sometimes sing the tune 'Dives and Lazarus', under the name of 'Kingsfold', to 'I heard the voice of Jesus say'. The folk song's very long: thirteen verses; but in the third verse the rich man says:

> 'Thou'rt none of my brothers, Lazarus,
> That liest begging at my door;
> No meat, nor drink will I give thee,
> Nor bestow upon the poor.'

The rich man was only interested in his family. But Lazarus was 'not one of us'; one of those people he 'wouldn't be seen dead with'. Only, to his surprise and regret, he *was* seen dead with him. Albert Schweitzer, the great Swiss theologian and musician, read this parable, and it changed his life. Africa's like the starving beggar lying at rich Europe's doorstep, he said. So he became a medical missionary, and founded the hospital in the African jungle at Lambaréné.

He didn't see him

The rich man passed Lazarus and didn't even see him. Well, he saw a body, but he didn't see a human being with needs and desires like his own, and the capacity to feel pain and question the world's injustice. One of the strongest motives for showing compassion in this life is the awareness that you may meet the needy person in the next life. How will you feel then, knowing that you have ignored them in this life and treated them as subhuman?

All-age worship

Find out as much as you can about Dr Albert Schweitzer; find or draw a picture of him working in his jungle hospital. (Try Google image search.)

Suggested hymns

My God, I love thee – not because; O God of earth and altar; O Lord of heaven and earth and sea; There is a land of pure delight.

Seventeenth Sunday after Trinity

Second Service   **Nehemiah – Standing Firm for God**

Ps. 134 Night-time in the Temple, 135 The acts of God; Neh. 2
Surveying the walls; John 8:31–38, 48–59 Jesus and Abraham

> *'Then the [Persian] king [Artaxerxes] said to me, "What do you request?" So I prayed to the God of heaven. Then I said to the king, "If it pleases the king, and if your servant has found favour with you, I ask that you send me to Judah, to the city of my ancestors' graves, so that I may rebuild it."' Nehemiah 2:4–5*

A fly on the wall

Do you sometimes wish you could have been a fly on the wall at the great events of history? Wouldn't it be wonderful to hear what the great heroes and heroines said, or better still to know what they were thinking? The Bible gives us short autobiographical fragments from David and Solomon, from the prophets and of course in the New Testament the letters of St Paul. To these we should add Nehemiah, who was Jewish, but an important official in the court of the Persian emperor. This was in about 445 BC, after the Jews returned from exile in Babylon. Nehemiah wrote an exciting first-hand account of what was said at court about the rebuilding of Jerusalem, and his own role in the rebuilding. Read his autobiography, in the Bible, and you really can become a fly on the wall.

Return from exile

For the Jewish nation, the experience of being defeated, then deported to Babylon in present-day Iraq, was traumatic. It changed their attitude to God. They had 70 years of misery to ask themselves why their God, who'd promised to protect them, had allowed them to be defeated; how long their punishment would last – or would it be for ever? – and how could you worship the LORD, when you couldn't visit the Temple in Jerusalem where he lived? 'By the waters of Babylon we sat down and wept,' they lamented, 'when we remembered Zion.'

But the day came, in 538 BC, when the Persian King Cyrus II conquered Babylon, and allowed the exiles to return to their own country. But neighbouring tribes opposed the rebuilding of the city walls – they were afraid that if the Jews could defend Jerusalem they'd begin to assert themselves. Cyrus was succeeded by Artaxerxes I, and Nehemiah, a Jew at the court of the Persian king, seized the providential moment to ask permission to rebuild Jerusalem. There can only have been time for a quick silent prayer, but it was enough, and God caused the king to say yes.

A ride round the ruins

The first thing Nehemiah did when he reached Jerusalem was to survey the ground and count the cost. Prayer's essential, yes, but it doesn't take the place of careful preparation before embarking on a new project. So, to avoid being seen by their enemies, who didn't want Jerusalem rebuilt, he set off with a few trusted friends on a moonlit night. He rode a small pony or a donkey, clambering over the scattered stones around the ruined walls. It's easy to picture him making mental measurements and calculating the cost in men and materials of repairing them. You can feel the tension and suspense in Nehemiah's account. When he reported back to the others, so persuasive was he that they all whispered with one voice, 'Let's start building!' But they had to build with trowel in one hand and sword in the other, for fear of a sudden attack by their enemies.

Jumbled documents

Although the documents are genuine, unfortunately they were worked over later by the same editor who compiled the First and Second Books of Chronicles, and he's jumbled the order of them a bit. The Books of Ezra and Nehemiah were originally a single book. The first part of the story is told in Ezra, chapters 1 to 6; then comes the beginning and end of Nehemiah, but chapters 8 to 11 belong with the end of the Book of Ezra, telling of how Ezra the priest came a generation later to Jerusalem and reimposed the Jewish Law. Despite that, it's a good read, and you admire the courage of the returning exiles.

Standing firm for God

You should never reapply what the Bible says about days gone by to changed circumstances today, and the story of Nehemiah rebuilding the walls has absolutely nothing to say for or against the present security fence in the Occupied Territories. However, you can see how brave the persecuted Jews had to be in Nehemiah's time, standing firm for God against the opposition of their neighbours. It's hard to see how, otherwise, the Jews could have survived as a nation until God was ready – ready to send his Son Jesus Christ to be born as one of them. There are times when each of us has to stand firm for God. We have to stand firm against opposition by persecutors, against ridicule by our friends, or against temptation from within ourselves, so that God's plans can be fulfilled and his promises can come true.

Suggested hymns

Christ is made the sure foundation/Blessed City, heavenly Salem; Come, my soul, thy suit prepare; Glorious things of thee are spoken; Who are these, like stars appearing?

Eighteenth Sunday after Trinity (Proper 22)
7 October
Principal Service   **Unprofitable Servants**
(*Continuous*): Lam. 1:1–6 The nation, suffering; *Canticle*: Lam. 3:19–26 New every morning; *or* Ps. 137 Suffering in Babylon; *or* (*Related*): Hab. 1:1–4; 2:1–4 A watchman; Ps. 37:1–9 Faith and justice; 2 Tim. 1:1–14 Faith and justice; Luke 17:5–10 Faith and obedience

> *'[Jesus said,] "When you have done all that you were ordered to do, say, 'We are worthless slaves; we have done only what we ought to have done!'"' Luke 17:10*

Servants

A cartoon in an old issue of *Punch* magazine dates from a different era – a different world, almost. A middle-class woman has just employed a new housemaid, and comes across her standing over a pile of objects on the landing. Everything in the house that can be picked up and carried is there: ornaments, lamps, books, dishes, all piled up higgledy-piggledy. 'What on earth is this?' the astonished employer asks her servant. 'But Ma'am,' replies the new housemaid, 'you said you liked a house where there's "a place for everything, and everything's in its place". Well Ma'am, *this* is the place!' The cartoon reminds us that employers expected their domestic servants to earn their wages by giving satisfaction – even doing more than their duty, by looking for tasks that needed doing, even before they were told to do them. Any who did less than this had failed to earn their keep: they were, in the words of the Authorized Version, 'unprofitable servants'.

Slaves

The parable that Jesus told dates from even longer ago, for the word it uses refers not to servants, but to slaves. No slave could ever earn a reward: he belonged body and soul to his master. No matter how well he did, his master never owed him anything. So, says Jesus, we can never put God in our debt. God doesn't work on a system of rewards and punishments, of 'nicely calculated less or more'. No matter how hard we work, we can never earn salvation. God's not obligated to admit us to heaven. If he does, it's out of his grace and kindness, not because we've earned it.

Duty

Jesus warns anyone who's proud of their achievements that they've no cause to boast. We're slaves of God, and when we've done all we can, we've only done our duty. Duty's not a common word these days: we hear more about rights than we do of responsibilities. Yet the poet Wordsworth called duty 'Stern daughter of the voice of God!', and Milton on his twenty-third birthday vowed to live 'as ever in my great Taskmaster's eye'. To call God a stern taskmaster's only part of the picture, but it's one we forget at our peril. The idea that when we've done our best, we've only done our duty, is a protection against pride. It stops us trying to wheedle one more favour out of God 'because I think I've earned it'. It prevents us complaining when life is not a bed of roses, because God never promised us a bed of roses, and we've done nothing to deserve one. It's a cure for self-pity. A mother moans, 'My work's never done.' A father may grumble, 'I'd have thought my children would be self-supporting by now.' The soldier complains, 'I've risked my life, but for what?' Even a saint may ask, 'Was it worth it?' Yet a slave doesn't ask those questions. A slave just gets on and does his duty without complaining, and not expecting any reward. And we are slaves of God. St Ignatius Loyola, the founder of the Jesuits, prayed:

Dearest Lord, teach me to be generous; teach me to serve you as you deserve; to give and not to count the cost, to fight and not to heed the wounds, to toil and not to seek for rest, to labour and not to ask for any reward, save that of knowing that I do your will.

Grace

But, as I've said, that's only part of the picture. God's not only a taskmaster, but a father, who forgives us when we stumble and picks us up when we fall. A father who gives us his grace to enable us to fulfil the tasks he sets us. God's a father whom it's a joy to serve, just to see the happy expression on his face, and hear him say, 'Well done, good and faithful servant, enter into the joy of your Lord.' Jesus told another parable whose message complements the one we've just read: 'Blessed are those slaves whom the master finds alert when he comes; truly I tell you, he will fasten his belt and have them sit down to eat, and he will come and serve them.'

All-age worship

Write out the prayer quoted above like an illuminated manuscript, or a wall plaque.

Suggested hymns

Awake, my soul, and with the sun; Father, hear the prayer we offer; From heaven you came, helpless babe (The Servant King); Will you come and follow me?

Eighteenth Sunday after Trinity
Second Service **Social Justice** Ps. 142 My portion in the land of the living; Neh. 5:1–13 Social justice; John 9 Spiritual blindness

'[Nehemiah said to the officials,] "I and my brothers and my servants are lending them money and grain. Let us stop this taking of interest. Restore to them, this very day, their fields, their vineyards, their olive orchards, and their houses, and the interest on money, grain, wine, and oil that you have been exacting from them."' Nehemiah 5:10–11

Economic breakdown

The situation in Nehemiah's time was complicated. On the one hand, the rebuilding of the walls of Jerusalem, which was surrounded by enemies, was costing a lot of money, which had to be raised by taxation. There seems to have been a period of drought. The two together meant that many of the poor farmers hadn't even enough income to feed their families properly. So they took the only course open to them: they mortgaged their land and the property. Some of them even sold their sons and their daughters, even themselves, into slavery to raise money. Fortunately the wealthy officials took on the responsibility of buying back those who had become slaves to the Gentiles. Only a fool, however, would pay out good money like that without security. So they seized the farmers' land, and charged them interest on the mortgage which took up so much of their income that once again they'd nothing left to buy food with. And if they didn't keep up the interest payments, the lender would foreclose on the mortgage. It was a vicious circle. As in all matters of politics, there was much to be said on both sides. The rich people may have regarded themselves as public benefactors, putting their wealth at the disposal of the poor. Yet the poor regarded the rich as their oppressors. There was complete economic breakdown in their society.

Compassion

But Nehemiah cut through these disputes like a knife cutting through butter. 'I was very angry when I heard this,' he wrote. He had compassion on the poor. He didn't regard them as a 'social problem'; he recognized that they were human beings like himself, with feelings like his, and a right to some self-respect. So he challenged the rich people publicly. God had power over them, just as they had power over the poor; didn't they fear God as much as the poor people feared the rich? Didn't they realize that by weakening their own people, they were putting the security of the nation at risk? The poor would have neither the strength nor the will to fight in defence of Jerusalem. It's always a temptation for anyone who has power to misuse that power, to feather their own nest, and to line the pockets of their family. We call it corruption, and it's the curse of any nation or organization where it's allowed to fester, because it destroys the respect in which the party or the company's held. Yet the corrupt official seldom sees it that way; he thinks he's just being sensible and looking after number one. Nehemiah had to put a stop to it at once.

Social justice

So he called a great assembly and charged them in public with their wrongdoing. Such was his moral authority that they backed down, and agreed to return their property to the poor and stop exacting interest at a rate the poor couldn't afford to pay. Nehemiah used his own money to help the needy, and made sure that his own household was above suspicion. Higher moral standards are required of those in authority, because they're an example to others. Whether they like it or not, other people will look to see how the powerful behave, and will copy them if there's any whiff of corruption or immorality. The same goes for their families: Julius Caesar is reputed to have said, 'Caesar's wife must be above suspicion.' And it applies to every Christian; people look at us, too. Jesus condemned the scribes who 'devour widows' houses, and for the sake of appearance say long prayers'. God won't welcome into his kingdom those who keep up religious appearances but neglect social justice. Love of God and love of your neighbour go together, and loving your neighbour isn't just about how you treat your friends. It requires scrupulous honesty in business, and a passionate concern for politics where it affects the well-being of those who can't defend themselves. Without social justice, we can't count on God being any more merciful to us than we are to the poor. Let Nehemiah's experience be a lesson to us all.

Suggested hymns

In a world where people walk in darkness (Let us light a candle); O God of earth and altar; Once to every man and nation; Where cross the crowded ways of life.

Nineteenth Sunday after Trinity (Proper 23)
14 October
Principal Service   **Gratitude** (*Continuous*): Jer. 29:1, 4–7
Support the city; Ps. 66:1–12 What God has done; *or* (*Related*):
2 Kings 5:1–3, 7–15c Naaman healed from leprosy; Ps. 111 The
works of the Lord; 2 Tim. 2:8–15 Suffering and perseverance;
Luke 17:11–19 The healing of a leper and his thanks

> *'[Jesus asked his disciples,] "Was none of them found to return and give praise to God except this foreigner?"' Luke 17:18*

The grateful leper

To reach Jerusalem, Jesus had to pass through the borderland region between Samaria and Galilee. But although there were people from both Jewish and Samaritan communities living there, they kept apart: 'the Jews had no dealings with the Samaritans'. Except that in adversity a group of lepers had been driven together; they had so much in common – all having been rejected by their own communities – that racial differences seemed unimportant. Of the ten, nine were Jews, one was a Samaritan. They weren't allowed to approach within breathing distance of healthy people, so they cried out to Jesus, from a distance, 'Jesus, Master, have mercy on us!' Jesus said to them, 'Go and show yourselves to the priests.' Now, that's what you were supposed to do *after* you were healed, to demonstrate the healthy flesh and prove the genuineness of the cure. But these ten weren't healed yet. Yet they trusted Jesus, and they believed that they would be healed eventually, in God's good time. So they set off towards the Temple. 'And as they went,' we read, 'they were made clean.' They showed themselves to the priests, and then one, and one only, of the ten returned to say 'thank you' to Jesus.

And he was a Samaritan

Jesus was astonished, not that the lepers would be grateful; that was only to be expected. He was amazed that only one returned to say so. How ungrateful and self-centred of the other nine, not to give praise to God! Yet many people have much to be grateful for, and never turn to Jesus to say 'thank you'. Many people whose lives are full of material wealth and spiritual blessings never give God a second thought. How often do *you* give thanks to Jesus for your home, your family, your money and the beautiful world we live in? Daily? I'm glad to hear it. It's often those who have least, who are most grateful for what little they have. Only one of the ten lepers thanked Jesus, 'and he was a Samaritan'. He was rejected by the racists because he was a foreigner. He was rejected by the healthy because he was sick, and they feared that he was infectious. Many diseases aren't as easily caught as people imagine, yet they shun the sick in their ignorance. And he was rejected by the religious, because they thought his misfortunes were a punishment sent from God. He had less than most people to be thankful for. Yet he was the only one who 'praised God with a loud voice'. 'And he was a Samaritan.'

As they went they were healed

Jesus told him that his faith had made him well. The faith that had led the lepers to set off for Jerusalem while they were not yet cured. The faith that trusted that their salvation would come eventually, although as yet they could see no sign of it. The Greek 'Stoic' philosophers used to stroll up and down the pillared colonnades, the 'stoas', discussing philosophical problems. When they began, no solution was in sight. But they had a saying, 'as we walk it will be solved'. So few Christians are as persistent as that. We want instant solutions. But God will give us our salvation only when he thinks we've shown by our faith and persistence that we're ready for it: 'God's time is best.'

The best motive

We've so much in life to be grateful for. When we look back at the dark times, we realize that it's only because we held our heads up and trusted God that we came through them. Job cries in his misery, 'Though he slay me, yet will I trust in him.' It's sometimes only when we thank God for what little we have, and trust him to do what's best for us, that he's able to give us the larger gifts that he's been storing up for us. Gratitude's the best motive for serving God. Not in order to 'get to heaven'; not from fear of punishment; but simply, like the Samaritan leper, because we're so grateful for what God has done for us already, that we're prepared to trust the future entirely to the hands of our ever-loving heavenly Father.

All-age worship

Make a collage of pictures from magazines of all the things you want to thank God for, and use it in a prayer.

Suggested hymns

Give thanks with a grateful heart; My God I love thee – not because; Now thank we all our God; Thank you Jesus, thank you Jesus, thank you Lord for loving me.

Nineteenth Sunday after Trinity

Second Service   **Friends of Jesus** Ps. 144 Prayer for peace; Neh. 6:1–16 Rebuilding the Temple; John 15:12–27 Friends of Jesus

> *'[Jesus said to his disciples,] "You are my friends if you do what I command you. I do not call you servants any longer, because the servant does not know what the master is doing; but I have called you friends, because I have made known to you everything that I have heard from my Father."' John 15:14–15*

Jesus calls the disciples his friends

Jesus said to his disciples, 'You are my friends.' Up until then they'd regarded him with awe. As a great teacher, a holy man, a spiritual superior, an intellectual giant, perhaps? He was their Master, but they never stopped putting him on a mental pedestal. And then Jesus said to his disciples, 'You are my friends!' My mates, my chums, my pals. I want you to regard me as an equal. Astonishing! Yes, and humbling too. Have you ever met somebody really famous, a celebrity, a sporting hero, a politician, and wished you were able to speak to them and ask them questions? 'Some hopes,' you thought. Or are you one of the lucky ones who can say, 'that person smiled at me, that person knows my name'. Then perhaps you understand why it was so amazing when Jesus, Jesus of all people, said to his disciples, 'You are my friends.'

Jesus calls us his friends

Now take it a step further. Those words are written in the Gospel because they don't apply only to the small number of folk who reclined beside Jesus at the Last Supper. They apply to everyone who reads the Gospel, everyone who calls themselves a Christian. So Jesus is speaking to *you* when he says to his disciples, 'You are my friends'! To you, personally, eyeball to eyeball, Jesus says, 'You . . . are . . . my . . . friend! Understand? Got it? It's *you* I'm talking about.' Jesus wants you to trust him and love him, as you would your best friend. Jesus wants you to carry on easy conversation with him, to chat to him at any old time when you've got something to say. Jesus calls us all his friends.

An awesome universe

What makes this even more awesome is that Jesus is speaking on behalf of God. Jesus said, 'I and my father are one.' Jesus is his Father's authorized spokesman. So if Jesus wants you as his friend, then God wants you to be his friend. Impossible! The word 'God' means the Creator of the universe. So Jesus says the universe is my friend! Sometimes the world around us seems very unfriendly; but if we can believe that behind the events of nature there lies a Person who loves us, then, even if we don't understand what's happening to us, it makes it easier to bear. 'Behind a frowning providence he hides a smiling face.'

Is God responsible?

Billy Connolly made a film called *The Man Who Sued God*. It took the insurance companies to task for refusing to pay up on what they call 'acts of God'. If they blame all the bad things that happen to us on God, then it should be possible to get compensation from God! Yet the Christian faith says that good and bad things alike are acts of God; he doesn't want bad things to happen to us, but he's not going to keep interfering with the forces of nature to stop them. Instead, God gives us the strength to endure the bad times, and works an amazing series of coincidences to make sure it all comes out right for us in the end: 'All things work together for good to those who love God.' This is because God loves us, as our Father and our friend; Jesus said to his disciples, on behalf of God, 'You are my friends'.

No other religion

No other religion makes this claim. Other religions proclaim much that's true, much that Christians can agree with. But no religion other than Christianity offers a God who, speaking through his Son, says, 'You are my friends.' That's why so many people have converted and are converting to Christianity; not because we criticize their religion, bribe or force them to become proselytes. Simply because we offer them a gospel: the good news that they can have Jesus as their friend.

Jesus is my friend

So take this message home with you, and take it to your heart. The simplest child can understand this:

'What are you doing, darling?'
'I'm talking to my friend Jesus.'
'Don't you feel lonely up there?'
'No, Mummy, 'cos my friend Jesus's here with me.'
'Aren't you frightened?'
'No, my friend Jesus will look after us.'

If that's true for children, it doesn't stop being true when we become grown-ups. Even when times are hard. Be happy! Smile! Jesus is your friend.

Suggested hymns

As the deer pants for the water; God moves in a mysterious way; Jesu, lover of my soul; O Jesus, I have promised.

Twentieth Sunday after Trinity (Proper 24)
21 October
Principal Service   **Persistence in Prayer** (*Continuous*): Jer. 31:27–34 The new covenant; Ps. 119:97–104 The Commandments; *or* (*Related*): Gen. 32:22–31 Wrestling Jacob; Ps. 121 Providence; 2 Tim. 3:14—4:5 The word of God; Luke 18:1–8 Persistence in prayer

> *'Jesus told them a parable about their need to pray always and not to lose heart.' Luke 18:1*

A funny story

Like many of the stories that Jesus told, the parable of the unjust judge has wit and humour. All we have in the Gospel is the bare bones of the story. Like most eastern storytellers, Jesus probably stretched it out, making the most of the comic potential. He probably had his audience in stitches by the time he'd finished. They knew all about situations like that. Who in a position of authority doesn't have to listen to complaints sometimes? To most of the moaners you can give a quick answer; some you can send away with a flea in their ear; and some you can just ignore. But some just won't take no for an answer. The poor widow was one of those. 'Hello,' thought the judge, 'we've another right one here!' Jesus tells us he was a dishonest judge. He'd have settled in her favour straight away if she'd slipped him a brown envelope with some cash in it. But she couldn't afford that. She went on and on with her complaint. She came back day after day, whenever the judge was open for business. Nothing he could say would shut her up. 'Of course,' he thought, 'if you once give in to people like her, it never stops. All the other moaners in town will be on my doorstep, asking me to deal with their gripes. And no more brown envelopes.' But then he realized that if he did nothing, the nuisance would never end. So eventually, with a sigh of despair, he gave in, looked into her problem, and did what she'd been asking him to do all along. If he'd only listened to her at the beginning he'd have saved himself a lot of heartache! The audience listening to Jesus tell the story must have chuckled with delight, seeing what a fool the corrupt judge had been. Honesty's the best policy; dishonesty costs you an awful lot of effort in trying to cover your tracks!

Is God like that?

Why did Jesus tell the story? At first it's not obvious. The parable of the Prodigal Son tells us that God's like a tolerant and forgiving father. Does this parable want us to believe that God's like a dishonest judge who tries to shirk his duty? No, that would be absurd, and those who were listening to Jesus knew it was absurd. The prophet Elijah poured scorn on the prophets of Baal, who kicked up a din to attract the attention of their god: 'Perhaps he's asleep,' mocked Elijah, 'or gone away on a journey!' Still today, some people pray as though God isn't really interested, and they have to bribe him by promising to be good or make some sacrifice if only God will give them what they're asking for. But the loving heavenly Father that Jesus spoke about is not like that. God is 'more ready to hear than we to pray'. But God wants us to take prayer seriously. Perhaps we should be looking not at the judge in the story, but at the widow.

Persistence in prayer

The widow kept on and on with her requests, because they were important to her – the most important thing in her life at that particular time. St Luke explains what the parable's about in the introduction: 'Jesus told them a parable about their need to pray always and not to lose heart.' Many people are very casual about prayer. Prayer's something they do when they're in trouble, or when they feel like it. There's an anonymous verse that runs:

> Whenever I pass an open church
> I always pay it a visit,
> in case, when I reach the pearly gates,
> the Lord should ask, 'Who is it?'

If you hardly ever talk to God, there's not much of a relationship between you. Much better to keep up a daily conversation with him. It's the relationship that matters.

Why pray?

God doesn't want you to spend time on your knees because he's difficult, or reluctant to give you what you need. But God does want you to realize that you depend totally on his love and generosity. We can never spend too much time in developing and deepening our love for God. That's why 'Jesus told them a parable about their need to pray always and not to lose heart.'

All-age worship

Make a list of the things you'd like to ask God for. If you were God, which things on the list would you mark with 'Yes', or 'No', or 'Wait'?

Suggested hymns

Come, my soul, thy suit prepare; Prayer is the soul's sincere desire; Spirit divine, attend our prayers; What a friend we have in Jesus.

Twentieth Sunday after Trinity
Second Service   Killing, for God's Sake

Ps. [146 Freedom] 149 Justice; Neh. 8:9–18 Rejoice in the law;
John 16:1–11 The Spirit of truth

> *'[Jesus said to his disciples,] "An hour is coming when those who kill you will think that by doing so they are offering worship to God."' John 16:2*

Persecution

Jesus predicted a time when the newborn Christian Church would find itself under persecution. Good people always run into opposition. It makes bad people really furious to see someone who's really good; it shows the bad people up for what they are, by contrast. Then they try to brush the good people under the carpet, so that they won't be an embarrassment to them. If that means killing them, so be it. But the persecutors always have to find a justification for what they've done, to calm their queasy consciences. So they always pretend that they've acted from the best possible motives. The person they've attacked was a danger to society, an unsettling influence. He, or she, was challenging the old ways, and introducing new and dangerous ideas. It was their duty to prevent this, wasn't it? So the bad people wipe the blood off their hands, and tell themselves they've done a really good day's work. Then they call God in as their publicity agent: God would have wanted them to act as they did, they really did it to please God. As Jesus said, 'An hour is coming when those who kill you will think that by doing so they are offering worship to God.'

Martyrdom

It's a great privilege to be a martyr. If you stand up for what you believe in, and it costs you your life, there's a place in heaven already with your name on it. Even if blowing the whistle costs you your job, you can live the rest of your life with a clear conscience, knowing that you did what you knew was right, and couldn't be bought. The Church soon found that not only did many martyrs die bravely, but also, more people were converted to Christianity by their example. So the saying was passed around, 'The blood of the martyrs is the seed of the Church!'

War

The word 'martyr' means a witness, and at first it was restricted to people who had died willingly as a witness to their faith. But it was soon realized that many die who have no choice in the matter. They stand on the side of right, they try to help their neighbours and they become innocent casualties of the struggle that's going on around them, 'collateral damage' as we call it. Innocent civilians bombed in wartime, passers-by caught in the crossfire, and their fellow citizens soon gave to them also the honour due to martyrs.

Schism

There were also wars between Christians, schism and division in the Church. So at the Reformation, Catholics burnt Protestants at the stake. They thought they'd abandoned the true faith, so they burnt them to save their souls. And Protestants burnt Catholics because they believed they were traitors, and were plotting to return their native land to the power of the Pope by force. Good and holy people on both sides thought that killing the others was their religious duty.

Crusades

Before that there were the Crusades. The original Arab Muslims tolerated Christian pilgrims visiting the Holy Land, but when they were replaced by the Seljuk Turks, the pilgrim caravans were attacked and robbed. The first crusade was called to defend Christian pilgrims. But soon the crusaders, eager for land and glory, attacked and killed Muslims, Jews and Greek Orthodox Christians indiscriminately. They wore the cross on their tunics, and said they were doing it in the name of Jesus.

Terrorism

Many people use religion as a convenient peg to hang their wickedness on. It does no good for the reputation of Christianity when the persecuted become the persecutors. So some nations turned the tables, and sought their revenge by attacking Christians with a variety of means that we call 'terrorism'. What the terrorists do is terribly wrong, and it can never succeed. Yet neither can the use of force by anti-terrorists ever bring it to an end. Force simply creates martyrs on both sides. It's clean contrary to the teachings of both Jesus and Muhammed to say that the suicide bomber, the person who dies in the process of taking the lives of others, is a martyr and will receive a reward in heaven. The prophet Muhammed said, 'The true Muslim is the one who hurts no one by word or deed.'

It's the victims of the terrorists whom we can be proud of, because, though they had no choice, they were innocent, and they wished no harm to others. True martyrs are those whom Jesus meant when he said, 'An hour is coming when those who kill you will think that by doing so they are offering worship to God.'

Suggested hymns

For all thy saints, O Lord; How bright these glorious spirits shine; Lo, round the throne, a glorious band; O God, thy soldiers' crown and guard.

Last Sunday after Trinity (Proper 25)   28 October

(Alternatively SS Simon and Jude, Bible Sunday or the Dedication Festival)

Principal Service   **Pride and Humility**

(*Continuous*): Joel 2:23–32 Harvest; Ps. 65 Harvest; *or* (*Related*): Ecclus. 35:12–17 Justice for the needy; *or* Jer. 14:7–10, 19–22 Repentance; Ps. 84:1–7 The Temple; 2 Tim. 4:6–8, 16–18 Fight the good fight; Luke 18:9–14 Pharisee's pride, taxman's humility

> *'[Jesus] told this parable to some who trusted in themselves that they were righteous and regarded others with contempt' Luke 18:9*

A good man and a bad man

The Pharisee, in the story that Jesus told, was a good man, and the tax-collector was a bad man. Let's make no mistake about that. The Pharisees took God seriously, and they tried very hard to live as God wishes us to. They read the Scriptures, they discussed them, they prayed, they were regular at the times of worship. They were respectable, law-abiding people. Just like you and me! The Pharisee was a good man. His problem was, he knew it, and was proud of it. The tax-collector, on the other hand, was a villain. The system in those days, as you probably know, was that the Emperor would put up for auction the right to collect taxes in each of the provinces of the Roman Empire. This way he got the money he needed immediately, without waiting for it to come in from late taxpayers. Those who bought the right to collect taxes in a certain province got their money back, and a little more, by auctioning the right to collect taxes in each of the towns. This was called 'tax-farming'. The local tax-collectors got *their* money back – and a *lot* more by way of profit – by overcharging the taxpayers. Property tax, customs dues, you name it, the tax-collector was the one who made the assessment of what was due, and the taxpayers had to pay what he asked, no arguing. Nobody likes paying tax, but when you know that the amount asked is extortionate, and there's nothing you can do about it, the resentment goes pretty deep. Then the taxes went to pay the Roman army, which was oppressing the land of Israel. You'll understand that the tax-collector was not a popular man. The popular phrase for the two worst categories of people in Israel was 'tax-collectors and sinners'.

The proud Pharisee

The story that Jesus told is fiction, but it was probably typical. Jesus tells us what the good man and the bad man said when they prayed in the Temple. The good man's prayer was a simple statement of fact. 'God, I thank you that I am not like other people: thieves, rogues, adulterers, or even like this tax collector. I fast twice a week; I give a tenth of all my income.' He hadn't broken any law, in fact he went beyond what the Law of Moses demanded. A good, law-abiding respectable citizen, you might say, and very religious. But his prayer, although addressed to God, was all about himself: every sentence beginning with the word 'I'. '*I* am not like other people . . . *I* fast . . . *I* give . . .' God knew that already, but the Pharisee couldn't resist telling him. His prayer wasn't really a prayer at all, it was a personal advertising campaign, with God as the target audience. His besetting sin was pride; he was self-centred. This isn't uncommon; most of us like talking about ourselves; we like to tot up the score of how well we're doing.

The humble tax-collector

So what about the really bad man? What did he pray? He didn't talk about how good he was, because he wasn't. He knew that he was a cheat, a rogue and a traitor. But somewhere he'd got the idea that God might be willing to overlook these facts, if only the tax-collector made a full and frank confession of them. So his prayer was humble, short and to the point: 'Lord, have mercy on me, a sinner.' The tax-collector may not have had many other virtues, but at least he was humble. And it was his humility that saved him.

Justification

'This [tax-collector]', said Jesus, 'went . . . home *justified* rather than the other.' 'Justified' is the word used for the winner in a court-case, the one who's declared 'not guilty'. Everyone would have expected the good Pharisee to be the one whom God regarded as righteous, but no, says Jesus, it's the very bad man, who's humble and penitent, who wins God's approval. If to be proud means being self-centred, then most of us need to repent of our pride. God forgives the penitent and humble sinner – but the proud are so busy talking about themselves that God can't get a word in edgeways!

All-age worship

Draw a picture to illustrate the proverb, 'Pride goes before a fall'.

Suggested hymns

Come, my soul, thy suit prepare; Just as I am, without one plea; O Lord, the clouds are gathering; Rock of ages, cleft for me.

SS Simon and Jude, Apostles   28 October
(or may be transferred to 29 October)
Foundations Isa. 28:14–16 A foundation stone; Ps. 119:89–96 I am yours, save me!; Eph. 2:19–22 The foundation of the apostles; John 15:17–27 You have been with me

> *'So then you are no longer strangers and aliens, but you are citizens with the saints and also members of the household of God, built*

Deep foundations

The foundations of a building are designed to bear the weight of the building and rest on a stable layer of earth or rock. They'll need to be particularly deep in areas subject to earthquakes, frost heave, strong winds or flooding. Disasters have occurred due to constructing a heavy building without adequate foundations. Jesus spoke a parable about two houses, one built on a rock foundation and the other built on sand. The apostle Paul wrote of the Christian community as resembling a temple building that needs firm foundations.

Living stones in God's house

St Peter wrote that each of us is like a stone in the walls of God's temple. But unlike the stones in a physical building, we are living human beings, 'living stones'. Each of us has a part to play in supporting the load. The work of the Church is too heavy to be born by just a few; it must be shared out among the whole community. If only a few stones are missing from the walls, the whole building will collapse. If only a few church members refuse to share their burden of responsibility, the Church can't do what God designed it for.

The apostles as foundation stones

So what are the deep foundations that the Christian community is built on? St Paul writes, 'You are no longer strangers and aliens, but you are citizens with the saints and also members of the household of God, built upon the foundation of the apostles and prophets, with Christ Jesus himself as the cornerstone.'

St Paul was an apostle – a 'missionary' is what the word means – but he wasn't one of the twelve apostles. He speaks of himself laying the foundations of new congregations during his pioneering missionary work, on which others have built. But this is a very appropriate reading for St Simon and St Jude's Day, because both of them *were* members of the Twelve. The Book of Revelation describes the heavenly Jerusalem and says, 'The wall of the city has twelve foundations, and on them are the twelve names of the twelve apostles of the Lamb.'

Simon and Jude

Not much else is known about Simon and Jude, apart from their names in the lists of the twelve apostles. Simon wasn't Simon Peter; he's described as 'Simon the Zealot'. This means that he was, or had been, a very zealous Jewish patriot; later the Zealots became what we would today call terrorists, fighting to drive out the Roman army. If Simon had been involved in violence, he must have renounced it when he became a disciple of Jesus. St Jude was that 'Judas, not Iscariot', who asked Jesus, 'Lord, how is it that you will reveal yourself to us and not to the world?' in John's Gospel. In Luke's Gospel and the Acts of the Apostles he is called 'Judas of James', which may mean that his father's name or his brother's name was James; he may be the author of the Epistle of Jude, but it's not certain. Many people identify him with Thaddaeus or Lebbaeus, who are mentioned in the lists of the apostles in Matthew and Mark. There's a book called *The Passion of Simon and Jude*, which describes how these two apostles preached together in Persia, where they were martyred together. Hence they're commemorated together on 28 October.

The foundations of a good life

When we describe the Christian Church as one, holy, catholic and apostolic Church, we mean that the apostles are the foundations of the Church. Our faith is based on what the twelve apostles taught. Many people believe that there is an unbroken line of bishops consecrating other bishops which stretches from the twelve apostles down to the bishops of today. This is called the 'apostolic succession'. Whether or not the facts are true, it's important that our faith and our community are continuous with the Christian Church in the early centuries, and not some innovative invention of our own. Most important of all, however, is that our personal life as Christians is based on firm foundations. The teaching of Jesus, transmitted to us by the apostles and the Church down the ages, is the only foundation that goes deep enough to ensure that we remain firm and stable as Christians, even when we're shaken and battered by the attacks of unbelievers and the temptations of modern life.

Captains of the saintly band; Christ is made the sure foundation; Christ is our corner-stone; Ye watchers and ye holy ones.

Fourth Sunday before Advent   4 November

(For use if the feast of All Saints was celebrated on 1 November, see page 346.)

Principal Service   **Lost Up a Tree** Isa. 1:10–18 Forgiveness; Ps. 32:1–7 Forgiveness; 2 Thess. 1:1–12 Justice; Luke 19:1–10 Salvation for Zacchaeus

> *'A man was there named Zacchaeus; he was a chief tax collector and was rich. He was trying to see who Jesus was, but on account of the crowd he could not, because he was short in stature. So he ran ahead and climbed a sycomore tree to see him, because he was going to pass that way. When Jesus came to the place, he looked up and said to him, "Zacchaeus, hurry and come down; for I must stay at your house today."' Luke 19:2–5*

Up a tree

Zacchaeus was lost. Not lost in a fog, nor in the dark, but in broad daylight, he was lost up a tree. Of course, he knew exactly where he was: up a tree in his home town of Jericho. It was a sycomore: not the same as the British (or American) sycamore, spelt with an 'a'; the sycomore with an 'o' is a type of fig tree, with broad spreading branches. But it felt to Zacchaeus as though he was, in modern parlance, 'up a gum tree'. He'd lost his way in life. The tax-collector *had* thought that all he had to do was to grow rich, and then he'd be happy. Now he was rich, very rich, and he wasn't happy at all. The delights of wealth had turned to ashes in his mouth; he had no job satisfaction; and he couldn't think what to do next. He was lost, and didn't know which way to turn.

Zacchaeus was a very little man

There's a song that children learn:

> Zacchaeus was a very little man,
> a very little man was he.
> He climbed up into a sycomore tree,
> for the Lord he wanted to see;
> and as the Saviour passed that way
> he looked up in the tree,
> and he said 'Zacchaeus, you come down
> for I'm going to your house today,
> for I'm going to your house today!'

Perhaps Zacchaeus appeals to children because he was small, like they are. It's not always easy being small. People naturally respect a tall person, and 'look up to them'. But with a small person, some people seem to look straight over their heads and ignore them. Zacchaeus must have suffered a lot from this in his life. So when he wanted to see Jesus, he couldn't even push his way to the front of the crowd. He did the only thing that was left to him, he 'went out on a limb', literally. Jesus was his last hope of finding a new direction in his life. It was self-respect he wanted – would Jesus be able to give that back to him?

A rich tax-collector

Zacchaeus was a chief tax-collector. Tax-collectors in Jesus's time could lie and cheat in the tax demands they made on people, and if they collected more than the government expected from them, they could pocket the difference. By cheating, Zacchaeus had become rich. Naturally, he wasn't at all popular with the people of Jericho, because it was their money that had made him wealthy. But it wasn't nice being despised because he was small, and hated because he was rich. He was desperately afraid that Jesus, too, would ignore him, or tell him off for being a sinner. But no, Jesus spotted Zacchaeus up the tree. Then, to everybody's surprise, Jesus invited himself to dinner with Zacchaeus.

Repentance

This made all the difference to Zacchaeus. At last, somebody'd treated him with respect. At last, he felt he mattered. Perhaps the new direction he was looking for was staring him in the face: he decided to go straight. No more cheating; no more fraud; he would collect as much tax as he was entitled to and no more. Then he made an astonishingly generous offer: he'd give away to the poor half the money he'd – er – accumulated. Not only would he pay people back what he'd cheated them of, but he'd pay back four times the amount! This was a completely new Zacchaeus they were seeing. Far more people are converted by being treated with love and respect than by being told off.

To save the lost

Jesus was delighted. Zacchaeus had been lost, and now he was found. He'd found his self-respect, he'd found a new purpose in life, and he'd found Jesus. 'That's good,' said Jesus. 'For the Son of Man came to seek out and to save the lost.' That's what Jesus is best at. The poet Heinrich Heine said on his deathbed, 'God will pardon me. It's his trade.' Zacchaeus's trade was collecting taxes. Jesus's trade is to seek and save those who think of themselves as lost souls, and to forgive them.

All-age worship

Draw a strip cartoon of the life of Zacchaeus.

Suggested hymns

Just as I am, without one plea; O God, by whose almighty plan; O Lord, the clouds are gathering; Rock of ages, cleft for me.

All Saints' Sunday   4 November
The Golden Rule

(These readings are used on the Sunday, or if this is not kept as All Saints' Sunday, on 1 November itself; see page 346.)

Dan. 7:1–3, 15–18 The people of God will receive power;
Ps. 149 The victory of God's people; Eph. 1:11–23 Christ rules with the saints; Luke 6:20–31 The sermon on the plain

   'Do to others as you would have them do to you.' Luke 6:31

Mrs Do-as-you-would-be-done-by

The saints were people who behaved bravely, and in a Christian way, towards other people. Charles Kingsley, in his novel *The Water Babies*, describes the fears of the children when they are told that a revengeful character called 'Mrs Be-done-by-as-you-did' is coming. How terrifying to think that we shall be treated in the same cruel, thoughtless way as we have treated other people! Yet when she actually appears, it turns out that she is, as Kingsley describes her, 'The loveliest fairy in all the world; and her name is Mrs Do-as-you-would-be-done-by'. She's the one who helps them to treat other people in the same way that they themselves would like to be treated. Kingsley based the name of his good fairy on the teaching of Jesus. The 'Sermon on the Mount', in Matthew's Gospel, and what we call the 'Sermon on the Plain', in Luke, both sum up the sort of character we find in the lives of the saints. Both include the words that Charles Kingsley used for ideal goodness: 'Do to others as you would have them do to you.'

The Golden Rule

It's known as 'the Golden Rule'. Jesus gave us a lot of positive directions, which are just that: they point us in the right direction and leave us to work out for ourselves what the next step's going to be. He summed it all up in two great commandments: love God, and love your neighbour. But what is love? How, in a difficult dilemma, do we decide which is the most loving course of action to take? Some people wear a little wristband with the letters 'WWJD', standing for 'What would Jesus do?' It's a good starting-point, because if you find in the Bible that Jesus faced a choice like one that you face today, you won't go far wrong if you take the decision that Jesus took. But many problems that we face today, Jesus never had to face. What would Jesus do when faced with a country you suspect to possess weapons of mass destruction? The question's meaningless, because Jesus, facing many problems that would be strange to us, never had to face that one in the society of his day. The only solution, the only guide, to all our moral dilemmas, is the Golden Rule: 'Do to others as you would have them do to you.'

Negative forms

Other teachers have proclaimed something like it, though usually in the negative form: 'Do *not* do to others what you would *not* like done to yourselves.' But none of them seems to have realized our need for positive guidance. We don't need telling what not to do, we know that already. But what action should we begin for ourselves? The answer is only given, in the positive form, in the Golden Rule.

Putting yourself in other people's shoes

The saints didn't only react to what other people did to them. They were 'pro-active', they went round looking for good things to do for other people. This requires a bit of imagination. It's no use saying, 'I would have liked my parents to have given me more money, therefore I'll spoil my children rotten and give them all the money they ask me for.' Because what they really want may not be your money so much as your time, your attention and your love. You have to put yourself in other people's shoes, to imagine what the world looks like from where they stand. You have to work out what their real needs are, as opposed to what you think they want, or even what *they* think they want. It's hard work being a Christian, and it needs mental effort. But it's the only way to be kind to people.

Saints

That's what the saints did: they put themselves into other people's shoes. And that's what we have to do for other people. We have to become incarnate in their heads and hearts, and see the world from their point of view, to see how they want us to treat them. That's what Jesus did. That's the Golden Rule for everybody: 'Do to others as you would have them do to you.'

All-age worship

Draw two columns. Write in one all the things you can think of that you'd like other people to do to you. In the other column write ways in which you could do those things, or something similar, for other people.

Suggested hymns

Awake, my soul, and with the sun; Father, I place into your hands; For all the saints who from their labours rest; Take my life, and let it be.

Third Sunday before Advent   11 November
Principal Service   At the Resurrection

(For a service which is not a Service of Remembrance.)

Job 19:23–27a My redeemer lives; Ps. 17:1–9 Prayer for salvation;
2 Thess. 2:1–5, 13–17 Perseverance; Luke 20:27–38 The wife of
seven brothers

> *'[Jesus said to the Sadducees,] "Those who are considered worthy of a place in that age and in the resurrection from the dead neither marry nor are given in marriage. Indeed they cannot die any more, because they are like angels and are children of God, being children of the resurrection."' Luke 20:35–36*

Sadducees

In Jesus's day, the Sadducees were the priestly party in the religious politics of Palestine. They opposed Jesus, because they were scared that he'd start a revolt. Then the Romans would impose military rule and the priests would be powerless. Apart from this, the Sadducees and the Pharisees were implacable rivals. The Pharisees had developed a set of traditions about how the Law was to be interpreted – the Sadducees would have none of this. The written law and nothing but the written law was what they stood by. Although there are hints about life after death in the Old Testament, it was the Pharisees who'd developed these into a doctrine of resurrection. Or perhaps it would be better to call their doctrine 'resuscitation', for they believed that the particles of dead bodies would come together again and stand up on earth, when the Messiah came, to live with him in an earthly kingdom. The Pharisees believed that, so the Sadducees disagreed, to annoy their rivals. The Sadducees said that the Pharisees' idea of resurrection was all rubbish: there's no life after death.

A trick question

The Sadducees thought they could defeat Jesus with a trick question. To understand the question, you have to know that in the Old Testament Law, if a man dies without leaving any children, the man's brother is compelled to marry the widow. Then, when she bears him a son, the lad will be counted as if he was the son of the dead brother: he'll take the dead man's name and inherit his property. This was called 'Levirate marriage', and it applied even if the surviving brother already had a wife and children of his own. So Jesus was asked to give judgement on a hypothetical case where a woman had been married to seven brothers one after the other. Not 'Seven Brides for Seven Brothers', but the same bride for all seven! At the end the seventh brother may have found himself with up to seven wives, poor man! Poor wives, too! The trick question was this: when everybody, according to the Pharisees, comes back to live on earth in the Messiah's kingdom, whose wife will this unfortunate woman be? Will she have seven husbands? Polygamy's allowed by Jewish law, but *seven husbands* are certainly not! Everybody laughed, probably. The Sadducees hoped that Jesus would be forced to say that the Pharisaic idea of resurrection was nonsense.

Literal interpretation

What Jesus, in fact, told them was that they'd got into this confusion by their insistence on literal interpretation of the Scriptures. Words that originally may have been meant literally very often take on a poetical or metaphorical truth when the original meaning's no longer considered reasonable. So although the Pharisees' doctrine of resurrection was poetically true, said Jesus, it doesn't describe a physical event.

What is resurrection?

So what is resurrection, according to Jesus? Jesus said to the Sadducees,

> Those who are considered worthy of a place in that age and in the resurrection from the dead neither marry nor are given in marriage. Indeed they cannot die any more, because they are like angels and are children of God, being children of the resurrection.

What Jesus meant was, the Sadducees were wrong when they said there's no life after death, but the Pharisees were also wrong. Life after death will be a spiritual experience in heaven, he says, where we shall be like the angels. That doesn't mean we'll have wings, but we *shall* have heavenly powers and abilities. We shall still be able to recognize each other, and talk to each other, and praise God. But purely physical considerations, like providing offspring to take your dead brother's name and his property, won't count any more. No earthly words are adequate to describe this supernatural existence, but we can be quite sure, however, that all that's good and wonderful in married love will find its fulfilment in heaven in some way or other. So the Sadducees' trick question has done us all a service, because it enabled Jesus to clarify what he understood by life after death. And that fills us with wonder, joy and hope for our own resurrection.

All-age worship

Draw a simple family tree, showing yourself, your brothers and sisters, your parents, uncles and aunts, and grandparents. What have you learnt from the other people in your family?

Suggested hymns

The voice that breathed o'er Eden; Love's redeeming work is done; O perfect Love, all human thought transcending; Ye holy angels bright.

Remembrance Sunday   11 November
Remembrance

(The readings of the day, or those 'In Time of Trouble' can be used. These readings are for 'The Peace of the World'.)

Micah 4:1–5 Swords into ploughshares; Ps. 85:8–13 God will speak peace; James 3:13–18 The harvest of peace; John 15:9–17 No greater love

> *'[Jesus said,] "No one has greater love than this, to lay down one's life for one's friends."' John 15:13*

Reasons for remembrance

The purpose of Remembrance Sunday is to remember – to remember those who've died, and to remember the reasons, good or bad, for which they died. Why did they die? There's usually no simple answer to that. Jesus said, 'No one has greater love than this, to lay down one's life for one's friends.' But did those who died in war voluntarily lay down their lives? No, they wouldn't have wished to die. But many of them, at some stage, took a decision which they hoped would bring peace for others, and risked involving the loss of their own life. The old soldier had had his right arm amputated in 1917. Whenever anyone said he had lost an arm in Belgium, he used to joke, 'To say I *lost* it sounds very careless; can't you say I *gave* it?' But even that's not true, because it wasn't a voluntary act on his part. Yet all those who died, or were injured or bereaved, deserve to be hailed as heroes and heroines, because they accepted their loss as being a sacrifice, however unwilling it may have been. And a sacrifice is also of benefit to others.

Reasons for war

In order to honour those who died as a result of war, we need to ask a few questions about war. Although many lessons can be learnt in wartime, and for some, though not all, it leads to a strengthening of character, nobody would disagree that peace is better than war. War happens when one group of people want what is not theirs. Yet there's usually an element of pride and selfishness on all sides, human beings being human in every nation. Patriotism, the love of your country, is good; but nationalism is immature; it's a failure to consider that others have rights as well. Some people are absolute pacifists, and say that you should allow your country to be overrun rather than offer forcible resistance. That's a position that should be honoured; yet pacifists should also honour the sincere reasons why some people believe equally strongly that to defend your country is the lesser of two evils. It's been said that nobody has learnt anything from history, except the fact that nobody learns anything from history! But we owe it to those who've died to look at the politics of the past, to see if past mistakes can be avoided in the future. The Greek word for truth literally means 'not forgetting'; we can only arrive at the truth about today by not forgetting what happened yesterday.

Alive in our memories

More important than remembering the politics, however, is to remember the people who died. Grieving mourners will say, 'I shall never forget him or her.' Yet life has to go on. Slowly we turn back to the business of living, and there just isn't time to be remembering the dead every minute of every day. Then with a guilty start we say to ourselves, 'Goodness, I haven't thought about him or her for days!' But there's nothing wrong with this; those who've died would surely want us to rebuild our lives. In that case, we need special days and anniversaries to bring them regularly back to our minds. Remembrance Sunday is one. For in a very true sense, the dead live on in our memories. The human brain's like a computer, it's a store of memories, together with a mechanism for bringing forward the memories we require at the moment we need them – for some forgetful people this doesn't work very well! We communicate with each other by sharing our memories. So when a writer or composer from the past communicates with us today, we can truly say, 'Mozart lives on in his music', and so on. Those who've died would like to think that they're remembered by those who survived, especially if those memories are proud ones. Jesus took bread and wine at the Last Supper and said, 'Do this in remembrance of me.' Jesus lives on in his Church whenever Christians remember him. Remembrance Sunday's important, because it gives those we honour a sort of immortality in our memories, which is the least we could do for them. Remembrance is a very powerful thing.

All-age worship

Make a garden of remembrance with small white crosses and poppies. Write the names of anybody who has died as a result of war on the crosses. What will you do if any of them were not Christians?

Suggested hymns

All people that on earth do dwell; Make me a channel of your peace; O God, our help in ages past; O valiant hearts, who to your glory came.

Second Sunday before Advent   18 November
Principal Service   **Perseverance** Mal. 4:1–2a Judgement;
Ps. 98 A new song; 2 Thess. 3:6–13 Perseverance in good works;
Luke 21:5–19 Perseverance

> *'[Jesus said to his disciples,] "By your endurance you will gain your souls."' Luke 21:19*

Luke

Once upon a time there were three Christians called Luke, Mark and Percy. (I warn you, some pretty awful puns are coming up.) Luke never got very excited about his religion. He went to church because it was the right thing to do, and he said his prayers for the same reason, but he never put his heart into it. His love for God was lukewarm. And that was his name: Luke Warm (first awful pun).

Mark

Luke Warm's friend was called Mark. He was better than Luke, he really cared about his Christianity, and said his prayers very devoutly. Nevertheless, Mark found going to church a bit boring, and he didn't like all these new services and modern hymns. Mark's faith didn't make much difference to his life at home or at work. The Bible readings in church sort of washed over him, leaving no trace, and he never read the Bible for himself at home. Perhaps that's why that he never seemed to make any progress in the Christian life. All Mark did was mark time. And the name of this Christian was (you guessed it) Mark Time (second awful pun).

Percy

But Luke Warm and Mark Time had a friend called Percy. It wasn't easy for Percy being a Christian. His family gave him no support, and his mates at work laughed at him. His daily prayer time felt as though he was talking into a telephone when nobody's listening on the other end of the line. But Percy kept at it, and read a few verses from the Bible every day. He really tried to practise his faith. Once there was a bit of a row among the worshippers at their church, and a number of the congregation left. Luke Warm's churchgoing had never meant very much to him anyway, and he never felt the loss of it when he stopped going. Mark Time decided to look for another church where he would get more out of the services. It didn't work, because what was stopping him from progressing was his own unwillingness to learn. So he stopped going to church altogether. The only churchgoer remaining out of the three of them was Percy. He'd promised to God at his confirmation that nothing except severe sickness would stop him being in church every Sunday till the end of his life. And when eventually Percy did die at a ripe old age, 'the trumpets sounded for him on the other side'.

Probably you've already worked out what the name of this persistent and indomitable Christian was. Yes, you're right: Percy Vere. Luke Warm, Mark Time and Percy Vere. (I warned you the puns were going to be pretty awful!)

The destruction of the Temple

Jesus spoke about perseverance. He said to his disciples, 'By your endurance you will gain your souls.' The disciples had been impressed by the beauty and the size of the Temple in Jerusalem which King Herod the Great had built. Jesus startled them by saying, 'As for these things that you see, the days will come when not one stone will be left upon another; all will be thrown down.' He went on to describe the suffering which would lead up to the destruction of the Temple. But persevere, he said, and keep the faith despite all the suffering you'll have to put up with. Then you'll save your life, and save your immortal soul as well.

Waiting idly

Thessalonica was one of the towns which the apostle Paul had visited. He told the Christians there that the Day of the Lord was coming soon. If that's the case, some of the Thessalonians thought, why go on working? They became idle, pious layabouts, sitting round, discussing religion and waiting for the world to end. Paul wrote to them, telling them they'd misunderstood what he'd said:

> For we hear that some of you are living in idleness, mere busybodies, not doing any work. Now such persons we command and exhort in the Lord Jesus Christ to do their work quietly and to earn their own living. Brothers and sisters, do not be weary in doing what is right.

Paul, too, told his followers to persevere.

Perseverance

So which sort of Christian are you going to be, Luke Warm, Mark Time or Percy Vere? The choice is yours. But remember that Jesus said to his disciples, 'By your endurance you will gain your souls.'

All-age worship

Draw a picture of Roman soldiers besieging Jerusalem in AD 70. *List the ways that innocent civilians suffer in wartime. See if you can find ways of helping the victims of recent wars.*

Suggested hymns

Awake, my soul, and with the sun; Father, hear the prayer we offer; Teach me, my God and King; Ye servants of the Lord.

Second Sunday before Advent
Second Service   The Lions' Den
Ps. [93 The Lord is king] 97 The Lord is king; Dan. 6 The lions' den; Matt. 13:1–9, 18–23 The parable of the sower

> *'Although Daniel knew that the document had been signed, he continued to go to his house, which had windows in its upper room open toward Jerusalem, and to get down on his knees three times a day to pray to his God and praise him, just as he had done previously.' Daniel 6:10*

Dare to be a Daniel

An atheist was asked to speak to a group of Christians. He began by saying, 'I feel like a lion thrown into a den of Daniels!' The story of Daniel in the lion's den is a popular one with children; it teaches the importance of courage in living the Christian life, and remaining faithful to God in times of difficulty. It's easy to visualize King Darius signing a 'law of the Medes and Persians which cannot be changed', and Daniel remaining faithful in his daily prayer in the upper room. Then he remains brave when thrown to the lions, although most people would be terrified, and God prevents them from biting him. So we learn to trust in God for his protection when we remain faithful to him, despite all opposition. The early Christians were taught that it's wrong to 'court martyrdom', to seek for suffering when it could be avoided, and we don't want to turn the children into little prigs. But if it becomes known that they pray and go to church, they'll receive plenty of mockery without seeking it. We need to encourage them to 'dare to be a Daniel'.

An old hymn

That's the refrain of an old hymn which was written by Philip Bliss
in 1873. Bliss wrote the song for his Sunday-school class at the First
Congregational Church of Chicago, Illinois.

> Dare to be a Daniel,
> Dare to stand alone!
> Dare to have a purpose firm!
> Dare to make it known.

It used to be very popular in Sunday schools, but you hardly hear
it now. The verses may be naïve, but they encourage Christians to
be bold:

> Standing by a purpose true,
> Heeding God's command,
> Honour them, the faithful few!
> All hail to Daniel's band!
>
> Many mighty men are lost
> Daring not to stand,
> Who for God had been a host
> By joining Daniel's band.
>
> Many giants, great and tall,
> Stalking through the land,
> Headlong to the earth would fall,
> If met by Daniel's band.
>
> Hold the Gospel banner high!
> On to vict'ry grand!
> Satan and his hosts defy,
> And shout for Daniel's band.

Defence, not attack

This and similar hymns are often criticized for being too militaris-
tic. Yet they don't encourage those who sing them to be aggressive;
only to be brave when they have to defend themselves against the
forces of evil. Defence, not attack. Life's a struggle between good
and evil. This is a helpful idea provided we don't divide people up
into categories in our minds, the good guys and the bad guys, the

white hats versus the black hats. If we're honest, we have to admit that there's a great deal of evil mixed up with the good in our own souls. We need to ask God to forgive that and cleanse us from it, before we can expect him to defend us against the evil in other people and in society at large.

Christians a threat to evil people

The reality of evil, however, can't be denied. William Pitt in 1770 said, 'Unlimited power is apt to corrupt the minds of those who possess it.' Lord Acton put it more succinctly a century later: 'Power tends to corrupt and absolute power corrupts absolutely.' The stronger a government becomes, the more frightened it is of those bold enough to dissent. Back in the nineteenth century the Sultan's grip on the Ottoman Empire was irresistible. Yet he did allow Christians to be self-governing in their own communities, or 'milets'. Nevertheless he would not allow any songs that seemed to threaten his authority, and it's reported that 'Dare to be a Daniel', together with 'Hold the Fort for I am coming', were prohibited by the Sultan from use anywhere in Turkey. Turkey's a changed country now, but there are many situations in the world, and in our own neighbourhood, where we need Daniel's courage to stand up to opposition when we're honest, and mockery when we persist in the habit of prayer. Will you 'dare to be a Daniel'?

Suggested hymns

Be bold, be strong; Fight the good fight with all thy might; He who would valiant be (Who would true valour see); Ye servants of God, your Master proclaim. (There is a midi-file of 'Dare to be a Daniel' on www.cyberhymnal.com)

Christ the King   25 November
Principal Service   **The Thief on the Cross** Jer. 23:1–6 Bad and good shepherds; Ps. 46 God is our refuge and strength; Col. 1:11–20 Forgiveness in the Son through the cross; Luke 23:33–43 The thief on the cross

> *'Then [the thief on the cross] said, "Jesus, remember me, when you come into your kingdom."' Luke 23:42*

The thief on the cross

The Bible doesn't tell us the name of the penitent thief, who was crucified next to Jesus. So it was necessary to invent one, and out of the Greek word for 'dying', the name Dismas was formed. He was undoubtedly a bad and vicious character, but legend has been busy smartening him up. Some legends make him a sort of Robin Hood, robbing the rich to give to the poor. Another says he was one of a band of robbers who attacked the Holy Family on their way from Bethlehem to Egypt. Young Dismas was so impressed by baby Jesus, however, that he set them free, saying to the baby, 'If ever there comes a time when you can have mercy on me, remember that I had mercy on you today.' But in spite of the legends, he was a brigand and he knew it, and he fully deserved the painful punishment of crucifixion.

To recognize a king

Was there irony in the words he said, 'Jesus, remember me, when you come into your kingdom'? Or did he really recognize something regal in the demeanour of the man on the next gibbet? Jesus's disciples had lost hope; they all deserted him and fled. But this villain believed, or at least partly believed, hoped against hope, that Jesus, after he died, would be resurrected and establish his kingdom on earth. Maybe the thief would be included in the resurrection event, he thought. Maybe he'd be granted some minor official position in the new government. It may have been a rather feeble faith, but it was better than no faith at all. He recognized that Jesus is a king, even though his crown is a crown of thorns.

'Today in paradise'

Jesus was and is indeed a king, but it was not a place in an earthly kingdom that he offered to Dismas. 'Truly I tell you,' said Jesus, 'today you will be with me in Paradise.' That was an astonishing promise to make to a wicked man. First because it was Paradise that was offered, and second because it was offered today. 'Paradise' is a Persian word meaning a walled garden. When a Persian king wanted to confer a special honour on one of his subjects, he gave him the title, 'Companion of the Garden'. This entitled him to walk in the king's private garden with him for intimate conversation. 'Paradise' was the word the Greek translation of the Old Testament chose to use for the Garden of Eden in Genesis. Originally the Jews thought that people who'd died would pass dreary years in a vast, drab waiting-room called Sheol, until the time came for their resurrection to earth. But a few writers suggested that at the end we return, as at the beginning, to a garden of delights, only this one's in heaven. St Paul and the Book of Revelation use the word 'paradise' in this way. Jesus promised the penitent thief that he could be a Companion of the Garden with the Saviour, spending eternity in delightful conversation with his Redeemer. He didn't have to wait till some far-off judgement day, either. The promise was for the very day on which he died, 'today'.

Penitence

Instant heaven, immediate redemption, paradise today! If eternity's timeless, there can be no hanging about. It's an amazing promise to make to anyone. Even to a good man. But this was made to a villain. Oh, I'm sure he had some redeeming features and saving graces, every sinner does. But it wasn't because of those that he was saved. It was because he was penitent. He admitted that he was no good, rotten to the core. But he still hoped that Jesus might do something with him. Jesus *can* do something with each of us, in spite of our failings and our shame. Not by making excuses for us, but by accepting our penitence and forgiving us. The promise to the penitent thief was a promise to each of us that, if we repent, on our dying day, 'Today, you shall be with me in Paradise.' That's why some people call the robber '*Saint* Dismas'.

All-age worship

Find a copy of a great master's paintings of 'the Earthly Paradise' (Jacopo Bassano or Jan Brueghel the Elder (www.doriapamphilj. it); Wenzel Peter (www.vaticanart.com)). List things we should do for the environment, and for other people, to help God's kingdom come on earth. Write a letter to a local newspaper about just one of the issues. Don't worry if they don't print it, the thought you put into writing it is what matters.

Suggested hymns

According to thy gracious word; Christ triumphant, ever reigning; For all the saints, who from their labours rest; To God be the glory, great things he hath done.

Christic the King

Second Service   **An Ideal King** Morning Ps. 29 Enthroned,
110 The king at your right hand; Evening Ps. 72 An ideal king;
1 Sam. 8:4–20 The demand for a king; John 18:33–37 My kingdom
is not of this world

> *'May his name remain for ever, and be established as long as the
> sun endures; may all nations be blest in him and call him blessed.'*
> *Psalm 72:17*

The demand for a king

For a long time, the tribes of Israel and Judah each appointed local
tribal leaders as and when they needed them. These are called
'Judges' in the Bible, but they had no legal function; today we might
possibly call them 'warlords'. Many of the neighbouring nations
who attacked them were led by experienced hereditary kings;
Pharaoh of Egypt is also described as a king. But the Israelites were
disorganized: the last verse in the Book of Judges tells us that 'In
those days there was no king in Israel; all the people did what was
right in their own eyes.' So the Israelites asked Samuel to appoint
a king for them. On the Lord's instructions, Samuel points out all
the disadvantages of having a king. What follows is an astonishing critique of the monarchical system. In very nearly every other
passage where the monarchy is mentioned, the idea is praised in
principle. Yet these two strands, for and against kingship, pro- and
anti-monarchy, coexist in the Scriptures, and not even the most
powerful king dared to cross out the portions that are critical.

The Madness of King George

In the film, *The Madness of King George*, the king, George III,
marvellously acted by the late Nigel Hawthorne, has one obvious
hang-up. Whenever he's about to talk about the American colonies,
which became independent during his reign, he stops and refers to
'something we mustn't mention'. The Americans were getting nothing out of the monarchical system, so they opposed it in principle
and in practice and fought for their independence. In Great Britain we've retained a hereditary monarchy but reduced its role to a
merely ceremonial one, a 'celebrity'. What does that say about our
attitude to kingship?

Failed kings

Most of the Bible writers were in favour of monarchy in principle, but appalled at the dreadful succession of kings they had. King Saul went mad; King David was an adulterer and a murderer; King Solomon worshipped idols; and after his death, in both the northern and southern kingdoms, the kings went from bad to worse. How could they believe in monarchy after that?

Hope for a Messiah

They solved the dilemma by dreaming of an ideal king. The seventy-second psalm doesn't apply in full to any actual king, but it holds up the ideal of what a king should be like.

> He shall judge the people righteously,
> and your poor with justice . . .
> In his time shall righteousness flourish,
> and abundance of peace till the moon shall be no more . . .
> He shall have pity on the weak and poor;
> he shall preserve the lives of the needy.
> He shall redeem their lives from oppression and violence . . .
> may all nations be blest in him, and call him blessed.

Nice idea in principle. Pity it never happened! But it would happen one day, they hoped. Surely. Won't it? This ideal king would be descended from the royal family of King David, he'd be the 'Son of David'. And he'd be anointed in the Temple in Jerusalem, like all the other kings before him. The Hebrew word for 'anointed' is 'Messiah', and that became their shorthand for the dream of an ideal king: the coming of the Messiah.

Christ the King

Jesus fulfilled these hopes and dreams. He was reluctant to use the word 'Messiah', because so many people thought of a military leader. But he was all the time talking about the kingdom of God, which he'd inaugurated. Christians translated Messiah into the Greek word for 'anointed' and called him 'the Christ'. But all the phrases used in Scripture about the ideal king seem made-to-measure for Jesus, and Christians obey Jesus as we would the best of kings. The Sunday before Advent has come to be called the Sunday of Christ the King. It's a good time to think about what ideal kingship means; to offer to Jesus our total obedience; to pray that others will come to see the value of doing the same, and pray for the building of his kingdom on earth. Sometimes you'll see a crucifix on which the figure of Christ is not the broken and suffering crucified Jesus, but wears a crown and a kingly robe. This is called a 'Christus Rex'. It was because Jesus was willing to be crucified for us, that we hail him as our king.

> And blessed be his glorious name for ever.
> May all the earth be filled with his glory. Amen! Amen!

Suggested hymns

Crown him with many crowns; Jesus is Lord! Creation's voice proclaims it; Judge eternal, throned in splendour; 'The kingdom is upon you!'

Sermons for Saints' Days and Special Occasions

St Stephen, Deacon, First Martyr   26 December 2006
The Death of Stephen 2 Chron. 24:20–22 The stoning of
Zechariah; *or* Acts 7:51–60 The death of Stephen;
Ps. 119:161–168 Persecuted without a cause; (*if the Acts reading
is used instead of the Old Testament reading, the New Testament
reading is* Gal. 2:16b–20 Crucified with Christ);
Matt. 23:34–39 Persecution predicted

> '*While they were stoning Stephen, he prayed, "Lord Jesus, receive
> my spirit." Then he knelt down and cried out in a loud voice, "Lord,
> do not hold this sin against them." When he had said this, he died.*'
> *Acts 7:59–60*

The appointment of the Seven

Jews brought up in Galilee and Judaea spoke Aramaic, a language
derived from the Hebrew of the Old Testament; they strongly
resisted the introduction of the alien Greek culture. Jews brought
up in the rest of the Roman Empire, known as the Dispersion, were
more liberal and mostly spoke Greek and read the Old Testament
in the Greek Septuagint translation. There was a dispute in Jerusalem between the Christians who spoke Aramaic and those who
spoke Greek. The Twelve, the original leaders of the Church, were
finding themselves snowed under by administration; they were all
Aramaic-speaking. The solution was to appoint seven men to help
them with the distribution of charity. The Seven spoke Greek, and
all have Greek names such as 'Stephen', the Greek word for a crown.
The Seven are often referred to as deacons, but not in the pages

of the New Testament. Stephen became involved in disputes with non-Christian Jews from the Synagogue of the Freedmen.

The Synagogue of the Freedmen

The Synagogue of the Freedmen may have been made up of descendants of Jewish captives taken into slavery in Rome by Pompey in 63 BC, and later set free. If they were Greek-speaking, they were suspected of being much more 'liberal' than the Hebrew-speaking congregations. To protect themselves against this accusation, many of them would have wanted to distance themselves from those of their members who went completely overboard and became Christians. The Christians appeared to reject the importance of the Temple and much of the Jewish Law. One of those from Cilicia who argued with Stephen may have been the Greek-speaking rabbi Saul from Tarsus, who was a completely orthodox Pharisee. A tablet inscribed in Greek was unearthed near the Pool of Siloam, south of the present-day walls of Jerusalem, referring to the officials of a synagogue who must have been Jews from the Dispersion; they all had Greek-sounding names, which they may have adopted from the slave-owners who set them free. Stephen gave a speech which subtly attacks those traditionalist Jews who had often rejected God's plan for them. In a rage, they stoned Stephen to death somewhere outside the city of Jerusalem.

The first martyr

Later, when many Christians accepted death rather than deny their witness to Christ, Stephen was looked back to as the first Christian 'martyr' – the word means 'witness'. What was Stephen witnessing to? He believed that Jesus was the expected Messiah, the anointed king of the Jews, who had come to save all who believed in him, no matter what language they spoke. This infuriated those who wanted to keep the Messiah as their own national hero. But Stephen was ready to die for his beliefs. Not many people are willing to do that.

The effect on St Paul

The executioners of Stephen folded their clothes and laid them at the feet of Saul of Tarsus. Saul, later called St Paul, will have remembered this day till the end of his life. Whatever thoughts were going through his head at that moment, they led to a complete change in his life; this was the beginning of a long process of learning new ideas and reassessing the old ones. As a zealous Pharisee he'll have seen it as his duty to make all Israel obey every one of God's laws. That was what they'd promised as their side of the covenant bargain. When they were all law-abiding, Saul believed that God would help his people to drive out the Romans under the leadership of a military Messiah. Then this would be followed by the resurrection of loyal Jews who had died. So Saul set out to destroy the heretic followers of Jesus of Nazareth. Later, when he was converted, Saul saw a vision of 'the Christ' (which is Greek for the Messiah), who compared Saul to an ox kicking against the goad which is being used to turn it into the right path. Saul, astonished to find that the resurrection had already taken place, then surrendered to the risen Lord whom Stephen had spoken of at his death. 'The blood of the martyrs is the seed of the Church.'

Suggested hymns

How bright these glorious spirits shine; Lo, round the throne, a glorious band; Palms of glory, raiment bright; Soldiers, who are Christ's below.

Alternative sermon

In Murder in the Cathedral, T. S. Eliot imagined the sermon that Becket would have preached on St Stephen's Day. For copyright reasons it cannot be printed here, but it could be read from the pulpit in place of the sermon on this day.

St John, Apostle and Evangelist   27 December
The Beloved Disciple Ex. 33:7–11a The tent of meeting; Ps. 117 Praise God, all nations; 1 John 1 The word of life; John 21:19b–25 The Beloved Disciple

> *'This is the disciple who is testifying to these things and has written them, and we know that his testimony is true.' John 21:24*

The mystery author

Who wrote the Fourth Gospel? It's a mystery, a real 'who-done-it?' The final verses tell us that it was the same person who reclined next to Jesus at the Last Supper. Or at least that those who actually wrote it down on paper depended on his testimony, so maybe he wrote a first draft. But who was that? The Gospel only calls him 'The disciple whom Jesus loved'. Now Jesus loves everybody, and he loved all his disciples. Being human he probably had some especially close friends, but they wouldn't boast about it. So it sounds more like modesty: 'I don't want to push my name forward, I'm just an anonymous disciple, the recipient of Jesus's love though quite unworthy of it.' Scholars call him the Beloved Disciple, or BD for short. He needn't necessarily have been one of the Twelve, so Nathanael and Lazarus have been suggested. But the most likely candidate is John the son of Zebedee. Jesus, as he hung on the cross, asked the Beloved Disciple to look after his mother Mary; and he was the first to enter the empty tomb after the resurrection. He may have written his draft of the Gospel near the end of a long life; some scholars have dated the Fourth Gospel as late as the second century, but the trend these days is towards a much earlier date.

Other writings

The three 'Letters of John' in the New Testament, referred to as 1 John, 2 John and 3 John, are by someone who simply refers to himself as 'the Elder'. Like the Gospel, they are in educated Greek with a few Hebrew turns of phrase, and they concentrate on similar themes such as love, light, water and the Word of God. So it's quite likely that they're by the same author as the Fourth Gospel. The Book of Revelation says that it's by someone called John, but John was a very common name, so we usually refer to this one as St John the Divine, an old English word for a theologian. Revelation's in a very rough Greek compared with the Gospel, though this is partly because it is packed full of quotations from the Old Testament. It's also in the style of visions which we call 'apocalyptic'. It's easier to imagine a Galilean fisherman writing Revelation, than expressing himself in the polished language of the Gospel. But as I said, John, son of Zebedee might have written the first draft. The idea that they were all written by the same person depends on a fifth-century book, based on late second-century traditions, called *The Acts of John by Prochorus.*

The Fourth Gospel

Today we are celebrating 'St John, Apostle and Evangelist', meaning 'one of the Twelve, and author of the Gospel'. Whether or not he was the son of Zebedee, it's important to take a look at what the author of the Fourth Gospel was doing. It tells the story of Jesus in a very different way from the other three. There are long speeches which would have been hard to memorize. All four Gospels are the fruit of theological reflection, but many see John as the result of a lifetime's meditation on the meaning of the events. Possibly the author took a saying of Jesus, such as 'You are the Light of the World' and wove it into a long discourse beginning 'I am the light of the World'. Many of these teaching sessions begin with the words 'I am', which is the name of God. Miracles are called 'signs', which point to God in action. So the Gospel is sometimes called the Book of the Seven Signs and the Seven 'I am's'. The author himself says:

> Jesus did many other signs in the presence of his disciples, which are not written in this book. But these are written so that you may come to believe that Jesus is the Messiah, the Son of God, and that through believing you may have life in his name.

The other three Gospels, with their accurate details, and John with his broad sweep, have been compared to a photograph and a portrait painting: the first is more factually true, the second brings out the truth of character. John's symbol is the eagle, with its penetrating eye and its wide vision. If the character of Jesus brought to you by the Fourth Gospel is attractive and brings you to believe in him, then the author, whoever he was, has achieved his purpose.

Suggested hymns

Be thou my vision; Disposer supreme, and Judge of the earth; O come, all ye faithful; Thou, whose almighty word.

Holy Innocents 28 December

Rachel Weeping Jer. 31:15–17 Rachel weeping for her children;
Ps. 124 When our enemies attacked us; 1 Cor. 1:26–29 God chose
what is weak; Matt. 2:13–18 The Massacre

> *'A voice is heard in Ramah, lamentation and bitter weeping. Rachel
> is weeping for her children; she refuses to be comforted for her
> children, because they are no more. Thus says the LORD: Keep your
> voice from weeping, and your eyes from tears; for . . . your children
> shall come back to their own country.' Jeremiah 31:15–17*

The death of Rachel

Jacob loved Rachel, and when, after seven years' labour, he was
tricked out of marrying her, he worked another seven years to win
her for his wife. She became the mother of Joseph and Benjamin,
the ancestors of three of the northern tribes, but died in childbirth.
Broken-hearted, Jacob buried her beside the road to Ephrath,
and some distance from there. Jeremiah locates Rachel's tomb at
Ramah, five miles north of Jerusalem, in the territory of the tribe of
Benjamin. Jeremiah was prophesying at the time when the northern
tribes had all been taken into exile by the Assyrians, and he pictures
her weeping for her lost descendants.

Rachel's tomb

However, distinct from Ephrath, there was another place called
Ephrathah, near Bethlehem, south of Jerusalem. It's mentioned in
connection with Bethlehem in the Books of Ruth and Micah. A
couple of notes in Genesis led to the confusion of the two, and
Matthew's Gospel tells the story of the massacre of the innocent
babies of Bethlehem and adds a reference to Rachel. Early Christian
settlers went looking for Rachel's tomb near Bethlehem, and in the
fourth century AD they identified a ruined Arab tomb as Rachel's.
The Crusaders built a fine structure on the site so that Christians
could worship there. After the Crusaders were defeated by Saladin,
it was adopted by the Arabs as a place to remember the daughter-
in-law of their ancestor Abraham. Then, in the nineteenth century,
a British Jew, Sir Moses Montefiore, bought the site, so that Jews
should have the opportunity to worship beside their Arab cousins
there. Until then it hadn't been a Jewish holy place. It's hard to

imagine what he would think now, to find that Christian and Muslim Arabs can't worship at the building called 'Rachel's Tomb', because of an Israeli security fence.

Weeping mothers

The Coventry Carol, 'Lully, lulla, thou little tiny child', is sung in the Coventry Mystery Play by the mothers of Bethlehem, just before Herod's soldiers rush in and kill all the babies. It seems as though mothers have always born the brunt of the suffering caused by war and politics, and their weeping echoes down the years. Their holy vocation is to create life, and their whole being is riven in two when the life they have brought into the world is taken away again. Jesus told us to weep with those who weep, and only someone with a heart of stone would be unmoved by the tears of a bereaved mother.

The tears of God

So how can the God of love possibly be unconcerned about the death of children? The answer is, of course, he's not unmoved at all. God weeps alongside the bereaved in every age. Many have asked, where was God during the Holocaust? A few brave souls have dared to answer that God was there in the gas chambers with the Jews who died. St John Chrysostom said that weeping Rachel is a parable for the tears of God. God is always weeping for his lost children, for those who are lost to him because they have turned their backs on him. And he sympathizes with his children when they weep. So why doesn't God do something about the death of innocent children? There's no simple answer. He won't take away our free will, because without freedom we can't love him. But free will also means that wicked men like King Herod are free to send their soldiers to kill. Nevertheless, God, while he weeps, does have an answer.

Your children shall come back

'Thus says the LORD: Keep your voice from weeping, and your eyes from tears; for . . . your children shall come back to their own country.'

This is God's promise to the bereaved. Just as the exiles return to their land, so those who have died will return to new life, not on this earth but in heaven. As King David said when his little son died, 'I shall go to him, but he will not return to me.' Weeping over the death of children is natural and right. But the time must come, eventually, when we dry our tears and rebuild our lives, looking forward to embracing them again in eternity.

Suggested hymns

In vain the cruel Herod's fear; Lully, lulla, thou little tiny child; There's a song for all the children; Unto us a boy is born.

Naming and Circumcision of Jesus   1 January 2007
The Covenant Community Num. 6:22–27 Aaron's blessing; Ps. 8 From the mouths of babes; Gal. 4:4–7 Born under the law; Luke 2:15–21 Naming and circumcision

> *'After eight days had passed, it was time to circumcise the child; and he was called Jesus, the name given by the angel before he was conceived in the womb.' Luke 2:21*

The covenant at Sinai

An Israelite at the foot of Mount Sinai who received a gobbet of warm cow's blood flicked into his eye would never forget it. In those days 90 per cent of them couldn't write, even to sign their own names. So if you were presented with a contract you couldn't sign it; instead it was sealed with blood. In this case, anyone who allowed the blood to fall on them had agreed. The contract at Sinai was somewhere between an international treaty and the insurance policy on a motor car. Treaties are between big nations and small nations; the big will protect the small provided they don't make any conflicting alliances. The insurance policy says the company will pay your repair costs and defend you in court, provided you pay your premiums. In either case, read the small print; total obedience to conditions is required. At Sinai the treaty or contract was called a covenant; it was between God and the Israelites: he would protect them provided they followed the small print, namely the Ten Commandments – the basic minimum rules for life together as a community. God can't do much for scattered individuals who go round killing each other and stealing each other's wives, but he can protect and guide them if they travel together as a community.

Other covenants

When the Israelites settled in the promised land, they soon realized they couldn't survive unless they co-operated. So the twelve tribes signed a covenant at Shechem, described in the Book of Joshua. David and Solomon were the only kings of this united federation of tribes. After Solomon's death they split into two kingdoms. When the remnant returned from exile in Babylon, they realized how much they needed each other. They didn't like each other, but they had to learn to accept differences. They even accepted that God would only sign a covenant with them to care for them, if they signed a covenant with each other to care for each other. So they called themselves 'the covenant community', the people who'd signed a contract with God and with their neighbours. Only if they kept the covenant could God help them.

A new covenant

However, nobody *could* keep the small print in the contract – the Commandments – and this failure to keep the conditions made the whole contract null and void. So Jeremiah dreamt of a new covenant written, not on stone, but on our hearts, one which we should *want* to obey. Jesus at the Last Supper said that the wine fulfils the same purpose as the blood of the animal sacrificed at Sinai: those who drank it were signing their willingness to obey God, not by laws but by love.

A non-exclusive covenant

In Jesus's time, the Jews said that circumcision is the sign of the covenant. When Jewish baby boys had this little operation, it made them members of the covenant community. Jesus was circumcised on the eighth day after he was born; if he was born on 25 December, that would be today; today Jesus became a member of the covenant community. It was just possible, in those days, for an uncircumcised Gentile to become part of the covenant community, but only if he was circumcised and obeyed all the Jewish laws. What was so shocking about St Paul's preaching was that he wanted to admit Gentiles to the covenant community, just as they are, despite their culture making them do things differently. The Christian Church is the new covenant community, it has no racial barriers, but welcomes everybody.

Baptism

In Paul's day baptism was an act of conscious decision by adults. He said we become members of the covenant community by baptism. In John Wesley's day this had been replaced by infant baptism, so he instituted a 'covenant service' to remind us that we're Christians only because we're all members of the same covenant community. Not by the accident of being born into a Christian family, but because we have decided to obey God and love our neighbours. So 1 January, the day when Jesus was circumcised and made a member of the community of Israel, is a good day for us to renew our own covenant with God, by renewing our baptism promises. But if you do, look carefully at the promises you made at your baptism or confirmation. They're not to be taken lightly; they may be life-changing, but they made you part of the covenant community, whom God has promised to love.

Suggested hymns

God is working his purpose out; How sweet the name of Jesus sounds; Lord, for the years your love has kept and guided; To the name of our salvation.

Epiphany   6 January

Gentile Wise Men Isa. 60:1–6 Bringing gold and incense; Ps. 72:[1–9] 10–15 Kings will bow before him; Eph. 3:1–12 Preaching to Gentiles Matt. 2:1–12 Visit of the Magi

> *'In the time of King Herod, after Jesus was born in Bethlehem of Judea, wise men from the East came to Jerusalem.' Matthew 2:1*

Gentile wise men

The wise men were Gentiles. A man recently chose the wrong word, when he remarked that he and his wife knew their first child would be a boy, because she had a scan and 'we could see the little fellow's Gentiles'! Actually, the word Gentiles means 'the nations'. For the Israelites, the nations around them were always their enemies. Gradually 'Gentiles' became the Jewish name for all the rest of the world. It's hard to exaggerate the mutual hatred and loathing between Jew and Gentile.

> Why are the nations in tumult,
> and why do the peoples imagine a vain thing?

ranted the Jews in the second psalm.

> The kings of the earth rise up,
> and the rulers take counsel together,
> against the Lord and against his anointed.
> He who dwells in heaven shall laugh them to scorn;
> the Lord shall have them in derision.
> Then shall he speak to them in his wrath,
> and terrify them in his fury.

There's not much love lost between Jew and Gentile there!

Dirty foreigners

God had made a contract or covenant with the Israelites; the sign
was circumcision. All the rest, the filthy outsiders, the Gentile dogs,
were the 'uncircumcised'. See how much scorn you can put into
that word! So when the Jews began to believe in resurrection, this
was obviously something Gentiles wouldn't share. If they did rise, it
would be to burn in hell while God's Chosen People gloated.

Nationalism

This extreme nationalism started to be a problem with Ezra, who
told the returned exiles to divorce their foreign wives. Foreign wives,
he said, were contaminating the pure Jewish race. There were pro-
tests against this Jewish racism: Jonah is a story about a prophet
who was rebuked for refusing to share his faith with the Gentiles of
Nineveh. Ruth is a novelette to remind Ezra and his pals that even
the great King David had a foreign great-grandmother. There are
scattered references in the Prophets and Psalms to Gentiles coming
to worship in Jerusalem. Isaiah says that the Servant of God shall
be 'a light to lighten the Gentiles'.

Jesus and the Gentiles

Jesus's attitude was much more tolerant. He healed the daughter of
the Gentile woman from Sidon, who'd teased him about the way
Jews referred to Gentiles as dogs. He healed the Roman centurion's

boy. He warned his fellow Jews that people from East and West would sit down to feast in the kingdom of God ahead of the children of Abraham. So we Gentiles get a rather 'better press' in the New Testament than the Old Testament. But the disciples were all Jews. What's important about the three wise men is that they were Gentiles. Magi were Persian astrologers, predicting the future from the stars. In old prayer books Epiphany is called the Manifestation of Christ to the Gentiles.

Apostle to the Gentiles

The Jews were shocked when Paul wanted to admit Gentiles to the covenant community. Without requiring them to be circumcised or adopt Jewish culture. This was the 'mystery' which Paul refers to in today's New Testament reading. This is why he was called the 'apostle to the Gentiles'. His *vision* was of a world united in love. The *means* he dreamt of, to achieve this, was through a church united in love, setting an example of love which transcends differences.

Missionaries

The word 'apostle' means a missionary. If it hadn't been for the Gentile magi – and St Paul, the apostle to the Gentiles – you and I, who are Gentiles, wouldn't be here today. But this has consequences in action. If the Christian faith is for us Gentiles, without requiring us to adopt Jewish culture, then it's for everybody of whatever culture. The worldwide mission of the Church is the concern of each of us. Everybody should be a missionary, or at least a supporter of missions. Missionaries had a bad name for being culturally insensitive, and dressing African or Indian children in western clothes. But recently, missionaries have done a great deal to build bridges between the races. They also encouraged the expression of Christian worship in Indian or African dance and chant, in churches built in local architectural styles. Sometimes you hear people say, 'Leave people with their own religion, it's more appropriate for their way of life.' But that's selfish. If you've found a good thing you must share it. Thank God for the missionaries who brought the gospel to our nation, and play your part in taking it to every nation.

Suggested hymns

As with gladness men of old; From the eastern mountains; Jesus shall reign where'er the sun; We three kings of orient are.

Week of Prayer for Christian Unity 18–25 January

That They May Be One Zeph. 3:16–20 Bring you home; Ps. 133 Brothers at unity; 1 John 4:9–15 We ought to love one another; John 17:11b-23 That they may be one

> *'Jesus prayed, "I ask not only on behalf of these, but also on behalf of those who will believe in me through their word, that they may all be one. As you, Father, are in me and I am in you, may they also be in us, so that the world may believe that you have sent me."'*
> *John 17:20–21*

Words mean different things

A teacher from the South of England went to teach at a school in the North. Finding dead flowers on her desk she went to look for the dustbin, and asked a passer-by, 'Where's the bin?' 'Ah've bin to 'ave me 'air cut, what's to do with thee?' was the astonished reply. Words can mean different things to different people; in case you hadn't realized, he thought that the teacher meant, 'Where hast thou just been to – where's tha bin?'

Unity between cultures

Jesus prayed that his followers might be one. That means that reunion of the followers of Jesus into one Church is not a side issue, but at the very heart of the gospel. Divisions between denominations may appear to be about important theological issues, but when you look closely at them, they are really because we have got used to doing things in different ways. We all have different 'cultures'. Unity between the divided churches is still a long way off. But what we can do something about now is unity between cultures. Then church unity will follow. This doesn't mean we all have to be of the same culture: Paul fought that we Gentiles shouldn't have to be circumcised, because that would have meant adopting Jewish culture. He knew that what Jesus was actually praying for was that different cultures should welcome and accept each other, and enjoy our diversity. The Eucharist, whether celebrated in a cathedral or in a wooden hut with chickens running over your feet, is still the Eucharist! But the split between the Eastern Orthodox Church and the Roman Catholic Church of the West was mainly because of language: 'substance' in Latin doesn't mean the same as the equivalent word in Greek. The Reformation was because the medieval empires in the South didn't understand the new nation states of the North. Similar misunderstandings happen in every age, between denominations and within denominations, which cause painful and unnecessary divisions. Usually, when it comes down to the nitty-gritty, they're only disagreements about the meaning of words.

Judge not

A Victorian novelist, Fanny Trollope, wrote a book criticizing American women as uncultured. Her son, the better-known novelist Anthony Trollope, tried to undo the damage his mother had caused by pointing out that it's not that some people are cultured and others not. Rather, there are *different cultures* of equal value, and you can't judge any culture from the outside. The New Testament wastes very little space criticizing the way people live – that never does any good anyway – but it does lambast those who judge others and criticize them because they're different: 'Judge not, that ye be not judged,' said Jesus; 'Revilers cannot enter the kingdom of heaven,' wrote Paul.

Think about our neighbours

Think for a moment about the other Christian bodies that worship in this neighbourhood. Have you taken the trouble to share in their worship, and find out what's important to them in the way they do things? Have you tried to find out what they believe, and asked yourself whether the apparent differences from what you believe are important questions that matter, or simply using words in a different way? If you don't do this, how can you be said to be taking seriously the prayer of Jesus, that his disciples might be one, as closely united as he is with his Father?

Enjoying our differences

When you meet a Christian from a different culture, don't judge or condemn them: thank God that he's called you and them to be his children. Pray for the grace to enjoy what makes you different, and to love your fellow Christians for who they are in the eyes of God. Jesus also prayed: 'I have other sheep that do not belong to this fold. I must bring them also, and they will listen to my voice. So there will be one flock, one shepherd.' There's no limit to the extent of that prayer – Jesus won't be satisfied until the whole world's united in love. We shall take the first steps towards that when you and I can learn to love each other in spite of, and because of, our differences.

Suggested hymns

Bind us together, Lord; In Christ there is no east or west; O Lord, who at thy Eucharist didst pray; Pray that Jerusalem may have.

Conversion of St Paul   25 January
What Resurrection? Jer. 1:4–10 The call of a prophet;
Ps. 67 Let all the peoples praise you; Acts 9:1–22 Saul's conversion;
(*if the Acts reading is used instead of the Old Testament reading, the New Testament reading is* Gal. 1:11–16a Called me through his grace); Matt. 19:27–30 The reward of eternal life

> *'He fell to the ground and heard a voice saying to him, "Saul, Saul, why do you persecute me?"' Acts 9:4*

Where was Paul coming from?

Where was St Paul coming from? Well, obviously, he was coming from Jerusalem. But what did Jerusalem signify to the young Pharisee, Saul of Tarsus? There's very little evidence for the beliefs of the Pharisees in the time of Jesus, apart from what the Gospels say about them. Actually, the letters of Saul of Tarsus, later known as St Paul, are themselves the best evidence for what he'd believed before he was converted. So, where he was coming from was from the heart of first-century Pharisaism.

The Pharisees

The Pharisees emerged shortly before the time of Christ as experts in the interpretation of the Law, and built up a body of traditions as to how to apply it. They probably believed that when every Jew kept every one of the laws for a whole day, then the Messiah would come, defeat the occupying Roman army, raise dead law-abiding Jews to new life, and usher in the kingdom of God. In Jerusalem.

What Saul hated about Christians

What Saul hated about Christians was that they told the ordinary people, whom the Pharisees derided as 'sinners', that keeping the Law doesn't matter; what matters is loving God and loving your neighbour. So the teaching of this new movement would make the Pharisees redundant, and worse still, the Messiah wouldn't come because God's people weren't keeping the laws. And if the Messiah didn't come, then there'd be no resurrection. So Saul, as an eager Pharisee, had to wipe out this dangerous heresy before it wrecked the whole future of the covenant community. He'd even heard it said that the Christians believed that the Messiah *had* come, that his name was Jesus of Nazareth, that he'd been crucified, and that the resurrection had already happened. The resurrection? What resurrection? To Saul of Tarsus, that was obviously nonsense; this wasn't the sort of resurrection he was waiting for.

Where was Saul heading for?

So Saul set out to destroy the young Christian movement. He was coming from Jerusalem. He was going to Damascus, because he knew that the overseas Jews of the Dispersion sat notoriously loosely to the Law and the covenant. He'd heard that the Christians promised resurrection to everyone: to sinners who ignored the Law, and even, it was whispered, to foreigners who weren't part of the covenant community at all. But on the way to Damascus his life was completely turned around. For he met Jesus, whom he knew perfectly well to be dead.

'I am Jesus, whom you are persecuting'

When Saul met this figure on the road to Damascus, who was very obviously alive, he asked who he was. 'I am Jesus, whom you are persecuting,' replied the Lord. Now Saul didn't think he was per-secuting Jesus, he thought he was persecuting the Church. Now he began to see that the members of the Church are what Paul later called 'the body of Christ'. So the resurrection wasn't an event in the future, conditional on obedience to the Law; it was an ongoing event in the present, the free gift of a loving God. Saul was destined, because of his Damascus Road experience, to become one of the leading followers of Jesus the Messiah. He would be a staunch defender of the right of Gentiles to be members of Christ's body, the community of the new covenant, without having to obey the Jewish Law – the very opposite of what he'd stood for until now!

Are we willing to change?

Are we willing to change, as Saul had to? Are we willing to throw out our cherished traditions and ideas about how the world's supposed to work? Are we willing to give up our insistence that everybody else must follow our strict code of morality? Are we willing to accept as our friends the very people whom up to now we wouldn't be seen dead with? In other words, to have our lives completely turned upside down? Are we willing to be completely dependent on God's kindness, his grace, not on any achievements of our own? Because even people who've thought of themselves as good religious people for years sometimes have a Damascus Road experience. Who knows where we're heading for? We just have to be willing to recognize Jesus in the most unexpected places, and go where and when God calls us, as Saul did. That'll be our first resurrection, and the second will follow.

Suggested hymns

Christ is alive! Let Christians sing; For I'm building a people of power; We sing the glorious conquest; Will you come and follow me?

Presentation of Christ in the Temple (Candlemas)

2 February *(or may be observed on 28 January in 2007)*
Never Too Old Mal. 3:1–5 The Lord shall come to his Temple; Ps. 24:[1–6] 7–10 Open the gates for the Lord; Heb. 2:14–18 Jesus became like the descendants of Abraham; Luke 2:22–40 The presentation of Christ in the Temple

'A light for revelation to the Gentiles.' Luke 2:32

A Christmas carol

A Christmas carol which we don't often sing is the one beginning, 'Where is this stupendous stranger?' It points out the craziness of God: if you wanted to conquer the world, who'd send a helpless baby? The incarnation's a paradox.

> Where is this stupendous stranger?
> Prophets, shepherds, kings advise;
> Lead me to my Master's manger,
> Shew me where my Saviour lies.
>
> O most Mighty! O most Holy!
> Far beyond the seraph's thought,
> Art thou then so mean and lowly,
> As unheeded prophets taught?
>
> O the magnitude of meekness!
> Worth from worth immortal sprung;
> O the strength of infant weakness,
> If eternal is so young!
>
> God all-bounteous, all creative,
> Whom no ills from good dissuade,
> Is incarnate and a native
> Of the very world he made.

Christopher Smart

The carol is by Christopher, or 'Kit', Smart, who lived from 1722 to 1771. His contemporaries thought he was completely mad, though Dr Johnson said:

Madness frequently discovers itself merely by unnecessary deviation from the usual modes of the world. My poor friend Smart showed the disturbance of his mind by falling upon his knees and saying his prayers in the street, or in any other unusual place. Now although, rationally speaking, it is greater madness not to pray at all, than to pray as Smart did, I am afraid there are so many who do not pray, that their understanding is not called in question . . . I did not think he ought to be shut up. His infirmities were not noxious to society. He insisted on people praying with him; and I'd as lief pray with Kit Smart as any one else.

The madness of God

Simeon was an interesting old priest. I'll bet the other priests thought he, too, was completely gaga. He'd reached a great age but he refused to die. Why? He said the Holy Spirit had told him he would see God's Messiah and 'the consolation of Israel'. Israel felt they were slaves to the Roman Gentiles. They looked for a military Messiah who would destroy the Gentiles and set Israel free. There was no indication that this was about to happen, but Simeon waited. What he saw was a 40-day-old baby boy. Has God gone mad? But Simeon had learnt to expect the unexpected when dealing with the God of surprises. He began to see that Israel needed to be set free, not from the Romans, but from resentment and hatred. Then he sings a song, a remarkable thing for an old man to do. His waiting's finished. He's now seen the 'glory of your people Israel' in a weak helpless baby. Also 'a light to lighten the Gentiles' – that's why we call this season Candlemas. So the Romans are not to be destroyed, but illuminated.

Old age, young minds

Simeon had 'seen the light' at a great age, he learned that 'you're never too old to learn'. We often assume 'you can't teach an old dog new tricks'. But you probably know old people who are open to new ideas, young at heart and well able to cope with change. Like Browning's Rabbi ben Ezra, they say: 'Grow old along with me; the best is yet to be.' There's no time left to speak of Anna the prophetess, another remarkable old person still open to change her ideas. God can never be contained in our presuppositions. God always catches us on the hop. You may have been a fairly conventional Christian for years, following the crowd, giving vague intellectual assent, then suddenly you see the light: God loves me, values me as an individual. This changes the priorities of your life and touches your heart, at the deepest level. It can happen at any age; you're never too old to learn. God may suddenly reveal his love for you in the place you least expect to see it: even in the smile of a helpless little baby. God is there, loving you, if you'll only recognize him, as Simeon and Anna did when they saw the light. God must be mad to come to us in that way, and not as a Messiah! Maybe it's only people who're a little mad, like Kit Smart, and you, and me, who can recognize the divine craziness of God's plan of redemption.

All-age worship

Young people can be involved in the Candlemas ceremonies; see The Promise of His Glory, www.oremus.org/liturgy/pohg/s6c. html.

Suggested hymns

Faithful vigil ended; Hail to the Lord who comes; In a world where people walk in darkness; Lord, the light of your love is shining (Shine, Jesus, shine).

St David, Bishop of Menevia, Patron of Wales
c. 601 1 March
A Goodly Heritage Ecclus. 15:1–6 Whoever holds to the law will obtain wisdom; Ps. 16:1–7 I have a goodly heritage; 1 Thess. 2:2–12 Entrusted with the gospel; Matt. 16:24–27 Take up your cross

> *'My share has fallen in a fair land; indeed, I have a goodly heritage.'*
> *Psalm 16:6* (Common Worship)

A choirboys' joke

There's an old joke in which a choirboy tells his friend, 'We sang the psalm about winning the lot at the fairground this morning.' 'Psalm about winning the lot at the fairground,' enquired the other, 'which one's that?' 'You know, Psalm 16,' replied the choirboy: 'The lot is fallen unto me in a fair ground.' In Common Worship it's translated, 'My share has fallen in a fair land; indeed, I have a goodly heritage.' I want to talk about heritage today, on St David's Day.

A pioneer of the faith

Among the many famous saints of Wales, St Cadoc was a pioneer, who taught St Illtyd. One of Illtyd's pupils was called Paul, and when he became an old man, the young David was his pupil at the White House in Carmarthen. Very few facts of David's life are known, but the legend has it that the Bishop of Llandaff had called together a synod at Trevi in Cardigan, and so many thousands attended that only David could preach loudly enough to be heard. He so charmed the crowds that he was elected to be the next

Archbishop of Caerleon – the alternative name for Trevi. Later he moved the centre of his see to his birthplace at Mynyu or Menevia. There he established an abbey, and there the cathedral of St David's now stands. It is three miles from the cliffs of St David's Head, the south-western tip of Wales. The life of the monks there was extremely strict and ascetic. It's very moving to kneel in the chapel of the cathedral, where St David's bones are housed in a casket, and feel that this great pioneer of the faith is still close to us in spirit. Just down the coast, on top of the cliffs, is the well of St Non, or Nonna, his mother. David travelled widely over South Wales and into western England.

Using our gifts

The Welsh are famous for their singing. If the legend's true, it was because St David had a strong and attractive preaching voice that he was made a leader in the Welsh church. It's not which gifts we have that matters, only God can decide that; what matters is our willingness to use our gifts in God's service. A voice can be trained. If we're called to use one of our gifts in God's service, and we imagine that it's not a very well-developed gift, are we willing to put the time and effort into developing it, so that we can be better servants of God?

St David preached against the Pelagian heresy. Pelagius, like David, was a Celt – his name in Celtic will have been Morgan. He seems to have taught the idea that we can pull ourselves up to heaven by our own bootstraps. There are not a few British people today who seem still to believe that 'if you're good you'll go to heaven'. But the Bible teaches that it's by God's grace that we're saved, not by our deeds. This was the orthodox teaching of the Church, which St David proclaimed. If we've been given any gifts by God, and are successful in using them in his service, it's 'not unto us', but to God that the praise must go; we must simply say that we are 'unprofitable servants'.

A goodly heritage

The pagan ancestors of the British people seem to have gladly embraced the Christian religion when it was preached to them. They already had a strong awareness of the presence of God in nature. When they became Christians they added to that a new sense of the presence of Christ and his saints, and wove it into their poetry and prayers. They were fiercely proud of the pioneer missionaries who had first preached the good news to them, and Welshmen and -women today are proud to belong to the 'Land of our Fathers', and to follow the faith that was taught by 'Dewi Sant'. While we must never narrow our horizons and forget that God loves the whole world, it's good to remember how much in our culture and character comes from God through the pioneers who taught our ancestors the faith in the early days. As the psalmist said, 'The boundary lines have fallen for me in pleasant places; I have a goodly heritage.'

Suggested hymns

Disposer supreme, and Judge of the earth; For all the saints, who from their labours rest; Guide me, O thou great Redeemer; Jesu, lover of my soul.

St Patrick, Bishop, Missionary, Patron of Ireland
c. 460   17 March
Wise as Serpents, Harmless as Doves Deut. 32:1–9 May my teaching drop like the rain; *or* Tob. 13:1b–7 In the land of my exile; Ps. 145:2–13 Make known to all peoples; 2 Cor. 4:1–12 This ministry; Matt. 10:16–23 Warnings for missionaries; *or* John 4:31–38 Ripe for harvest

> *'[Jesus said,] "See, I am sending you out like sheep into the midst of wolves; so be wise as serpents and innocent as doves."' Matthew 10:16*

Autobiography of a missionary

St Patrick is the patron saint of Ireland, yet he was born in England. The lives of the saints of old gather to themselves all sorts of later legends, some believable and some less so. But in the case of St Patrick, we have a firsthand account from his own hand. His *Confessions* and *The Letter to Coroticus* are unique in the history of the early Celtic church. What we have in our libraries are later copies, but the originals were almost certainly written by Patrick himself, telling in his own words the history of his life as a missionary. He was born somewhere in western England in the fourth century AD, in a Christian family, and when he was about seventeen he was kidnapped by slave-traders and taken to Ireland, and sold as a cattle-hand. Yet he loved the rough Irish people who were his masters, and longed to share with them the Christian faith that he had learnt at home, and of which they knew nothing.

Wise as serpents, harmless as doves

Patrick escaped from Ireland in a ship carrying dogs to France. There he trained for the priesthood and was ordained. He soon took the courageous step of travelling back to Ireland as a missionary. There he suffered much opposition, and felt that he was sent by Christ 'like a sheep into the midst of wolves'. He wasn't stupid, he knew exactly what he was up against. But he refused to use trickery to gain his own way, and eventually won supporters by his charm. Christian missionaries often have to be 'wise as serpents and harmless as doves'.

Christian mission today

There are some countries today where Christians receive violent opposition to their faith. In most of these, the overseas missionary's not involved in direct evangelism, but is supporting the local Christians in practical ways, in medicine, agriculture or technology. Any Christian who leaves her or his own country to help the Church in another country is a missionary. Jesus knew all about the dangers when a single wolf enters a flock of sheep, so there was a striking ironic humour in his warning that his followers were to go out like a single sheep into a flock of wolves! Jesus kept the memorable animal metaphors flowing when he advised them to be as cunning and worldly-wise as snakes in assessing the challenges that face them, yet as harmless as doves in their refusal to use the devil's methods of threat and bribery to gain converts.

Gentleness and charm

Most of us will never meet violent persecution for our faith; we are more likely to be ignored, dismissed as irrelevant to modern life, and mocked openly or behind our backs for our stupidity in sticking to such an old-fashioned set of beliefs. We mustn't underestimate the strength of this opposition; we must be wise as serpents. Yet we are still called to be missionaries. It is all too easy to shrink into a purely private faith, which we never mention in public so as to avoid being made fun of. Jesus won't allow us to do this, but sends each one of us out as sheep among wolves to bear witness to our faith, and to share the love of God with those who may never have heard that God loves them. Yet we shall fail if we become aggressive, nobody wins converts that way; we have to win people by our gentleness and charm, as Patrick did in Ireland.

Patrick's prayer

There's a short evening prayer which is attributed to Patrick, and which expresses his quiet confidence in the protection of God:

> May your angels, holy Son,
> Guard our homes when day is done,
> When at peace, our sleep is best:
> Bid them watch us while we rest.
>
> Prince of everything that is,
> High Priest of the mysteries,
> Let your angels, God supreme,
> Tell us truth dressed as a dream.
>
> May no terror and no fright
> Spoil our slumber in the night;
> Free from care our eyelids close;
> Spirit, give us prompt repose.
>
> We have laboured through the day:
> Lift our burdens when we pray,
> Then our souls in safety keep,
> That our sleep be soft and deep.

> *(Versification © 1999 by Michael Counsell
> in 2000 Years of Prayer, Canterbury Press)*

Suggested hymns

Captains of the saintly band; God is working his purpose out; For all the saints, who from their labours rest; I bind unto myself today.

St Joseph of Nazareth   19 March

The Patient Stepfather 2 Sam. 7:4–16 Descendants of David;
Ps. 89:27–36 David's line; Rom. 4:13–18 Abraham's descendants;
Matt. 1:18–25 Joseph's dream

*'When Joseph awoke from sleep, he did as the angel of the Lord
commanded him; he took [Mary] as his wife.' Matthew 1:24*

Patience

Although the other Gospels refer to Jesus as the son of Joseph, most
of the detail about Joseph is found in Matthew. This Gospel traces
Jesus's ancestors through Joseph, which is correct in Jewish Law,
because Joseph, even though he wasn't the natural father, formally
adopted his stepson. The purpose of the genealogy was to show
that Jesus was the Messiah, the longed-for king of the Jews, and the
successor of King David, not only metaphorically but from the legal
bloodline. Marriage took place in two stages: first the couple were
betrothed, which was a legally binding commitment to proceed to
the second stage of full marriage later. If a woman was found to have
committed adultery while she was betrothed, she could be stoned to
death if the innocent husband demanded it. So when Joseph found
that his betrothed fiancée Mary was pregnant, although he'd had
no relations with her, he'd have been quite justified under the Law
in demanding her execution. But Joseph didn't do that. He was
a righteous man, a good man, and he loved his apparently erring
fiancée. So to avoid the possibility of legal proceedings against her,
he decided to break off the engagement – this was equivalent to
divorcing a wife – but quietly, so that nobody should ask the reason
why. This was remarkably patient of him.

Mystery plays

In the Middle Ages, cycles of mystery plays were performed, telling
the story of the Bible from Creation to Judgement Day, in church or
on stages and carts around the town. The text of the plays performed
in Coventry, York and Chester has survived complete. In the section of the Mystery Plays dealing with the birth of Jesus, Joseph
is treated with broad medieval humour. If he's not the father of
Mary's child, he wants to know who *on earth* is the father? Who is
the man who's cuckolded Joseph? And this makes Joseph's patience
all the more surprising and admirable.

Called to be a stepfather

Then Joseph had a dream. The angel of the Lord told him that nobody '*on earth*' was the father of Mary's child; he was to be born 'not of blood or of the will of the flesh or of the will of man, but of God' (John 1:13). So Joseph hadn't been cuckolded after all; instead he was to be called to a very special and difficult vocation, to care for a stepson as if the child were his own son. It was an important task, because the child Jesus was in fact the Son of God. In the mystery of the incarnation, Christians have learnt to describe Jesus as fully human and fully divine. The human child needed the patient care of loving parents, and when Jesus later spoke about love, we know that he was describing what he himself had experienced in the gentle arms of his parents. When Jesus disappeared in the Temple at the age of 12, Joseph didn't shout and argue or beat him, but patiently took him home again. Joseph patiently taught the boy Jesus the trade of a carpenter, which involved anything from carving a wooden yoke so that it would sit easily on the shoulders of an ox, to building a complete house on firm foundations. Jesus knew what he was talking about, and he learnt his trade from Joseph. We can be sure that when Jesus made a table, it stood level and firm.

In loving memory

Joseph doesn't appear in the gospel stories of the adult life of Jesus. He'd probably died before Jesus started his ministry. This doesn't necessarily mean that Joseph was much older than Mary, as was later assumed: the expectation of life in those days was quite brief. Yet although Joseph was dead, he lived on in the loving memory of Jesus. Jesus told many stories about fathers and sons, and we can be sure that he had a mental picture of Joseph the carpenter as he spoke. Jesus's favourite word for talking about God was as a father, especially in the parable of the Prodigal Son. God is not, as so many people think, a distant and fierce judge, said Jesus; he's more loving than the most patient father you can possibly imagine. Who can Jesus have been thinking of then, other than the patient carpenter and stepfather in Nazareth, Joseph, the husband of the Virgin Mary? We honour Joseph and keep him in loving memory, because we too owe a great deal to his patience.

Suggested hymns

As Joseph was a-walking; Joseph dearest, Joseph mine; Lord of the home, your only Son; Rejoice in God's saints, today and all days.

Annunciation of our Lord to the Blessed Virgin Mary

(Transferred to 26 March; see page 98.)

St George, Martyr, Patron of England c. 304   23 April
George and the Dragon 1 Macc. 2:59–64 Be courageous; *or* Rev. 12:7–12 Michael fights the dragon; Ps. 126 Restore our fortunes; 2 Tim. 2:3–13 A soldier of Christ; John 15:18–21 They will persecute you

> *'The great dragon was thrown down, that ancient serpent, who is called the Devil and Satan, the deceiver of the whole world – he was thrown down to the earth, and his angels were thrown down with him.' Revelation 12:9*

St George of Chivalry

Courage and valour are great virtues, especially in standing up for what is right. Patriotism is to be encouraged, so long as it doesn't turn into narrow nationalism. These virtues are fostered by repeating year by year the romantic legends of St George the dragon-killer, who defended the life of the maiden. Like the stories of King Arthur and the knights of the round table, we know that these legends are romantic and poetic elaborations of the truth, but they are none the worse for that, provided that they can encourage young men and women to be brave and virtuous. Just as Arthur was a historical figure, so was St George, but we know very little about either of them. As a change from all the chivalry, this year let's look into the history of the cult of St George.

Lydda

George is believed to have been a martyr, dying for his faith during the third century AD in Lydda, in the Holy Land. This is where St Peter healed a paralysed man; the Bible says that all the residents of

Lydda saw this and turned to the Lord. Obviously a strong church was founded there, which became a target for persecution in the third century. George must have been a Christian there who refused to deny his faith, probably refused to sacrifice to the Roman Emperor as a god, and was executed for so doing. Lydda is now the site of Lod airport.

Bringer of fertility

For some reason, probably by identification with a pre-Christian god, George became what is called a 'green saint', a bringer of fertility to the crops and the herds. William Dalrymple, in his marvellous travel book *From the Holy Mountain*, describes one Middle-Eastern shrine of St George where barren women, both Christian and Muslim, pray side by side to St George asking that they may be able to have a baby.

Joppa

Lydda is a short distance inland from Joppa, which was an important port in Old Testament times. It was from Joppa that the prophet Jonah embarked when he was trying to run away from God's call to be a missionary. St Peter was called from Lydda to go to Joppa because a much-loved embroideress called Dorcas had died there; Peter raised her from the dead. Joppa became known as Jaffa, where Jaffa oranges come from. Now it's a suburb of the Israeli metropolis of Tel Aviv-Yafo. Joppa's always had a fine natural harbour, where the ships are protected from the waves by a spit of land, at the end of which there still rises today what is left of a rock known as 'Andromeda's Rock'.

Perseus

Andromeda, in Greek mythology, was the beautiful daughter of the King and Queen of Joppa. Her mother Cassiopeia offended the sea nymphs by boasting that she was more beautiful than they were. In revenge, the sea god Poseidon sent a great sea monster to devastate the kingdom. The only way to appease the gods was to sacrifice Andromeda. So she was chained to the rock at the entrance to the harbour, and left there to be devoured by the monster. The Greek hero Perseus flew by on the winged horse Pegasus, fell in love with Andromeda, and asked for her hand in marriage. Her father agreed, and Perseus slew the monster.

George and the dragon

This was too good a story to waste, so in the sixth century it was transferred to the otherwise unknown St George of nearby Lydda, who became a warrior-saint, slaying the dragon to rescue the maiden. So popular was the story that the Crusaders who fought in that area adopted George as their patron saint and brought the cult back to England with them. He became recognized as England's patron saint when King Edward III made him the patron of the newly founded Order of the Garter. Generations of English people have been inspired to defend their nation by the legend of St George and the dragon. Jan Struther wrote a hymn, 'When a knight won his spurs', one of the most popular in schools today, which updates the legend and gives it a contemporary moral:

> So let faith be my shield and let hope be my steed,
> Against the dragons of anger, the ogres of greed;
> And let me set free, with the sword of my youth,
> From the castle of darkness the power of the truth.

Suggested hymns

And did those feet, in ancient time; I vow to thee, my country; O God of earth and altar; When a knight won his spurs.

St Mark the Evangelist   25 April

Early Days Prov. 15:28–33 Good news; *or* Acts 15:35–41 Paul rejects Mark; Ps. 119:9–16 How can young people keep their way pure?; Eph. 4:7–16 The gift of an evangelist; Mark 13:5–13 Staying-power

> *'How can young people keep their way pure? By guarding it according to your word.' Psalm 119:9*

What we know about St Mark

Who wrote the Gospel of Mark? Actually, we know quite a lot about St Mark. That is, assuming that a number of unprovable assumptions are true. These are the assumptions:

1 the man carrying a water-pot was Mark;

2 the Upper Room where Jesus held the last supper was the room
   in John Mark's mother's house where the disciples continued to
   meet after the resurrection;
3 Mark was the anonymous young man who ran away naked in
   Gethsemane;
4 this John Mark was the nephew of Barnabas who accompanied
   St Paul on his first missionary journey;
5 the second-century traditions that Mark became Peter's translator
   and wrote the Gospel of Mark are reliable historical memories.

If these assumptions are true, and it's quite likely that they are, we
know more about the life of young John Mark than about many
people who are referred to in ancient history books. There's enough
here to fill three sermons; this year let's concentrate on Mark's early
days.

A young man

It's tough being a teenager. There's so much you need to know in
adult life, and it's hard to know where to find it. 'How can young
people keep their way pure?' asks the psalmist, and answers his own
question thus, 'By guarding it according to [God's] word.' Young
John Mark didn't have much time to study the Scriptures. That's
because his mother was a widow; she must have been, because
people called her home 'John Mark's mother's house' – without
giving his father's name. So if she was a poor widow, she couldn't
afford to employ servants: she and her son would have to do all the
housework between them. Even carrying the water-pots from the
well, which was women's work, was something Mark had to do
to help his mother. The only time of year when they could make a
bit of pocket-money was at Passover. Then they could rent out the
upper room of their home in Jerusalem to people willing to pay for
somewhere inside the city boundaries to eat the Passover lamb. The
arrival of Jesus and his disciples, and the women who paid the bills
for him, was a godsend to poor John Mark and his mother, in more
ways than one.

The Last Supper

According to Mark's own Gospel, Jesus told the disciples that a
young man carrying a water-pot would lead them to the room
where they should prepare the Passover meal. How did Jesus know

that they were going to meet a man doing women's work? Possibly he'd already spotted Mark on the edge of the crowd, when he came to listen to him, and found out about their precarious housekeeping arrangements. So Mark could well have been there at the Last Supper, and followed Jesus to Gethsemane. After Jesus was arrested, according to a story which is recorded in Mark's Gospel only, 'A certain young man was following him, wearing nothing but a linen cloth. They caught hold of him, but he left the linen cloth and ran off naked.' Why should Mark bother to report such a trivial incident, unless it was something that happened to him? Perhaps he was the young man concerned?

John Mark's mother's house

The first time Mark's named in the Bible, however, is in the Acts of the Apostles. An angel had released Peter from prison. Immediately Peter went to the house of Mary, the mother of John Mark, 'where many had gathered and were praying'. Then follows the funny incident about the maid called Rhoda – by now, they could afford a servant – who left poor Peter standing on the doorstep. It sounds like an eyewitness account. Probably the house had been the meeting-place for the disciples ever since the Last Supper and the day of Pentecost.

Mark's life's work

So if young Mark was in the background at all these events, and taking it all in, he was preparing himself for his life's work, without even realizing it. It was early days yet. Mark was taking in the word of God by listening to Jesus and his disciples. His way in life, in the future, would involve writing that word down in the form of a Gospel. He was the first person to write one.

Who knows what tasks God may have in mind for each of us, young or old? The only way we can prepare ourselves for what God demands of us is by soaking ourselves in the words of the Lord Jesus, as young John Mark did.

Suggested hymns

Break thou the bread of life; Disposer supreme, and Judge of the earth; Lord, thy word abideth; The saint who first found grace to pen.

SS Philip and James, Apostles   1 May

Fame Isa. 30:15–21 This is the way; Ps. 119:1–8 The way of the Lord; Eph. 1:3–10 The mystery of forgiveness; John 14:1–14 Show us the Father

> *'Philip said to him, "Lord, show us the Father, and we will be satisfied." Jesus said to him, "Have I been with you all this time, Philip, and you still do not know me? Whoever has seen me has seen the Father. How can you say, 'Show us the Father'?"' John 14:8–9*

Fame

To read the newspapers today you'd think the only thing that matters is to become a celebrity. The gossip columns are full of the doings of celebrities, and some newspapers seem one long gossip column. Television programmes are made with no more claim to interest us than that the people who take part are celebrities. A German drama critic, Georg Lichtenberg, wrote:

> The journalists have constructed for themselves a little wooden chapel, which they also call the Temple of Fame, in which they put up and take down portraits all day long and make such a hammering you can't hear yourself speak.

How ironic, then, that the names of the two apostles whom we celebrate today should be known to everybody, but we know very little else about them.

Philip the apostle

Today's dedication is to 'Philip and James, Apostles', so you'd assume that each of them was one of the Twelve, 'who were also called apostles'. One of the Twelve was called Philip; he came from Bethsaida, just the other side of the River Jordan from the province of Galilee, in the Greek-speaking area of ten towns known as the Decapolis. He it was who brought Nathanael to Jesus; and later some Greeks approached Philip, perhaps because he had a Greek name, and he took them to meet the Master. At the Last Supper, Philip asked Jesus to show them the Father. The answer he received is full of teaching about the unity between God the Father and Jesus his Son, and the unity between Jesus and those who pray in his name.

How many Philips?

Yet the word 'apostle' isn't restricted to the Twelve in the Bible; Paul and many others who weren't members of the Twelve are called apostles. There was also a Philip who was one of the Seven, appointed to relieve the Twelve of the burden of the charitable distributions made by the Church. They were later referred to as deacons. Then there was 'Philip the evangelist', who preached in Samaria, baptized the Ethiopian official, and together with his four daughters gave hospitality to Paul, Luke and their companions. St Luke's quite clear in his own mind that Philip the evangelist was one of the Seven. But Papias, writing in the second century, who met Philip's daughters, insists that Philip the evangelist was the apostle, one of the Twelve, and that he was buried at Hierapolis! Hierapolis is now called Pamukkale, a popular tourist resort in Turkey, and the remains of Philip's tomb are there. In the sixth century, Philip's bones were taken to Rome, and placed together with the bones of St James in a new church there, which was dedicated on 1 May 560, which is why this is St Philip and St James's Day. But which Philip? And which James?

St James

James is a very common name in the New Testament; it's the English form of Jacob. There are two Jameses mentioned in the lists of the Twelve. One of them, a Galilean fisherman, was the brother of John, son of Zebedee, and was present at the transfiguration and in Gethsemane. He was killed by King Herod, and is celebrated on 25 July. The other James, whom we celebrate today, is often known as James the Less or 'Little James'. He was the brother of Matthew, and the son of Alphaeus and Mary. One of the brothers of Jesus, who tried to dissuade him from his ministry, was also called James. 'James the brother of the Lord' was the leader of the church in Jerusalem. According to the Jewish historian Josephus he was called James the Just and was martyred on the orders of High Priest Annas II around AD 60–62. Then there's the author of the Letter of James. They were all probably different people, but we can't be sure, and there are no special days for the others.

Almost anonymous

So the answer to the question 'Whom do we celebrate on St Philip and St James Day?' is 'We don't know, and it doesn't matter.' How good to celebrate two people who were so little concerned with being celebrities that nothing certain's been passed down to posterity except their names. Perhaps all those who long for their 'fifteen minutes of fame' have something to learn from them.

Suggested hymns

Christ is the world's light, he and none other; Rejoice in God's saints, today and all days; To God be the glory; Twin princes of the courts of heaven.

St Matthias the Apostle   14 May
Added to the Eleven Apostles Isa. 22:15–25 Eliakim

replaces Shebna; Ps. 15 Who shall dwell in your house?;
Acts 1:15–26 Matthias replaces Judas; (*if the Acts reading is used instead of the Old Testament reading, the New Testament reading is* 1 Cor. 4:1–7 Stewards of God's mysteries); John 15:9–17 I have appointed you to go

> *'And they cast lots for them, and the lot fell on Matthias; and he was added to the eleven apostles.' Acts 1:26*

Apostle spoons

Have you ever seen a set of 'apostle spoons'? They're teaspoons or coffee-spoons, with the figure of a saint cast into the end of the handle. They should always be in sets of twelve. 'Because', people will tell you, 'there were twelve apostles in the Bible.' Only unfortunately that's not true. Certainly there are lists of twelve names in Matthew, Mark and Luke, and in the Acts of the Apostles. But there were many others whom the Bible calls apostles, who weren't included in the lists of the Twelve. The most famous was St Paul, 'the Apostle to the Gentiles', who was not one of the Twelve. He refers to many of his companions as apostles, including at least one woman apostle, Junia. The word simply means someone who's been 'sent out'; in other words a missionary.

The Twelve

Yet the Twelve were important. Often the Gospels refer to them simply as that, 'the Twelve', and we often write it with a capital T. In one place they are described as 'the Twelve, who were also called apostles'. One theory is that Paul the apostle himself gave the name of 'apostles' to them, when they left Jerusalem and started doing missionary work, to show that they were all equal in God's service. And yet the number twelve was very significant; so significant, in fact, that when Judas Iscariot, who'd been one of the Twelve, committed suicide, the others thought it was important enough to appoint an immediate replacement. They didn't want to take a vote for anything so important. They used the ancient method of writing the names of each candidate on the two sides of a piece of wood and throwing it onto the ground. This was called 'casting lots'; depending on whether it came up 'heads or tails', they felt that God had made the decision.

Why twelve?

Matthias was chosen, and he's the saint we commemorate on 14 May. We know nothing else about him at all, except that he fulfilled the conditions for being an apostle, that he'd been with Jesus and was a witness to the resurrection. So why was it so important to keep the number up to twelve? Jesus told the Twelve, 'You who have followed me will also sit on twelve thrones, judging the twelve tribes of Israel.' The twelve tribes were the descendants of the twelve sons of Jacob. So the twelve apostles symbolized the twelve patriarchs; that, incidentally, is the only reason why there were no women among them, because a woman can't symbolize Reuben, Simeon, Levi, Judah, Dan and so on. 'Judging' means ruling, so the Twelve were to be the rulers of the Jewish church after the resurrection of Jesus; others, like Paul, would take care of the Gentile church. That's why it was necessary to appoint Matthias; otherwise the symbolism of the twelve sons of Jacob would be lost.

Symbolism

You may ask, 'What's that to do with us?' The appointment of Matthias teaches us the importance of symbolism and of willingness. Never dismiss anything as 'merely symbolic'. Symbols are important to people, they're how they define their identity and proclaim their loyalty; symbolic language may be the only way to proclaim truths that are too deep for prose. Never pour scorn on somebody else's symbols. As the Irish poet W. B. Yeats put it, 'Tread softly because you tread on my dreams.'

Willingness

The second lesson is that we never know what God's going to demand of us. Matthias never dreamt that he'd become one of the leaders of the Jewish church. But when the call came, and 'the lot fell upon Matthias', he was willing to do whatever God expected of him, and go anywhere that God called him to. You don't know whether God's going to call you to a position of responsibility, or to pursue a boring but demanding life of service to others, where nothing will be remembered about you but your name. But if you've 'been with Jesus', in regular prayer, worship and Bible reading, and if you can witness to the power of the resurrection in your own life, then God will give you that power, to enable you to do whatever you have to. All you need is to be willing, as Matthias was.

Suggested hymns

Jesus, take me as I am; O thou who camest from above; Strengthen for service, Lord, the hands; Thy way, not mine, O Lord.

Visit of the Blessed Virgin Mary to Elizabeth   31 May
Christian Domesticity Zeph. 3:14–18 Sing, daughter Zion;
Ps. 113 Making her a joyous mother; Rom. 12:9–16 Hospitality;
Luke 1:39–49 [50–56] Magnificat

'Let love be genuine . . .' Romans 12:9

Christian domesticity

Some Christians are called to live heroic lives of outstanding virtue in the public eye. For the Virgin Mary that would come later. Apart from the inevitable gossip that began when it became evident that she was expecting a baby before she was married, her pregnancy was a quiet one. So she decided to visit her cousin. Elizabeth was much older than her, and past the change of life; yet, amazingly, she too was expecting. They must have been genuinely fond of each other, for it was a difficult journey from Nazareth to the Judaean highlands for a woman in Mary's condition. But she went, so that they could compare notes and be quietly happy together. Mary's song, the Magnificat, is all about the importance in God's eyes of ordinary poor people. Together, Mary and Elizabeth looked forward to lives of Christian domesticity. St Paul gives a picture of what this is like, in the second reading today. It's amazing how much the well-travelled and socially awkward apostle understands about the everyday life of ordinary Christians! It's worth going through his advice line by line.

Let love be genuine.
The love between the cousins Mary and Elizabeth was open and sincere; we need to show love to our family and friends which has no trace of hypocrisy in it.
Hate what is evil.
This doesn't tell us to hate evil people, but to hate those tendencies in society and in ourselves which tempt others into doing wrong.
Hold fast to what is good.
Time to be together as a family, time for relaxation, time for prayer; we should hold on to these things.
Love one another with mutual affection.
This is a pointer towards balanced relationships, with neither husband nor wife dominating over the other, and children and parents respecting each other.
Outdo one another in showing honour.
The only rivalry there should be between Christians is to see who can be most successful in affirming and praising others.
Do not lag in zeal, be ardent in spirit, serve the Lord.
Our prayer, our worship, and our church work should arise from a strong desire in our hearts to serve Jesus in return for what he has done for us.
Rejoice in hope.
There will be sad times for everybody when disappointment or bereavement come. But gradually we learn to look forward joyfully to the time when we shall all be reunited in heaven.
Be patient in suffering.
Similarly, most people have times of physical pain and mental agony; but if we trust in God's love we don't need to be constantly complaining about them.

Persevere in prayer.
We should be regular in our times of prayer, even when we don't
feel like praying.
Contribute to the needs of the saints.
We can give money discretely and secretly to people in need, and to
Christian charities.
Extend hospitality to strangers.
However small your home, most people can manage to invite people
in, sometimes. The Greek word for a stranger is *xenos*; this phrase
is also a rebuke to the rampant 'xenophobia' which seems to afflict
so many today.
Bless those who persecute you; bless and do not curse them.
This is a challenge to love our enemies.
Rejoice with those who rejoice, weep with those who weep.
We must adjust our style according to who we're talking to. How-
ever much we may want to run away when a friend is in sorrow, all
they need is a listening ear.
Live in harmony with one another.
Christians are not very good at this: different denominations and
different parties within the Church criticize each other, when what
the world needs is to see how we can live in harmony despite our
differences.
Do not be haughty, but associate with the lowly.
There's no place for snobbery in church; it's one of the few places
where different social classes can mix on equal terms.
Do not claim to be wiser than you are.
Oh, how good we are at pretending to know it all, and how reluctant we are to listen to other people's opinions!

The example of Mary and Elizabeth

These down-to-earth instructions remind us all of the importance
of being loving in the details of our behaviour, and send us back to
the example that Mary and Elizabeth showed in Christian domesticity. 'Let love be genuine,' wrote St Paul. If only our love was as
genuine as theirs!

Suggested hymns

*Brother, sister, let me serve you; From heaven you came, helpless
babe (The Servant King); Tell out, my soul, the greatness of the
Lord!; Ye watchers and ye holy ones.*

Day of Thanksgiving for the Institution of Holy Communion (Corpus Christi)   7 June

Living Bread Gen. 14:18–20 Melchizedek brought bread and wine; Ps. 116:12–19 The cup of salvation; 1 Cor. 11:23–26 The Last Supper; John 6:51–58 Living bread

'[Jesus said,] "I am the living bread that came down from heaven. Whoever eats of this bread will live forever; and the bread that I will give for the life of the world is my flesh."' John 6:51

'You are what you eat'

Ludwig Feuerbach was a nineteenth-century German philosopher. The only thing he's famed for is saying 'You are what you eat,' which is a pun in German but falls rather flat when translated into English. Recently it became the title of a series of television programmes. On the physical level it's obviously true: the cells of our bodies are made up of molecules from the food we consume. It also seems that people who pick at their food have a different personality from those who eat a daily roast; those who eat frogs' legs are culturally different from those who eat Yorkshire pudding! Jesus says that in a spiritual sense, our souls are formed by what we absorb as spiritual nourishment.

Corpus Christi

This is highlighted by his words at the Last Supper, which we commemorate on Maundy Thursday. It was felt, however, that there's so much else happening in Holy Week, that the Lord's Supper, Holy Communion, Eucharist or Mass – call it what you like – when we commemorate and re-enact the Last Supper, didn't receive enough attention. So a new feast was instituted, when the Easter season was over, on the Thursday after Trinity Sunday, and called Corpus Christi, which means the Body of Christ. St Thomas Aquinas, the great thirteenth-century theologian, wrote a complete set of hymns and prayers to be used on this day. They express in beautiful poetry his devotion to the sacrament of the Eucharist. The spirituality and the language are timeless; unfortunately the philosophy of Aristotle on which they are based is now seen by many as rather dated. There's no time to go into the complicated issue of transubstantiation; Queen Elizabeth I wrote a piece of appalling verse, which is

sound common sense, saying that she was willing to leave it to Jesus
to decide what he meant by the words 'This is my body':

> 'Twas God the word that spake it,
> He took the bread and brake it;
> And what the word did make it;
> That I believe, and take it.

Spiritual food

So, like her, we can leave others to argue over what the bread and
wine actually are; Jesus himself said that it's their spiritual symbolism that matters. A few verses after the passage set as today's
Gospel he says, 'It is the spirit that gives life; the flesh is useless. The
words that I have spoken to you are spirit and life.' The symbolism
of eating's very helpful in this way. To receive the power of Jesus
for ourselves, we must feed on him – there's no other word which
expresses it so well – we must absorb his teaching, his character, his
mind, his ways. Ask yourself constantly, 'What would Jesus do in
my place?' and do it; allow Jesus to love other people *through you*.
Then Jesus will be in you and you in him, just as closely as the food
we eat becomes a part of us. Jesus is our spiritual food. Without
him dwelling in us we are powerless. When Jesus is in us we are
transformed. A great Scottish preacher said he first really believed
that Jesus is alive today when he saw the expression on his father's
face as he returned from receiving Holy Communion.

The Church, the Body of Christ

Perhaps it was when the first Christians repeated the words of
Jesus, 'This is my body', as they gathered together to worship, that
it dawned on them that they themselves were becoming the Body of
Christ. St Paul frequently appeals to this metaphor: we're like limbs
and organs in Christ's body, each of us different, but each with a
part to play in doing Christ's work in the world. St Paul appeals to
this, to teach his divided congregations to be tolerant of each other.
However much you reverence the bread and wine in the sacrament,
you should reverence your fellow-worshippers as much. It would be
a little impractical to genuflect to each other as we leave the church,
but really we ought to! For all the other communicants have now
absorbed Christ into themselves, and each of them has become the
Body of Christ, just as truly as the bread is; 'you are what you

eat'. Even the church members whom you resent, despise or ignore: Christ is in them. They have become, for you, the Body of Christ, and will remain so all week. Treat them with reverence and respect, for if you don't, you'll be blaspheming the Body of Christ.

Suggested hymns

God is here! As we his people; I am the bread of life; Now, my tongue, the mystery telling; The church of God a kingdom is.

St Barnabas the Apostle   11 June
Good cop–bad cop Job 29:11–16 Like one who comforts; Ps. 112 Generous; Acts 11:19–30 Barnabas encourages Saul; (*if the Acts reading is used instead of the Old Testament reading, the New Testament reading is* Gal. 2:1–10 Barnabas and me); John 15:12–17 Love one another

> *'Then Barnabas went to Tarsus to look for Saul, and when he had found him, he brought him to Antioch.' Acts 11:25–26*

The 'son of encouragement'

The name of Barnabas probably means 'son of prophecy'. But in Acts it's translated as 'son of encouragement' – or 'son of consolation' in the old translations. This was probably based on a similar word, used as a nickname, and a well-deserved one at that, meaning someone who comforts and encourages others. He owned a field, which he sold, and brought to the leaders of the Jesus movement the money which was realized, for them to distribute to the poor. Maybe it was they who, impressed by his encouraging generosity, first gave him his nickname – 'Dear old Barnabas, he's such an encouragement to us.' He came from Cyprus, where the Jews spoke Greek fluently. So when a church grew up in Antioch with many Greek-speaking Jews among its members, naturally they sent for Barnabas to be one of their preachers. He encouraged many to become Christians, and the congregation grew so much that they needed help in the leadership team. Well, Barnabas had met, during one of his visits to Jerusalem, a Greek-speaking Jew from Tarsus called Saul. Barnabas went to Tarsus to find Saul, and bring him to Antioch. Barnabas encouraged Saul to become his assistant.

Sent out as missionaries

They worked so well together as a team that the church in Antioch decided to send them out as missionaries together. So they both became known as apostles; it's the usual Greek word for somebody who's 'sent out'. Barnabas and Saul's first journey was to Cyprus. Dear old Barnabas was on his home stamping ground there, and he arranged a tour of the synagogues where he was probably already well known. Perhaps he was told to keep an eye on the young firebrand to keep him on the straight and narrow. If so he failed, because after a conversation with Sergius Paulus, the Roman Governor of Cyprus, Saul, now known as Paul, set off on a mission of his own, taking Barnabas, his former boss, as *his* assistant.

Good cop–bad cop

What was the secret of the successful partnership between Paul and Barnabas? In the American television series, Starsky and Hutch were two policemen who would sometimes have difficulty getting information out of a suspect. Then, with an unseen wink to their partner, they would embark on a well-rehearsed routine which they called 'Good cop–bad cop'. One of them would become extremely threatening. He'd threaten the suspect with suffering, imprisonment, separation from his family, whatever it took to make him thoroughly alarmed and frightened. Then the other policeman would take the suspect aside saying, 'Don't worry, I'll look after you and see you come to no harm.' The suspect was so grateful that he'd 'spill the beans', and tell the 'good cop' whatever he wanted to know! I wonder whether dear old Barnabas and the aggressive Saul of Tarsus played a variation on the good cop–bad cop routine? Stern young Saul would preach threateningly, warning of the dangers of hellfire to those who failed to keep the terms of God's covenant. And then dear old Barnabas would say, 'Never mind. God loves you, and, in Christ, God will forgive you for all the things Saul has made you feel guilty about!' Then the hearers would be converted, in a way they would never have been if Saul hadn't softened them up first, and if Barnabas, the 'son of consolation', hadn't followed up with the good news of Christ. Stern young Saul and dear old Barnabas – bad cop–good cop? It's an interesting speculation!

Missionary methods – Paul's or ours?

In the early twentieth century Roland Allen wrote a book with the challenging title, *Missionary Methods – Paul's or Ours?* He was arguing that western missionaries were mistaken in building large schools and hospitals and not handing over authority to local Christians. Many would say that what happened following the collapse of colonialism proved him right. But may we not also learn other lessons from Paul's missionary methods? If we're right in speculating about the complementary ministries of Paul and Barnabas, doesn't that teach us that both are needed? We should challenge believers and unbelievers to aim for the highest standards of morality. We should also reassure them that God loves all, and forgives all. God accepts us as we are, trusting us to grow in grace as time goes by.

Suggested hymns

Christ is the world's light, he and none other; Disposer supreme, and Judge of the earth; God, whose city's sure foundation; Lord, it belongs not to my care.

Birth of St John the Baptist   24 June
(see page 173)

SS Peter and Paul, Apostles   29 June
On This Rock Zech. 4:1–6a, 10b–14 Two anointed ones;
Ps. 125 Stand fast for ever; Acts 12:1–11 Peter released from prison;
(*if the Acts reading is used instead of the Old Testament reading,
the New Testament reading is* 2 Tim. 4:6–8, 17–18 Poured out);
Matt. 16:13–19 Peter recognizes the Messiah; **or for Peter alone**:
Ezek. 3:22–27 Preaching to his own; Ps. 125; Acts 12:1–11; (*if the
Acts reading is used instead of the Old Testament reading, the New
Testament reading is* 1 Peter 2:19–25 Suffering for God);
Matt. 16:13–19

> *'[Jesus said,] "I tell you, you are Peter, and on this rock I will build
> my church, and the gates of Hades will not prevail against it."'*
> *Matthew 16:18*

A nickname

Peter's real name was Simon or Simeon; Peter (in Greek), or Cephas (in Aramaic), was a nickname given by Jesus. Perhaps Peter's house in Capernaum was built on a rock foundation. Perhaps it was the original Jesus had in mind when he told the parable of the house built on the rock, and that was why he gave Peter his nickname. It was, after all, a most unsuitable nickname. A rock is something firm and immovable – heavyweight boxers are nicknamed 'Rocky' – but Peter was vacillating and impetuous. When Jesus predicted his own crucifixion, Peter tried to persuade him against it, and got rebuked as a 'tempter': 'you Satan'. At the transfiguration Peter started babbling about building shelters. At the Last Supper he refused to have his feet washed; then he threatened to stick by Jesus till death, and tried to defend him with a sword. Yet when he was challenged by a chit of a servant girl, he denied that he even knew who Jesus was. Don't forget that all these criticisms of Peter are recorded in St Mark's Gospel, and Mark is traditionally regarded as Peter's secretary and translator. So Peter was open and honest when preaching about his own faults. Perhaps his nickname was a joke; Jesus knew all about his instability of character, and teased him in order to build his character up. Jesus knew that Peter would fail him, but that he was capable of learning from his failures. If that describes a rock, it must be a very crumbly one.

On this rock

Yet at Caesarea Philippi, Peter was the first to recognize that Jesus was the long-awaited Messiah. The Messiah was supposed to be a general who would drive out the occupying Roman army. Only Peter recognized that the carpenter and healer, the preacher of love and forgiveness, was truly the one anointed by God to bring in his kingdom. Immediately after this, Jesus said, 'I tell you, you are Peter, and on this rock I will build my church.' It's a very surprising verse. Only twice in the Gospels does Jesus use the word 'church', though it's the usual word in Greek for the 'congregation of Israel'. Because Roman Catholics have used this verse to defend the supremacy of the popes, Protestants have argued that it is on the rock of Peter's faith that the Church is to be built. Or interpreters may say that if Peter was indeed the leader of the early Jewish church, there's no evidence that he was entitled to pass on his authority to his successors as bishops of Rome.

The gates of Hades

Be that as it may, this passage is a great encouragement to us all. Jesus doesn't build his Church on super-heroes. He builds it on ordinary, all-too-human, unreliable, vacillating and – I almost said 'fallible' – people like Peter. And like me, and like you. Jesus knows our faults, and how undependable we are, yet still he can use us. Still he can succeed, even with such rotten raw material, in building a fabric which will survive. Jesus finishes his promise to Peter about the Church, 'on this rock I will build my church, and the gates of Hades will not prevail against it.' Hades (in Greek) or Sheol (in Hebrew) is where all people, good or bad, were thought, up until that time, to go. It wasn't thought of as a place of punishment, or where the Devil lives. We might as well say, 'the gates of death'. Now, whoever heard of gates getting up and attacking a rock? So the thought must be of the rock attacking the gates, like a battering ram or a demolition ball. The rock of the Church will attack the gates of death, and the Church will win. By spreading the good news of the resurrection of Jesus, the Church will give to millions and millions of souls down the ages the hope of eternal life. That sounds like a good organization to belong to, even if you're only a crumbly rock like Peter. Or like me, or like you. The 'Church that conquers death'. A good gang to be in, that!

Suggested hymns

Firmly I believe and truly; Forsaken once, and twice denied; 'Thou art the Christ, O Lord'; 'Tis good, Lord, to be here.

St Thomas the Apostle   3 July
Doubt and Faith Hab. 2:1–4 The righteous live by faith;
Ps. 31:1–6 I trust in the Lord; Eph. 2:19–22 The foundation of the apostles; John 20:24–29 Doubting Thomas is convinced

> *'[Jesus] said to Thomas, "Put your finger here and see my hands. Reach out your hand and put it in my side. Do not doubt but believe." Thomas answered him, "My Lord and my God!"' John 20:27–28*

The twin

Thomas is a nickname; it's Hebrew for 'the twin'; St John's Gospel also gives the Greek word for twin, 'Didymos', but nobody knows what his real name was or who his twin brother or sister was. We call him 'doubting Thomas', because he said 'I will not believe unless I see'. That's unfair, in view of what happened a week later. But first, a true story.

Faith and tolerance

A group of students arrived at a theological college from a world where they were surrounded by doubt. They were hoping to become more settled in their faith. A series of sermons was delivered in the college by some former students, each of whom had moved on from dogmatic doctrine to a more tolerant approach to intellectual exploration. The result was seven sermons one after another, all based on the lines from Tennyson, 'There is more truth in honest doubt than in all the creeds.' Now that was not what the students wanted to hear, at least not seven times on the trot! The college organist wickedly put down for the hymn after the last sermon, 'Firmly I believe and truly . . .'. Seldom has it been sung with such enthusiasm! But we change as we grow older. The core of faith grows stronger, but the things on the fringes become less important. We come to believe more and more strongly in fewer and fewer things.

The scientist's hero

In this way a mature Christian's a bit like a scientist. The job of a scientist is to be sceptical, and believe only what you can reason out for yourself, and test by experiment. So doubting Thomas is a scientist's hero: he wouldn't accept the words of other people about the resurrection, and needed to see for himself; he needed proof. He got it a week later, when he met in the upper room rather reluctantly with the other ten. Then he became 'believing Thomas', for he was the first to call Jesus God: 'My Lord and my God'. Those who begin with certainty often end in doubt, whereas those who begin with doubt will often end in faith.

What is faith?

What is faith? Faith isn't assent to propositions, because propositions are words, and God's too big for words. Faith is trust in a person. Thomas trusted Jesus, because Jesus trusted Thomas. Then Thomas realized that in some way Jesus is God. So from a position of doubt and gloom he moved to firm trust that God loved him. Knowing that you are loved gives you confidence to do things. The Christian experience of being loved by God gives us the power to love others for his sake, and to let his love flow through us. This is a fact of experience, which we can prove for ourselves. The experience is true, but try to describe it in words and you're into difficulties, for no words are adequate to describe the experience of loving and being loved.

Freedom and commitment

Bishop Hensley Henson in the first half of the twentieth century wrote of the necessity for the individual to be free, but for 'the institution to be something'. The Church must have a creed; but Christians mustn't be excommunicated if they can't yet assent to the words that the Church has traditionally used to describe the good news. Faith isn't assent to propositions, it's trust in a person. So doubting Thomas should be the patron saint of all of us, because he didn't clutch his doubts to himself, but met with others to discuss them, and eventually he was convinced that Jesus is alive.

Believing in Jesus

To be a Christian, you're not required to 'believe' any particular form of words, but to 'believe in', put your trust in, the person of Jesus, and believe that God loves you. Don't worry if you can't understand some of the words we use; there's nothing wrong with doubt over words, provided you're prepared to work through your doubts like Thomas did, and come to a relationship of trust in Jesus.

Suggested hymns

Firmly I believe and truly; In the Lord I'll be ever thankful (Taizé); Jesu, my Lord, my God, my all; Lead, kindly light, amid th'encircling gloom.

St Mary Magdalene   22 July (see page 192)

St James the Apostle   25 July

Ambition Jer. 45:1–5 Seeking greatness; Ps. 126 Sow in tears, harvest in joy; Acts 11:27—12:2 Herod kills James; (*if the Acts reading is used instead of the Old Testament reading, the New Testament reading is* 2 Cor. 4:7–15 Treasure in clay pots); Matt. 20:20–28 Seeking greatness

> *'[Jesus said,] "Whoever wishes to be first among you must be your slave." ' Matthew 20:27*

James the apostle

James is the English form of Jacob. There are up to six Jameses mentioned in the New Testament. The one known as James the Less or 'Little James' is celebrated on 1 May together with St Philip. But the one we celebrate today is James the brother of John; they were Galilean fishermen, and the sons of Zebedee. They were both members of the Twelve apostles, and present at the transfiguration and in Gethsemane. These two were nicknamed by Jesus 'the sons of Thunder' because of their stormy temperament. As today's reading from Acts tells us, this James was killed by King Herod Agrippa I.

To sit at your right hand

According to St Matthew's Gospel, the mother of James and John came to Jesus asking that her two sons might sit on Jesus's right and left in his kingdom. She meant this very literally; she hadn't yet realized that, as Jesus told Pilate, 'My kingdom is not of this world.' She thought he was going to become an earthly king, drive out the Romans and rule over the nation of Israel in Jerusalem. So she wanted to make sure that when that happened, her two boys would have the leading positions. She envisaged Jesus literally sitting on a throne, with James and John sitting on slightly smaller thrones on either side of him, giving orders about how the new kingdom was to be run – and probably taking a few bribes from people asking them for favours. Certainly being treated with great honour and respect. She was very ambitious for her boys, as any good mother would be. Only she was jumping to conclusions; Jesus said it wasn't going to be like that at all. In Mark's Gospel it's James and John themselves who make the request. They were very ambitious for themselves. There's nothing wrong with ambition, they thought.

Good ambition

They were right, of course; there's nothing wrong with ambition. Everyone wants to make their mark in the world. If there's an important job that you can do well, it's to everybody's benefit that you should go after it. Positions of authority can give you power, and power *can* be misused to harm other people, but power can also be used to run an organization well, to rule benevolently over a kingdom, or to prevent vice and crime, and everybody's better off if those things are done efficiently. So there's a good form of ambition, which seeks the power to be of service to others.

Bad ambition

But there's also a bad form of ambition. The other apostles were angry with James and John, because if they were given power, it would mean that the others were deprived of it. They'd be climbing to the top on other people's shoulders, and if the other people got trampled down in the process, that was no concern of theirs. In the oft-quoted words of Lord Acton, 'Power tends to corrupt, and absolute power corrupts absolutely.' The hunger for greater and greater power becomes an end in itself. When the important position has been obtained, the priority becomes a struggle to hold on to it. Harold Wilson once remarked, 'People say I don't know what's going on. I know what's going on – *I'm* going on!' Yet the life of a politician, the constant butt of criticism by others, is in many ways such a thankless one, that anybody would be a fool to go in for it unless they enjoyed, to some extent, the trappings of power.

Jesus on ambition

So how are we to choose between good ambition and bad ambition? Jesus put his finger on the difference, when he told James and John that they must be ambitious to serve. 'Whoever wishes to be first among you must be your slave,' he said. The proudest title given to the popes is 'servant of the servants of God'. Achieving power, so that you can be the slave of everybody, at the constant beck and call of those who need you, is a very worthy ambition. But it's not very common! In considering what position in life you hope to occupy, the only yardstick is where you could be of most service to others. In this way you'll be a true follower of Jesus, who said, 'The Son of Man came not to be served but to serve, and to give his life a ransom for many.'

Suggested hymns

Brother, sister, let me serve you; For all thy saints, a noble throng; From heaven you came, helpless babe (The Servant King); Lord, who shall sit beside thee?

The Transfiguration of our Lord   6 August
Cloud on the Mountain Dan. 7:9–10, 13–14 The Son of Man;
Ps. 97 Clouds are around him; 2 Peter 1:16–19 We saw;
Luke 9:28–36 The transfiguration

> *'A cloud came and overshadowed them; and they were terrified as they entered the cloud. Then from the cloud came a voice that said, "This is my Son, my Chosen; listen to him!"' Luke 9:34–35*

Clouds are around him

Many people today see visions; many more dream dreams. The difference between a vision and a dream is whether you're awake or asleep, and if they're caused by God the difference isn't important. If it's caused by someone wanting to appear to you, it's a vision. Hardly surprisingly, every visionary describes what they've seen in terms of their own culture. Peter, James, and John went up a mountain with Jesus and saw a vision which they knew to be of God. Only no Jew would ever say that they'd actually seen God. So they used one of the symbols from the Old Testament. They said a cloud had come down on the mountain and surrounded them. Imagine you're on a mountaintop when the mist comes down, so that you can't see your hand in front of your face. It's said to be a very frightening experience, but quite beautiful, too. Awesome, in fact. So Peter, James and John were terrified when they entered the cloud; but they had an additional reason to be in awe, derived from the symbolism that was ingrained in their upbringing. The cloud was the sign of the presence of God.

Cloud on the mountain

As the Israelites travelled through the wilderness they were led by God in a pillar of cloud by day, which turned into a pillar of fire by night. The glory of God was in the cloud, symbolized by a bright light. The cloud came down on Mount Sinai when God gave the Ten Commandments, and God spoke to Moses from the cloud. The cloud covered the tent of meeting, for this was where Moses met with God as a friend. Later, the cloud filled the Temple in Jerusalem when it was dedicated, to show that this was where God's presence was now to be found. In Daniel the Son of Man came to God on the clouds. God spoke to the disciples from the cloud on the mountain of transfiguration. Finally, Jesus returned to the presence of his Father at the ascension, when a cloud received him from their sight.

The presence of God

The Jews had a special word, the 'shekinah', for the bright cloud that symbolized the presence of God. When the cloud came and overshadowed them on the Mount of Transfiguration, no wonder the disciples were afraid! Of course, God's present everywhere, but we usually don't recognize him. When he wants to make his presence known, he uses the symbol of the cloud. When the disciples heard a voice speaking to them from the cloud, they knew it was God speaking.

Who is Jesus?

What did God tell them from the cloud on the mountain? He spoke about Jesus. 'This is my Son, my Chosen; listen to him!' These are titles given to the Messiah in the Old Testament. The disciples were to understand that Jesus was the long-expected king who would rule justly over his people. In the second Psalm, God says to the king of Israel, 'You are my Son, today I have begotten you.' First, if Jesus is the Son of God, we must obey him, do what he tells us, listen to his teaching and believe it because it comes with the authority of God behind it. Second, if Jesus is the Son of God, then the love that we see in his character must be the character of God. Jesus is like God the Father, and God the Father is like Jesus. When Jesus tells us God loves us, we must believe him, because he shows that love in his own life. Jesus wants us to be his friends, and speak to him in prayer as one friend speaks to another. If Jesus is the Son of God, that means that like Moses we can speak to God as a friend. We don't need a cloud on a mountain to remind us of the presence of God. God is present every time we talk to Jesus, and his love surrounds us whenever we pray. Prayer is a very awesome experience, but it's also a very beautiful one. That's what the words that Peter, James and John heard on the Mount of Transfiguration should teach us – that God is near us when we pray, and that God the Creator loves us as much as Jesus does.

Suggested hymns

Immortal, invisible, God only wise; Jesus, these eyes have never seen; Lord, the light of your love is shining (Shine, Jesus, shine); 'Tis good, Lord, to be here.

The Blessed Virgin Mary   15 August
All Glorious Within Isa. 61:10–11 As a bride; *or*
Rev. 11:19—12:6, 10 A woman in heaven; Ps. 45:10–17 You shall
have sons; Gal. 4:4–7 Born of a woman; Luke 1:46–55 Magnificat

> *'The king's daughter is all glorious within; her clothing is embroidered cloth of gold.' Psalm 45:13* (Common Worship)

A charming novel

There's a charming novel about a humble Catholic priest in a slum parish in Scotland. His church is nothing much to look at from the outside, and neither is he. He's mocked and ridiculed by his neighbours, ignored by those in authority, and his parishioners make impossible demands on him. But he goes on saying Mass, hearing confessions and praying for the people whom it's his task to love into faith. Due to his constant care, the church building's not unattractive on the inside, and his delight is to stand and pray to the Blessed Virgin Mary and ask her protection over them all, for he knows that the blessed mother has a loving heart. His meditations are based upon Psalm 45, the psalm written for a royal wedding:

> Hear, O daughter; consider and incline your ear:
> forget your own people and your father's house.

> So shall the king have pleasure in your beauty:
> he is your Lord, so do him honour.

It's suitable for a royal wedding, true, but he sees that it also applies to the Virgin Mary, chosen by God the King to be the mother of his Son.

> The king's daughter is all glorious within;
> her clothing is embroidered cloth of gold.
> She shall be brought to the king in raiment of needlework:
> after her the virgins that are her companions.

The priest thinks of those who've followed Blessed Mary in the way of celibacy. The psalm continues:

> Instead of your fathers you shall have sons,
> whom you shall make princes over all the land.

Mary's Son was King Jesus, and he has chosen Christians to be his brothers and sisters. The psalm speaks to us not only of Mary, but of the Christian Church which she symbolizes. 'The king's daughter is all glorious within.' The family of the Church, like the building where it worships, may not look impressive to those who scoff from outside the Church. But from within, for those who are faithful members of the Church and who love the Church their mother, for them the Christian Church, with all its faults, is 'all glorious within'. That's the title of the novel, by Bruce Marshall: *All Glorious Within*.

Truth from a mistranslation

The phrase is in fact a mistranslation. In the psalm, it means that the princess is still within the palace being robed in the cloth of gold, ready to be brought out to meet her new husband. But that's no matter, for the novel brings a profound truth out of it. As God said when he chose a shepherd boy and turned him into the mighty King David, 'The LORD does not see as mortals see; they look on the outward appearance, but the LORD looks on the heart.' Talking to the Virgin Mary may seem like superstition and delusion to some, but to those who are 'within', within the Christian Church, she is glorious because Jesus loved her and she's become our mother also. Some say that to honour the Virgin is to take away the honour that belongs to Jesus alone, but Mary wants to bring us closer to her Son. Some allege that devotion to the Virgin results from looking for a tender feminine heart in Mary, because those who fear a masculine God can't find tenderness there; but the Christian says that Mary is our constant reminder that there is a feminine side to God.

A symbol of the Church

Mary symbolizes the Church for us. She contained God in her womb, and the Church contains Christ within it, and carries him to the world. At Christmastime we pray to Jesus, 'Be born in us today'. The Church is the Body of Christ. There are many things wrong with the Church, as an institution, and those who are within can see them more clearly than those who stay outside to criticize. From within, we can try to reform the institution and put right its faults, because we love the Church our mother. From the outside, you can't see how all-glorious Mother Church is to those who love Jesus. From within, we can see how essential the Church is to God's plan of spreading his love throughout the world. It's sad that those who mock can't see this, but the loss is theirs. The Church our mother, like Mother Mary, never stops caring for us; she is 'all-glorious within'.

Suggested hymns

Her virgin eyes saw God incarnate born; Shall we not love thee, Mother dear?; Ye watchers and ye holy ones; Ye who own the faith of Jesus.

St Bartholomew the Apostle   24 August
Nathanael Bartholomew Isa. 43:8–13 My witnesses; Ps. 145:1–7 Speak of your wondrous acts; Acts 5:12–16 The apostles heal; (*if the Acts reading is used instead of the Old Testament reading, the New Testament reading is* 1 Cor. 4:9–15 The shame of the apostles); Luke 22:24–30 Judging the twelve tribes

> *'[Jesus said,] "You are those who have stood by me in my trials; and I confer on you, just as my Father has conferred on me, a kingdom, so that you may eat and drink at my table in my kingdom, and you will sit on thrones judging the twelve tribes of Israel."' Luke 22:28–30*

Nathanael Bartholomew

Bartholomew is a surname: it means 'son of Tolmae'. What was his first name? Well, the name 'Bartholomew' occurs in the lists of the Twelve apostles in the Gospels of Matthew, Mark and Luke, and in the Acts of the Apostles; apart from that we know nothing about him. But Bartholomew isn't mentioned in St John's Gospel. Yet St John has a lot to say about a disciple named Nathanael, who was obviously one of Jesus's closest friends. Nathanael, meaning 'God gave', was a fairly common first name. Many people think, therefore, that one of the Twelve had the full name of Nathanael Bartholomew.

Nathanael under the fig tree

In the first chapter of St John's Gospel we read:

> Philip found Nathanael and said to him, 'We have found him about whom Moses in the law and also the prophets wrote, Jesus son of Joseph from Nazareth.' Nathanael said to him, 'Can anything good come out of Nazareth?' Philip said to him, 'Come and see.' When Jesus saw Nathanael coming toward him, he said of him, 'Here is truly an Israelite in whom there is no deceit!' Nathanael asked him, 'Where did you get to know me?' Jesus answered, 'I saw you under the fig tree before Philip called you.' Nathanael replied, 'Rabbi, you are the Son of God! You are the King of Israel!' Jesus answered, 'Do you believe because I told you that I saw you under the fig tree? You will see greater things than these.' And he said to him, 'Very truly, I tell you, you will see heaven opened and the angels of God ascending and descending upon the Son of Man.'

The rabbis said that under a fig tree was a good place to meditate on the Scriptures. Apparently Nathanael was reading the story of Jacob's ladder, on which angels took the prayers of God's people up to heaven, and brought the messages from God down to earth, at a place called 'Bethel', which means the house of God. But Nathanael was not only reading the Scriptures, he was meditating on them and trying to apply them to his own day. Where was the House of God now? Where could he talk to God and God talk to him? Surely some important spokesman for God, coming from a great city, perhaps the Messiah himself, would be the intermediary.

'We've found the Messiah'

Then Philip came to him and said they had found what they were looking for. The answer to Nathanael's searching was a carpenter from an obscure village called Nazareth. 'Nazareth? Don't make me laugh!' But when they met, the carpenter said, 'I saw you under the fig tree' (so Jesus knew about his meditation – was this some supernatural knowledge which sees into people's souls?). Then this *was* the Messiah, the King of Israel! Nathanael went further – he was the first to call Jesus 'the Son of God'. Jesus confirmed that Nathanael had got it right. Jesus was Bethel, the place where our prayers are taken up to God, and where we hear God speaking to us his messages of love.

Nathanael on Lake Galilee

Nathanael's named once more in St John's Gospel, after the resurrection of Jesus. He was among a group of disheartened disciples who went back to their old trade of fishing. 'They went out and got into the boat, but that night they caught nothing. Just after daybreak, Jesus stood on the beach; but the disciples did not know that it was Jesus.'

Things had changed irreversibly, they couldn't go back to the way it was before they met Jesus. It's no use any of us trying to reconstruct the past. Once you've met Jesus, the only way is forward.

The inevitability of change

So Nathanael had accepted, from the beginning of the gospel to its end, the inevitability of change. If the Messiah comes from an obscure place like Nazareth, then you must put away your prejudice and welcome him. If the Messiah is crucified, you mustn't try to turn the clock back: you've got to go forward, and maybe you'll meet the risen Christ as you go about your work. Nathanael Bartholomew has a lot to teach us.

Suggested hymns

As Jacob with travel was weary one day; Blessed assurance, Jesus is mine; Hark, my soul, it is the Lord; The Son of God his glory hides.

Holy Cross Day   14 September

Such Love! Num. 21:4–9 The bronze serpent; Ps. 22:23–28 All the earth shall turn to the Lord; Phil. 2:6–11 Obedient to death on the cross; John 3:13–17 God so loved the world

> *'"And just as Moses lifted up the serpent in the wilderness, so must the Son of Man be lifted up, that whoever believes in him may have eternal life."' John 3:14–15*

Foreshadowing

The Gospel-writers believed that the crucifixion was predicted in the prophecies of the Old Testament. 'Coming events cast their shadows before them.' So in today's Gospel reading, the evangelist compares it to Moses lifting up the serpent in the wilderness. The story's told in the first reading. The Israelites looked at the bronze serpent, lifted up on a pole; they believed in God and they were saved from death. So those who believe in the cross of Christ will be saved from eternal death. When Jesus was lifted up on the cross, he was truly lifted up onto a throne from which he can rule the earth. But it's not only the verbal coincidences between the Old and New Testaments that constitute prophecy. The Old foreshadows the New because the nature of God is unchanging. Through violent centuries the People of God had gradually learnt that God doesn't desire punishment, as they had originally assumed. God wants love. God wins our love by saving us out of our disasters. But God saves us at great cost to himself. Jacob Boehme, a seventeenth-century mystic, wrote that 'There is a cross in the heart of God.' There's a cross in the heart of God because the cost of love is suffering. God's love is an unconditional love. Self-sacrifice is the nature of God. So all that the Old Testament says about God comes true on Calvary, because that's the sort of God he is. There was a cross in the heart of God before ever the wood was raised on Calvary.

The site of Calvary

When the Romans destroyed Jerusalem in AD 70, Skull Hill where Jesus had been crucified was levelled like everywhere else. The Christians of Jerusalem were forced out, but before long some of them drifted back, and revisited the site of Golgotha. They started worshipping the crucified Saviour there, so to prevent this, the

Emperor Hadrian erected a statue of Jupiter and a temple to Venus over Calvary. 'That'll fix these Christians,' he thought, but unwittingly he thereby identified the site for all time. The first Christian emperor, Constantine, in the fourth century, demolished the Temple of Venus and found underneath it a small, skull-shaped lump of rock, and opposite it, a number of cave-tombs in the wall of a quarry. Constantine removed the surrounding rock and built a roof over Calvary to form a place where pilgrims could pray. Today we call it the Church of the Holy Sepulchre, although it has several times been rebuilt.

The true cross

Constantine's mother, the Empress Helena, visited Jerusalem and had a dream in which an angel told her that she would find the true cross, on which Jesus was crucified, at the bottom of a certain well. She sent workmen to dig in the well, and on 3 May they came up with two large pieces of wood. Whether or not they were the real thing we shall never know. Enemies of Christianity often allege that if all the relics of the true cross in all the churches round the world were put together they would build a house, but that is simply not true, most of them are only tiny fragments. In the Book of Common Prayer, 3 May was called the feast of 'The Invention (meaning the discovery) of the Cross'. But the Church of the Holy Sepulchre was consecrated on the 14 September, so today was called Holy Cross Day. In addition to Good Friday, it was felt that we need another day to mediate on what the cross means to us. If the cross is at the heart of God, it must be at the heart of the faith of Christians, who believe in an infinitely loving, self-sacrificing God.

Suggested hymns

Faithful cross, above all other (part of *Sing, my tongue, the glorious battle*); *Such love; Were you there when they crucified my Lord?; When I survey the wondrous cross.*

St Matthew, Apostle and Evangelist   21 September

More Precious than Jewels Prov. 3:13–18 Wisdom more
precious than jewels; Ps. 119:65–72 Better than gold; 2 Cor. 4:1–6
The open statement of the truth; Matt. 9:9–13 The call of Matthew

*'Happy are those who find wisdom, and those who get under-
standing, for her income is better than silver, and her revenue better than gold. She is more precious than jewels, and nothing you
desire can compare with her.' Proverbs 3:13–15*

A Jewish gospel

St Matthew begins his Gospel with the words: 'An account of
the genealogy of Jesus the Messiah, the son of David, the son of
Abraham.' He doesn't just have a dry-as-dust interest in family
trees, though Matthew chapter one is not an exciting place to begin
reading the Bible! He wants to give Jesus his place in history. In
particular, Matthew wants to show the Jewish roots of the Christian gospel. St Matthew's has been described as the most Jewish of
the Gospels. He never misses a chance to show how the events of
Jesus's life are a fulfilment of patterns and predictions in the Old
Testament. Jesus is the climax of the process which began with the
Jewish kings, prophets and lawgivers.

Wise people

But there was another strand in Jewish religion which we often
forget about, and which Jesus also fulfilled. These were the wise
people – although all of them were male, I daren't call them 'wise
men' or you'll immediately think of the three wise men who visited
Bethlehem, but those were non-Jewish. These that I'm referring to
were secretaries in the court of the Jewish kings. Because their job
was reading and writing they were often called 'scribes'. They probably based their job on the example of the Egyptian courts. There,
the scribes of the Pharaohs wrote books describing the wisdom that
was needed by those who were to advise the monarch, often in the
form of proverbs or wise sayings. The Jewish scribes in the court of
King Solomon, which had close contacts with Egypt, made collec-
tions of wise sayings, several of which appear in the biblical Book
of Proverbs under the name of the scribe who gathered them. Matthew may have seen himself as standing in this tradition; he alone

reports the saying of Jesus: 'Therefore every scribe who has been trained for the kingdom of heaven is like the master of a household who brings out of his treasure what is new and what is old.'

Wisdom

What then was this wisdom that the scribes wrote about? To a large extent it was practical common sense. The scribes probably learnt to write by copying out proverbs written by their predecessors, and in the process they learnt how to be a good adviser to the king. As well as the Book of Proverbs, they wrote several others such as Job, Ecclesiastes and several in the Apocrypha, which we call 'the Wisdom Literature'. Many of these contain poems in praise of Wisdom, who is imagined as if she was a wise teacher. Today's first reading includes one of these from the Book of Proverbs:

> Happy are those who find wisdom,
> and those who get understanding,
> for her income is better than silver,
> and her revenue better than gold.
> She is more precious than jewels,
> and nothing you desire can compare with her.

The moral teaching of Jesus

St Matthew's Gospel then probably regards the moral teaching of Jesus as not only fulfilling the Jewish Law, but taking on the mantle of the teachers of wisdom. His wise advice on loving God and loving your neighbour *is* common sense. The teaching of Jesus, as presented by St Matthew, could justly be called 'the New Wisdom'.

Only by grace

Yet Matthew knew perfectly well that it's impossible to put it into practice. On our own, that is. As St Paul said, describing his days as a Pharisee, 'I do not do the good I want, but the evil I do not want is what I do.' It's impossible to follow the wise teaching of Jesus, until we receive grace. So in the second part of his Gospel, Matthew moves on from wise teaching and describes the death and resurrection of Jesus. His suffering and his triumph bring us the grace that enables us to obey his commandments, and to behave wisely. Without the cross, wisdom is just wishful thinking. With the cross at its centre, the Christian teaching is not just wisdom but gospel, the good news that God loves us. It's this that elicits our love for God in response, and gives us the grace to serve him with wisdom. Thank you, Matthew, for writing your Gospel to bring us the good news of God's grace, which is more precious than jewels, and nothing we desire can compare with it.

Suggested hymns

Come sing, ye choirs exultant; Disposer supreme, and Judge of the earth; He sat to watch o'er customs paid; Immortal, invisible, God only wise.

St Michael and All Angels   29 September
Michael Fought the Dragon Gen. 28:10–17 Jacob's ladder; Ps. 103:19–22 Bless the Lord, you angels; Rev. 12:7–12 Michael fought the dragon; (*if the Revelation reading is used instead of the Old Testament reading, the New Testament reading is* Heb. 1:5–14 Higher than the angels); John 1:47–51 Angels descending on the Son of Man

> *'War broke out in heaven; Michael and his angels fought against the dragon. The dragon and his angels fought back, but they were defeated, and there was no longer any place for them in heaven.'*
> *Revelation 12:7–8*

Fantasy literature

There's been a great vogue recently for what's loosely called 'fantasy literature': books that retell old myths, or invent new ones, and films based on them. From Greek myths to Arthurian legend to *The Lord of the Rings* to Harry Potter, stories are told which, without claiming to be a statement of fact, are welcomed as a proclamation of truth. Some truths can only be conveyed by fiction. Some of the heroes and heroines had a basis in history, but they were redrawn to accentuate a tendency in human nature. From *Aesop's Fables* to the latest soap opera on the television, the purpose of fiction is to make us identify with the characters, or pass judgement on their behaviour. In this way we learn how to behave when crises big or small confront us in our daily lives.

Belief in angels

Today we celebrate St Michael and All Angels. The Book of Revelation paints the picture this way: 'War broke out in heaven; Michael and his angels fought against the dragon. The dragon and his angels fought back, but they were defeated, and there was no longer any place for them in heaven.' In the later books of the Old Testament, such as the Book of Daniel, written after the captivity of the Jews under the Persians, the talk of angels seems to be influenced by Persian beliefs that every nation on earth had its guardian angel, representing the nation before the throne of God in heaven. So in Daniel chapter ten, a heavenly figure says, 'the prince of the kingdom of Persia opposed me twenty-one days. So Michael, one of the chief princes, came to help me'; and in chapter twelve:

> At that time Michael, the great prince, the protector of your people, shall arise. There shall be a time of anguish, such as has never occurred since nations first came into existence. But at that time your people shall be delivered, everyone who is found written in the book.

Michael is the heavenly representative of the nation of Israel, who defeats the heavenly representative of Persia. This can hardly have been intended as a description of earthly events, but it gives an eternal meaning to the struggle that is taking place on the earth. So, do angels exist? We can only reply with Shakespeare, 'There are more things in heaven and earth than are dreamt of in thy philosophy.'

The cosmic struggle

But that isn't really the important question. From Greek myths to Arthurian legend to *The Lord of the Rings* to Harry Potter, the important thing is to emphasize that there's a struggle going on between good and evil: that's a fact, whether or not the story is fiction. And the struggle that you see taking place in your classroom or your neighbourhood or on the stage of international events isn't just a local struggle. These conflicts all matter, because they're all part of the cosmic struggle between good and evil.

Good and evil

The threads of good and evil are frequently tangled, so that some actions may be partly good and partly evil. Nobody's completely good or completely bad. Often we're faced with choosing the lesser of two evils; often the evil we have to fight against is within ourselves. But there really is a distinction between good and evil, and we have to choose which side we're on.

Our part to play

Our choices do matter. You may be only a Hobbit in the Shire, or a trainee wizard at Hogwarts, but your little decisions can have long-term consequences. Looking back at the end of a long life, you may be able to say, 'On such and such a day I made a decision which changed my life. I didn't know it at the time, but now I can see why it mattered.' Can you believe, then, that all those seemingly unimportant choices added together can change the history of the world? Their effects are multiplied, until it can be seen that we too have a part to play in the cosmic struggle between good and evil. So, whether it's fact or fiction, to read that the archangel Michael defeated the Devil teaches you that even in seemingly trivial cases, choosing the good is important, and the decisions you make do matter.

Suggested hymns

Angels voices, ever singing; Around the throne of God a band; Hark! hark, my soul! angelic songs are swelling; Ye holy angels bright.

St Luke the Evangelist   18 October
God Heals the Broken-hearted Isa. 35:3–6 Healing in the new age; *or* Acts 16:6–12a The Macedonian call; Ps. 147:1–7 God heals the broken-hearted; 2 Tim. 4:5–17 Only Luke is with me; Luke 10:1–9 Sending out the seventy

> *'The Lord builds up Jerusalem, and gathers together the outcasts of Israel. He heals the brokenhearted, and binds up all their wounds.'*
> *Psalm 147:2–3*

St Luke, the beloved physician

In his Letter to the Colossians, St Paul refers to 'Luke, the beloved physician'. The author of the Gospel according to St Luke, and the Acts of the Apostles, which is the sequel to the Gospel, was a doctor. Mind you, medical science wasn't very far advanced in those days, and he may not have been able to offer much beyond a few herbs, the ability to set a fracture and to put back a dislocation (without anaesthetic!). And prayer. St Luke agreed to travel round with St Paul as his personal medical attendant. Paul was apparently not in good health, and small wonder considering the number of beatings and shipwrecks he endured, so a physician, who was also a believer, would have been an invaluable companion.

The importance of the doctor

There's a tendency among some Christians to think that if you have faith, you don't need a doctor. Well, Paul had more faith than most of us, and he needed St Luke. Faith and prayer will do wonders in healing the sick, but it's cruel to tell anyone not to make use of the help the doctor can give. It's cruel, it's a sin, and it may be a crime, if it causes them to die unnecessarily. It's a sin because if the sick person doesn't recover, they will come to think that it's because their faith is too weak, and from there it's only a short step to believing that God's not interested in healing them because they're not good enough. Weak Christians may be driven into despair, and away from Christ, because they've been discouraged from using conventional medicine. St Luke wouldn't have approved. There's a book in the Apocrypha called the Wisdom of Jesus son of Sirach, and often known as Ecclesiasticus. It contains a long passage (38:4–14) showing how the physician's skill comes from God; let me read it to you:

> The Lord created medicines out of the earth,
> and the sensible will not despise them.
> Was not water made sweet with a tree
> in order that its power might be known?
> And he gave skill to human beings
> that he might be glorified in his marvellous works.
> By them the physician heals and takes away pain;
> the pharmacist makes a mixture from them.
> God's works will never be finished;
> and from him health spreads over all the earth.

My child, when you are ill, do not delay,
but pray to the Lord, and he will heal you.
Give up your faults and direct your hands rightly,
and cleanse your heart from all sin.
Offer a sweet-smelling sacrifice,
and a memorial portion of choice flour,
and pour oil on your offering,
as much as you can afford.
Then give the physician his place,
for the Lord created him;
do not let him leave you,
for you need him.
There may come a time when recovery lies in the hands of
    physicians,
for they too pray to the Lord
that he grant them success in diagnosis and in healing,
for the sake of preserving life.

Healing is God defeating evil

The Bible's in no doubt that sickness is evil, and healing is a sign
that God is at work. So Isaiah had predicted:

Strengthen the weak hands,
and make firm the feeble knees.
Say to those who are of a fearful heart,
'Be strong, do not fear! Here is your God.
. . . He will come and save you.'
Then the eyes of the blind shall be opened,
and the ears of the deaf unstopped;
then the lame shall leap like a deer,
and the tongue of the speechless sing for joy.

Jesus fulfilled this by his healings; St Luke fulfilled it with his medi-
cines. When you're in conflict with the forces of evil, you throw
against them every weapon you've got. If you're fighting sickness
and disease, you need to use both prayer and medicine.

God heals the broken-hearted

Every doctor will agree, however, that when a patient's in a low
mental condition, it slows their recovery. Mind and body are
intimately related. St Luke wrote his Gospel, laying special empha-

sis on Jesus's care for the weak. God's love surrounds us at all times, and especially when we're sick. So the healing work of the beloved physician continues to our day, in his ministry to the sad. God's not interested in just the body or just the soul, he wants to heal them both together.

Suggested hymns

As water to the thirsty; At even, ere the sun was set; Give thanks with a grateful heart; Peter and John went to pray.

SS Simon and Jude, Apostles   28 October
(see page 258)

All Saints' Day   1 November

(If 4 November is not kept as All Saints' Sunday, the readings on page 263 are used on 1 November. If those are used on the Sunday, the following are the readings on 1 November.)

Come to Jesus Isa. 56:3–8 My house for all people; *or* 2 Esd. 2:42–48 Crowned by the Son of God; Ps. 33:1–5 Rejoice, you righteous; Heb. 12:18–24 Come to Zion; Matt. 5:1–12 The Beatitudes

> *'You have come to Mount Zion and to the city of the living God, the heavenly Jerusalem, and to innumerable angels in festal gathering.' Hebrews 12:22*

A bishop's humour

At his enthronement as Bishop of London in 1956, Henry Montgomery Campbell arrived in his splendid robes outside the great west door of St Paul's Cathedral. Before a crowd of onlookers, he lifted up his crozier and, as is traditional on such occasions, hammered on the closed door with it to demand admission. But something had gone wrong with the timing, and the Dean hadn't yet reached the other side of the door to fling it open. Nothing happened, and after a longish pause the Bishop turned to his chaplain and was heard to say, 'Do you think we've come to the wrong place?'

The right place

I can assure you that by coming to this church today, you have come
to the right place. For the Letter to the Hebrews says that because
you're a Christian,

> You have come to Mount Zion and to the city of the living God,
> the heavenly Jerusalem, and to innumerable angels in festal
> gathering, and to the assembly of the firstborn who are enrolled
> in heaven, and to God the judge of all, and to the spirits of the
> righteous made perfect, and to Jesus, the mediator of a new
> covenant, and to the sprinkled blood that speaks a better word
> than the blood of Abel.

A letter to Jewish Christians

The Authorized Version heads it 'The Epistle of Paul the Apostle to
the Hebrews'. But that wasn't the title in the early manuscripts, and
it almost certainly wasn't written by St Paul. Nobody knows who
did write it, and a better translation of the title would be 'A Letter
to Jewish Christians'. It makes many references to the Jewish Scriptures, but was written in Greek, and seems to take up Plato's idea
of heaven as a world of ideas and ideals. It could have been written
by a Jew from the Egyptian city of Alexandria, which was famous
as a place where Jewish teachers studied Greek philosophy. Maybe
it was written by Apollos, a Jew from Alexandria whom St Paul
mentions as one of his friends.

Heaven

In the Letter to the Hebrews, heaven's like the ideal pattern of
God's Temple, of which the Temple on Mount Zion in Jerusalem on
earth is just a copy. The sacrifice being offered there is the sacrifice
of Jesus on the cross, and Jesus is both the sacrificial victim, and
also the priest who offers the sacrifice. The congregation in the
heavenly Temple consists of all the saints and angels, says the Letter. Christians who've died are described as 'the spirits of the righteous who've been made perfect'. Righteous means good people,
but cheer up, there's a place in heaven for you, even if you're not
particularly good. When the heavenly account books are balanced
up, to see whether you've done more good things than bad things
in your life, a share in the goodness of Jesus is transferred to your

account! With that sort of accountancy, all your imperfections can be washed away, and you can enter the next life as a perfect human being. Imagine all your friends and family meeting the new you, without any of the faults that annoyed them so much on earth!

All Saints

So if we've all been made perfect when we get to heaven, we shall all be saints. It's good to have heroes and heroines, great Christians of the past who've lived admirable lives which we can aspire to copy, and to call them St This and St That. We remember all the saints on this day, and we shall meet them all in heaven. But by that time there'll be no distinction, because we too shall have been made perfect. Then we shall all be saints; we shall be all saints.

Come to Jesus

Then we shan't be ashamed to meet Jesus. Jesus said, 'Come to me, all who are weary and carry heavy loads.' We can come to him now, in faith, and we shall come to him when we die, in heaven. When we come to church, we've come to the right place, because we come to share in the heavenly worship of the saints and angels, we are gradually being made better, and we come to Jesus. And when we die, we also come to share in the worship of the saints and angels, we are made perfect, and we come to Jesus. Isn't that good news?

Suggested hymns

All ye who seek for sure relief; I heard the voice of Jesus say; O for a heart to praise my God; Rejoice in God's saints, today and all days.

Commemoration of the Faithful Departed
(All Souls' Day)   2 November
I Will Raise Them Up Lam. 3:17–26, 31–33 New every morning; *or* Wisdom 3:1–9 Souls of the righteous; Ps. 23 The Lord my shepherd, *or* 27:1–6, 16–17 He shall hide me; Rom. 5:5–11 Christ died for us; *or* 1 Peter 1:3–9 Salvation ready to be revealed; John 5:19–25 The dead will hear his voice; *or* John 6:37–40 I will raise them up

'[Jesus said,] "This is indeed the will of my Father, that all who see the Son and believe in him may have eternal life; and I will raise them up on the last day."' John 6:40

Life after death

Very few of the people who write in the newspapers or speak on the television seem to believe in life after death, which is sad. It takes a particularly brave form of stoicism to grit your teeth and carry on trying to do good and make friends when you believe there'll be nothing left to show for it in the long run. It's also sad, because 'the chattering classes', as they're sometimes called, influence the opinions of those who read and watch. Whether other people are so sceptical it's hard to tell. Speaking in a group and subject to peer pressure, many people may be ashamed to admit what they believe. But get them on their own, and most people, even those who say they don't believe in God, have a wistful longing to believe that they'll meet again with those who've died. Because so much scorn has been poured on the churches, who are the witnesses to the resurrection, many people turn to superstition and séances instead, to give them the reassurance they need. But the offer of eternal life which Jesus brought is far more satisfying than the half-existence of a ghost.

All Souls' Day

The Church founded All Souls' Day to reassure people about the state of those who've died. All Saints' Day was there on 1 November, with its joyful, triumphant message about the life of the saints in heaven. 'But what about my Bert?' bereaved people asked. 'He was no saint, but he believed in God in his own way. Isn't there any hope for him?' The promise of Jesus is clear; yes, there's hope for Bert and all like him. Jesus said, 'This is indeed the will of my Father, that all who see the Son and believe in him may have eternal life; and I will raise them up on the last day.' So the day after All Saints' Day was set aside to remember all those who've died. We want to honour them by mentioning their names again. We want to reassure ourselves that there *is* hope for them. And we want to ask God to care for them and look after them till we meet again.

Purgatory and time

Jesus promised eternal life to all who believe; and we have his own word for it that 'faith which is as small as a grain of mustard-seed' is sufficient. What about those who didn't believe in Jesus? Well, Jesus told a parable about those who never had a chance to believe in him. We know it as the parable of the sheep and the goats. What many people fail to notice is that it begins with all the nations gathered for judgement – 'the nations', not the Chosen People. They are judged on their kindness to those in need. So the Church in the Middle Ages taught that all the souls of those who've died will spend a time of purification in purgatory, while they're made ready to enter the presence of God. Nowadays, when we believe that time's relative, some people see no need to talk about a waiting period in eternity, where all is timeless. But it's good to keep All Souls' Day for remembering all those who've died, even those of whom we're not certain whether they're in heaven or not.

Raised in hope

If you don't believe in life after death, this life's a pretty gloomy affair. But Jesus rose from the dead; many people saw him alive; he listens to and answers our prayers. So he raises up the downcast, and gives them new life with hope and meaning.

Raised to life

Then, when we die, Jesus will raise us up to the new and eternal life of heaven. Trust me, he says, that's a promise. How sad that the sceptics can't bring themselves to accept that offer, since it's guaranteed for everybody, the good people who believe, and the not-so-good people who are sorry. So we'll pray today for the souls of everybody who's died, that Jesus will keep his promise to those who believed, and find a way to break through with his love to those who doubted.

Suggested hymns

Abide with me, fast falls the eventide; Give rest, O Christ, to thy servant with thy saints; I am the bread of life, he who comes to me shall not hunger; Sweet is the work, my God, my king.

The Saints and Martyrs of (our own nation)

8 November

Patriotism Isa. 61:4–9 Build up the ancient ruins; *or*
Ecclus. 44:1–15 Let us now praise famous men; Ps. 15 Who may
dwell in your tabernacle?; Rev. 19:5–10 A great multitude invited;
John 17:18–23 To be with me to see my glory

> *'Let us now praise famous men, and our fathers that begat us.'*
> *Ecclesiasticus 44:1* (Authorized Version)

Serving your nation

If a nation is to survive, its people must be eager to serve their nation.
This may be by seeking a post of influence so as to improve other
people's lives. Or it may simply be by praying for their homeland,
and casting their vote at an election having considered what will be
best for the nation as a whole, rather than what makes a comfortable life for themselves.

Knowing its history

The best way of ensuring that people want to serve their nation is
to teach them its history. This shouldn't be a history that disguises
the nation's faults in the past, but it should explain how the nation
came to be as it is, and if possible why. History teaching – which
includes teaching in schools, teaching adults by means of television
series, and teaching ourselves by reading – should focus on the land
where we live, but not exclusively so. They say that history's always
written by the winners, and we must guard against subjectivity by
listening to those on the losing side also; but it's no good replacing
a bias in one direction with a greater bias in the other.

Loving its people

We must also learn to love the people of our own nation, past and
present. Some of our fellow citizens have, or had, characteristics
that make us feel ashamed to belong to the same nation. But others,
in all generations, have shown distinctive national characteristics
of which we can be proud. For this reason ruin several denominations, 8 November, a week after All Saints' Day, has been set aside
for remembering the saints of our own nation: in the Church of

England it's a festival called 'The Saints and Martyrs of England', but other churches have a similar opportunity for remembering their own local heroes.

Famous men

'Let us now praise famous men,' writes Jesus son of Sirach, in the book in the Apocrypha which is often called Ecclesiasticus, 'and our fathers that begat us.' Forgive me if I use the Authorized Version. Even modern translations fail to mention famous women, but for anyone who has heard or sung Ralph Vaughan Williams's haunting unison setting of these words, the Authorized Version is engraved on their consciousness.

> And some there be, which have no memorial; who are perished, as though they had never been; and are become as though they had never been born; and their children after them. But these were merciful men, whose righteousness hath not been forgotten.

The famous and the almost forgotten, the heroes of the past and the obscure teachers who've influenced our own growing personalities, their memory should be treasured in our hearts.

Martyrs on all sides

As we look back over the history of the church in our nation, there will be occasions of pride and occasions of shame. Particularly in the Reformation period, there were people on all sides who were willing to die for what they believed in. So we can *all* be proud of *all* the martyrs of the past, whichever denomination they belonged to.

Immaturity

But our pride must always be a critical one. Many schoolchildren are proud of the school they belong to. When they're immature, they think their school's perfect, every other school is appalling, and they'll fight other children simply because they don't attend '*my* school'. Later a child will begin to see faults in their own school and virtues in others. When they reach a degree of maturity, however, they'll be ready to admit that there's a lot which '*my* school' can learn from others; but they're still proud of their own school, with all its faults, simply because it's 'mine'. The same growth in maturity is required in dealing with other nations, other races, other religions. Sadly, many people never achieve even the first stages of maturity in those fields.

'Patriotism is not enough'

Edith Cavell was an English nurse who became a popular heroine during the 1914–18 war. She was arrested for assisting Allied soldiers to escape from German-occupied Belgium. In October 1915 she was shot. Her last words were, 'I realize that patriotism is not enough. I must have no hatred or bitterness towards anyone.'

We must guard against the descent of patriotism into narrow and intolerant nationalism. A critical pride in your own nation is a fine thing; but the desire to kill the people of other nations, simply because they differ from you, is the work of the Devil.

Suggested hymns

In our day of thanksgiving one psalm let us offer; Judge eternal, throned in splendour; Lord of lords and King eternal; Lord, while for all mankind we pray.

St Andrew the Apostle   30 November
Strategy for Evangelism Isa. 52:7–10 The messenger who announces peace; Ps. 19:1–6 The heavens declare God's glory; Rom. 10:12–18 God's messengers reconcile Jew and Greek; Matt. 4:18–22 The call of the fishermen

> *'For there is no distinction between Jew and Greek; the same Lord is Lord of all and is generous to all who call on him. For, "Everyone who calls on the name of the Lord shall be saved." But how are they to call on one in whom they have not believed? And how are they to believe in one of whom they have never heard? And how are they to hear without someone to proclaim him?' Romans 10:12–14*

A bilingual disciple

St Andrew, like his brother Simon Peter, was born in Bethsaida Julias. Extensive remains of this town have been recently found on the east bank of the River Jordan where it enters Lake Galilee. It was in the mostly Greek-speaking area known as the Decapolis. The brothers later settled to the west of the Jordan, in the tiny fishing village of Capernaum. This was in the province of Galilee, where most people spoke Aramaic, a dialect of Hebrew. People living near the border were probably bilingual and spoke both Aramaic and Greek. Andrew has a Greek name; Simon's is Aramaic. Andrew's first appearance on the stage of the gospel story is when Jesus calls him; then Andrew fetches his brother Peter.

The hardest form of evangelism is to share the good news with members of your own family. Some people pray for their relations for years before they're ready to listen, but there must have been something infectious about Andrew's joy in discovering Jesus, for his brother was converted straight away. They were called to be fishers for people, evangelists.

Andrew was one of the inner circle of disciples who were present at the transfiguration and close to Jesus in Gethsemane. His bilingual background meant that he was one of those who brought some Greeks, who were enquiring about Jesus, to meet him. Jesus was so moved to find that his words were attracting, not just the tiny nation of the Jews, but the whole Greek-speaking Roman Empire, that he exclaimed: 'The hour has come for the Son of Man to be glorified.'

St Andrew in Patras

We don't have any details in the Bible about what happened to Andrew after that. But there's a very strong tradition that he went to Patras in Greece. Patras is now an important port in the Peloponnese, where the ferries land from Italy, and at the southern end of the impressive new bridge which joins the western part of that peninsula to the Greek mainland. We can't be absolutely certain that Andrew went there, but with his interest in boats and Greeks it seems quite likely. The tradition continues by describing his crucifixion there on an X-shaped cross, as punishment for baptizing Maximilla, the wife of the Roman Governor of Patras, who was named Egaes. Poor Andrew's bones weren't left in peace but dragged all over Europe, to Constantinople, the Vatican and Amalfi, and some of them to St Andrew's in Scotland, which is why the red X-shaped cross of St Andrew is part of the Union Flag of the United Kingdom.

A strategy for evangelism

St Paul built on Andrew's foundations in trying to evangelize the Greeks, and bind them into one church with the Jews. Paul probably never went to Patras; his strategy was to establish strong churches in the provincial capitals, in this case the nearby city of Corinth, and rely on the Christians from these cities to take the good news of the gospel out to the surrounding towns. When he wrote from Corinth to the Christians in Rome, he emphasized the importance of those who were willing to carry the good news of Jesus to others: 'How are they to call on one in whom they have not believed? And how are they to believe in one of whom they have never heard? And how are they to hear without someone to proclaim him?' Yet some were trying to deny that Greeks could be members of what was at that time a mostly Jewish church. Paul, like Andrew, saw that this was a denial of the gospel message: 'For there is no distinction between Jew and Greek; the same Lord is Lord of all and is generous to all who call on him. For, "Everyone who calls on the name of the Lord shall be saved."'

If Paul and Andrew hadn't insisted on this principle, you and I wouldn't be Christians. Just think: if that's true, shouldn't we also be willing to bring people to Jesus, no matter what language they speak, or what their national, ethnic or religious background, as Andrew was?

Suggested hymns

Jesus calls us—o'er the tumult; I danced in the morning when the world was begun; Take up thy cross, the Saviour said; Will you come and follow me?

Sermon for Harvest Festival
The Food that Lasts Deut. 26:1–11 First fruits; Ps. 100 Enter his gates with thanks; Phil. 4:4–9 Rejoice!; *or* Rev. 14:14–18 The harvest of souls; John 6:25–35 Work for the food that lasts

> *'[Jesus said,] "Do not work for the food that perishes, but for the food that endures for eternal life, which the Son of Man will give you."' John 6:27*

Hard work in agriculture

Most 'townies' probably don't realize how much hard work's needed on a farm. It's not just the physical effort, it's the long hours and the unremitting demands of the seasons. Those who buy their food from a supermarket find it hard to understand the amount of labour that has gone into producing it. In the olden days, most people grew at least some of their own food. They knew what their food cost, not in money terms, but in back-breaking toil.

The pangs of hunger

In many parts of the Third World today, the situation's life-threatening. Many people in poorer countries spend morning to night working in the fields, yet even so they can't raise enough food to feed themselves and their families, let alone to sell in the market. They know the pangs of hunger – real hunger, aware that they'll die if they can't get something to eat. The hunger that comes from not having eaten anything for a whole day or more. By comparison with that, for us to say, 'Oh, I do feel hungry, I could just do with a sandwich,' is almost obscene. Third World people know what food costs, for the absence of food may cost them their life. Harvest Thanksgiving is a chance for us to give thanks to God for the growth of the crops that produce our food, and also for the hard labour of those in many countries who work in the fields and the factories to grow it and process it; the drivers and the shop-workers who've brought it to us. When we realize what it's cost them, we should be all the more grateful.

Materialism

Jesus knew what he was talking about when he spoke of people working for their food. Even if we've never felt the pangs of absolute hunger, we know that if you want something enough, you'll work hard to get it. Unfortunately, it's mostly material things that people are prepared to work for: food, clothing, a house, a car, a computer, things we use in our leisure activities. The trouble with these things is they don't last; or if they do, we're no longer satisfied with them and want to upgrade to a better one. Have you ever left food unwrapped in a cupboard or on a shelf, and come back to find it going mouldy? That's what Jesus meant when he spoke of working for food that perishes. It's futile.

Save and share

We don't realize that our food has cost other people in the currency of hard work, so we're incredibly wasteful. You throw food away if it's rotten, but did you need to buy so much in the first place? By spoiling our environment, we make it harder and harder for the land to produce enough food. How could we share our food with those who haven't enough? Giving away the harvest offerings to a local home or hospital is a start. Giving money to charities that work in the Third World is a step further. But we need to look into the whole question of fair trade if we are to find any long-term solutions. There are two words that can be made out of the letters in the word HARVEST. All the letters in the word SAVE are there in the word HARVEST. And so are all the letters in the word SHARE. A lesson we can take away from our harvest festival is that each of us can look into ways of saving the world's food supplies, and sharing it with those in need.

Hungering for eternal life

But material things perish. What can we work for that doesn't perish? Jesus said, 'Don't work for the food that perishes, but for the food that lasts for eternal life, which the Son of Man will give you.' We don't often think about eternal life, living with Jesus for ever in heaven. Jesus says we should be as hungry for that as a starving farmer in Africa is for a good meal. We should be willing to put as much hard work into gaining the harvest of eternal life as goes into producing our food. We should save and share: save our souls by believing in Jesus. And share not only our food, but the promises of eternal life with others.

All-age worship

Find out as much as you can about what will happen to the harvest goods after the service. Could you arrange a visit to the place where they are sent?

Suggested hymns

Come, ye thankful people, come; Praise and thanksgiving, Father, we offer; To thee, O Lord, our hearts we raise; We plough the fields, and scatter.

Sermon for a Wedding
What is Love?
1 Cor. 13

'Love is patient; love is kind; love is not envious or boastful or arrogant or rude. It does not insist on its own way; it is not irritable or resentful; it does not rejoice in wrongdoing, but rejoices in the truth. It bears all things, believes all things, hopes all things, endures all things.' 1 Corinthians 13:4–7

'All you need is love'

Couples get married because they are in love. For most couples, when they fall in love, it's the most wonderful experience in their lives. But in a good marriage, it goes on getting better, as they learn to grow in love as the years go by. The Beatles were close to the truth when they sang, 'All you need is love'. But what is love? The word has many meanings, from 'I love strawberries' through 'I love my country' to 'I love you with all of my heart for ever and ever'. Some of those meanings are rather selfish. 'I love to have power over other people' is not usually a generous sort of love. Some people love what they can get, and that sort of love is no basis for a happy marriage.

Love songs

You can't talk about love in prose. A great composer was once asked to explain what his music meant. 'If I could have explained it in words,' he replied, 'do you think I would have taken all that trouble to put it into notes?' Similarly, if it was possible to explain love in prose, how come there are so many love-songs? Even when the Bible talks about love, the prose takes wings and quickly becomes a form of poetry.

Jesus on love

Jesus tells us, in the Bible, that we should love God with all our heart and all our mind and all our soul and all our strength, and we should love our neighbours 'as ourselves'. Those are not alternatives. You can't choose either to love God or your fellow human beings; you have to love both. Sometimes you're overwhelmed by the fact that somebody else loves you, even though you don't deserve it. Then you love your lover, in return, in gratitude for the love you've received. Your heart becomes so full of love, that it overflows with love onto other people you meet. Often they become better people. If you truly realize that God loves you, even though you don't deserve it, then that can be overwhelming too. So in gratitude to God for his many blessings, you want to give him something in return. But there's nothing that God needs, so, instead, you love other people for God's sake.

St Paul on love

St Paul, when he wrote to the Christians in Corinth about love, gave the most beautiful description of true love that's ever been written. You'll notice that the love which St Paul describes is utterly unselfish:

> Love is patient; love is kind; love is not envious or boastful or arrogant or rude. It does not insist on its own way; it is not irritable or resentful; it does not rejoice in wrongdoing, but rejoices in the truth. It bears all things, believes all things, hopes all things, endures all things.

Try putting your own name in place of the word love in that sentence, like this:

> Michael's patient; Michael's kind; Michael isn't envious or boastful or arrogant or rude. Michael doesn't insist on his own way; Michael isn't irritable or resentful; Michael doesn't rejoice in wrongdoing, but rejoices in the truth. Michael bears all things, believes all things, hopes all things, endures all things.

Is that true? Sadly, most of us would have to admit that although it's sometimes true, most of the time it's not. Which just shows how much we all have yet to learn about love.

How to love

But the Bible doesn't only tell us about love: it shows us how to love. Jesus sacrificed his life for those he loved; Jesus died because he loves you. Jesus said there's no greater love than to lay down your life for those you love. When we realize that this is how much Jesus loves us, then we can love each other in the same, self-sacrificing way. If you love your husband or your wife, not for what you can get but for what you can give, in the way of your time, your effort, your willingness to compromise, then that'll be true love indeed. As the American song says, 'If that ain't loving me, God didn't make little green apples.'

Suggested hymns

Gracious Spirit, Holy Ghost; Lord of all hopefulness, Lord of all joy; Love divine, all loves excelling; O love that wilt not let me go.

A wedding hymn

Morning has broken: wedding day morning;
Jesus has spoken, if we will hear:
blessing our new love at its first dawning,
nurturing true love, calming our fear.

Nothing but Jesus' total self-giving –
nothing else frees us, touching each heart;
so we must follow, caring, forgiving;
let each tomorrow form a fresh start.

Hear when we pray, Lord, answer our calling;
stay close each day, Lord, all through our life;
'till, like rain showering, blessings are falling,
richly empowering each man and wife.

Michael Counsell © 1993

(If printing this on a service sheet please report it to Christian Copyright Licensing International as 'Morning has broken – Wedding version'.)

Sermon for a Funeral or Memorial Service
Room for All

John 14:1–6

> *'[Jesus said to his disciples,] "Do not let your hearts be troubled. Believe in God, believe also in me. In my Father's house there are many dwelling places. If it were not so, would I have told you that I go to prepare a place for you?"' John 14:1–2*

Troubled

Jesus gathered his friends in the upper room for the Last Supper, and told them he was going to die. Quite naturally, he found them puzzled and frightened by this. So he reassured them with these words, which we find in the fourteenth chapter of St John's Gospel:

> Do not let your hearts be troubled. Believe in God, believe also in me. In my Father's house there are many dwelling places. If it were not so, would I have told you that I go to prepare a place for you?

The purpose of a funeral

There are a number of reasons for holding a religious service when somebody's died. The first is to pay tribute to the person who's died, and to give thanks for their life. There may be some regrets, so we can tell God in the secrecy of our hearts if we're sorry for anything, certain that God will forgive us. It's a deeply emotional time, and to have a form of ritual enables us to express our grief. Feelings of grief can fester and produce trouble later if they're bottled up, and although everyone grieves in their own way and at their own pace, the funeral can be the beginning of a healing process. A funeral's a chance to say goodbye to the person who's died, and ask God to look after them. We can tell the bereaved of our love, and offer our support.

Reassurance

Then the funeral can also be a time for reassurance. Many of us put off thinking about death, and when we're bereaved we may not be quite sure what we believe. Even those who call themselves

Christians sometimes find their faith a bit shaky at times of loss. So it's good to turn back to the Bible, to see what Jesus said about it. His message for his disciples was clearly one of reassurance, for them and for us.

Trust

First, he invites us to trust him. He said that he came from God, and anyone who says that is either mad, bad, or telling the truth. Jesus clearly wasn't mad or bad so he must have been telling the truth. He said that he was going to prepare a place for us in heaven, and appeals to our judgement of his character. Does Jesus seem to you like a liar, someone who would deliberately mislead those he loves? On a matter of vital importance like life after death? Would he have told us that there is life after death, unless he'd been absolutely certain? Would he have accepted the inevitability of his own death, if he hadn't trusted God, his heavenly Father, absolutely? 'Believe in God, believe also in me,' he said.

Room for all

Then he reassures us concerning what life after death is like. Of course, it's so much better than this life, that he could no more describe it to us than you can describe the joys of adult life to a child. So he uses a picture, a metaphor. Where have you been most happy? Of course there are sad exceptions, but for those who've had a reasonably safe upbringing, the answer would probably be, 'at home, in my parents' house'. Well, says Jesus, that's what heaven's like: 'In my Father's house there are many dwelling places.' There's room for all in heaven. You don't need to be superhumanly good, just to have faith no bigger than a grain of mustard seed, that'll see you through.

Dwelling places

The word Jesus uses for dwelling places is the same word that he used when making arrangements to hold the Last Supper in the upper room: it means a guest room. Those we love, if they had even a little faith amid their doubt, have gone to a guest room that Jesus has prepared specially for them. Of course you're sad when they die; of course you never 'get over it'. But what they would want most is for us, in due time, to pick up the pieces and get on with living a good life, so that they can be proud of us. Then, one day, maybe many years from now, we shall meet them again. 'Do not let your hearts be troubled,' said Jesus. 'Believe in God, believe also in me. In my Father's house there are many dwelling places.' There's room for all in heaven.

Suggested hymns

Jesus lives! Thy terrors now; Lead kindly light, amid th'encircling gloom; The Lord's my Shepherd, I'll not want; Thine be the glory.

Sermon for a Baptism or Christening
Let the Children Come to Me
Matt. 19:13–15

> *'Then little children were being brought to [Jesus] in order that he might lay his hands on them and pray. The disciples spoke sternly to those who brought them; but Jesus said, "Let the little children come to me, and do not stop them; for it is to such as these that the kingdom of heaven belongs." And he laid his hands on them and went on his way.' Matthew 19:13–15*

The chosen people

The Jews were, and are, God's Chosen People. Jesus was a Jew, so most of what Christians believe has its roots in the Jewish faith. Little Jewish boys became members of the Chosen People when they were eight days old, at circumcision. Little girls were members of the Chosen People from the day they were born. If grown-ups, who weren't born Jews, wanted to join the Chosen People, they could, but it was a difficult process. The climax was when you washed away all your pagan wrong beliefs and wrong deeds, and came into the new faith fresh and clean for a new start in life. The Greek word for washing is 'baptism'.

John the Baptist

Who can tell me the name of Jesus's cousin? That's right, John the Baptist. He, of course, was also a Jew. He said to his fellow Jews,

'It's no use thinking that having a Jewish mother makes you one of the Chosen People. You've got to choose for yourself. Choose to be one of the Chosen. So,' said John the Baptist, 'I want you to go through the same process you make the non-Jews go through. Come down to the River Jordan and join the Chosen People by being washed.' That's why they called him John the Baptist: it means 'John the Washer'. Then John's cousin Jesus came and asked if he could be baptized. 'But you haven't done any wrong things to be washed clean from,' objected John. 'It isn't really about that,' answered Jesus. 'I want to choose to be one of the Chosen People.' So John baptized Jesus in the River Jordan, and then Jesus took over as the leader and John faded into the background.

Becoming a Christian

From then on, anyone who wanted to become a follower of Jesus did so by baptism. That's why we also call it christening, which means Christian-ing, or making somebody a Christian. Of course, mostly it was grown-ups who chose to follow Jesus. But sometimes they brought their whole family: 'He was baptised with his whole household,' we read in the Bible. We know that St Peter was married, because Jesus healed Peter's mother-in-law when she had a fever, and a man can't have a mother-in-law unless he has a wife! So when Peter was baptized, presumably the kids came too. If Jews joined the Chosen People at eight days old, how could you tell children they couldn't become Christians until they were old enough to understand?

Godparents

But, of course, as soon as you start baptizing little babies you're doing what John the Baptist told us not to do: letting people think they can become members in the People of God by having the right parents, and missing out altogether on the element of choosing for themselves. To avoid this problem, the Church said you must choose friends to be godparents. Then the mother and father of the baby, helped by the godfathers and godmothers, can promise to bring the child up in a Christian way. They can promise to tell the child about Jesus, and encourage the child to make their own choice to follow Jesus later, at what we call a Confirmation Service. By bringing your child to be christened, or agreeing to stand as a godparent, that's what you agree to promise: to teach the child about Jesus, teach them to pray, bring them with you to church, and encourage them to be confirmed.

The service

Jesus loves your children as much as you do. We read in St Matthew's Gospel:

> Then little children were being brought to [Jesus] in order that he might lay his hands on them and pray. The disciples spoke sternly to those who brought them; but Jesus said, 'Let the little children come to me, and do not stop them; for it is to such as these that the kingdom of heaven belongs.' And he laid his hands on them and went on his way.

So I hope you'll enjoy this service, and take your promises very seriously. We, on our part, the church congregation, will promise to pray for the children who are baptized here, and to support you in the Christian upbringing of your child in every way we can.

Suggested hymns

Give me oil in my lamp, keep me burning; He's got the whole wide world in his hands; O Jesus, I have promised; When Jesus came to Jordan.

Acknowledgements

DIETZ, Howard, 'Triplets'. Words & Music by Howard Dietz and Arthur Schwartz © 1937 Chappell & Co. Administered by Warner/Chappell Music Ltd, London W6 8BS. Reproduced by permission.

DUDLEY-SMITH, Timothy, 'I lift my eyes'. Text copyright Timothy Dudley-Smith in Europe (including UK and Ireland) and Africa, and in all territories not controlled by Hope Publishing Company, USA. Copyright permission granted by Hope Publishing for the rest of the world.

FIELDS, Dorothy, 'Nothing's impossible', from *Swing Time*. Copyright not traced.

FLANDERS, Michael, 'Oh what a beautiful scene', from *Captain Noah and his Floating Zoo*. Copyright © Music Sales, London. Reproduced by permission.

FLANDERS, Michael, 'Playing on the status symbols', from *The Songs of Michael Flanders and Donald Swann*. Copyright administered by Warner/Chappell Music Ltd, London W6 8BS. Reproduced by permission.

HARBURG, Yip, 'No matter how I probe and prod', from *The Agnostic* by E. Y. 'Yip' Harburg. Reprinted by permission and published by Glocca Morra Music administered by Next Decade Entertainment, Inc. All rights reserved.

HARNICK, Sheldon, 'If I were a rich man', from the musical *Fiddler on the Roof*. Words by Sheldon Harnick, Music by Jerry Bock. Copyright © 1964 (Renewed) Mayerling Productions Ltd. (Administered by R&H Music) and Jerry Bock Enterprises for the United States and Alley Music Corporation, Trio Music Company, and to Jerry Bock Enterprises for the world outside of the United States. Used by permission. All rights reserved.

MACLENNAN, Gene, 'Put your hand in the hand'. Copyright not traced.

RICE, Tim, 'The Last Supper', from *Jesus Christ Superstar*. Copyright © Universal/MCA Music Publishing Ltd. Permission sought.

STRUTHER, Jan, 'When a knight won his spurs'. Words by Jan Struther (1901–53) from *Enlarged Songs of Praise 1931* by permission of Oxford University Press.

USTINOV, Peter, from *Dear Me*, by Peter Ustinov, published by William Heinemann. Copyright © 1977 by Pavor, S.A. Reprinted by permission of the Random House Group Ltd, for UK and Commonwealth except Canada; and throughout the US, Territories, Philippines and Canada by permission of Little, Brown & Co., Inc.

Russell Plaice
& Partners

Scripture Index to Sermon Texts

Subject Index

Entries in *italics* are sermon titles

Abba 40
Absentee landlords 233
Adam leaving Eden 54
Added to the eleven apostles 314
Adders 164
Adoption 39
Advocate 152
All glorious within 332
Ambition 328
Angels 342
Answers to prayer 70, 196
Anti-Semitism 235
Apostles 314
Apostolic succession 260
Arranged marriages 184
Aristotle 145
Ask, seek, knock 194
At early dawn 113
At the resurrection 266
Atheists 181
Atonement 111
Awesome universe 250

Balance sheet 204
Baptism 44, 290, 363
Belief 122
Beloved disciple 93, 283
Bible interpretation 53, 267
Bible study 38
Birth by drowning 43
Birth of the Baptist 173
Blessed are the dead 12
Book of life 204
Brahms' Requiem 12
Broken-hearted 345

By royal appointment 109

Calvary 337
Children 37, 48, 161, 206, 287, 364
Christian domesticity 316
Church 82, 231, 333
Chosen people 363
Circumcision 289
Cloud on the mountain 330
Cloud took him 144
Come to Jesus 346
Comforter 152
Coming of the Son of Man 9
Communication 201
Conscience 215
Corinth 55, 118
Cornerstone 211
Council of Jerusalem 165
Counting the cost 82
Covenant 17, 288
Covenant community 288
Creation 65, 67
Crooked corn-merchant 169
Crucifixion 112
Crusades 255
Cultures, class, change and castaways 231, 293

Daniel 273
Darwin, Charles 180
Dead son 161
Dealing with atheists 180
Death 12
Death benefits 205

371

Author Index

Have you ordered your 2007 editions of...   Quantity

CANTERBURY CHURCH BOOK & DESK DIARY (cased).........**£16.99** + p&p*

CANTERBURY CHURCH BOOK & DESK DIARY (organiser)......**£16.99** + p&p*

CANTERBURY PREACHERS COMPANION.................................**£16.99** + p&p*

ORDER FOR THE EUCHARIST... **£7.99** + p&p*

**Ask for details of discounted prices for bulk orders of 6+ copies
of any individual title when ordered direct from the Publisher**

ADVANCE ORDER: **Please supply the following 2008 editions on publication** *(May 2007)*
                                                                        Quantity

CANTERBURY CHURCH BOOK & DESK DIARY 2008 - Cased...................... £16.99 + p&p* *

CANTERBURY CHURCH BOOK & DESK DIARY - Personal Organiser.......... £16.99 + p&p* *

CANTERBURY PREACHERS COMPANION 2008.. £16.99 + p&p* *

ORDER FOR THE EUCHARIST 2008.. £7.99 + p&p* *

SAVE 20% - Order a complete set of CANTERBURY CHURCH BOOK AND DESK DIARY
(either cased or personal organiser edition), CANTERBURY PREACHERS COMPANION and
ORDER FOR THE EUCHARIST at the combined **advance order price of £33.58** + p&p*

***Please add £2.50 to each order under £50.00 to cover post and packing in the UK.
All orders totalling £50.01 or over are sent POST FREE in the UK.**
For details of overseas carriage charges, please contact the publisher's Norwich office shown below.

ALL ORDERS ARE SUBJECT TO STOCK AVAILABILITY

I wish to pay by...

...**CHEQUE** for £...................... made payable to **SCM-Canterbury Press Ltd**
To include post and packing as applicable. (see above*)

...**CREDIT CARD**   Visa, Delta, MasterCard and Switch accepted (delete as appropriate)
Your credit card will not be debited until the books are despatched.

Card number:.. Expiry: ___/___

Switch Issue No: __ __   Valid from: ___/___

Signature of
cardholder:.. Security code: ___ ___ ___
Last three digits on the signature panel

Please **PRINT** all details below.

Title:............ Name:...

Delivery address:...

....

....

.... Post Code:..................

Telephone:... Date:.........................

Return this order form - with details of payment - to

Canterbury Press Norwich,
St Mary's Works, St Mary's Plain, Norwich NR3 3BH, UK

Telephone 01603 612914 Fax 01603 624483 Website www.scm-canterburypress.co.uk

Please provide the following catalogues (✓)

CANTERBURY PRESS *   SCM PRESS *   RELIGIOUS AND MORAL EDUCATION PRESS (RMEP) *

Canterbury Press Norwich, SCM Press and RMEP are divisions of SCM-Canterbury Press Ltd,
a subsidiary of Hymns Ancient & Modern Ltd. Registered Charity No.270060